D0929838

A Publication Sponsored by
the Society for Industrial and Organizational Psychology, Inc.,
A Division of the American Psychological Association

Other books sponsored by the Society include:

The Changing Nature
of Performance

The Changing Nature of Performance

Implications for Staffing, Motivation, and Development

Daniel R. Ilgen

Elaine D. Pulakos

Editors

Foreword by Sheldon Zedeck

Jossey-Bass Publishers • San Francisco

HF
5549.5
.P35
C48
1999

The epigraph on page 1 is from *Job Shift* by William Bridges. Copyright © 1994 by William
Bridges and Associates, Inc. Reprinted by permission of Perseus Books LLC.

Substantial discounts on bulk quantities of Jossey-Bass books are available to
corporations, professional associations, and other organizations. For details and
discount information, contact the special sales department at Jossey-Bass Inc.,
Publishers: (415) 433–1740; Fax (800) 605–2665.

Jossey-Bass Web address: http://www.josseybass.com

 Manufactured in the United States of America on Lyons Falls Turin Book.
This paper is acid-free and 100 percent totally chlorine-free.

Library of Congress Cataloging-in-Publication Data

The changing nature of performance : implications for staffing,
   motivation, and development / Daniel R. Ilgen, Elaine D. Pulakos,
   editors.
       p.   cm.
   Includes bibliographical references and indexes.
   ISBN 0-7879-4625-7
   1. Performance standards.   I. Ilgen, Daniel R.   II. Pulakos,
Elaine Diane.
HF5549.5.P35C48   1999
658.3'125—dc21   98-56199

FIRST EDITION
HB Printing   10 9 8 7 6 5 4 3 2 1

A joint publication in
The Jossey-Bass
Business & Management Series
and
The Jossey-Bass
Social & Behavioral Sciences Series

Frontiers of Industrial and Organizational Psychology

Contents

Part Two: The Effect of Change on Three Key Processes—Staffing, Motivation, and Employee Development

Part Three: Concluding Remarks

Foreword

The Society for Industrial and Organizational Psychology established the Frontiers of Industrial and Organizational Psychology series in 1982, in part to advance the scientific status of the field. The series was designed to include volumes that would each deal with a single topic considered to be of major contemporary significance in the field. Each volume editor, a leading contributor to the topic, would take responsibility for developing the volume with the goal of presenting cutting-edge theory, research, and practice in chapters contributed by individuals doing pioneering work on the topic. Each volume was to be aimed at members of the Society for Industrial and Organizational Psychology—researchers, practitioners, and students. The volumes were to be published on a timely basis rather than on a fixed schedule, though at a projected rate of one volume per year.

The first editor of the series was Raymond Katzell, who was followed by Irwin Goldstein. I began my term as series editor in May 1993. The practice of choosing volume topics and editors that I am following is the one successfully established by my predecessors. Specifically, the topics and volume editors are chosen by the *Frontiers* series editorial board. There is considerable exchange between the board and the volume editor in the planning stages of each volume. Once the volume is under contract, the series editor works with the volume editor to coordinate and oversee the activities of the board, the publisher, the volume editor, and the volume authors.

Under the excellent leadership and guidance of Raymond Katzell, three major volumes were developed and published: *Career Development in Organizations,* edited by Douglas T. Hall (1986); *Productivity in Organizations,* edited by John P. Campbell and Richard J. Campbell (1988); and *Training and Development in Organizations,* edited by Irwin L. Goldstein (1989). Under the equally excellent stewardship of Irwin Goldstein, four additional volumes were produced:

Organizational Climate and Culture, edited by Benjamin Schneider (1990); *Work, Families, and Organizations,* edited by Sheldon Zedeck (1992); *Personnel Selection in Organizations,* edited by Neal Schmitt and Walter Borman (1993); and *Team Effectiveness and Decision Making in Organizations,* edited by Richard A. Guzzo and Eduardo Salas (1995).

Since my term began, we have published three volumes: *The Changing Nature of Work,* edited by Ann Howard (1995); *Individual Differences and Behavior in Organizations,* edited by Kevin Murphy (1996); and *New Perspectives on International Industrial/Organizational Psychology* edited by P. Christopher Earley and Miriam Erez (1997). The success of the series is evidenced by the high number of sales (more than thirty thousand copies have been sold), the excellent reviews written about the volumes, and the frequent citation of volumes and chapters in papers by scholars.

The present volume, *The Changing Nature of Performance: Implications for Staffing, Motivation, and Development,* edited by Daniel R. Ilgen and Elaine D. Pulakos, continues the tradition of publishing volumes that are designed to move the field forward and present new thinking and approaches. The general purpose of this volume is to provide a discussion of the relationship between the changing nature of work and the understanding, measurement, and influence of human performance. More specifically, the volume addresses how seven key changes in the nature of work—changes in technology, job design, type of workforce, training methodology, external control, leadership, and work structure—affect how job performance is viewed and measured. Three human resource domains are emphasized: staffing, motivation, and training and development (learning). A key premise of the volume is that though there have been changes in work and in the environment, the importance of employee performance has not changed. The authors of the volume's chapters address the changes and the relationship of those changes to understanding performance. The goal of the volume is not only to present greater understanding of the changing nature of performance but also to offer concrete ways in which to deal with the change.

The volume editors, Daniel Ilgen and Elaine Pulakos, have done an excellent job of identifying the topics, selecting a diverse group of authors, and working with them to provide a focused volume that is sure to direct research for many years to come. The Society owes

Ilgen and Pulakos and their chapter authors a considerable debt of gratitude for undertaking such an ambitious volume. We anticipate that it will serve as an important stimulus for researchers seeking to move forward in understanding behavior in today's environment.

The production of a volume such as this one requires the cooperation and efforts of many individuals. The volume editor and chapter authors and the series editorial board all played an obvious major role. They deserve our sincere appreciation and thanks for devoting their time and efforts to a task that was undertaken for the sole purpose of contributing to the field without any remuneration whatsoever. Thanks are also due to Cedric Crocker, editor of the Business and Management Series, and his colleagues at Jossey-Bass, especially Julianna Gustafson, who took the manuscript through production without a hitch.

January 1999   SHELDON ZEDECK
                                 University of California at Berkeley
                                 Series Editor

Preface

In 1995, Ann Howard edited a book in the Frontiers of Industrial and Organizational Psychology series titled *The Changing Nature of Work*. In that book, she and the authors described a number of major changes that had already occurred or that were in the process of occurring that were having a major impact on the way work is done in organizations. At that time, both of us were involved in projects in which the measurement of performance was critical. Reading the book when we were struggling with defining and measuring performance made evident to us that many of the changes occurring at work were likely to create even greater problems for measuring performance than we were experiencing in our own work. In fact, the potential effects of some of the changes went beyond problems of measurement. They brought into question many of the ways in which performance was typically construed. Discussing these issues led us to look directly at potential effects of the changing nature of work on performance.

Our assumptions underlying the development of the present book are simple; the problems are not. First, we assume that the performance of individuals in organizations is critical to the effectiveness of organizations. Technology, markets, and other factors influence the proportion of variance in organizational effectiveness that is affected by peoples' performance, but as long as people are part of organizations, how they perform will be important.

The second assumption is that three key human resource processes affect human performance and depend on knowledge about it. These processes are staffing, motivation, and training and development. Central to selection, placement, and other staffing functions is having an understanding of human performance and of the demands of jobs and tasks in order to match the characteristics of people to those of their jobs. Efforts to motivate employees require that behaviors be observed and evaluated in order to encourage the display of desirable behaviors and discourage undesirable ones. Finally, training and development attempt to provide people with the knowledge, skills, and other characteristics they need at work. Without some means of determining what are or are not desirable behaviors, and whether or not training and development experiences affect these behaviors, little of value can be accomplished through training or development. In sum, we see no reason to question the central role of human performance at work; although the nature of work may be changing, the need to understand and measure human performance is not.

The dilemma that the changing nature of work presents is that understanding, measuring, and influencing human performance is just as important today as it was in the past. We believe, however, that the changes that are taking place are altering how we view and measure performance in ways that question some of the traditional views of performance. For that reason, we have brought together a number of authors to focus specifically on the implications of change for performance at work.

The book is best construed as a matrix. The rows of the matrix—technology, contingent employees, the changing nature of jobs, customer defined performance, and other features of modern organizations—represent the sources of changes that affect performance. The authors of the chapters in Part One of the book describe a wide variety of changes in each of these domains. The columns that cross the rows of the matrix are major human resource functions—staffing, motivation, and training and development. The authors of the chapters in Part Two of the book were presented with each of the content (row) chapters and then asked to reflect on the impact that the conditions described in those chapters have had on their particular functions. Finally, in Part Three John P. Campbell, whose model of performance has had a great deal of influence on how industrial and organizational psychologists in the 1990s view performance at work, reacts to the result of this process. For us, the volume's editors, the exercise has broadened our view of performance and encouraged us to look for more complex ways of responding to the ever-present need to understand the performance of people at work. We hope it does the same for you.

January 1999

Daniel R. Ilgen
East Lansing, Michigan

Elaine D. Pulakos
Arlington, Virginia

The Authors

DANIEL R. ILGEN is John A. Hannah Professor of Organizational Behavior at Michigan State University in the departments of psychology and management. He received his Ph.D. degree (1969) in industrial and organizational psychology from the University of Illinois. Prior to his present position, he served on the psychology faculty at Purdue University. He is a past president of the Society for Industrial and Organizational Psychology. His current research examines decision making in hierarchical teams composed of persons with differing levels of expertise. He is presently the editor of *Organizational Behavior and Human Decision Processes*.

ELAINE D. PULAKOS is director of the Washington, D.C., office of Personnel Decisions Research Institutes. She received her B.A. degree (1980) from the Pennsylvania State University and her M.A. (1983) and Ph.D. (1984) degrees from Michigan State University. Pulakos is currently serving as president of the Society for Industrial and Organizational Psychology. Her research and consulting interests are in the areas of personnel selection and performance appraisal, and her research has appeared in several scholarly journals. She has also worked with numerous public and private sector clients designing and implementing customized human resource systems such as selection systems, performance management systems, and individual development systems. She is a fellow of the American Psychological Association and the Society for Industrial and Organizational Psychology.

DAVID E. BOWEN is professor of management in the Department of World Business, Thunderbird/American Graduate School of International Management, Phoenix, Arizona. He has previously been on the faculties at Arizona State University West and the University of Southern California. He received his Ph.D. degree (1983) in business administration from Michigan State University. His research, teaching, and consulting focus on the organizational dynamics of delivering service quality and on the effectiveness of human resource management departments. His articles have appeared in *Academy of Management Review, Academy of Management Journal, Academy of Management Executive,* and *Human Resource Management.* He coedited the *Academy of Management Review*'s 1994 special issue on Total Quality Management. He has published six books on service management, including *Winning the Service Game* (1995, with Ben Schneider). He serves on the editorial review boards of the *Journal of Management Inquiry, Human Resource Management,* the *Journal of Quality Management,* the *Journal of Market-Focused Management,* and the *International Journal of Service Industry Management.*

JOHN P. CAMPBELL received his Ph.D. degree (1964) in psychology from the University of Minnesota. He is professor of psychology and industrial relations at the University of Minnesota, where he has been since 1967. From 1964 to 1966 he was assistant professor of psychology at the University of California at Berkeley. He served as president of the Division of Industrial and Organizational Psychology of the American Psychological Association from 1977 to 1978, and as associate editor and then editor of the *Journal of Applied Psychology* from 1974 to 1982. In 1971 he authored the first chapter on training and development in the *Annual Review of Psychology.* He also coauthored *Managerial Behavior, Performance, and Effectiveness* (1970, with M. Dunnette, E. Lawler, and K. Weick); *Measurement Theory for the Behavioral Sciences* (1978, with E. Ghiselli and S. Zedeck); *What to Study: Generating and Developing Research Questions* (1984, with R. Daft and C. Hulin); and *Productivity in Organizations* (1988, with R. Campbell). He was awarded the Society of Industrial and Organizational Psychology's Distinguished Scientific Contribution Award in 1991. He also served as principal scientist for the comprehensive, multiyear selection and classification project known as Project A (sponsored by the Army Research Institute). Current research interests are in performance measurement, personnel selection and classification, and the modeling of personnel decision making.

THERESA M. GLOMB received her B.A. degree (1993) in psychology from DePaul University and her Ph.D. degree (1998) in industrial and organizational psychology from the University of Illinois. She has published in the areas of anger and aggressive behaviors in organizations, emotional expression in organizations, sexual harassment, contingent workers, and job attitudes and behaviors.

STANLEY M. GULLY is an assistant professor in the Department of Human Resource Management, School of Management and Labor Relations, Rutgers University. He received his Ph.D. degree (1997) in industrial and organizational psychology from Michigan State University. His applied work has included the development of guidelines for training leaders of interdependent work teams, the creation of multisource feedback systems for leaders in hospital settings, and the design of training modules for increasing employee safety in manufacturing firms. His research interests include identification of key factors that influence leadership and team performance, development and creation of more effective training and instructional systems, organizational learning, and novel applications of research methodologies to the investigation of multilevel phenomena. His research has appeared in *Advances in Interdisciplinary Studies of Work Teams, Research in Personnel and Human Resource Management,* and the *Journal of Applied Psychology.*

BERYL HESKETH received her Ph.D. degree (1982) in psychology from Massey University, New Zealand. She is currently professor of psychology at Macquarie University, where she has been since 1994, having previously been on the faculty at the University of New South Wales. She chaired the Inaugural Australian Industrial and Organizational Psychology conference in Sydney in 1995 and was the recipient of the Australian Psychological Society College of Organizational Psychologists' Elton Mayo Award in 1997 in recognition of her significant contributions to industrial and organizational psychology in Australia and internationally through her research and professional activities. She has published widely in international journals, was associate editor of the *Journal of Vocational Behavior* in 1996 and 1997, is an associate editor of the *International Journal of Selection and Assessment,* and serves on the editorial board of several other journals. She is a member of the Australian Research Council's Large Grants Committee and is chair of the Heads of Departments and Schools of Psychology Association. Her research interests are in selection, training, and career decision making, as well as measurement issues generally.

CHARLES L. HULIN received his B.A. degree (1958) in psychology from Northwestern University and his Ph.D. degree (1963) in industrial and organizational psychology from Cornell University. Except for sabbatical leaves, he has been at the University of Illinois since 1962. Currently he has joint appointments at the Institute of Labor and Industrial Relations and the Aviation Institute. He is coauthor of four books and is currently editing a book on applications of computational modeling in organizational research. He has published in the areas of job attitudes, behaviors, sexual harassment in work organizations, temporary workers, computational modeling, and translations of scales into foreign languages. He was associate editor of the *Journal of Applied Psychology* from 1975 to 1982. He received the Ghiselli Award for Excellence in Research Design in 1989 and 1997, and the Career Scientific Contributions Award from the Society for Industrial and Organizational Psychology in 1997.

SUSAN E. JACKSON is professor of management and organizational behavior at the Stern School of Business, New York University. She has previously held appointments in New York University's Department of Psychology, the University of Michigan's Department of Organizational Behavior, and the University of Maryland's Department of Psychology. She received her Ph.D. degree (1982) in organizational psychology from the University of California at Berkeley. Her research interests include team composition, workforce diversity, and the design of strategic human resource management systems. She has authored or coauthored numerous articles and books on these and related topics. She is a fellow of the American Psychological Association and of the Society for Industrial and Organizational Psychology, where she served as a member of the executive committee for several years. She has served as editor of the *Academy of Management Review* and as president of the Academy of Management's Division of Organizational Behavior, and is currently a member of the board of governors for the Center for Creative Leadership.

STEVE W. J. KOZLOWSKI is professor of organizational psychology at Michigan State University. His major interests include organizational innovation and change, and the processes by which people adapt to novel and challenging situations. His theory and research writings address organizational downsizing, technological innovation, continuous learning, adaptive performance and expertise, leadership, team development, climate, and socialization. Kozlowski's current research program, which focuses on adaptability and team development, is a collaboration with the Naval Air Warfare Center Training Systems Division and the Air Force Office of Scientific Research. He is a fellow of the American Psychological Association and of the Society for Industrial and Organizational Psychology. He serves on the editorial boards of the *Journal of Applied Psychology, Organizational Behavior and Human Decision Processes,* and the *Academy of Management Journal.* Kozlowski received his B.A. degree (1976) in psychology from the University of Rhode Island and his M.S. (1979) and Ph.D. (1982) degrees in industrial and organizational psychology from the Pennsylvania State University.

KURT KRAIGER received his Ph.D. degree (1983) in industrial and organizational psychology from the Ohio State University. He is professor of psychology at the University of Colorado at Denver and director of the university's Center for Applied Psychology. His research interests include training evaluation, training theory and learning, performance measurement, and organizational assessment. He is currently editor of the *Training Research Journal,* an international, multidisciplinary scholarly journal, and coeditor (with K. Ford, S. Kozlowski, E. Salas, and M. Teachout) of the book *Improving Training Effectiveness in Work Organizations* (1997). He was elected as a fellow of the Society for Industrial and Organizational Psychology in 1996.

MANUEL LONDON received his Ph.D. degree (1974) in industrial and organizational psychology from the Ohio State University. He is professor and director of the Center for Human Resource Management in the Harriman School for Management and Policy, State University of New York, Stony Brook. From 1974 to 1977 he taught in the business school at the University of Illinois, Champaign-Urbana. From 1977 to 1989 he held a variety of research and human resource management positions at AT&T. He moved to Stony Brook in 1989. His research interests are principally in the areas of employee and management development (including career motivation, employee development, performance evaluation, and multisource ratings). Two of his recent books are *Self and Interpersonal Insight: How Individuals Learn About Themselves and Others in Organizations* (1995), and *Jobs, Careers, and Economic Growth* (1995). He has been associate editor of the *Academy of Management Journal;* has been on the editorial boards of the *Academy of Management Review,* the *Journal of Applied Psychology, Personnel Psychology,* and *Administrative Science Quarterly;* and has served as senior editor of the Society for Industrial and Organizational Psychology's Professional Practice Series.

ROBERT G. LORD received his Ph.D. degree (1975) in psychology from Carnegie-Mellon University. He is professor of psychology and chair of the Department of Psychology at the University of Akron, where he has been since 1974. He served as associate editor of the *Journal of Applied Psychology* from 1988 through 1994 and coauthored (with K. Maher) the book *Leadership and Information Processing: Linking Perceptions and Performance* (1991). His research interests include leadership perceptions, leadership and its impact on group and organizational performance, control theory and self-regulation, information processing and social perceptions, perceptions of minorities, and social justice theory.

EDWARD M. MONE has twenty years of experience in career, leadership, and organization development. Currently he is director of people processes and systems at Booz-Allen & Hamilton, Inc. Formerly HR division manager for strategic planning and development at AT&T, he has held a variety of human resource and organization development positions since 1982. Before that he was a partner in an outplacement and career management firm based in New York City. He has also served as an adjunct faculty member at the Harriman School for Management and Policy at the State University of New York, Stony Brook. He holds an M.A. degree (1977) in counseling psychology, has completed doctoral-level coursework in organizational psychology, and is currently an Ed.D. candidate at Teachers College, Columbia University, where he researches individual, team, and organization learning. He has coauthored and coedited books, book chapters, and articles in the areas of human resources and organization development. He also maintains a limited consulting practice.

STEPHAN J. MOTOWIDLO received his Ph.D. degree (1976) in industrial and organizational psychology from the University of Minnesota and is now Huber Hurst Professor of Management and director of the Human Research Center at the University of Florida. His research interests include work attitudes, occupational stress, selection interviews, job simulations, performance appraisal, and models of the performance domain. Motowidlo served on the editorial board of the *Journal of Applied Psychology* and currently serves on the editorial boards of *Human Performance* and the *Journal of Management*.

KEVIN R. MURPHY is professor of psychology at Colorado State University. He received his B.A. degree (1974) from Siena College, his M.S. degree (1976) from Rensselaer Polytechnic University, and his Ph.D. degree (1979) from the Pennsylvania State University, all in psychology. He has served on the faculties of Rice University and New York University, and as a visiting researcher at the University of California at Berkeley, at the University of Stockholm, and at the Navy Personnel Research and Development Center. Murphy has served as president of the Society for Industrial and Organizational Psychology. He is editor of the *Journal of Applied Psychology* and serves as a member of the editorial boards of *Human Performance* and the *International Journal of Selection and Assessment*. He is the author of more than seventy articles and book chapters, and author or editor of seven books: *Psychological Testing: Principles and Applications* (1988, with C. D. Shofer), *Psychology in Organizations: Integrating Science and Practice* (1990, with F. Saal), *Performance Appraisal: An Organizational Perspective* (1991, with J. Cleveland), *Understanding Performance Appraisal: Social, Organizational, and Goal-Oriented Perspectives* (1995, with J. Cleveland), *Honesty in the Workplace* (1993), *Individual Differences and Behavior in Organizations* (1996), and *Statistical Power Analysis: A Simple and General Model for Traditional and Modern Hypothesis Tests* (1999, with B. Myors). Murphy's areas of research include personnel selection and placement, performance appraisal, and honesty in the workplace.

PATRICE R. MURPHY is a doctoral student in management and organizational behavior at New York University. Her research interests include learning in organizations and cross-cultural issues in organizational behavior, particularly relating to workforce diversity and performance management. Murphy received her B.A. (1984) and M.B.A. (1990) degrees from the University of Melbourne, Australia, and a master's degree (1994) in labor law and relations from the University of Sydney. Prior to commencing doctoral studies, Murphy worked as a strategic human resource management consultant with MTIA Australia.

EARL R. NASON received his Ph.D. degree (1995) in psychology from Michigan State University. He is now a staff officer in the Personnel Policy Directorate Headquarters, U.S. Air Force. From 1995 to 1997 he was assistant professor and research director for the department of behavioral sciences and leadership at the U.S. Air Force Academy. His research interests include selection, experiential learning, and team processes performance. His work for the Air Force focuses on testing for personnel selection, promotion, and qualification, and the use of surveys for organization development.

ANDREW NEAL received his Ph.D. degree (1996) in psychology from the University of New South Wales. He is currently lecturer in organizational and cognitive psychology in the School of Psychology at the University of Queensland. His research interests include human performance, situation awareness, implicit learning, categorization, safety climate, and safety behavior.

MARK J. SCHMIT received his Ph.D. degree (1994) in industrial and organizational psychology from Bowling Green State University. He is a consultant with Personnel Decisions International. He previously served as a member of the organization development staff at Payless Shoe Source and as an assistant professor of management at the University of Florida. His research interests include personality measurement, psychometrics, job-related employee selection systems, job analysis, and performance modeling.

ELEANOR M. SMITH received her Ph.D. degree (1996) in industrial and organizational psychology from Michigan State University and is now senior consultant at Aon Consulting. Her research interests include training and development, team processes, and newcomer socialization.

WENDY GRADWOHL SMITH received her Ph.D. degree (1997) in industrial and organizational psychology from the University of Akron and is now assistant professor of psychology at Auburn University. Her research interests include leadership perceptions and gender bias, implicit stereotypes and cognitive categories, dynamic models of social cognition, self-schemes, work motivation, and work attitudes.

DAVID A. WALDMAN received his Ph.D. degree (1982) from Colorado State University. Since then, he has taught at the State University of New York, Binghamton, and at Concordia University in Montreal. He is presently professor of management at Arizona State University West. His accomplishments include the book *The Power of 360-Degree Feedback: How to Leverage Performance Evaluations for Top Productivity* (1998). He has published more than fifty scholarly articles and book chapters, has received approximately $400,000 in grant money, and currently holds editorial board memberships for the *Journal of Applied Psychology* and the *Journal of Quality Management*. His research focuses on 360-degree feedback processes, aging and work behavior, leadership, and cross-cultural human resource management issues. His articles have appeared in such publications as the *Journal of Applied Psychology,* the *Academy of Management Journal,* the *Academy of Management Review,* the *Academy of Management Executive, Personnel Psychology,* and *Research in Personnel and Resources Management.* Waldman's activities have included consultation for a number of private firms and government agencies in the United States, Canada, and Mexico.

The Changing Nature
of Performance

CHAPTER 1

Introduction
Employee Performance in Today's Organizations

Daniel R. Ilgen
Elaine D. Pulakos

*No longer the best way to organize work, the traditional job
is becoming a social artifact.*
WILLIAM BRIDGES

The last quarter of the twentieth century has witnessed dramatic changes in the way goods and services are produced. These changes go beyond simple alterations of form and intensity. Just as the transition from agrarian to industrial society was revolutionary, so has been the change from an industrial to a postindustrial (Naisbit, 1982) or postmodern (Featherstone, 1991) world that has occurred in the last quarter of the twentieth century. Technological, social, political, and economic forces have brought about significant changes in how people live and how work is done.

The impact of these forces is perhaps no better illustrated than by the views of William Bridges (1994a, 1994b) on jobs. Traditionally, jobs are basic units around which work is organized and the means by which individuals are linked to organizations (Ilgen, 1994). Duties and responsibilities are bundled together and labeled "jobs" on the basis of interactions between tasks that the organization needs to have accomplished and the capabilities and limitations of people assigned to the jobs. Once jobs are created and given descriptive labels, the labels themselves serve as efficient means to communicate what needs to be done in the jobs and what experience, skills, abilities, and other personal characteristics are necessary to perform well in them. Often, simply mentioning the job title—whether bus driver or oral surgeon—gives a rough idea of what people in that job do and what skills are needed to do it. In addition, the cost of labor to fill the job, the status of the job-holder both on and off the job, and many other concerns that are important both to organizations and to individuals are associated with jobs. Thus, to suggest that a job is a "social artifact," as Bridges has, shakes the very foundation on which work is structured and organized, and the fabric of the societies of those whose lives are interwoven with work organizations.

From Bridges's perspective, flattening organizations, self-managed work teams, reengineering, telecommuting, and other organizational practices currently in vogue are symptomatic responses ("cure-alls of the day," according to Bridges, 1994a, p. 68) to the fact that it is much more difficult than it used to be, and in some cases no longer possible, to draw reasonable boundaries around a limited set of specific duties and responsibilities and then assign them to individuals. These trends are evidence that organizations are moving along a path toward "dejobbed" work. Unfortunately, those who make decisions about how work should be organized do not fully recognize the nature of the path on which they travel or the implications of the current route for future destinations.

It is not necessary to accept all of Bridges's thesis or to call on hackers to mount a Luddite assault on what Upton and McAfee (1996) call the "virtual factory" in order to recognize that work is undergoing major changes and that these changes have many implications for the behavior of people in organizations. In an earlier volume in the series in which the present volume appears, Howard (1995) argued that technological and social forces are reshaping work, workers, and working. She identified a number of changes, and three domains (work, workers, and working) in which the factors influencing these changes originate. Other writers have focused on specific conditions that are likely to have an impact on work—from commonly recognized sources of potential impact, such as workforce diversity (Jackson, 1992; Offermann &

Gowing, 1990), to less obvious sources, such as the softening of national boundaries in multinational organizations (Davis, 1995). This is not a time for "business as usual."

Whereas other authors (such as Howard, 1995) have provided excellent discussions of a number of conditions and consequences that lead to and result from changes in the nature of work, our purpose for the present book is more limited. We accept the fact that changes are occurring in the structure and processes for accomplishing work. We hold firm, however, on one critical condition that has not changed—that is, the importance of employee performance. The performance of people at work remains a critical factor both in the viability of organizations and in the well-being of their members. In even the most automated organizations, human beings still staff critical functions, and their performance has impacts on the effectiveness of those organizations. Although performance is as central to organizational effectiveness today as it was in the past, key changes in the world of work are having significant impacts on how we conceptualize and assess human work performance. In this book, we examine these changes; their impact on performance, definition, and measurement; and their implications for the development of human resource systems in organizations.

We begin below with a discussion of three key human resource processes—staffing, motivation, and learning—and the central role of performance in these processes. Following this discussion, we describe seven significant changes in the nature of work, provide examples of how these changes are affecting work performance, and examine their implications for design of the three key human resource processes. In the final section of the chapter we present an overview of the remainder of the book.

Human Resource Systems in Organizations

Critical to performance effectiveness in work organizations is linking human beings to the production process. People work. They design production systems, and they populate, operate, and modify those systems. They are the human resources essential to advanced industrialized societies. People make the place (Schneider, 1987).

Three key human resource processes link people to production, whether the outcomes of that production are goods, services, or some combination of the two. These three processes are *staffing,* employee *motivation,* and employee *learning.*

Staffing involves linking human knowledge, skills, abilities, and dispositions to the demands of the work setting. People differ in the personal characteristics they bring to the work setting, and work settings differ in what they require to accomplish their goals. Some jobs require complex and highly specialized skills that take years of formal education to acquire. Other jobs require the strength and physical endurance that is most frequently found in young adults. Still others need workers who possess particular interpersonal skills, customer service skills, or other temperament attributes. In all cases, central to performance effectiveness is a good match between the demands of the job and the organization, and the characteristics of the jobholder. Staffing policies and practices address this match.

Regardless of the quality of the match between work demands and human capacities, however, people must be willing to invest the time and effort required to perform a job well. Thus, the second key human resource process that links people to production is employee motivation—the willingness to perform job duties effectively. Leadership, supervision, incentive plans, job design, and other features of the work setting create and maintain employees' willingness to come to work and do the work well.

Finally, both staffing and employee motivation deal with good fits between peoples' capabilities and desires and the demands of the jobs in which they find themselves. Yet the abilities, skills, and even motivation needed today may not be the same as those that will be needed in the future. Staffing and motivational systems, once established, work best when job demands remain constant, when job applicants continue to bring to the job needed skills and abilities, and when the likes and dislikes of people do not change much. But such stability exists neither in the work environment nor in people. Thus, a third cluster of human resource activities links people to production by ensuring that members of the workforce develop and learn important skills that are required to meet changing technological or other demands in today's work environments. People and the organizations in which they work must develop ways to support and encourage continuous learning in order to stay current, competitive, and effectively prepared for the future. The formal mechanism for such employee learning is training and development initiatives that confront change by focusing on changing people and, specifically, what they are able to do effectively on a job.

Ironically, although the nature of work has changed in some significant ways, the fundamental processes through which people are linked to their work remain the same. Staffing, motivation, and learning are as important today as they were in the past. That is not to say, however, that the staffing, motivation, and learning practices in today's organizations should be like those of the past. In fact, shifts are needed, have begun, and will continue to occur in these key human resource practices in response to changes in work processes and the nature of work. Within a generation, the demand for skills involving physical strength and stamina declined dramatically as skills involving cognitive and analytical ability replaced them. The practices and procedures used to appraise performance are being reconsidered and redesigned to attempt to cope with changing demands brought on by complexities in the nature of performance itself (Hedge & Borman, 1995). Systems are being designed to provide information to leaders and managers from multiple stakeholders using 360-degree feedback (London & Beatty, 1993). These changes, along with others that are described throughout the book, are attempts to respond to the changing nature of work as it affects individual performance and, in turn, the primary human resource systems in organizations (staffing, motivation, and learning).

The Centrality of Performance in Human Resource Functions

Staffing, employee motivation, and employee learning are often seen as three distinctively different core processes through which people are linked to work. The subcomponents of these processes can be arrayed chronologically along a continuum. Recruiting and selection, for example, two key mechanisms for staffing, occur before individuals can be placed in positions in which they will experience conditions that influence their motivation or that give them the opportunity to learn new behaviors. Many of the activities involved in each process are also distinct. Testing and conducting interviews, for example, are very different from establishing reward systems, influencing the members of a team, or conducting a training or mentoring program. In spite of these differences, there are also many commonalities and a number of places where the human resource systems overlap and intersect. During the recruitment and selection process, for example, applicants are learning about the organization as well as about themselves. The nature of this early interaction with the organization has been shown to have strong effects on motivation as reflected in commitment to the job and the organization, if the applicant is hired (Weitz, 1956).

Similarities and differences aside, all three key human resource functions share a critical focus on enhancing employee performance, and therefore also rely on performance assessment to evaluate their effectiveness. Effective implementation of recruitment and selection practices requires organizations to understand what constitutes employee performance and what differentiates good from poor performance in order to identify what knowledge, skills, abilities, and temperaments individuals must possess to perform effectively in the jobs for which they are hired. In turn, the effectiveness with which employees perform on a job is the primary criterion for judging the effectiveness of selection processes. Similarly, motivation does not occur in a vacuum; it requires one to ask, Motivation for what? Typically, the behaviors that are the objects of motivation are those that relate to how effectively individuals perform. Finally, effective training and development programs require thorough understanding of the kinds of behaviors that need to be learned. At some point when one is designing training and development experiences it is necessary to ask, What behaviors are important? and How are these behaviors recognized in people? To identify such behaviors raises, by necessity, the issue of defining performance standards and developing ways to measure whether or not those who received the training have or have not learned to behave in a way that meets these standards. More generally, successful development certainly requires an accurate assessment of individuals' strengths and weaknesses so that appropriate job experiences and training can be provided to enhance needed skills. The main point is that without an understanding of what constitutes effective job performance and without mechanisms to assess performance effectiveness accurately, none of the three primary human resource functions can be accomplished in organizations.

The Specification and Measurement of Performance

Due to the critical role of employee performance in organizations, a great deal of attention has been paid to its specification and measurement. Volumes have been written on the subject by human resource specialists and managers, and a great deal of research and writing has been focused on it by psychologists and other behavioral scientists. With respect to specifying the meaning of performance, complex problems arise in attempting to define the domain of the construct in such a way as to include all of the important and relevant dimensions of effectiveness while also excluding elements that go beyond the individual's performance or those that may be outside of his or her control. Such problems are often labeled "criterion problems," stemming from the use of performance as the critical variable to be predicted by a selection system. Most recently, Campbell's theory of performance (Campbell, 1990; Campbell, McCloy, Oppler, & Sager, 1993) has provided an overarching framework that partitions the domain of performance-relevant human characteristics into declarative and procedural knowledge and motivation. This framework has guided a number of recent approaches to construing work performance. More is presented on the model later in this chapter.

Measures for assessing performance effectiveness run the gamut from objective tabulations of individual output on the job—such as measures of sales volume or number of pounds of fish delivered to the dock at the end of the day—to subjective opinions of employee effectiveness recorded on standard performance appraisal rating scales. Not uncommonly, combinations of several measures are used. Regardless of the measures used, the objective is to create reliable and valid measures that adequately sample the domain of a person's job performance and do so in a manner that is not contaminated by conditions that are beyond the influence of the person whose performance is being assessed. Meeting the objective of measuring performance fairly, accurately, and effectively is far more difficult than it may appear to those who have not attempted to construct such measures.

Changes in the Nature of Work

The focus of this book is on seven key changes that are occurring today in the nature of work and how it is organized, on the implications of these changes for performance specification and measurement in organizations, and on implications for the design of human resource systems whose primary goal is performance enhancement. Although organizations vary in the extent to which they are characterized by these changes, many if not most of today's organizations are experiencing one or more of the following trends to some degree:

- Interweaving of technology and jobs
- Changes in the design of jobs
- Integration of contingent workers into the workforce
- Increased emphasis on continuous learning
- External control of performance standards by customers
- Limitations on leadership and supervision
- Changes in the structure of work from individuals to teams

The Interweaving of Technology and Jobs

There are at least two ways that technology affects performance. The first way is the confounding of individual and technological contributions to performance. More and more jobs are integrated with technology, and technology has a great influence on performance. Disentangling the contributions of the jobholder from the contributions of technology when assessing performance is becoming increasingly more difficult. If the effects of technology were relatively constant across jobs that have the same job description, isolating the variance due to technology would be relatively easy. In theory we understand the partitioning of variance due to persons and variance due to technology. Costs and other factors, however, are such that in practice the levels of technology vary a great deal among persons holding the same jobs. Consider, for example, a clerical job classification at a university. Due to the costs of technology and to the fact that budgetary responsibility for hardware and software purchasing and updating is left to each individual department, the differences in quality among the work stations within a single job classification are large. These differences can have major effects on the performance of the person assigned to the work station. The advantage of being able to isolate individual contributions to performance in such situations is no different than it was in the past. However, the combination of the high cost of technology, rapid change in technology, and the extent to which technological components have spread to almost all job classifications has made addressing this problem far more critical today than it was in the past. The problem will only become more pronounced as we move into the future and may require that we rethink our models of the human-technology interface.

The second aspect of technology that plays a major role in performance is the increasing sophistication of the technology used to monitor job incumbent performance. In many jobs that are characterized by a technological component, it is possible to track employee behavior through the technology and to use this information to assess individual performance. Similarly, monitoring devices can be installed that track performance. Unintended consequences of this monitoring, ethical considerations, and other issues may arise, however, that were not present when the world or work was characterized by less sophisticated technology.

Finally, the impact of information technology affects both of these issues. It also spreads them to a far wider array of jobs than was the case in the past. Many workers today have access to information, databases, references, and so on far beyond what was available in the past and, for most people, without ever leaving their desks. Certainly workers who have Internet access, for example, will be able to perform some job tasks much more efficiently and effectively than workers who do not have such access. Workers who are appropriately equipped can communicate with one another quickly, efficiently, and at all hours without ever having to "talk." Of course these interactions and the use of such systems can be monitored by the organization and by others. The main point is that the explosion in information technology has left almost no job beyond its grasp. This trend, which will only continue, presents challenges with respect to isolating and assessing individual performance.

Changes in the Design of Jobs

A key feature of the "old world" was that jobs were relatively stable over time, and the elements of jobs were common to a relatively large number of people (that is, enough to do analyses using the statistical procedures with which industrial-organizational psychologists are comfortable). A number of forces are reducing the extent to which jobs are stable and job elements are common. Some of the forces for change are weaker unions (and therefore weaker forces to codify and lock in job classifications for long periods) and increased tailoring of jobs to fit people (such as the Americans with Disabilities Act, job sharing, and so on). Some researchers have even speculated that there will be no stable jobs in the future; rather, work will be organized around specific projects and initiatives that employees will move into and out of (Ilgen, 1994).

Although the performance of critical tasks will be just as important as ever, as the number of job commonalities decreases we see two primary implications for performance. First, it may be more costly to measure performance because less standardization in jobs and hence less standardization in performance measures for those jobs will be possible. Second, observed behavior will be increasingly confounded with specific situations, such that isolating variance due to the person versus the situation will be much more difficult. Traditional approaches to performance assessment require that there first be a good understanding of the job and its specific requirements. As it becomes harder to define what a person's job is and as the number of jobs with common job descriptions decreases within an organization, the present job-specific methods of performance measurement will accommodate the new conditions less effectively. Obviously, changes in the direction we are suggesting will have repercussions for all of the human resource functions that rely on performance assessment.

Integration of Contingent Employees into the Workforce

Increased competition has led to another trend in today's organizations that is likely to continue to grow in the future—namely, the use of contingent workers (that is, temporary, contract, part-time, and seasonal employees). Contingent employees offer organizations many benefits, ranging from flexibility in staffing that may be required to meet varying business cycles and needs, to economic advantages that result from lower costs of training and benefits. Of course, along with these advantages are several potential costs, including possibly lower performance levels, less organizational commitment, and a reduced pool of full-time workers from which to draw future organizational leaders.

Although there have always been contingent workers in the workforce, their numbers are steadily increasing, particularly in highly skilled positions. In addition, if jobs were relatively stable and isolated units to which individuals could be assigned (the traditional model), it would be somewhat less of an issue whether the individuals assigned to them are full-time or part-time employees; regardless of the nature of the employment contract, employee performance could be assessed independently. With the breakdown of individual jobs, the use of teams constructed of both part-time and full-time employees, and all the other changes already mentioned, commitment to the organization and organizational commitment to employee learning and development as they relate to the nature of employment become issues. Defining, motivating, and managing the performance of contingent workers in organizations characterized by the types of changes discussed here raises a number of issues that were not as salient in organizations of the past.

Increased Emphasis on Continuous Learning

In the past, performance was based entirely on previous behavior. A period was defined (such as the past twelve months) and standards for performance during that time were used to judge individual effectiveness. Now, as part of the definition of performance, organizations are asking how the job could be done in a way that allows for continuous learning. Continuous learning is important in light of the changes that are occurring in organizations and that will continue to occur. For some organizations, continuous learning must become part of the culture if the organization is to survive in the present environment (Tracey, Tannenbaum, & Kavanagh, 1995). As discussed previously, one of the changes that necessitates continuous learning is technological advancement, which changes the nature of work and the skills individuals must possess to perform tasks as they become automated. In addition, downsizing, higher demands for quality, corporate restructuring, and streamlining also require employee relearning to be competitive for different jobs, and that organizations be constantly looking for discrepancies between current and required skill levels (that is, skill gaps) in the workforce.

Although most of the continuous learning models can be mapped onto the standards-driven performance of the past, creating standards that rely on inferences about a person's ability to handle future states is somewhat different. One key issue is how to define effectiveness. If continuous learning is an important criterion for individual and organizational effectiveness, then it seems that one's ability or willingness to engage in continuous learning and actually learn effectively should be a formal aspect of performance definition and assessment. Specific criteria for evaluating performance effectiveness may not be tied so much to how well new tasks are performed and how new situations are handled, because initial performance when learning will often be poor. One aspect of effectiveness may thus be the extent to which workers demonstrate change from previous states. The process of defining and assessing this type of effectiveness is not well specified or understood at this time.

Control of Performance Standards by Customers

In the past, the definition of performance tended to follow an industrial revolution–oriented model in which internally set and internally relevant standards were used to define effectiveness. When this was the case, good and poor performance were relatively straightforward to define, and such definition was typically accomplished by task and subject matter experts within the organization. This made sense in a world where business revolved primarily around production of goods. In recent years, however, the U.S. economy has been characterized by a boom in the services industry, and customers have become critical in defining how employee performance is defined and assessed. The Total Quality Management movement has also resulted in a focus on customer expectations. In this case, however, "customers" are not only external purchasers but also internal coworkers that an employee may be serving in one capacity or another.

Many issues that are relevant to performance measurement and assessment have resulted from this change to a customer-focused world of work. For example, how does one reconcile possible differences in internal management and external customer performance standards, and how does one deal with the resulting differences in performance expectations? Whereas in the old world employees primarily needed to put pieces together to form quality products, the product is now much more intangible and is often a function of the partnership between the employee and his or her customer. The interpersonal and consulting behaviors that contribute to high levels of performance in these types of work situations and to the requisite skills that underlie them are much different than they were in the past. The issue of how to accurately evaluate the fuzzy and less tangible customer service performance raises numerous definition and measurement issues.

Limitations on Leadership and Supervision

All of the factors described in the preceding sections not only have a great impact on workers but they also have implications for managerial and supervisory roles in organizations. Traditional supervisory roles suitable for hierarchical organizations are much less apt to fit well in organizations that are characterized by self-directed work teams or high levels of employee flexibility with respect to the tasks performed, the hours worked, the location where work is performed, and so forth. In addition, the supervision of employees who have less stable jobs or who are working on multiple project teams that are not within the supervisor's direct purview presents some distinct challenges. The role of supervisor as an employee developer, rewarder, motivator, and appraiser may need to be reconceptualized and reoperationalized to deal with the changing nature of work.

Changes in the Structure of Work from Individuals to Teams

The structure of work is changing from being organized around individuals to being structured around work groups or teams (Guzzo, 1995; Ilgen, 1994). Traditionally, a job was mapped onto each employee. In that approach, it was possible to isolate relatively well the duties and responsibilities of each individual, as well as to conduct a job analysis to specify the cluster of activities performed. The job analysis could then be used to describe the duties and responsibilities of jobholders, to identify the knowledges, skills, abilities, and other characteristics required for the job, and to develop performance standards.

Alternatively, the team approach maps jobs onto the teams and allows for considerable fluidity over time and among persons in the way duties and responsibilities are associated with team members. This makes it far more difficult to isolate, and hence to evaluate, reward, and develop, individual performance. In addition, from a staffing perspective more or different skills and abilities (such as interpersonal skills and social intelligence) are likely required for workers to operate effectively in team environments than in traditional work environments that have the individual as their primary focus. Finally, individuals may be members of more than one team at a time, which requires them to be adaptable to different group processes, goals, and customers of their work. How to resolve conflicts and contribute effectively to group solutions are important performance requirements for individuals working within a team structure.

Plan of the Book

As long as people are engaged in producing goods and services, their performance is critical to organizational effectiveness. A fundamental objective of all human resource practices is to ensure that members of the organization can perform effectively and contribute to the organization's objectives. Defining, assessing, predicting, and changing performance is as critical today as it ever was. Yet we have argued that a number of changes in the nature of work have altered the way performance is viewed and made it considerably more difficult to define, assess, predict, and affect performance. This introductory chapter has touched on a few of these issues.

The remainder of the book elaborates on performance in organizations from two perspectives. First, the seven chapters in Part One describe in detail the seven key changes, introduced in this chapter, that are strongly influencing work and work settings and discusses their implications for performance. Beryl Hesketh and Andrew Neal begin this discussion in Chapter Two by focusing on technology. They explore the implications of understanding human performance when it is inextricably entangled with technology. They also consider technology as a medium through which the performance of people is observed and measured. Stephan Motowidlo and Mark Schmit, in Chapter Three, raise the issue that all task or job performance occurs in the context in which the job is imbedded. To what extent behavior directed toward the context is or is not part of performance and how such behavior should be construed is the subject of their chapter.

In Chapter Four, Charles Hulin and Theresa Glomb address the fact that the workforce is shifting from one consisting almost exclusively of full-time employees to one populated with high proportions of contingent workers. To understand the performance of the total workforce, we are going to have to understand contingent workers in terms of both their individual performance and the effect of the intermingling of contingent and noncontingent employees throughout the organization.

An increase in the pace of change places demands on all employees to update their skills to keep up with that change. Given this critical need to update, successful job performance is limited not only to how well people meet current job demands but also to how well they prepare themselves for future conditions, some of which may not be well understood in advance. In Chapter Five, Manuel London and Edward Mone look at continuous learning, both in terms of its role in preparing for future performance and as a part of present performance.

In traditional organizations, what constitutes performance is typically determined by the tasks that people do and by other people within the organization, such as supervisors, who design jobs, specify standards for good performance, and evaluate the extent to which the standards are met. The recent attention given to customer needs and desires shifts responsibility for defining performance from within to outside the organization. In some cases, performance itself is a function of customers' behavior, such as when the cleanliness of a fast-food establishment depends in part on how well customers carry out their role and throw away their trash. Chapter Six, by David Bowen and David Waldman, looks at the role of customers in performance.

Robert Lord and Wendy Gradwohl Smith, in Chapter Seven, and Steve Kozlowski, Stanley Gully, Earl Nason, and Eleanor Smith, in Chapter Eight, conclude Part One by directing attention to social changes in the nature of work as they affect performance. Lord and Gradwohl Smith consider leadership as an emergent social process that is only partially under the influence of the leader. Kozlowski, Gully, Nason, and Smith focus on teams and the dynamic nature of their change over time. Performance in the team at any given time is a complex mix of task, interpersonal, and individual factors considered against the background of the team's past and members' beliefs about its future.

Taking the conditions described in Chapters Two through Eight as givens, Part Two—Chapters Nine through Eleven—shifts the focus to the three human resource processes in which performance and performance measurement are central. Not all seven of the conditions examined in the earlier chapters affect each of the three processes, but each process is affected by several of the seven. In Chapter Nine, Kevin Murphy begins the discussion with a look at staffing, paying particular attention to selection processes in which individual performance has classically been considered the criterion against which the quality of selection should be assessed. Murphy addresses a number of interesting problems that the changes affecting performance may create, but he also cautions that we should not overestimate the level of change that is likely to occur over the long run.

In Chapter Ten, Patrice Murphy and Susan Jackson focus on motivational effects of performance change. They argue that jobs and roles are socially constructed realities in which the influence of the jobholder or roleholder is increasingly making it harder to define performance and more likely that conflict and misunderstandings will occur among people.

Finally, Kurt Kraiger, in Chapter Eleven, asks how changes in the nature of performance are likely to affect individuals' ability to learn, change, and keep pace with the new demands of their jobs. All of the conditions discussed in Chapters Two through Eight point to accelerated change and the need for adaptability. Kraiger addresses ways of meeting this need.

Part Three concludes the book with a chapter by John Campbell. Throughout the book, the authors frequently rely on Campbell's model of performance (Campbell, 1990; Campbell et al., 1993). In Chapter Twelve, Campbell examines the conditions described in Chapters Two through Eight and reacts to them. He also examines the effects on the human resource process discussed in Part Two as they relate to our ability to cope with the changing nature of performance at work.

References

Bridges, W. (1994a). The end of the job. *Fortune, 130*(6), 62–74.

Bridges, W. (1994b). *Job shift.* Reading, MA: Addison-Wesley.

Campbell, J. P. (1990). Modeling the performance prediction problem in industrial and organizational psychology. In M. D. Dunnette & L. M. Hough (Eds.), *Handbook of industrial and organizational psychology* (Vol. 1, 2nd ed., pp. 687–732). Palo Alto, CA: Consulting Psychologists Press.

Campbell, J. P., McCloy, R. A., Oppler, S. H., & Sager, C. E. (1993). A theory of performance. In N. Schmitt & W. C. Borman (Eds.), *Personnel selection in organizations* (pp. 35–70). San Francisco: Jossey-Bass.

Davis, D. D. (1995). Form, function, and strategy in boundaryless organizations. In A. Howard (Ed.), *The changing nature of work* (pp. 112–138). San Francisco: Jossey-Bass.

Featherstone, M. (1991). *Consumer culture and postmodernism.* London: Sage.

Guzzo, R. A. (1995). Introduction: At the intersection of team effectiveness and decision making. In R. A. Guzzo & E. Salas (Eds.), *Team effectiveness and decision making in organizations* (pp. 1–8). San Francisco: Jossey-Bass.

Hedge, J. W., & Borman, W. C. (1995). Changing conceptions and practices in performance appraisal. In A. Howard (Ed.), *The changing nature of work* (pp. 451–482). San Francisco: Jossey-Bass.

Howard, A. (1995). A framework for work change. In A. Howard (Ed.), *The changing nature of work* (pp. 3–44). San Francisco: Jossey-Bass.

Ilgen, D. R. (1994). Jobs and roles: Accepting and coping with the changing structure of organizations. In M. G. Rumsey, C. B. Walker, & J. H. Harris (Eds.), *Personnel selection and classification* (pp. 13–22). Hillsdale, NJ: Erlbaum.

Jackson, S. E. (1992). *Diversity in the workforce: Human relations initiatives.* Washington, DC: American Psychological Association.

London, M., & Beatty, R. (1993). 360-degree feedback as a competitive advantage. *Human Resource Management, 32,* 353–372.

Naisbit, J. (1982). *Megatrends: Ten new directions transforming our lives.* New York: Warner Books.

Offermann, L. R., & Gowing, M. K. (1990). Organizations of the future: Changes and challenges. *American Psychologist, 45,* 95–108.

Schneider, B. (1987). The people make the place. *Personnel Psychology, 40,* 437–453.

Tracey, J. B., Tannenbaum, S. I., & Kavanagh, M. J. (1995). Applying trained skills on the job: The importance of the work environment. *Journal of Applied Psychology, 80,* 239–252.

Upton, D. M., & McAfee, A. (1996). The real virtual factory. *Harvard Business Review, 74*(4), 123–133.

Weitz, J. (1956). Job expectancy and job survival. *Journal of Applied Psychology, 40,* 245–247.

PART 1

Changes in Work That Impact Performance

CHAPTER 2

Technology and Performance

Beryl Hesketh
Andrew Neal

Through the centuries, technology has been a major influence on change in the workplace. This change is sometimes incremental, but it may also offer radical departures from traditional ways of working. Although many would argue that the current information-based technological revolution is little different from earlier technological revolutions, it has resulted in a major change to the nature of work. In the past and particularly now, technology has influenced how people work, what they do, and how their performance is monitored and evaluated. In this chapter we treat technology in a broad sense, although most of our examples are drawn from manufacturing and computer-based technologies, particularly those that have contributed to the extended way in which information is able to be used. We do not offer a single definition of technology, but we have been influenced by the view of Sproull and Goodman (1990) that technology includes "knowledge of cause-and-effect relationships embodied in machines and methods" (p. 255). The difficulty of obtaining agreed-on definitions of technology is evident in the processes that have been followed in the "Technology for All Americans" project (Satchwell & Dugger, 1996), which aims to introduce technology as a core subject in the school curriculum. In an attempt to define the concept, these authors draw on the work of Johnson, Foster, and Satchwell (1989), who suggest that technology is applications-oriented applied science and applied human knowledge that extends human capability and exists in both hardware (tools, equipment, and so on) and software (such as the Internet). A broad view of technology such as this one fits the purpose of this chapter, the major emphasis of which is on understanding the ways that technology extends human capability and performance.

Technology has invaded all areas of work, including education, finance, banking, retailing, hospitality, tourism, and manufacturing. Milbank (1993) draws attention to the shift within traditional blue collar work by which 40 percent of the workforce is now employed in "New Collar" work (blue collar work in a white collar setting). Manufacturing has become automated, with increased electronic monitoring of the automated processes. These developments pose a major challenge to traditional ways of conceptualizing and assessing performance, while also offering new ways of measuring it. For example, electronic monitoring of automated systems provides a basis for electronic monitoring of the human operators of these processes. In many instances management may be less interested in how output is achieved, as long as the combination of technology and people effectively attains production or reaches other goals. The blurring of the people-and-technology contribution to measurable performance output poses a major threat to traditional ways of dealing with criteria in industrial and organizational psychology, where the primary interest is in the contribution of the person. Although conceptually it may remain important to maintain a pure definition of performance, obtaining actual measures of this that are unconfounded by technology may become increasingly difficult. In this chapter we examine the relations between technology and performance, with a particular emphasis on understanding the components of performance that have traditionally been used as criteria in industrial and organizational psychology.

Isolating the components of performance that are useful in criterion measurement requires an understanding of the main effects of people and technology, as well an understanding of the person-by-technology interaction. We use Campbell's model of performance (1990) as a starting point, but apply person-technology (P-T) fit and interaction ideas to it, highlighting possible ways of modeling the contributions of people and technology to performance. In doing this, we argue that it may no longer be possible to assume that technology is not a direct determinant of individual performance. We argue, rather, that technology can be both a determinant and an antecedent of performance. We draw on the broader person-by-situation debate, and on recent response surface approaches to person-environment (P-E) fit (Edwards & Van Harrison, 1993), to illustrate the effects of technology at each level of the Campbell model.

Our discussion of the Campbell model is informed by ideas from the personality literature relating to weak and strong situations (Adler, 1996), from the cognitive literature relevant to problem solving and skill acquisition (Anderson & Fincham, 1994; Hesketh, 1997; Neal & Hesketh, 1996), and from the literature on attribution theory (Kelley & Michela, 1980). We review the ways in which people integrate information derived from electronic monitoring with traditional judgmental data, and comment on the consequences of electronic monitoring for motivation and stress. Finally, throughout we suggest practical ways of assessing performance when it is confounded by technology. Although we argue for a new view of performance that acknowledges that technology is an integral component of observed performance, we do provide suggestions for ways of partialing out direct influences of technology on performance when this is necessary.

Modeling Performance

The Campbell Model of performance offers a comprehensive framework for understanding performance in an organizational context.

The Campbell Model of Performance

Campbell (1990) defines performance as a set of behaviors that are relevant for the goals of an organization. Effectiveness, conversely, is defined as the outcomes that stem from these behaviors. Campbell argues that performance consists of at least eight separate components: job-specific task proficiency, non-job-specific task proficiency, written and oral communication task proficiency, demonstration of effort, maintenance of personal discipline, facilitation of coworkers, leadership and supervision, and management and administration. This eight-factor model is argued to represent the highest level of abstraction that is sufficient to describe all of the jobs in the *Dictionary of Occupational Titles*. A similar model has been developed by Borman and Motowidlo (1993), who propose that these eight factors can be grouped into two broad clusters of behavior: task performance and contextual performance. Campbell (1990) argues that because performance is under the complete control of the individual, it can have only three determinants: declarative knowledge (knowledge of facts), procedural knowledge (automated skills), and motivation. These determinants are in turn influenced by a range of individual and situational antecedents. Individual antecedents include ability, experience, and personality. Situational antecedents include such factors as job design and leadership.

A substantial body of evidence derived from Project A (Campbell, McHenry, & Wise, 1990) and other defense-related research (Kanfer & Ackerman, 1989) supports the Campbell model. Ability and experience are strong predictors of task proficiency, while personality constructs, such as achievement orientation and dependability, predict contextual performance (McHenry et al., 1990; Motowidlo & Van Scotter, 1994; Wise, McHenry, & Campbell, 1990). Furthermore, ability and experience predict declarative and procedural knowledge, while personality constructs predict motivation (Ackerman, 1992; Borman, White, & Dorsey, 1995; Borman, White, Pulakos, & Oppler, 1991; Campbell, Gasser, & Oswald, 1996; Kanfer & Ackerman, 1989; McCloy, Campbell, & Cudeck, 1994).

A key assumption of the Campbell model is that behaviors used as measures of performance must be under the complete control of the individual. The model assumes that situational factors, such as technology, cannot act as direct determinants of performance. Instead, situational factors such as technology are thought to act as antecedents of performance (by influencing motivation, for example), as direct determinants of effectiveness, or as moderators of the relationship between performance and effectiveness. Although this approach is theoretically neat, we argue that it may no longer be practically applied in many jobs. It is often extremely difficult to generate measures of individual performance that are not contaminated by technological factors. Given this confounded relationship between performance and technology, we believe that it is not appropriate to restrict the definition of performance to behavior that is completely under the control of the individual. Instead we argue that individual and technological influences need to be addressed at all levels of the model. P-E fit and interaction models, and the person-by-situation debate in personality, provide one way of conceptualizing these influences. In the next section we draw on the conceptual features emerging from the P-E fit literature to gain further insight into the ways in which the person-by-technology (P × T) interaction may influence various components of performance.

Person-by-Technology Interaction in Performance

Recent developments in conceptualizing fit offer insight into ways of dealing with the P × T confounded relationship and suggest a new way of conceptualizing performance (Edwards, 1991; Hesketh & Gardner, 1993; Edwards & Van Harrison, 1993). Edwards (1991) has drawn attention to problems with traditional P-E fit models in which fit has been conceptualized in a simplistic form, such as a difference score or some other composite index, without any thought being given to the nature of the direct effects of the person or the environment, or to the type of interaction between the two. Edwards argues that researchers need to specify the precise nature of the three-dimensional relationship between P, E, and the outcome measure of interest. This involves using polynomial regression terms, along with interactions, to test for linear and nonlinear main effects. The same logic can be used to examine the influence of the person and technology at different levels in the performance model. Rather than excluding the effects of technology, Edwards's response surface approach highlights the importance of considering the manner in which the individual person's contribution can interact with technology.

The literature on weak and strong situations (Weiss & Adler, 1984) provides one basis for developing predictions about the form of the interaction between the person and technology. Adler (1996) reviews a decade of research including meta-analytic studies that show how situations affect the strength of relationship between personality and performance. Weiss and Adler (1984) draw attention to the contribution of situational flexibility to the validity of personality tests in a selection context. Where a situation is highly predictable and controlled (a strong situation), there is little opportunity for personality to be expressed. Where the situation is more flexible, however, permitting the expression of individual differences (a weak situation), validities are likely to be higher. Barrick and Mount (1993) have shown that conscientiousness, extroversion, and agreeableness are stronger predictors of job performance where employees enjoy greater autonomy (a weak situation). Extrapolating from this research, we predict that in a strong technology environment there may be insufficient scope for individual differences to express an influence on performance. Weaker technology environments, however, may offer greater opportunities to detect a person's contribution.

The contribution of strong and weak situations and the interaction of individual and situational factors can be illustrated using a sporting analogy. Anabolic steroids (considered a form of technology for purposes of this illustration) are known to interact with individual differences in skill levels and with individual differences in the amount of practice needed to influence performance in sports such as swimming or weight lifting. They make no direct contribution, however, to performance. Although steroids facilitate performance in the presence of practice and skill, they may impair performance, or have no influence, in the absence of practice or skill. Anabolic steroids amplify the contribution of individual differences to performance, but the increments in performance arising from drugs could not have been achieved without skill and extended training. We would argue that this interaction should be considered a part of the person component. A view such as this is controversial in the sporting arena, where every effort is made to reduce the variance in the technology-drug contribution in assessing a person's uncontaminated performance. There can be few work contexts, however, where it would make sense to handicap performance to provide an even playing field for employees in order to facilitate the measurement of performance. Although there may be occasions when it is desirable to partial out the direct effects of the technology, the component of performance that arises from an interaction between variations in levels of technological sophistication and individual differences (such as ability or personality) indicates that some individuals are capable of benefiting from technological enhancements, a feature that should interest management in both selection and training contexts.

More complex three-dimensional relationships between the person, technology, and performance are also possible. An example from tennis illustrates one such complex interaction. Let us assume that there is a direct linear relationship between individual differences in skill or tennis ability and tennis proficiency; a small, accelerating relationship between technology (sophistication of the racquets) and proficiency; and a significant interaction between the differing levels of technology and tennis ability among individuals. Racquet technology may have an important influence among individuals with more skill (advantages accrue with a good racquet), but among less skilled players, poor racquet technology may have little influence on performance. Individual differences (predominantly in procedural skills for this example) may have a direct linear relationship with tennis performance, and it may interact with skill such that a skilled player is able to gain incremental benefits from improved racquet technology. This interaction, we argue, represents an important domain of performance for purposes of selection and training.

To summarize the argument this far, we suggest that Campbell's model (1990) may require modification to accommodate the contribution of technology in components other than effectiveness. Edwards's emphasis (1991) on the importance of understanding both direct and interacting influences of person and environment on outcomes can be applied to the P × T contribution to performance. A complete picture of the P × T interaction requires measures of main effects as well as their interactions. In the next section we take this core idea from Edwards and apply it more specifically to the antecedents and determinants of performance in Campbell's model. We also use the opportunity to unpack these components of the Campbell model, drawing on recent developments in cognitive psychology in relation to problem solving and categorization.

Technology as an Antecedent of Performance

There is reasonable evidence to suggest that technology can act as an antecedent of performance, through its direct effect on motivation and knowledge, and possibly through interactions with variables such as ability and experience.

Motivation

It is commonly assumed that technology can influence performance through its effects on job design and individual motivation (Wall & Martin, 1987). Few consistent findings, however, have emerged from field studies investigating these links (Cordery, Mueller, & Smith, 1991; Wall, Kemp, Jackson, & Clegg, 1986). The reason for these inconsistent findings could be that these studies have focused on task performance rather than on contextual performance. Technology has been found to exert meaningful effects on job control, cognitive demand, and production responsibility (Jackson, Wall, Martin, & Davids, 1993). For example, the introduction of advanced manufacturing technology (AMT) can lead to operator dissatisfaction and strain if it reduces operator control or increases job demands beyond the operator's capacity (Blumberg & Gerwin, 1984; Martin & Wall, 1989; Wall et al., 1990). Although there is no evidence to suggest that these affective reactions to technology influence task proficiency, they may well influence motivation to perform contextual behaviors. Furthermore, technology may also interact with individual difference variables, such as self-efficacy, to influence motivation (see, for example, Martocchio, 1992; Mathieu, Martineau, & Tannenbaum, 1993) and possibly contextual performance.

Procedural and Declarative Knowledge

Technology can also be a determinant of procedural knowledge. Wall, Jackson, and Davids (1992) found that AMT systems that include the operator in the control loop have less downtime than systems that do not include operator control. Jackson and Wall (1991) demonstrated that the reduced incidence of downtime stemmed from the operators learning to anticipate and prevent the incidence of faults. This skill appeared to be learned implicitly, because it was acquired directly from experience and was not associated with declarative knowledge about the complex cause-and-effect relationships embedded within the system (see Chmiel & Wall, 1994; Neal & Hesketh, 1997). These studies also demonstrate the importance of examining the direct effect of technology on system effectiveness. Wall, Jackson, and Davids (1992) found that only moderate periods of downtime were preventable. The large-scale breakdowns were directly attributable to the technology and could not be prevented by the operators.

Technology as a Determinant of Performance

The literature on expertise, problem solving, and categorization can be used to illustrate how technology can act as a direct determinant of performance. Research across a range of problem domains demonstrates that people typically perform difficult tasks by classifying the problem according to the types of procedures needed for solution, retrieving one or more prior examples, mapping the correspondences between the examples and the problem, and then developing a set of procedures, based on those used in the earlier examples, to solve the current problem (Medin & Ross, 1989; Reeves & Weisberg, 1994). Repeated practice on a task is thought to produce an improvement in speed and accuracy by allowing the individual to retrieve the solution directly from memory rather than deliberately abstracting a new solution each time (Anderson & Fincham, 1994; Logan, 1988).

The major determinant of performance that has been emphasized within the cognitive literature is prior knowledge (Wisniewski & Medin, 1994). There are two types of prior knowledge that individuals can use to perform a task: *abstract knowledge* and *instance-based knowledge*. Abstract knowledge is knowledge of the underlying structure of the problem domain, and instance-based knowledge is knowledge of prior examples. Experts are thought to perform well because they have more complex forms of abstract knowledge and because they have more examples stored in memory. The following section outlines how technology can interact with these cognitive processes.

Supplementing Prior Knowledge

Technology can act as a direct determinant of performance by supplementing prior knowledge. Many people treat computer-based information as an extension of their own abstract and instance-based knowledge. For example, the way information is structured in information technology may give hints or clues about how to develop solution procedures, eliminating the need to retrieve prior examples and map correspondences. Developments in computer science address these issues by examining ways in which language and graphics can assist problem solving. Clever interface designs mimic user knowledge structures, or provide an extension of these, presenting a situation that confounds performance and technology to a high degree. Law provides an example relevant to the role of instance-based knowledge. A key feature of expert lawyers used to be their capacity to draw on memories of instances of case law to solve current problems. Now these cases are stored on databases and do not have to be retrieved from memory. Technology, in the form of variations in the adequacy of the store of examples, the structure for organizing these, and the user interface, is a direct determinant of performance in these situations.

These forms of technology may also interact with individual differences in factors such as prior knowledge, memory, and ability. For example, prior knowledge may aid an individual's ability to search a database or use an expert system appropriately, particularly if the knowledge structures embedded in the technology match those that are represented in the user's memory. Furthermore, the design of human-computer systems has progressed to the point where the system can adapt to and compensate for the knowledge held by the individual (Rencken & Durrant-Whyte, 1993). Adaptive aiding can involve transforming the data displayed to the human operator to better suit the individual user, partitioning the tasks to be undertaken by the operator or the computer, and providing expert system advice during problem solving. It is surprising that in the past little attention has been given to the implications of these ergonomic interventions for the actual measurement of performance.

In practice, disentangling technology-based and human-based knowledge in an example such as this is complex, and may even be unnecessary for purposes of selection and training. Rather, work sample tests can be used to assess individual differences in how quickly people adapt to and make use of computer-based extensions to their own knowledge, while training will need to focus on facilitating this process. Similarly, tests can be developed to determine how well individuals search databases for instances of knowledge. Finally, measures of knowledge structure, such as concept mapping (Novak, 1990) and Pathfinder (Cooke, Durso, & Schvaneveldt, 1986), can be used to evaluate the compatibility between a user's knowledge structure and the structure of the technological domain. These measures can be used to predict or evaluate training success (Dorsey & Foster, 1996; Kraiger, Ford, & Salas, 1993).

Influencing Task Complexity

Technology may also act as a determinant of performance by influencing the complexity of the tasks that the operator must perform. For example, AMT has dramatically increased the complexity of many of the problems that operators solve. The complexity of these problems is determined by the nature of the underlying cause-and-effect relationships within the system, and by the design of the user interface. Technologies that require operators to process lagged effects, or to integrate large amounts of separate information, are known to impair performance (Chmiel & Wall, 1994).

Drawing on ideas from the P-E fit literature, we suggest that the interaction between the complexity of the technology and the complexity of the knowledge that operators use may also influence performance. Several commentators have emphasized the importance of abstract knowledge when dealing with complex technologies (Reason, 1990; Weick, 1990). Abstract knowledge allows operators to transfer prior knowledge to new examples, even when the surface features of the two problems differ. This characteristic of abstract knowledge is useful for operators when the system is operating outside the bounds of their experience, particularly during emergencies (such as the Chernobyl disaster). Unfortunately, the problem with using abstract knowledge is that many technologies are so complex that operators cannot develop a complete understanding of the complex cause-and-effect relationships within the system. Laboratory studies have demonstrated that humans simplify these types of complex relations by using incomplete or fragmentary rules (Palmeri & Nosofsky, 1995; Perruchet & Pacteau, 1990). In these situations, it may be more appropriate to rely on instance-based knowledge. Instance-based knowledge allows the individual to respond to local contextual factors that cannot be captured in general rules (Brooks, 1987), and may be used in a relatively effortless and automatic manner (Neal, Hesketh, & Andrews, 1995). Unfortunately, the difficulty with using instance-based knowledge is that it may not transfer to novel situations quite as well as rule-based knowledge. Furthermore, in highly complex systems the user interface often presents information at a high level of abstraction and impairs access to instance-based information. This occurs in complex automated cockpits, in control systems in manufacturing, and in air traffic control. A technology layer that helps transpose real instances into intuitive and understandable symbolic instances may facilitate learning; it may also open up dangers associated with system failure as operators no longer know how to deal directly with the plant or equipment.

As is the case with P-E fit measures, measuring the complexity of technology and the complexity of knowledge on a commensurate scale will facilitate untangling the P × T interaction. Unfortunately, the construct of complexity has proven to be extremely difficult to operationalize. One possibility is to operationalize complexity in terms of the number of elements that are needed to represent a given relationship in memory. Halford and colleagues (1994) have developed a system for classifying complexity levels of data representations in memory. The simplest levels of representation are associative (elemental and configural associations). Associative representations are capable of accounting for many forms of learning (such as conditional discrimination), but they cannot be used for reasoning and higher cognitive processes. More complex representations include explicit relations between the elements. Humans have been shown to be able to represent from one (for unary relations) to five (for quinary relations) elements in an explicit relationship. It should be possible to use a taxonomy such as this to measure the complexity of both the knowledge structures used by individuals and the technological environment with which they deal. For example, simple forms of technology, such as typewriters, require the operator to represent elemental associations (between keys and letters). Complex types of technology, such as air traffic control systems, require operators to represent higher order relationships (such as speed, altitude, flight path, aircraft type, and call sign). By measuring the complexity of knowledge and technology on the same metric, it becomes easier to apply P-T fit analysis for purposes of untangling the individual person's contribution. The analysis-of-variance method discussed shortly would require commensurate measurement of this sort.

Technology and Error

Finally, technology can act as a determinant of performance by influencing human error. The cognitive literature reviewed earlier suggests that technology can influence error by causing operators to misclassify problems, retrieve the wrong examples, map the wrong correspondences between the prior examples and the current problem, or apply the wrong procedure. For example, during the Three Mile Island disaster, the operators failed to recognize that a relief valve was stuck open and that high temperature radioactive water was pouring into the basement. This error represented a misclassification of the problem. Technology was largely responsible for this error, because the warning light did not show the actual status of the valve (Reason, 1990). This type of research into human faultfinding and problem-solving procedures has informed the development of integrated manufacturing systems that combine human factors with system variables to increase effectiveness and efficiency of fault finding (Morrison, 1994). Partitioning the variance in performance into person and technology components in these situations is extremely difficult, even though conceptually it may remain desirable to do so.

Technology can offer a complementary role in prompting people when they make errors (Zapf & Reason, 1994). This form of feedback compensates to some extent for a lack of self-awareness on the part of human operators. If used correctly technology-based error detection and feedback could help increase the accuracy of self-assessment and enhance skill acquisition (Ohlsson, 1996). Alternatively, if automated error detection and correction is readily available, there is a danger that operators would cease to engage in self-regulation of their performance and rely exclusively on automated monitoring. Under these latter circumstances, technology may interfere with the development of metacognitive skills associated with accurate self-assessment that are known to increase as expertise improves. No doubt the solution lies in encouraging the active processing required for human error detection, but with the safeguard of technology-based error detection as feedback and as a basis for error recovery.

This discussion illustrates again how technology extends the individual determinant, making it somewhat difficult to disentangle contributions, particularly for purposes of validating selection measures and training interventions. In the next section we outline suggestions for ways of assessing the contributions of both people and technology as well as their interactions.

Measuring Individual and Technological Contributions to Performance

In this section we draw on attribution theory, the measurement of performance in relation to expectations or goals, and control theory to suggest ways in which performance might be measured when technology interacts with the contribution of the person. We highlight ways in which one may attempt to understand the direct contributions of both the individual and technology to performance, as well as to understand the P-T interaction. We believe that the component of variance accounted for by the interaction is important for purposes of criterion development and performance assessment, because without the contribution of the person, this interaction could not exist. There may, however, be situations in which one wishes to partial out the direct contribution (main effect) of the technology, particularly when obtaining criterion data for research.

Attributional Processes in Partitioning Variance Judgment

Judgmental data will remain the major source of information about performance, and hence there is a need to develop practical methods of partitioning the variance in performance to distinguish between the person component (both directly and in interaction with technology) and the component due purely to technology. Untangling the respective contributions to performance of the person, technology, and their interactions involves a causal analysis and requires asking those providing the performance ratings to make an attribution for output either to the person, to the technology, or to some interaction of the two (Kelley & Michella, 1980). For example, assume the existence of multiple meat-processing plants, half of which are equipped with modern technology and the other half having to manage with dated and frequently faulty equipment. Assume also that traditional individual difference variables in the form of ability, personality, and other relevant attributes exist among the meat workers in all of these plants. It would be unfair to attribute all differences in performance levels in these two types of plants to individual differences, unless there were systematic differences in general ability or other relevant attributes between the two groups of plants. Even within one plant, or on one process line, isolating the contribution of performance independent of technology is difficult, yet this is what is asked of a rater in completing a performance assessment.

Early in the development of attribution theory, Feldman (1981) drew attention to its relevance in the process of making performance inferences of this sort. Kelley's covariation attribution model (Kelley & Michela, 1980) provides an analysis of variance framework for teasing out causal contributions. Specifically, Kelley would claim that where a particular level of performance arises in association with low consensus (others do not perform similarly on the same equipment), low distinctiveness (an individual performs at a particular level across a range of situations or types of equipment), and high consistency (a person performs consistently at a particular level over time), then the level of performance can be attributed to the individual. Where everyone, however, performs at a particular level on the equipment (high consensus) and the individual does not show this level of performance in different situations (high distinctiveness) nor consistently across occasions (low consistency), a technology attribution is more likely. There are of course other combinations of levels of consistency, consensus, and distinctiveness, with extensive research suggesting likely attributions (Kelley & Michela, 1980). Although attribution theory suggests a way of partitioning the variance and attributing causes, in practice it is difficult to obtain sufficient and relevant information in applied contexts to permit these inferences. Nevertheless, the framework is a useful one because it suggests an experimental approach to partitioning the variance so that the person's direct contribution and his or her contribution in interaction with technology can be identified, independent of the direct contribution of technology.

Systematic variation of the contribution of technology may provide a basis for understanding its influence over performance. A hypothetical example may help illustrate this point. Assume that within an organization one has three types of personal computers and associated software that vary in terms of the speed with which word processing operations can be performed and in the nature of the aids to report-writing that are available in the software. Assume also that within the organizations there are standard individual differences among employees on factors such as typing speed and general ability. These differences can be treated as a continuous or grouped factor. Assume also that individuals are asked to prepare three different but equivalent reports, one on each of the computers. These reports can be assessed in terms of timeliness, overall quality in appearance, and accuracy. Using an analysis of variance, or multiple regression framework, it may be possible to determine the main effect or direct contribution for the level of technology; the direct contribution of individual differences among the employees on, say, a measure of ability; and the interaction between the individual difference factor and the level of technology. As discussed earlier, we would argue that, unlike the traditional moderator role of technology, the interaction between technology and individual differences is to some extent under the control of the person, and hence belongs to "performance." To ignore the main effect for the technology, however, may result in unfair comparative judgments of performance, and hence the direct contribution of technology (independent of the interaction) is worth assessing. Extending the example to obtain actual measures of performance may require building on a work-sample approach to assessing performance. Although we would argue that this has merit, work samples tend to assess maximal rather than typical performance, and task rather than contextual performance. It would also be a costly way of trying to partial out technology contributions. These limitations would need to be kept in mind.

Errors provide another salient source of performance information that is available to raters in making attributions about performance and that is subject to P × T interactions. Technology has a role both in creating errors (system errors, failure of hard disks, and so on) and in providing a basis for error management through the detection of errors after they are made (such as spelling checkers) and through error recovery (such as undo facilities; Frese, 1991). Error analysis requires careful disentangling of the human and technology factor. Accident investigators are adept at this type of analysis, although the fundamental attribution error (Kelley & Michela, 1980) is not unusual. Aircraft accident or incident analysis in Air Traffic Control involves systematic attempts to attribute blame to either pilot, air traffic controller, or other human error (either directly or in combination with technology), or to some form of equipment or technology malfunction over which the person had no control. Accurate attributions of errors, incidents, or accidents are critical in the future development of appropriate air traffic controller, pilot, and cockpit training, or of selection systems.

Aircraft or other major accidents justify the time involved in carrying out the detective work to make accurate attributions. In many work contexts, day-to-day analysis of this sort is neither cost-effective nor likely, even though it may be necessary to isolate contributing factors. Nevertheless, every rater will need some of the skills required to engage in the detective work necessary to make accurate attributions about errors and other aspects of performance, and to integrate the information into performance judgments.

Whether those responsible for performance appraisal are capable of making complex attributions, about either performance or errors, that rely on interpreting interactions, controlling for technology's main effects as well as dealing with nonlinear relations remains an empirical question. Research is needed to determine whether rater training can alert raters to the direct effects of technology and to the $P \times T$ interactions and allow them to make moderately accurate attributions. In keeping with the new view of performance, raters would be expected to include the technology-by-person interaction as part of the performance being rated, although they may need to partial out direct contributions of the technology.

Measuring Performance Against Expectations That Adjust for Technology

Another way of overcoming the difficulty of partitioning the performance variance between the person (including the $P \times T$ interaction) and technology is to measure performance in relation to individual or group targets or goals that have been set with an understanding of the extent to which technology directly enhances or inhibits performance in a particular job or context. The use of expectations that take into account the technology contribution (main effect) has several advantages. First, it builds on goal setting, which is known to have motivational implications. Second, it has the possibility of overcoming a focus on past behavior in assessing performance; instead, it stresses striving and future performance. Third, expectations-based performance assessment can be used at the team, division, or any aggregate level, providing a coherence to performance assessment across these levels. Finally, there are technologies for scaling expectations (Hesketh, 1993) both at the individual level—such as Goal Attainment Scaling, or GAS (Kiresuk & Sherman, 1968)—and at the group or team level—such as the Productivity and Measurement Enhancement System, or ProMES (Pritchard et al., 1989).

GAS is a scaling technique that permits comparison of outcomes across individuals when there are different expected levels of outcome and even different dimensions or weights for dimensions. Specifically, in relation to performance this would mean setting expected performance goals in different domains and, if desired, weighting the importance of those domains. Typically, anticipated measurable performance outcomes would be specified for five levels of performance assumed to have the characteristics of a standardized z-score (much better than expected, better than expected, expected, worse than expected, and much worse than expected). In setting expected levels of performance, the direct contribution of the technology to performance output can be taken into account. Because the aim is to isolate criterion-relevant components of performance (any direct contribution of the person or contribution arising from an interaction with technology), the expectations should be set for a given job and its associated technology. Actual performance would be rated subsequently against the a priori specified levels of expected performance.

The scaling technique outlined by Kiresuk and Sherman (1968) provides a basis for integrating outcomes across performance domains and converting these to a T score. Modifications to the formula may be needed, as it assumes a correlation of about .3 among different dimensions. In the performance appraisal field these intercorrelations are likely to be much higher. The scaling procedure is not unlike that outlined subsequently by Pritchard and colleagues (1989) when presenting the ProMES. The origin of GAS was clinical and community psychology, where it was designed to capture individualized goals and yet allow for group interpretations of outcomes. The use of GAS to capture expected levels of performance for an individual job and its associated technology could also be adopted to deal with performance at a group level.

ProMES was originally developed as both a motivational system and a way of measuring performance at a group level. It too involves assessing performance in relation to expected outcomes. Providing that the expectations were established taking into account the direct contribution of technology, ProMES provides a basis for assessing performance after partialing out a main effect for technology. ProMES can be adapted to deal with an individual-level contribution as well. Either GAS or ProMES could be used to deal with the earlier example of technology difference in meat-processing plants. In each case the expected level of outcome would take into account what could realistically be achieved through direct human effort or through human effort interacting with technology, allowing for the main effect of technology to be partialed out.

Control Theory

Control theory provides another approach for partitioning the contributions to performance of the person, technology, and their interactions. Most modern control theory aims to develop a model of the system that is to be the focus of control. It is this model-building component of control theory that offers possible insights into understanding the role of technology in performance. At a simple level, control theory involves having a set point (or goal), with measurements being taken of the discrepancy between the output and the goal or desired performance (Lord & Levy, 1994). This discrepancy or distance from set point activates an intervention to improve output. In most control theory applications, several factors interact, sometimes in nonlinear fashion, to produce the actual output, making it difficult to know which of the various input factors should be targeted for change to improve overall performance. The P × T interaction discussed earlier presents a similar dilemma. Assuming that the aim is to improve overall man-machine system performance, control theory offers a way of deciding where to put the change effort in order to achieve maximum increases. The dynamic and time-varying nature of most industrial control systems makes it easier to use regression-based procedures (across time as distinct from across people) to work out where to alter the process. Systematic experimentation is often carried out on the plant to provide sufficient variability to capture a model of the system through regression. Artificial perturbations may be used that permit a stronger inference about the contributions to overall performance of different input components. Furthermore, the modeling component provides a basis for developing simulations of the system that provide an off-line opportunity for experimentation about the system.

In the P-T interaction, a similar solution could be tried. Specifically, this would involve a variant of the work-sample approach currently used as both a predictor and a performance measure. If one is unsure whether the overall performance is due to the person, to technology, to the interaction, or some combination thereof, then it may make sense to test what happens when one alters one component of the situation. This might be achieved by swapping staff on different technology or computer systems, handicapping temporarily a more sophisticated computer system to assess the influence on performance, or temporarily providing an individual working on old technology with an updated version. Experimentation of this sort may permit a clearer partitioning of the P-T variance in understanding contributions to performance, particularly if the experimentation follows a response surface approach such as that of Edwards and Van Harrison (1993) or an analysis of variance framework of the sort outlined in Kelley's covariation model (Kelley & Michela, 1980), which was discussed earlier. Of particular interest here is the responsiveness of the person to technology. Some individuals may perform well but not demonstrate benefits from technology (no interaction). Others may both perform well and with enhanced technology show exceptional improvement. Clearly it is this responsiveness to technology (the interaction between the person and the technology) that will be of growing importance, and that should be incorporated into any model of performance.

The examples just presented rely on work-sample tests that emphasize task performance and do not capture typical performance or cover the contextual domain (Sackett, Zedeck, & Fogli, 1988). Other approaches may be needed to tap into the typical levels of performance sustained by individuals over longer periods, as well as those aspects of performance falling into the contextual domain. Measures of typical performance can be obtained through electronic monitoring, which can cover longer periods. As will become evident, however, the motivational influence of technology and electronic monitoring on performance depends on the way it is used and introduced.

Electronic Monitoring

Computerized performance monitoring (CPM) involves the use of new technology to record, store, retrieve, and present information relevant to human and system performance. It can provide information about attendance, speed, errors, and completion rates. CPM is increasingly being used in the United States in areas such as insurance, communication, transportation, and banking. Its use outside the United States is less widespread at this stage.

Advantages and Disadvantages of CPM

The role of CPM in the performance appraisal process has been analyzed within a cognitive model of the performance appraisal (Kulik & Ambrose, 1993b). The continual recording of computer-driven behavior provides potentially more accurate recording and recall of performance, which should increase the objectivity of performance assessment. Electronically produced data about performance, however, must still be used by individuals in making judgments and must often be integrated with other judgmental data. This need has given rise to a body of research concerned with the processing of electronically derived performance information, the relative advantages of different types of formats for its presentation, and different time spans and levels of detail contained in the electronic summary of performance (Ambrose & Kulik, 1994; Kulik & Ambrose, 1993b). Although research is in its early stages, some findings are available. For example, blocks of information facilitate integration but may also obscure patterns of improvement or decline over time.

Other advantages of CPM may be ease in giving feedback based on more objective information, reduction in potential litigation, and more comprehensive assessment over time. Despite these purported advantages, however, there are several unintended consequences of the use of CPM (Nussbaum & Du Rivage, 1986). Concern has been expressed that quality suffers where performance is monitored electronically, that CPM may have a negative influence on occupational health and well-being, and that there are implications for perceived control.

Aiello (1993) gives an example of how operators who were monitored for the number of calls they handled were able to achieve their targets by cutting off any callers they anticipated would take time (namely those with accents or who had a hearing problem). Subsequently, the operators were rewarded for reaching their target by sacrificing customer service, while operators who provided good customer service but handled fewer calls were not rewarded. Under these circumstances, it could be argued that electronic monitoring has affected quality.

Galinsky and Schleifer (1995) examined the use of CPM and feedback for data entry clerks trying to achieve speed goals. Baseline data were collected for the first day, then participants either were or were not provided with feedback in relation to preestablished standards. In this particular study, although speed goals were approached, there was an increase in errors. Goal setting is a powerful manipulation, and in combination with electronic monitoring, if speed goals are emphasized it is not surprising that quality suffers. It might also, however, have been possible to emphasize quality as well as speed.

The issues discussed here are not new to industrial and organizational psychologists who have long drawn attention to the pitfalls of blind reliance on purportedly objective measures of performance that fail to capture important aspects of performance (that is, they suffer from criterion deficiency). Those aspects of behavior that are noted, measured, and rewarded are likely to increase. If electronic monitoring captures only a component of performance, then only that component will be enhanced. Studies such as those of Aiello (1993) and Galinsky and Schleifer (1995) seem to suggest a problem with electronic monitoring in terms of its failure to capture quality with primary emphasis on quantity. This, however, is not a necessary consequence of electronic monitoring, which could be designed also to capture error rates and sample qualitative data. Shell and Allgeier (1992) suggest that regularly collected data from customer service questionnaires, although not performance monitoring as such, could be fed into a computerized system for feedback and used in incentive systems. It is not unreasonable to assume that in the future banks, restaurants, and other service organizations will set up at the exit door a brief computerized customer service questionnaire that will provide a form of electronic monitoring that does capture service quality. The information obtained could be related back to particular tellers or service personnel.

Shell and Allgeier (1992) describe the experiences of a particular organization that implemented a CPM system and associated incentive scheme only after extensive consultation and involvement of staff, and by following best practice with respect to incentive systems. The results were positive. The same system implemented within a different climate and following different procedures may not have succeeded. It is not electronic monitoring per se that is either good or bad but the way in which it is used. Dissatisfaction with electronic monitoring occurs when ethical concerns are not taken into account, when it is introduced without consultation, and when it is perceived as an infringement on the limited amount of personal control that staff experience in work contexts.

Electronic Performance Monitoring and Stress

Caryon (1993) outlines the impact of electronic monitoring on job demands, job control, and social support, all of which are important in understanding affective responses to technology. In a laboratory study, Aiello and Kolb (1995) found that electronic monitoring induced feelings of stress. This occurred while controlling for job design and social support. Previous findings of the impact of electronic monitoring had been attributed to the nature of the job design and to the reduction in social support. These studies could not, however, rule out the possibility that participants in an electronically monitored group perceived the design of their job differently than those who were not electronically monitored. Negative reactions to electronic monitoring may arise from perceived loss of control associated with closer monitoring. Employees dislike constant surveillance, and electronic monitoring leaves a feeling of lack of trust (Westin, 1992). If electronic monitoring is to be used, there should be perceived opportunity to dispute the results produced, or to provide alternative information that can feed into judgmental data.

Little attention has been given to the impact of electronic monitoring on supervisors as distinct from its impact on those being monitored. Although many may see the purported objectivity of electronic monitoring as an advantage, it does reduce one source of supervisor power, namely, reward power. The supervisor-employee work relationship is influenced by supervisor power, which is reduced through electronic monitoring. This means that employees no longer have the potential to use social skills, ingratiation, or other upward influence tactics aimed at affecting their supervisors' perceptions of performance. This is one aspect of control lost to the employee through the introduction of electronic monitoring. These types of reactions may well be implicit; they are often an intuitive part of the social fabric of the interpersonal environment at work. As such, the issues may not be voiced and addressed during discussions about the introduction of electronic monitoring, yet they are likely to influence attitudes toward the systems.

Di Tecco, Cwitco, Arsenault, and Andre (1992) surveyed telephone operators whose performance was monitored electronically. Because shorter call times were considered desirable, and because the time was monitored, operators were under considerable pressure to reduce call time. This together with the difficulty of serving a customer well contributed substantially to feelings of stress. Seventy percent of the participants saw this pressure as contributing to stress to a very large extent. It may not have been the electronic monitoring as such, however, that contributed to the stress, but the inappropriate allocation of call time objectives that were unachievable for some operators and that resulted in a reduction in quality.

As has been shown in relation to technology generally, it is usually not the technology as such that causes the stress but the organizational context or the manner in which the technology is introduced. Korunka, Weiss, Huemer, and Karetta (1995) were able to demonstrate that the introduction of technology resulted in psychosomatic complaints only where the jobs were extremely monotonous and where there was little involvement in the process of introducing technology.

Not all stress is necessarily bad. There is a suggestion that electronic monitoring provides a form of social facilitation, thus enhancing performance levels. Aiello and Kolb (1995) examined the impact on individual and work groups of manipulating electronic monitoring (in a laboratory context). Electronic monitoring appeared to offer a social facilitation effect and reduced social loafing. Even in a laboratory context, however, the nonmonitored participants, particularly those in cohesive groups, were the least stressed.

Integration of Judged and Electronic Performance Monitoring

If electronic monitoring captures only a component of performance—probably typical task-related performance—the current concern relates to how this information might be integrated with judgmental performance information about other areas, such as contextual performance. Research is needed to determine whether raters will be able to keep the two components separate, and to determine the extent to which the medium used to present the information influences the rating.

Kulik and Ambrose (1993a) draw attention to the role of prior knowledge and categorization in performance appraisal judgments. The model of performance outlined earlier in the chapter can be used to understand the influence of technology on the actual appraisal judgments and on the prior knowledge about performance that underlie the judgments (Fenner, Lerch, & Kulik, 1993). Traditional performance appraisal tends to be based on holistic judgments (Feldman, 1981), which probably reflect the use of instance-based knowledge rather than abstract knowledge (Neal et al., 1995). It is possible that electronic monitoring data could provide a supplement to the appraiser's prior instance-based knowledge. Depending on its presentation, however, the provision of information derived from electronic monitoring may lead to a more analytic approach to performance assessment, with possible consequences for accuracy. Kulik and Ambrose (1993a) investigated the impact of electronic monitoring on appraisal processes and found that electronically based data did supplement visual information but the visual data were weighted more strongly. These issues are currently under investigation, and the area will continue to be a fruitful one for future research (Ambrose & Kulik, 1994; Barker & Banerji, 1995). In the future it may be possible to develop rules for integrating information about performance derived from different sources.

Video Technology

Although not strictly within the category of electronic monitoring, the role of video technology, which is increasingly being digitized and used in connection with computerized systems, offers another form of monitoring and information for performance judgments. Doerr, Mitchell, Klastorin, and Brown (1996) videotaped the performance of employees in a fish processing plant. Seventy hours of videotape were collected, and activity samples were analyzed for measures of effort, persistence, and attention. The availability of software packages to facilitate this type of scoring (such as Noldus) point to the possibility of using technology for off-line assessments of performance. Similar approaches have been used for monitoring the performance of assessment-center activities (Bray & Byham, 1991). Off-line assessments of assessment-center activities permit the use of multiple raters, thus increasing the reliability of assessments, and provide an opportunity to analyze specific behaviors in much more detail. Ryan and colleagues (1995) found that assessors able to replay a video were more accurate in deciding whether a particular behavior was present or absent. No improvements were obtained, however, in the validity of the video ratings over live observations of a group's interaction. Nevertheless, we suggest that more detailed analysis of yet-to-be-determined gestures and behavior may provide a better basis for assessing performance for use as both a predictor and a criterion.

Using Electronic Monitoring to Detect Rating Style

Electronic monitoring may provide a valuable basis for calibrating performance ratings given by different raters. Rating style is an issue that has seldom been controlled in the use of performance ratings. Typical validation studies involve many different raters, with some rating a number of employees and others rating only one. The statistical nonindependence of raters and ratees is usually ignored, because of the difficulty of disentangling rating style from real group differences (such as between different divisions or units). It seems likely that where electronic monitoring is available, it may help to determine whether there are systematic differences between raters. In a large selection study, we recently included a dummy person that was rated by all raters in order to calibrate their different rating styles. Electronic monitoring was not an option, but we see no reason why performance monitoring could not be used when available as a basis for taking into account rater styles—an issue that to date has been ignored in the industrial and organizational psychology literature.

Adaptive Performance

Although change and the importance of adapting to it have always been features of work environments, technology has increased the salience of this aspect of performance. The rapid pace of change in job requirements arising from technological innovations places employees in a situation where they constantly need to demonstrate a capacity to engage in new learning and cope with change. Under these circumstances, one is no longer assessing absolute performance; rather, the focus is on responsiveness to changing job demands. In a sense one is assessing the extent to which an employee is able to keep relatively close to a moving trajectory or target. In control theory terms, what is needed is tracking control.

The first part of this chapter dealt with the need to update the Campbell (1990) model to take account of a more complex view of technology and performance that goes beyond merely seeing technology as a moderator. The domains of performance identified in the Campbell model and in the simplified Borman and Motowidlo (1993) model may also need to be updated. We suggest that the current partitioning of the performance domain into task and contextual performance should be extended to include a new component—namely, adaptive performance (Allworth & Hesketh, 1996).

To test this idea, Allworth and Hesketh (1996) and Hesketh, Allworth, and Considine (1996) adapted the Fuzzy Graphic Distributional Performance measures (Hesketh & Challis, 1994) to assess a broad range of performance domains. In several large selection studies (Allworth & Hesketh, 1996; Hesketh et al., 1996), adaptive performance could be separated from task and contextual performance and, in some cases, was predicted by a set of constructs different from those relevant to the two traditional measures of performance. Adaptive performance covered features such as ease of learning new tasks, confidence in approaching new tasks, and flexibility and capacity to cope with change. These studies also demonstrated that carefully constructed biodata scales measuring past experience of change, coping strategies, and self-efficacy for change predicted adaptive performance comparatively well.

Although the idea has not been tested, it seems likely that rated adaptive performance will relate to the interaction component of the $P \times T$ confounded relationship. The interaction component captures individuals who are able to benefit from technological innovations, an ability that is conceptually related to the adaptive domain of performance that we are assessing via ratings. Experimental studies will be needed to determine whether this link between the partitioned interaction component of the variance and rated adaptive performance can be established.

Conclusion

Technology has always posed a threat to industrial and organizational psychologists in search of a pure measure of performance for use as a criterion in selection, training, and career development programs. Surprisingly little attention has been given to the issue, however, and where it has, the traditional view has been to treat technology as confounding measures of performance. In this chapter we have argued that from the perspective of an employer, if not that of an industrial psychologist, the extent to which an individual is able to use technology to enhance output is an important component of performance. Using this view, we have suggested a modification of the Campbell (1990) model of performance aimed at accommodating the wider influence of technology. Specifically, we have outlined how technology can affect performance directly, and not only its impact on effectiveness. Drawing on P-E fit ideas, analysis of variance frameworks (such as the covariation model of attribution; Kelley & Michela, 1980), and control theory, we suggested a way of modeling and hence measuring the $P \times T$ contribution to performance. Although we accept that there are times when it is necessary to partial out the direct contribution of technology to assess performance, we argue that the performance-by-technology interaction is under the control of the person, and hence is able to be predicted and trained, suggesting that it belongs in the performance domain. We are not arguing against the need to retain a conceptually clear view of performance, unconfounded by technology, but we do suggest that future developments in technology will make it increasingly difficult for raters to make such judgments.

A second theme in the chapter relates to the role of electronic monitoring. Early signs point to the need to be cautious in how monitoring is introduced, and to avoid simplistic reliance on it as a comprehensive source of performance information. We predict that this is an area that will develop extensively, both in terms of innovative ways of using technology to capture and assess performance, and in relation to research on how best to use the information and integrate it with other data.

Finally, we highlighted a recent development that has involved an extension of the Borman and Motowidlo (1993) model of the performance domain to include adaptive performance (Allworth & Hesketh, 1996). We predict that this aspect of performance will become increasingly important, and that it may relate to the $P \times T$ confounder highlighted in the earlier part of the chapter.

In summary, we believe that it will not be possible to go back to the traditional view of performance, which aimed to remove all variance due to technology. We predict, instead, that in the future a major aspect of performance that will be of interest to employers is adaptive performance—namely, the component of performance that includes people's responsiveness to technology and their capacity to take advantage of it to enhance interactive performance.

References

Ackerman, P. L. (1992). Predicting individual differences in complex skill acquisition: Dynamics of ability determinants. *Journal of Applied Psychology, 77*, 598–614.

Adler, S. (1996). Personality and work behavior: Exploring the linkages. *Applied Psychology, 45*, 207–224.

Aiello, J. R. (1993). Computer-based work monitoring: Electronic surveillance and its effects. *Journal of Applied Social Psychology, 23*, 499–507.

Aiello, J. R., & Kolb, K. J. (1995). Electronic performance monitoring and social context: Impact on productivity and stress. *Journal of Applied Psychology, 80,* 339–353.

Allworth, E. A., & Hesketh, B. (1996). *Construct-based biodata and the prediction of adaptive performance.* Paper submitted to the Twelfth Annual Conference of the Society for Industrial and Organizational Psychology, St. Louis, MO.

Ambrose, M. L., & Kulik, C. T. (1994). The effect of information format and performance pattern on performance appraisal judgments in a computerized performance monitoring context. *Journal of Applied Social Psychology, 24,* 801–823.

Anderson, J. R., & Fincham, J. M. (1994). Acquisition of procedural skills from examples. *Journal of Experimental Psychology: Learning, Memory and Cognition, 20,* 1322–1340.

Barker, P., & Banerji, A. (1995). Designing electronic performance support systems. *Innovations in Education and Training International, 32,* 4–12.

Barrick, M. R., & Mount, M. K. (1993). Autonomy as a moderator of the relationships between the Big Five personality dimensions and job performance. *Journal of Applied Psychology, 78,* 111–118.

Blumberg, M., & Gerwin, D. (1984). Coping with advanced manufacturing technology. *Journal of Occupational Behavior, 5,* 113–130.

Borman, W. C., & Motowidlo, S. J. (1993). Expanding the criterion domain to include elements of contextual performance. In N. Schmitt & W. C. Borman (Eds.), *Personnel selection in organizations* (pp. 71–98). San Francisco: Jossey-Bass.

Borman, W. C., White, L. A., & Dorsey, D. W. (1995). Effects of rates task performance and interpersonal factors on supervisory and peer performance ratings. *Journal of Applied Psychology, 80,* 168–177.

Borman, W. C., White, L. A., Pulakos, E. D., & Oppler, S. H. (1991). Models of supervisory job performance ratings. *Journal of Applied Psychology, 76,* 863–872.

Bray, D. W., & Byham, W. C. (1991). Assessment centers and their derivatives. *Journal of Continuing Higher Education, 39,* 8–11.

Brooks, L. R. (1987). Decentralized control of categorization: The role of prior processing episodes. In U. Neisser (Ed.), *Concepts and conceptual development: Ecological and intellectual factors in categorization.* Cambridge: Cambridge University Press.

Campbell, J. P. (1990). Modeling the performance prediction problem in industrial and organizational psychology. In M. D. Dunnette & L. M. Hough (Eds.), *Handbook of industrial and organizational psychology* (Vol. 1, 2nd ed., pp. 687–732). Palo Alto, CA: Consulting Psychologists Press.

Campbell, J. P., Gasser, M. B., & Oswald, F. L. (1996). The substantive nature of performance variability. In K. R. Murphy (Ed.), *Individual differences and behavior in organizations* (pp. 258–299). San Francisco: Jossey-Bass.

Campbell, J. P., McHenry, J. J., & Wise, L. L. (1990). Modeling job performance in a population of jobs. *Personnel Psychology, 43,* 313–333.

Caryon, P. (1993). Effect of electronic performance monitoring on job design and worker stress: Review of the literature and conceptual model. *Human Factors, 35*(3), 385–395.

Chmiel, N., & Wall, T. D. (1994). Fault prevention, job design, and advanced manufacturing technology. *Applied Psychology, 43,* 455–473.

Cooke, N. M., Durso, F. T., & Schvaneveldt, R. W. (1986). Recall and measures of memory organization. *Journal of Experimental Psychology: Learning, Memory and Cognition, 12,* 538–549.

Cordery, J. L., Mueller, W. S., & Smith, L. M. (1991). Attitudinal and behavioural outcomes of autonomous group working: A longitudinal field study. *Academy of Management Journal, 34,* 464–476.

Di Tecco, D., Cwitco, G., Arsenault, A., & Andre, M. (1992). Operator stress and monitoring practices. *Applied Ergonomics, 23,* 29–34.

Doerr, K. H., Mitchell, T. R., Klastorin, T. D., & Brown, K. A. (1996). Impact of material flow policies and goals on job outcomes. *Journal of Applied Psychology, 81,* 142–152.

Dorsey, D. W., & Foster, L. L. (1996). *An application of knowledge structure assessment in the computer domain: Relations with experience and implications for training.* Paper presented at the Eleventh Annual Conference of the Society for Industrial and Organizational Psychology, San Diego, CA.

Edwards, J. R. (1991). Person-job fit. In C. L. Cooper & I. T. Robertson (Eds.), *International review of industrial and organizational psychology* (Vol. 6, pp. 257–283). New York: Wiley.

Edwards, J. R., & Van Harrison, R. (1993). Job demands and worker health: Three dimensional reexamination of the relationship between person-environment fit and strain. *Journal of Applied Psychology, 78,* 628–648.

Feldman, J. M. (1981). Beyond attribution theory: Cognitive processes in performance appraisal. *Journal of Applied Psychology, 55,* 127–148.

Fenner, D. B., Lerch, F. J., & Kulik, C. T. (1993). The impact of computerized performance monitoring and prior performance knowledge on performance evaluation. *Journal of Applied Social Psychology, 23,* 573–601.

Frese, M. (1991). Error management or error prevention: Two strategies to deal with errors in software design. In H. J. Bullinger (Ed.), *Human aspects in computing: Design and use of interactive systems and work with terminals* (pp. 776–782). Amsterdam: Elsevier.

Galinsky, T. L., & Schleifer, L. M. (1995). The influence of performance standards and feedback on speed and accuracy in an electronically monitored data-entry task. *International Journal of Human-Computer Interaction, 7,* 25–36.

Halford, G. S., Wilson, W. H., Guo, J., Gayler, R. W., Wiles, J., & Stewart, J. E. M. (1994). Connectionist implications for processing capacity limitations in analogies. In K. J. Holyoak & J. Barnden (Eds.), *Advances in connectionist and neural computational theory: Vol. 2. Analogical connections* (pp. 363–415). Norwood, NJ: Ablex.

Hesketh, B. (1993). Measurement issues in industrial and organizational psychology. In C. L. Cooper & I. T. Robertson (Eds.), *International review of industrial and organizational psychology* (Vol. 8, pp. 133–172). New York: Wiley.

Hesketh, B. (1997). Dilemmas in training for transfer and retention. *International Review of Applied Psychology: Research and Practice, 46,* 317–339.

Hesketh, B., Allworth, E., & Considine, G. (1996). *Preliminary report on phase one of the selection project for the Hilton Hotel.* Unpublished paper, Department of Psychology, Macquarie University, Sydney, Australia.

Hesketh, B., & Challis, H. (1994). *Using fuzzy ratings to capture performance variability.* Paper presented at the Society for Industrial and Organizational Psychology, Nashville, TN.

Hesketh, B., & Gardner, D. (1993). Person-environment fit models: A reconceptualization and empirical test. *Journal of Vocational Behavior, 42,* 315–332.

Jackson, P. R., & Wall, T. D. (1991). How does operator control enhance performance of advanced manufacturing technology? *Ergonomics, 34,* 1301–1311.

Jackson, P. R., Wall, T. D., Martin, R., & Davids, K. (1993). New measures of job control, cognitive demand and production responsibility. *Journal of Applied Psychology, 78,* 753–762.

Johnson, S. D., Foster, W. T., & Satchwell, R. (1989, July). *Sophisticated technology, the workforce and vocational education.* Springfield: Department of Adult, Vocational and Technical Education, Illinois State Board of Education.

Kanfer, R., & Ackerman, P. (1989). Motivation and cognitive abilities: An integrative/aptitude-treatment approach to skill acquisition. *Journal of Applied Psychology, 74,* 657–690.

Kelley, H. H., & Michela, J. L. (1980). Attribution theory and research. *Annual Review of Psychology, 31,* 475–501.

Kiresuk, T. J., & Sherman, R. E. (1968). Goal attainment scaling: A general method for evaluating comprehensive community mental health programs. *Community Mental Health Journal, 4,* 443–453.

Korunka, C., Weiss, A., Huemer, K. H., & Karetta, B. (1995). The effect of new technologies on job satisfaction and psychosomatic complaints. *Applied Psychology, 44,* 123–142.

Kraiger, K., Ford, J. K., & Salas, E. (1993). Application of cognitive, skill-based and affective theories of learning outcomes to new methods of training evaluation. *Journal of Applied Psychology, 78,* 311–328.

Kulik, C. T., & Ambrose, M. L. (1993a). Category-based and feature-based processes in performance appraisal: Integrating visual and computerized sources of performance data. *Journal of Applied Psychology, 78,* 821–830.

Kulik, C. T., & Ambrose, M. L. (1993b). The impact of computerized performance monitoring design features on the performance appraisal process. *Journal of Managerial Issues, 5,* 182–197.

Logan, G. D. (1988). Toward an instance theory of automatization. *Psychological Review, 95,* 492–527.

Lord, R. G., & Levy, P. E. (1994). Moving from cognition to action: A control theory perspective. *Applied Psychology, 43,* 335–398.

Martin, R., & Wall, T. D. (1989). Attentional demand and cost responsibility as stressors in shopfloor jobs. *Academy of Management Journal, 32,* 69–84.

Martocchio, J. J. (1992). Microcomputer usage as an opportunity: The influence of context in employee training. *Personnel Psychology, 3,* 529–552.

Mathieu, J. E., Martineau, J. W., & Tannenbaum, S. I. (1993). Individual and situational influences on the development of self-efficacy: Implications for training effectiveness. *Personnel Psychology, 46,* 125–147.

McCloy, R. A., Campbell, J. P., & Cudeck, R. (1994). A confirmatory test of a model of performance determinants. *Journal of Applied Psychology, 79,* 493–503.

McHenry, J. J., Hough, L. M., Toquam, J. L., Hanson, M. A., & Ashworth, S. (1990). Project A validity results: The relationship between predictor and criterion domains. *Personnel Psychology, 43,* 335–354.

Medin, D. L., & Ross, B. H. (1989). The specific character of abstract thought: Categorization, problem solving and induction. In R. J. Sternberg (Ed.), *Advances in the psychology of human intelligence* (Vol. 5, pp. 189–223). Hillsdale, NJ: Erlbaum.

Milbank, D. (1993, September 9). New collar work. *Wall Street Journal,* p. 1.

Morrison, D. L. (1994). Fault diagnosis and computer integrated manufacturing systems. *IEEE Transactions on Engineering Management, 41,* 69–83.

Motowidlo, S. J., & Van Scotter, J. R. (1994). Evidence that task performance should be distinguished from contextual performance. *Journal of Applied Psychology, 79,* 475–480.

Neal, A., & Hesketh, B. (1996). *The adaptability and resistance of abstract and exemplar-based knowledge to subsequent rule changes.* Paper presented at the Eleventh Annual Conference of the Society for Industrial and Organizational Psychology, San Diego, CA.

Neal, A., & Hesketh, B. (1997). Episodic knowledge and implicit learning. *Psychonomic Bulletin and Review, 4*(1), 24–37.

Neal, A., Hesketh, B., & Andrews, S. (1995). Instance-based categorization: Intentional versus automatic forms of retrieval. *Memory and Cognition, 23,* 227–242.

Novak, J. D. (1990). Concept maps and Venn diagrams: Two metacognitive tools to facilitate meaningful learning. *Instructional Science, 19,* 29–52.

Nussbaum, K., & Du Rivage, V. (1986). Computer monitoring: Mismanagement by remote control. *Business and Society Review,* 16–20.

Ohlsson, S. (1996). Learning from performance errors. *Psychological Review, 103,* 241–262.

Palmeri, T. J., & Nosofsky, R. M. (1995). Recognition memory for exceptions to the category rule. *Journal of Experimental Psychology: Learning, Memory and Cognition, 21,* 548–568.

Perruchet, P., & Pacteau, C. (1990). Synthetic grammar learning: Implicit rule abstraction or explicit fragmentary knowledge? *Journal of Experimental Psychology, 119,* 264–275.

Pritchard, R. D., Jones, S. D., Roth, P. L., Stuebing, K. K., & Ekebert, S. E. (1989). The evaluation of an integrated approach to measuring organizational productivity. *Personnel Psychology, 42,* 341–359.

Reason, J. T. (1990). *Human error.* Cambridge: Cambridge University Press.

Reeves, L. M., & Weisberg, R. W. (1994). The role of content and abstract information in analogical transfer. *Psychological Bulletin, 115,* 381–400.

Rencken, W. D., & Durrant-Whyte, H. F. (1993). A quantitative model of adaptive task allocation in human-computer interfaces. *IEEE Transactions on Systems, Man, and Cybernetics, 23,* 1073–1090.

Ryan, A. M., Daum, D., Bauman, T., Grisez, M., Mattimore, K., Nalodka, T., & McCormick, S. (1995). Direct, indirect and controlled observation and rating accuracy. *Journal of Applied Psychology, 80,* 664–670.

Sackett, P. R., Zedeck, S., & Fogli, L. (1988). Relations between measures of typical and maximal performance. *Journal of Applied Psychology, 74,* 336–342.

Satchwell, R. E., & Dugger, W. E. (1996). A united vision: Technology for all. *Journal of Technology Education* [on-line], 7(2). Available: http://scholar.lib.vt.edu/ejournals/JTE/jte-v7n2/satchwell.jte-v7n2.html

Shell, R. L., & Allgeier, R. G. (1992). A multi-level incentive model for service organizations. *Applied Ergonomics, 23,* 43–48.

Sproull, L. S., & Goodman, P. S. (1990). Technology and organizations: Integration and opportunities. In P. S. Goodman & L. S. Sproull (Eds.), *Technology and organizations* (pp. 254–265). San Francisco: Jossey-Bass.

Wall, T. D., Corbett, J. M., Martin, R., Clegg, C. W., & Jackson, P. R. (1990). Advanced manufacturing technology, work design and performance: A change study. *Journal of Applied Psychology, 75,* 691–697.

Wall, T. D., Jackson, P., & Davids, K. (1992). Operator work designs and robotics systems performance: A serendipitous field study. *Journal of Applied Psychology, 75,* 691–697.

Wall, T. D., Kemp, N., Jackson, P., & Clegg, C. (1986). Outcomes of autonomous work groups: A long-term field experiment. *Academy of Management Journal, 29,* 280–304.

Wall, T. D., & Martin, R. (1987). Job and work design. In C. L. Cooper & I. T. Roberston (Eds.), *International review of industrial and organizational psychology* (Vol. 2, pp. 61–91). New York: Wiley.

Weick, K. E. (1990). Technology as equivoque: Sense making in new technologies. In P. S. Goodman & L. S. Sproull (Eds.), *Technology and organizations* (pp. 1–44). San Francisco: Jossey-Bass.

Weiss, H. M., & Adler, S. (1984). Personality and organizational behavior. In B. M. Staw & L. L. Cummings (Eds.), *Research in organizational behavior* (Vol. 6, pp. 1–50). Greenwich, CT: JAI Press.

Westin, A. F. (1992). Two key factors that belong in a macroergonomic analysis of electronic monitoring: Employee perceptions of fairness and the climate of organizational trust or distrust. *Applied Ergonomics, 23,* 35–42.

Wise, L. L., McHenry, J., & Campbell, J. P. (1990). Identifying optimal predictor composites and testing for generalizability across jobs and performance factors. *Personnel Psychology, 43,* 355–366.

Wisniewski, E. J., & Medin, D. L. (1994). On the interaction of theory and data in concept learning. *Cognitive Science, 18,* 221–281.

Zapf, D., & Reason, J. T. (1994). Introduction: Human errors and error handling. *Applied Psychology, 43,* 427–432.

CHAPTER 3

Performance Assessment in Unique Jobs

Stephan J. Motowidlo
Mark J. Schmit

We begin with the premise that the technical, economic, cultural, and business environments of work organizations are changing at an accelerating rate and becoming less and less predictable. It is becoming more difficult to anticipate technological opportunities, customers' demands, and the availability of resources far enough in advance to prescribe standard operating procedures for bringing in raw materials, transforming them into products and services that will satisfy customers, and distributing them throughout the marketplace. Traditional organizational forms based on mechanistic assumptions, bureaucratic structures, and rigid hierarchical management that might have been effective and efficient in more stable environments will probably not be as functional as they used to be because they are not nimble enough to adapt to fast change and take advantage of fleeting business opportunities.

If current environmental trends continue, they foretell dramatic changes in the structure of work and organizational forms. We expect that organizations will become less bureaucratic, less mechanistic, and more organic. They will probably be flatter, with fewer layers of management. Decision-making authority will be pushed down the organizational hierarchy to allow local control and flexibility. We expect that teams composed of individuals representing different functional specialties will bear primary responsibility for enforcing patterns of individual behavior necessary for accomplishing team goals. Instead of relying on direct supervision as in traditional bureaucratic organizations, team members will have to share commitment to team goals and enforce patterns of individual behavior within the team out of a sense of mutual accountability that will reinforce the notion that coworkers in interdependent networks are their own (internal) customers. They will have to be vigilant in identifying their internal customers' shifting needs and demands. In addition, of course, they will also have to monitor closely the needs and demands of their external customers and tailor the goods and services they provide accordingly. We expect that individuals will be assigned to teams as changing circumstances dictate, to multiple teams simultaneously, and to different teams over time. Within team structures, individuals will have considerable latitude over what they do to contribute to team goals.

These assumptions imply that jobs in the future will be less rigidly programmed and more flexibly "unique." (In this chapter we use the term *unique* in its loose sense to mean uncommon, rare, or unusual, not in its more formal sense to mean unlike absolutely anything else.) If people perform different sets of tasks in the different teams to which they are assigned, what one person does during any given performance period will be different from what most other people do during the same period, and different too from what that same individual is likely to do in the next performance period. Differences such as these in work activities will be exaggerated further by increased autonomy and decision-making authority that will allow individuals considerable latitude in exercising idiosyncratic preferences for activities within the scope of broad organizational objectives and team goals. Also, changing assignments from team to team will make it difficult to retain traditional models of performance monitoring and evaluation that have relied on judgments by a single supervisor.

We expect that two critical issues will present special problems for performance assessment. They present challenges even in relatively structured jobs in traditional organizational forms, but we expect they will present even more difficult challenges as jobs become more unique. The first issue is deciding what aspects of incumbents' behavior should be represented in measures of the degree to which they contribute to organizational objectives.

The second issue is finding sources who can provide information about targeted aspects of incumbents' behavior.

This chapter speculates about the nature of performance assessment in a working world where jobs are much more varied than they are today, and about ways to address the two issues just mentioned. The chapter is organized into three sections. First, it presents a theory of individual differences in task and contextual performance that forms the basis for our discussion about assessing performance in such jobs. Second, it describes some implications of the theory for important issues in assessing performance in unique jobs. Third, it discusses alternatives to performance assessment for some kinds of personnel decisions that might be better guided by information about knowledge, skills, and work habits instead of by information about individuals' histories of actual contributions to the accomplishment of organizational objectives.

A Theory of Individual Differences in Task and Contextual Performance

The following theory of individual differences in task and contextual performance was described in detail in another publication (Motowidlo, Borman, & Schmit, 1997). We summarize it briefly here to establish a conceptual framework for our discussion of performance assessment in unique jobs.

Basic Assumptions About Performance

Starting from the conventional wisdom that job performance is essentially the degree to which an individual helps the organization reach its goals (Campbell, 1983), the theory of individual differences in task and contextual performance makes four important assumptions about the performance construct:

1. *Performance is a behavioral construct.* Performance is behavior that can be evaluated as positive or negative for individual or organizational effectiveness. We distinguish performance from the results of performance, which are the states or conditions of people or things that are changed by individual behavior. The theory deliberately focuses on the behavioral foundation of performance because apparent results of performance are usually affected by

many factors in addition to configurations of behavior that are under an individual's control.

2. *Performance behavior is episodic.* The theory assumes that during the course of a work day people perform many discrete actions, each with its own identifiable beginning and ending. Some of these actions or behavioral episodes make only a trivial difference, if any at all, to organizational goal accomplishment. Such behaviors have little or no effect on people's performance. Other behavioral episodes help or hinder the organization in accomplishing its goals in significant ways. Following Campbell (1990), the theory assumes that only behavioral episodes that make a difference to organizational goal accomplishment are part of the performance domain.

3. *Performance behavioral episodes are evaluative.* The theory assumes that performance behavioral episodes can have varying degrees of positive or negative effects on organizational goal accomplishment. The theory then defines job performance as the aggregated value to the organization of the discrete behavioral episodes that an individual performs during a particular period.

4. *The performance domain is behaviorally multidimensional.* There are many different kinds of behavior that would advance or hinder organizational goals. Lumping them all together produces a psychologically intractable hodgepodge. It thus becomes important to identify behaviorally homogeneous clusters of behavioral episodes in the performance domain and to aggregate the contribution value of behaviors within such clusters. This yields multiple job performance scores for each incumbent, each score representing the net value of his or her behaviors in a single category aggregated over a particular period.

Task and Contextual Performance

One way to develop behavioral categories of job performance is according to the reasons that behavioral episodes either contribute to or detract from organizational goal accomplishment. In fact, this is the basis for the distinction that Borman and Motowidlo (1993) made between task performance and contextual performance.

Borman and Motowidlo discussed two types of task performance. One type consists of activities that transform raw materials into the goods and services that are the organization's products.

These include activities such as selling merchandise in a retail store, operating a production machine in a manufacturing plant, teaching in a school, performing surgery in a hospital, and cashing checks in a bank. A second type of task performance consists of activities that service and maintain the technical core by replenishing its supply of raw materials, distributing its finished products, or providing important planning, coordination, supervising, or staff functions that enable it to function effectively and efficiently. Thus task performance bears a direct relation to the organization's technical core, either by executing its technical processes or by maintaining and servicing its technical requirements.

Contextual performance, according to Borman and Motowidlo, does not contribute through the organization's core technical processes but maintains the broader organizational, social, and psychological environment in which the technical core must function. Contextual performance includes activities such as helping others, following rules, endorsing organizational objectives, persisting, and volunteering, which promote the viability of the social and organizational network and enhance the psychological climate in which the technical core is embedded.

The defining difference between task performance and contextual performance is that task performance contributes to organizational objectives through the technical core while contextual performance contributes by supporting the social, organizational, and psychological context of work. This distinction suggests the following hypotheses about other differences between task and contextual performance that enrich the nomological net surrounding the constructs (Organ, 1997) but without being part of the basic definitions of task and contextual performance:

1. Task activities are more varied from one job to another while contextual activities are more similar across many or even all jobs (Borman & Motowidlo, 1993, 1997).
2. Task performance is more strongly related to individual differences in ability while contextual performance is more strongly related to individual differences in personality (Borman & Motowidlo, 1993, 1997; Motowidlo & Van Scotter, 1994; Van Scotter & Motowidlo, 1996).

3. Task performance is more in-role or role-prescribed while contextual performance is more extra-role or discretionary (Borman & Motowidlo, 1993, 1997; Organ, 1997).

Contextual performance shares similarities with several other behavioral patterns related to prosocial behavior (Brief & Motowidlo, 1986); organizational citizenship behavior (Organ, 1988, 1997; Smith, Organ, & Near, 1983); organizational spontaneity (George & Brief, 1992; George & Jones, 1997); personal initiative (Frese, Kring, Soose, & Zempel, 1996; Speier & Frese, 1997); the model of soldier effectiveness described by Borman, Motowidlo, Rose, and Hanser (1985); and the multifactor model of job performance described by Campbell, Gasser, and Oswald (1996) and by Campbell, McCloy, Oppler, and Sager (1993). Specific points of similarity between the taxonomy of contextual performance dimensions offered by Borman and Motowidlo (1993, 1997) and the dimensional elements in these other behavioral patterns are as follows:

Contextual performance: Persisting with enthusiasm and extra effort as necessary to complete tasks successfully

Prosocial organizational behavior: Making extra effort on the job (Brief & Motowidlo, 1986)

Personal initiative: Having a goal and action orientation and persisting in the face of barriers and setbacks (Speier & Frese, 1997)

Model of soldier effectiveness: Maintaining perseverance and conscientiousness (Borman et al., 1985)

Multifactor performance model: Demonstrating effort (Campbell et al., 1996)

Contextual performance: Volunteering to carry out tasks that are not formally part of one's own job

Prosocial organizational behavior: Suggesting organizational improvements (Brief & Motowidlo, 1986)

Organizational spontaneity: Making constructive suggestions and developing oneself (George & Brief, 1992; George & Jones, 1997)

Personal initiative: Being self-starting and proactive (Speier & Frese, 1997)

Model of soldier effectiveness: Showing initiative and taking on extra responsibility (Borman et al., 1985)

Multifactor performance model: Demonstrating effort (Campbell et al., 1996)

Contextual performance: Helping and cooperating with others

Prosocial organizational behavior: Helping coworkers and customers (Brief & Motowidlo, 1986)

Organizational citizenship behavior: Showing organizational courtesy (Organ, 1988, 1997), sportsmanship (Organ, 1988), altruism (Smith et al., 1983), and helpfulness (Organ, 1997)

Organizational spontaneity: Helping coworkers (George & Brief, 1992; George & Jones, 1997)

Model of soldier effectiveness: Assisting coworkers (Borman et al., 1985)

Multifactor performance model: Facilitating peer and team performance (Campbell et al., 1996)

Contextual performance: Following organizational rules and procedures

Prosocial organizational behavior: Complying with organizational values and policies (Brief & Motowidlo, 1986)

Organizational citizenship behavior: Being conscientious (Smith et al., 1983; Organ, 1997)

Model of soldier effectiveness: Following orders and regulations and showing respect for authority (Borman et al., 1985)

Multifactor performance model: Maintaining personal discipline (Campbell et al., 1996)

Contextual performance: Endorsing, supporting, and defending organizational objectives

Prosocial organizational behavior: Staying with the organization during hard times and representing the organization favorably to outsiders (Brief & Motowidlo, 1986)

Organizational spontaneity: Protecting the organization (George & Brief, 1992; George & Jones, 1997)

Model of soldier effectiveness: Showing concern for unit objectives (Borman et al., 1985)

Multifactor performance model: Managing and administering (Campbell et al., 1996)

These many similarities between behavioral elements that make up dimensions of contextual performance and behavioral elements in other prominent and widely cited patterns of work behavior reinforce the theoretical importance of the behavioral elements.

Individual Differences

The theory of individual differences in task and contextual performance also predicts causal relations between individual difference variables, task performance, and contextual performance. It borrows liberally from ideas developed by Hunter (1983), Campbell and colleagues (1993), and McCrae and Costa (1996) and from a paper by Schmit and colleagues (1996) that attempted to explain mechanisms through which personality might affect job performance.

Empirical and theoretical contributions by Hunter (1983), Campbell and colleagues (1993), and McCrae and Costa (1996) have in common the idea that the effects on job performance of basic individual difference variables such as ability and personality are mediated by other variables. In Hunter's model the mediating variables are knowledge and skill (work sample performance); in Campbell and colleagues' model they are declarative knowledge, procedural knowledge and skill, and motivation; and in McCrae and Costa's model they are characteristic adaptations that include variables such as knowledge, skill, and habits.

Based on these ideas, the theory maintains that individual differences in personality and cognitive ability, in combination with learning experiences, lead to variability in knowledge, skill, and work habits, which are the most immediate determinants of job performance. An especially important aspect of this theory is that the traits, knowledge, skills, and habits that are related to task performance are different from those that are related to contextual performance. Cognitive ability is presumed to affect primarily task performance through its effects on task knowledge, task skills, and task habits, while personality traits are presumed to affect primarily contextual performance through their effects on contextual knowledge, contextual skills, and contextual habits.

Task knowledge is knowledge of facts, principles, and procedures related to the job's technical core. Contextual knowledge is knowledge of facts, principles, and procedures for maintaining and developing the social, organizational, and psychological context of work. Examples of contextual knowledge include knowing how to cooperate with a diverse group of people; how to calm an upset worker; how to work productively with difficult peers, supervisors, and subordinates; how to present a favorable image of the organization to outsiders; and how to defend a supervisor's actions.

Task skill is skill in using technical information, principles, and procedures to carry out core technical functions smoothly, quickly, and without error. Similarly, contextual skill is skill in helping and cooperating with others, abiding by organizational rules and procedures, supporting organizational objectives, persisting to overcome obstacles, and taking the initiative to perform activities that are not formally required.

Task work habits are responses to task situations that either facilitate or interfere with the performance of task behaviors. They include characteristic ways of using technical information, performing technical procedures, making decisions, and so on that may or may not be consistent with what the performers know are the most effective way to do these things. They also include motivational task habits such as characteristic tendencies to exert high or low levels of effort, to focus sustained effort on a task, to fall prey to distraction, and to set challenging personal goals. Contextual work habits are responses that either facilitate or interfere with effective performance in contextual work situations. They include characteristic tendencies to approach or avoid various types of interpersonal and group situations, preferred ways of handling conflict, interpersonal and political styles such as Machiavellianism, and characteristic communication styles.

Implications for Performance Assessment

The theory of individual differences in task and contextual performance has several implications for performance assessment. Although these implications apply generally to performance assessment in both traditional and unique jobs, they are especially relevant for unique jobs.

Both Task Performance and Contextual Performance Are Important to Assess

The importance of task performance for accomplishing organizational objectives is straightforward; people who perform tasks effectively contribute directly either to the goods and services produced through the technical core or to the technical core's capacity to produce goods and services. Borman and Motowidlo (1993) argued that contextual performance is also important for accomplishing organizational objectives, but for different reasons; people who perform contextual activities effectively help develop and sustain a viable social, organizational, and psychological context for the technical core.

Two lines of empirical research support the organizational importance of contextual performance. First, results of several studies (Borman, White, & Dorsey, 1995; Ferris, Judge, Rowland, & Fitzgibbons, 1994; MacKenzie, Podsakoff, & Fetter, 1991; Motowidlo & Van Scotter, 1994; Van Scotter & Motowidlo, 1996; Werner, 1994) show that ratees' contextual performance significantly affects supervisors' judgments about the ratees' overall job performance, which presumably reflects their overall value to the organization. Second, results of several other studies (Podsakoff, Ahearn, & MacKenzie, 1997; Podsakoff & MacKenzie, 1994; Walz & Niehoff, 1996) show that contextual performance is correlated with indices of organizational effectiveness. Contextual performance might contribute to organizational effectiveness through several routes. It might facilitate coworkers' and managers' productivity, free up resources for other productive purposes, help coordinate work activities between individuals and groups, make it easier to attract and keep high-performing employees, make the organization's productivity more stable, and help the organization adapt to changes in the environment (Podsakoff & MacKenzie, 1997).

Contextual performance is likely to become even more important if organizations and jobs change in the ways we think they will in response to ever more turbulent organizational environments. Several specific changes mentioned earlier argue for the increasing importance of some aspects of contextual performance.

For instance, one expected organizational change is toward increased reliance on teams instead of individual work assignments. People will have to work more and more cooperatively with others over an extended period of time to accomplish assigned group objectives. Teams will often include individuals from diverse functional areas who will bring different perspectives, priorities, and types of functional expertise. Working effectively in such teams will require well-developed interpersonal and conflict resolution skills. Thus the trend toward more team-based work assignments will put a special premium on the helping and cooperation dimension of contextual performance.

Teams will frequently be self-managed, without the close and direct supervision that was typical in traditional, bureaucratic organizations, so mutually accountable team members will essentially have to exert and accept influence over one another. To ensure that the norms that teams develop and enforce are consistent with organizational objectives, it will become even more important for individuals to perform effectively in the contextual dimension of endorsing, supporting, and defending organizational objectives. It will also become more important for them to perform effectively in the contextual dimension of following organizational rules and procedures as they are translated into norms that prescribe acceptable behavior for team members.

Another expected organizational change is that decision-making authority will be pushed down to lower organizational levels, as close as possible to the points where they are actually implemented. As people become more autonomous and responsible for decisions about their work, it will become more important for them to know and accept organizational objectives so that their decisions and choices can reflect those objectives. For this reason, effectiveness in the contextual performance dimension of endorsing, supporting, and defending organizational objectives will become more important. For the same reason, people will also have to show more initiative and willingness to take on extra responsibility. This means that the contextual dimension of volunteering to carry out task responsibilities that are not formally part of the job will become more important.

Still another expected change is that people will move from one assignment or project to another and will have to adapt frequently to new work settings. They will also have to be flexible and open to different ways of operating in different work settings, and willing to learn new skills demanded by changing assignments and projects. Thus, self-development and flexibility, as reflected in the contextual dimension of volunteering to carry out tasks that are not part of the job, will become more important.

A final example of an expected change is that organizations will put more and more emphasis on serving customers instead of on just developing, producing, and marketing excellent products and services. People will have to pay more attention to customer needs and preferences, and work harder to satisfy them. This will accentuate the importance of the contextual performance dimension of helping and cooperating with others.

One implication, therefore, for performance assessment is that if a measure of job performance is to take into account all consequential opportunities for individuals to contribute to organizational objectives, that measure should include both task elements and contextual elements. The contextual elements will likely become even more important for organizational effectiveness and survival as jobs change to become more unique.

Different Dimensions of Task Performance Are Relevant for Different Jobs

Jobs have traditionally been defined and distinguished from each other according to sets of tasks. These distinctions allow individuals to specialize in performing only some of the many specific tasks that need to be carried out to produce the services or goods that are the organization's products. But differences between jobs in terms of their task components will become even greater if our speculations are correct about how organizational and job structures are likely to change in response to changes in organizational environments.

In mechanistic organizations designed for relatively stable environments, it is possible to identify specific tasks that need to be performed and organize them to take advantage of the efficiencies that result from division of labor, because the same technological recipe for transforming raw materials into goods and services and distributing them in the marketplace can be followed over an extended period when an organization's environment is stable and predictable. Necessary tasks can be identified beforehand, divided into logical groupings, and assigned to individuals who perform much the same set of tasks while they occupy the same job. Importantly, although there are substantial differences between jobs in terms of the tasks they involve, each job might be performed by several individuals who carry out many of the same activities.

In organic organizations that must be ready to adapt quickly to changes in their turbulent and unpredictable environments, however, it is not possible to count on the same technological recipe for all changing circumstances. That is why we expect that organizations will make more use of team-based work assignments, with individual team members exercising greater control over what specific tasks they perform. The team can adjust to rapidly changing circumstances by performing different sets of tasks as dictated by changes in the availability and nature of raw resources, changes in technological developments, and changes in customer needs and preferences. If individuals are assigned to multiple teams at the same time and to different teams over time, this too will make it difficult or impossible to anticipate what tasks any individual will be required to perform. As a result, the tasks performed by an individual over a particular period will be different from those performed by most other individuals over the same period, and jobs will become more unique with respect to the tasks performed.

Although jobs in traditional, mechanistic organizations are differentiated according to a division of labor that assigns different sets of tasks to different groups of individuals, there is still considerable homogeneity in these organizations because the same set of tasks is performed by multiple people who occupy the same job. In addition, people in mechanistic organizations perform the same job with much the same set of prescribed tasks over a lengthy period that might last for several years. In organic organizations of the future, however, the differences between jobs in terms of their tasks will be greatly magnified. Each person will probably carry out a largely unique set of activities that are different from the set of tasks performed by most other people and different from the tasks the person is likely to perform in the future.

This is not to say that there will be no structure at all to the sets of tasks performed by different individuals. We are not arguing that everyone in a work organization is equally likely to perform every task that must be performed. For instance, we do not expect that people in the computer industry who are responsible for writing sophisticated programs will also be equally responsible for running machinery that produces computer hardware components, for negotiating prices with suppliers who provide raw materials for the manufacturing process, and for drafting legally binding contracts for the sale of large batches of personal computers to government agencies. We also do not expect that people in the health care industry who are responsible for performing brain surgery will also be equally responsible for delivering babies, preparing food for patients, and laundering linens. Many tasks that must be performed require knowledge and skills that take time and special abilities to develop. It is not likely that everyone will have the ability to acquire the knowledge and skills needed to perform successfully every necessary task, even if their interests and preferences are broad enough to dispose them to want to perform every necessary task. Thus, individual differences in ability, personality traits, knowledge, skills, work habits, and occupational interests will still channel people toward some kinds of tasks and away from others, even in unique jobs.

As a result, we expect that although jobs will become more unique, people will still be primarily responsible for domains of tasks within the total set of tasks that must be performed in the organization, and multiple people will be primarily responsible for the same task domains. For lack of a better term, we call these task domains *work categories*. Work categories are different from traditional jobs in three important ways. First, they are considerably broader than traditional job descriptions. Second, their boundaries are less rigid and less well defined. And third, they represent only tasks that someone *might* be required to perform at some time, not tasks that people are definitely required to perform on a regular basis. Therefore, although several people might be responsible for the same domain of tasks, over any given period of time they might actually have to perform very different subsets of activities within the domain. This implies that task dimensions will be different for people in different work categories, for different people in the same work category during the same period, and for the same person over different periods.

The process of identifying task dimensions for performance assessment in unique jobs might be somewhat more complicated than in traditional jobs, but it should not entail drastically different procedures. The theory of individual differences in task and contextual performance argues that assessments of task performance must represent the aggregated value to the organization of behavioral episodes in the task side of the performance domain. In traditional organizations operating in relatively stable environments, the content of these behavioral episodes can be reasonably well defined by standard methods of job analysis that examine activities and performance requirements for individual incumbents in positions grouped according to their content such that each homogeneous grouping is considered a job. Because several individuals perform the same job, and because each individual performs the same job over an extended period that might be several years in duration, a job analysis leads to a behavioral definition of the task performance domain that can be applied to all individuals in the same job category for as long as they remain in that category. Usually this behavioral definition takes the form of a set of dimensions that cover the important tasks in the job. In a nutshell, job analysis for traditional jobs assumes that the same set of task dimensions applies to everyone in the same job, it studies task requirements for people in the same job, and it identifies task dimensions for that job accordingly.

A job analysis strategy for unique jobs can be carried out in much the same way, but with a few important differences. It would assume that the same set of task dimensions are *potentially* relevant for everyone in the same work category, it would study tasks actually performed by people in the work category, it would identify task dimensions for the work category accordingly, and it would determine which subset of these task dimensions apply to each individual for any given performance period. Task performance dimensions for a work category could be developed through standard job analysis procedures. For example, interviews and meetings with a large sample of incumbents in the same work category, coupled with on-the-job observation, would generate a list of tasks that could form the basis for a task checklist questionnaire that could be used to ask for information about the importance of these tasks and the amount of time spent on them. The list of activities would probably be longer and more diverse than those typically developed for jobs that vary less now than we expect they will in the future. Also, ratings of importance and time spent will probably vary from incumbent to incumbent, again because their jobs will be more varied than they are now. Nevertheless, such an approach should be able to identify an exhaustive set of task dimensions that anyone in the work category might be required to perform at one time or another, even if no one actually performs all the task dimensions in any given performance period.

Once the task dimensions for a work category are defined, an individual's performance would be assessed in two steps. In the first step, information would be collected about the appropriateness of each task dimension for the individual's performance during the period in which the rater had an opportunity to observe the ratee's task performance. This first step is essentially an analysis of the ratee's unique job during the period embraced by the performance assessment. In the second step, information would be collected about how effectively the individual performed each task that was judged as part of his or her job during the performance period.

The Same or Similar Dimensions of Contextual Performance Are Relevant for All Jobs

The theory of individual differences in task and contextual performance implies that the same or similar configurations of contextual behavior episodes are likely to be important in nearly all jobs, even if the jobs vary significantly in their task requirements. The reason that contextual performance is presumed to be universally important is that most jobs are embedded in organized social structures. Most jobs are part of a collective effort to attain organizational objectives that are larger than the specific objectives of any single job and that involve interactions between individuals and groups who have different specific objectives but who share the larger organizational objective.

Everyone who works in an organization has the opportunity to act in ways that either improve or worsen the social, organizational, and psychological environment for others in the organization. In addition, although there might be some differences from organization to organization and from individual to individual in the kinds of opportunities that become available for contextual performance, behavioral episodes that improve the organizational, social, and psychological environment in one organization and job setting generally are likely to be very similar to behavioral episodes that improve it in other organizations and job settings.

Thus, the categories of contextual performance defined by Borman and Motowidlo (1993) should serve to guide the development of contextual dimensions for performance assessment in unique jobs. Specific behavioral definitions can be adjusted according to the kinds of opportunities that people in a particular work category and organization have for performing contextual behaviors, but in general these dimensions should cover contextual elements of helping and cooperating with others, following organizational rules and procedures, endorsing organizational objectives, persisting with extra enthusiasm, and volunteering.

Performance Varies Partly Because of Main and Interaction Effects of Situations

Another implication of the theory of individual differences in task and contextual performance is that some portion of the variability in individual performance is attributable to situational variability. In the framework of analysis of variance, there should be (1) main effects of individuals on performance, because some people are likely to be better performers overall than other people; (2) main effects of situations on performance, because it should be easier for most people to perform effectively in some situations than in other situations; and (3) interaction effects between individuals and situations, because some people are most effective in some situations while other people are most effective in other situations.

The theory predicts both main and interaction effects of situations because many elements of task and contextual knowledge, skill, and habits, which are the intervening variables in the theory, are learned in connection with specific situations. In large part, these intervening variables represent knowledge of facts, procedures, and actions that are likely to be effective in specific situations; skill in carrying out actions and procedures known to be effective in certain situations; and habitual effective responses to specific situations. In addition, whether someone possesses these sets of knowledge, skills, and habits depends in part on opportunities to be in the situations where they can be learned. As a result, the behavioral episodes in the performance domain for a particular individual, distributed over a particular period, will vary in their contribution values partly according to the nature of the situations in which they occur.

Main and interaction effects of situations on performance are likely to increase when jobs become more unique because situational variability will increase. If we are correct in assuming that people in unique jobs will be assigned to constantly changing projects and to teams because of efforts by the organization to adapt to a changing environment, they will find themselves in a much wider variety of work situations than did people working in traditional, mechanistic organizations. Situational differences in an individual's job performance will therefore be even more pronounced.

Variability in performance across different work situations is not necessarily a source of error in the assessment of job performance. Job performance can vary legitimately from situation to situation. This creates special challenges for assessing performance in unique jobs because we expect that supervisors or others who are in a position to observe and evaluate someone's job performance will be confounded with the situation. One performance rater in one job situation will have direct access to information about performance episodes only in that situation. Others who might also be in a position to rate the same individual's performance will probably have direct access only to information about performance episodes in different situations. Therefore, if different raters disagree about someone's job performance, that might not necessarily indicate rater error; instead, it might simply indicate that the individual actually performed more effectively in one job situation than in another, perhaps because he or she had knowledge, skills, or work habits that fit one situation better than another.

Performance Measures Must Accurately Represent the Distribution of Behavioral Episodes in the Performance Domain

The theory of individual differences in task and contextual performance defines job performance as the aggregated value of an individual's behavioral episodes over a period. This means that to be administratively practical, procedures for assessing performance will probably have to involve judgments from people who are in a position to observe an individual's behavior during a performance period. According to an information processing model of personnel decisions developed earlier (Motowidlo, 1986), such judgments are accurate to the extent that they faithfully represent the distribution of effective and ineffective behavioral episodes in the performance domain.

In a laboratory study simulating managerial work, Mero (1994) tested whether ratings of job performance varied according to the number of effective and ineffective performance episodes that raters observed. He found that ratings of effectiveness on separate performance dimensions were strongly correlated with the proportion of effective to ineffective performance episodes presented in relation to each dimension.

Judgments about job performance can be distorted, however, by factors that bias the sample of behavioral episodes that judges observe and input to memory, by factors that bias the sample of behavioral episodes they retrieve from memory when called upon to evaluate performance, and by factors that affect their motivation to record judgments that accurately represent the sample of behavioral episodes they retrieve from memory (Motowidlo, 1986). Thus, a major challenge in collecting assessments of job performance is to help judges sample, retrieve, and record their judgments accurately.

In another study, Mero (1994; Mero & Motowidlo, 1995) found that raters who were made to feel accountable for their ratings by expecting to have to explain them at the end of the study rated simulated subordinates more accurately than raters who were not made to feel especially accountable. This suggests that it is possible to improve rating accuracy, defined as the correspondence between performance ratings and distributions of effective and ineffective behavioral episodes in the performance domain, by holding raters accountable for their ratings.

The requirement that performance ratings accurately reflect the distribution of behavioral episodes in the performance domain has two special implications for performance assessment in unique jobs. One implication has to do with the source of the ratings. Traditionally, formal performance appraisals for administrative purposes are often made by a single supervisor annually or semiannually or according to some other standard schedule. If made annually, for instance, the supervisor's ratings represent the aggregated value of behavioral episodes over the previous year. Rating all incumbents over the same period makes it possible to compare them to each other according to their contributions to the organization during the standard period and then to allocate pay raises or other organizational rewards and make personnel decisions such as promotions or assignment to training opportunities differentially on that basis.

As jobs become more unique, however, because of constant assignment and reassignment to different projects and teams, it will probably not be reasonable to expect a single supervisor to be able to capture the distribution of effective and ineffective performance episodes in his or her appraisals over a standard period such as six months or a year. No single supervisor will be able to observe an individual's performance over enough of the many different work situations in which the individual will perform to be in a good position to form judgments of performance based on reasonably adequate samples of the individual's behavioral episodes. This problem is especially acute if differences in the task requirements of the various work situations are great enough that they require substantially different kinds of task knowledge, skills, and habits for effectiveness. In that case, a single supervisor might have firsthand knowledge about an individual's performance in the few situations he or she can observe, but not know about performance in other situations in which the individual's performance could well be considerably more or less effective.

The solution to this problem is to collect performance judgments from multiple raters (Hedge & Borman, 1995), each of whom has access to information about performance episodes in different team and project situations, and have them appraise an individual's performance during only that period in which they were able to observe the ratee's behavior. The multiple raters might include supervisors or task force leaders from different project teams, peers, subordinates, customers, and virtually anyone else who observed the ratee's performance. If ratings from multiple judges are collected in this way, they will have to be combined somehow, perhaps by weighting them by the length of time represented in each rating, in order to derive a performance score that will have the same meaning across ratees and allow fair comparisons between them.

Readers will recognize the strategy of collecting performance judgments from multiple raters as the core of what has come to be called 360-degree feedback. It is a procedure for collecting performance information from multiple informants at different hierarchical levels (supervisors, peers, and subordinates) and feeding it back to the targets of evaluation to encourage development and performance improvement. Murphy and Cleveland (1995) noted that disagreements between sources are to be expected and can create difficulties if the information is used for evaluative instead of developmental purposes. They also noted that although research results indicate that people do not necessarily mind getting upward feedback (from their subordinates), it should be balanced with other sources of feedback. They recommend that performance feedback from nontraditional sources such as subordinates should be provided in the form of an anonymous average of the group of raters, not in the form of individual observations.

The other special implication for unique jobs has to do with holding raters accountable. When a single supervisor is solely responsible for appraising an individual's performance, as in many or most traditional jobs today, it is a relatively simple matter to hold the supervisor accountable; such supervisors can simply be required to review and justify their appraisals and performance ratings with their own supervisors. Having to give face-to-face feedback to ratees is another way that supervisors are traditionally made to feel accountable for their evaluations.

If performance ratings for an individual are made by multiple raters, however, including coworkers, subordinates, and customers in addition to multiple supervisors, holding all these raters accountable becomes much more complicated. If multiple ratings are collected anonymously and then compiled as an average across raters—in the same way, for instance, that student evaluations of teacher performance are typically made on American campuses and that customer evaluations of service providers are often made in service industries—it is hard to see why raters should feel particularly accountable for their judgments under these circumstances. It is not likely that customers, or subordinates especially (Murphy & Cleveland, 1995), and probably not even peers, can realistically be required to give their evaluations directly to ratees in face-to-face meetings. But another way to encourage at least some feelings of accountability in assessing performance in unique jobs might be to require multiple raters to meet as a group to discuss their ratings, to justify them to one another, and to come to a consensus evaluation, much like the procedures that are often followed for evaluations in formal assessment centers. Of course this adds a tremendous administrative burden to the process of performance appraisal, probably more than most organizations are likely to be willing to accept.

Alternatives to Assessing Job Performance

We have argued that main and interaction effects of situations contribute to performance variability in traditional jobs and will contribute even more to performance variability as jobs become more unique. Along with what we believe will be a trend toward more frequent assignment and reassignment to different teams and projects, situational effects on performance will make it difficult to rely on a single supervisor for performance evaluations, so multiple raters will probably have to be involved. But this introduces other assessment problems, such as how to hold raters accountable for their ratings, especially raters from nontraditional sources, such as peers and subordinates; how to deal with differences between raters in their evaluations; how to combine ratings provided by raters who observe ratees for different periods in different job situations; and how to derive performance scores that can be fairly compared between ratees to guide personnel decisions about them. These problems are not necessarily insurmountable, but the additional administrative burden imposed on the performance appraisal process will probably prove discouraging for many organizations.

It might be possible to avoid this burden for some kinds of personnel decisions for which job performance is often measured by substituting measures of other constructs that might be less costly or administratively burdensome. For instance, decisions about individual development or training needs that could be made on the basis of assessments of job performance might actually be better made on the basis of sound measures of relevant knowledge, skills, and work habits. Similarly, decisions about promotions that are often made on the basis of assessments of job performance might also be better made on the basis of assessments of knowledge, skills, and habits, this time in relation to effective performance in the job to which a promotion is being considered. Knowledge, skill, and work habits are the real constructs of interest for personnel decisions such as these. When job performance is measured instead, it is just a surrogate for knowledge, skill, and work habits.

Job performance is conceptually different from its antecedents in knowledge, skill, and work habits in that it is the accumulated value to the organization of an individual's behaviors. Knowledge, skills, and work habits, conversely, are individual difference characteristics that affect only a person's potential for behaving in ways that contribute organizationally. Another conceptual difference is that job performance is affected by motivational states that can be altered through supervisory practices, administrative policies, group dynamics, and other factors on the job. Motivational factors represented in work habits are trait factors that might change to some degree through the effects of learning, but they are nevertheless relatively stable.

An important advantage of measuring knowledge, skills, and work habits instead of job performance is that they can be measured by standardized tests in a single administration without requiring observations and evaluations from multiple judges in multiple situations. It might be more expensive to develop procedures for testing knowledge, skills, and work habits than to develop forms for collecting judgments of job performance. However, as jobs become more unique and as performance assessment requires a correspondingly larger number of different raters for each incumbent, the costs of developing standardized testing procedures might be less than the costs of requiring many raters to participate in the assessment of an individual's job performance.

The first step in developing such testing procedures is to develop a taxonomy of relevant knowledge, skills, and work habits. One approach might be to start with general performance or competency models that would suggest possibilities for necessary knowledge, skills, and work habits. For instance, the dimensions of contextual performance defined by Borman and Motowidlo (1993, 1997) offer one taxonomy that might be used in this way.

Another model that should be very useful for this purpose is the multifactor performance model developed by Campbell and colleagues (1993). Their model divides the performance domain into eight factors: job-specific task proficiency, non-job-specific task proficiency, written and oral communication tasks, demonstrating effort, maintaining personal discipline, facilitating peer and team performance, supervision, and management and administration. These factors are designed to be sufficient to describe the latent performance structure of all jobs in the *Dictionary of Occupational Titles*.

In addition, some human resource consulting firms offer general competency models for analyzing training needs, for developing selection devices and performance appraisal procedures, and for conducting succession planning and job evaluation. The models often include dimensions that heavily represent contextual content, such as facilitating team performance, teamwork and cooperation, and championing continuous improvement (Development Dimensions International); building relationships, promoting corporate citizenship, and leveraging networks (Personnel Decisions International); and possessing interpersonal understanding, flexibility, and organizational commitment (Hay/McBer). They also include task-like dimensions such as feedback and improvement planning, judgment and problem solving, and planning and organizing work (Development Dimensions International); use of financial and quantitative data, use of technical/functional expertise, and development of systems and processes (Personnel Decisions International); and information seeking and directiveness (Hay/McBer).

If a general taxonomy of knowledge, skills, and work habits can be extracted from performance and competency models such as these, the next step would be to use such a taxonomy as a framework for identifying specific knowledge, skill, and work habit requirements for a particular job or work category.

The approach just described starts with generic, theoretical models of job performance and moves from there to specific knowledge, skill, and work habit requirements. An alternative approach would be to start with a detailed job analysis of specific contextual and tasks performed by incumbents of a job or work category, then to collect time-spent and frequency ratings from subject matter experts, and finally to infer knowledge, skill, and work habit requirements in the usual way. Either approach should produce a workable taxonomy of knowledge, skill, and work-habit requirements for a job or work category at a level of detail useful for guiding the development of procedures for measuring individual differences in these characteristics. The taxonomy should be at a fine enough level of detail to capture important elements of knowledge, skill, and work habits specific to a particular job or work category, but it should also be broad enough to represent requirements in a range of situations that occur with some frequency on the job.

Knowledge can be assessed through written or oral tests of facts, information, and procedures that are necessary for effective performance in various situations. Such tests are widely used to tap task or technical knowledge (Dye, Reck, & McDaniel, 1993). To measure knowledge of correct procedures or the most effective action to take in difficult situations, such tests are sometimes in the form of low-fidelity simulations in which candidates are presented with written, oral, or visual portrayals of a problem situation and asked how they would handle it. Low-fidelity simulations in the form of situational (paper-and-pencil) inventories (Motowidlo, Dunnette, & Carter, 1990; Motowidlo & Tippins, 1993; Stevens & Campion, 1997) and situational interviews (Latham, 1989; Latham, Saari, Pursell, & Campion, 1980; Latham & Skarlicki, 1995) that focus on social, interpersonal, or motivational problems can be used to tap knowledge related to contextual performance.

Skills can be assessed through high-fidelity simulations that require candidates actually to perform a response to a problem situation instead of just describing what they would do if they were in the situation. Job sample tests are well known for assessing skills on the task side of the performance domain (Asher & Sciarrino, 1974). High-fidelity simulations such as in-basket exercises, group discussion exercises, role-play exercises, and other simulations involving social, administrative, interpersonal, or organizational elements can be used to measure contextual skills.

Finally, work habits related to either task performance or contextual performance can be assessed through structured interviews that ask applicants to describe how they have handled certain kinds of problem situations in the past (Janz, 1982, 1989; Motowidlo et al., 1992).

Conclusion

As organizations adapt to accelerating change in their environments, we expect to see major adjustments in how jobs are structured. They will probably become increasingly varied and unique because individuals will become responsible for larger and less well defined domains of work. We expect that people will be assigned to teams with responsibility for projects of varying duration, to multiple project teams simultaneously, and to different teams over time.

Both task and contextual elements of job performance are important for organizational effectiveness and survival, but the contextual elements will probably become even more important than they are now because the new job structures will demand more in the way of interpersonal helping and cooperation, persistence, initiative, volunteering to do whatever is necessary, willingness to comply with organizational rules and procedures, and support for organizational objectives. Contextual dimensions of performance will be the same or similar for all (or nearly all) jobs because all (or nearly all) are embedded in organized social structures with the same kinds of needs for support and maintenance. Task dimensions, however, will vary greatly between jobs. Thus, to the extent that jobs are becoming more varied and unique, we argue that their uniqueness will be primarily in their task elements, not in their contextual elements.

One challenge for performance assessment in such jobs is how to define task performance dimensions relevant for an incumbent over a particular performance period. We have suggested that it should be possible to define exhaustive sets of task dimensions for categories of work (which are broader and less well defined than traditional jobs) with the expectation that they include all task functions that anyone in that work category might ever be required to perform. It should then be possible to identify a subset of these dimensions that are relevant for a particular incumbent for the period embraced by his or her performance assessment.

We have also argued that main and interaction effects of situations on job performance will increase when jobs become more unique because situational variability itself will increase. This suggests that a second major challenge for performance assessment in unique jobs will be to find sources of information who can provide assessments that accurately reflect the distribution of effective and ineffective behavioral episodes in the performance domain. It will probably become necessary to rely on multiple sources of performance information for each incumbent, but this introduces problems related to rater accountability and raises the question of how information from multiple raters can be combined to yield performance scores that mean the same for different incumbents so that they can be fairly compared to one another.

The problems related to the use of multiple sources of performance information might be too burdensome for many organizations. We therefore have suggested that some kinds of personnel decisions might not really require information about incumbents' job performance if information about their knowledge, skills, and work habits can be collected. Such an approach would call for the development of general and specific taxonomies of relevant knowledge, skills, and work habits. These can be measured through paper-and-pencil tests of job knowledge; through low-fidelity simulations in paper-and-pencil, interview, or video formats; through high-fidelity simulations such as work sample tests and assessment center procedures; and through interview formats that use structured questions about behavior in past situations that is similar to situations that are likely to occur on the job for which the person is being evaluated.

References

Asher, J. J., & Sciarrino, J. A. (1974). Realistic work sample tests: A review. *Personnel Psychology, 27,* 519–533.

Borman, W. C., & Motowidlo, S. J. (1993). Expanding the criterion domain to include elements of contextual performance. In N. Schmitt & W. C. Borman (Eds.), *Personnel selection in organizations* (pp. 71–98). San Francisco: Jossey-Bass.

Borman, W. C., & Motowidlo, S. J. (1997). Task performance and contextual performance: The meaning for personnel selection research. *Human Performance, 10,* 99–109.

Borman, W. C., Motowidlo, S. J., Rose, S. R., & Hanser, L. M. (1985). *Development of a model of soldier effectiveness* (Institute Report No. 95). Minneapolis, MN: Personnel Decisions Research Institutes.

Borman, W. C., White, L. A., & Dorsey, D. W. (1995). Effects of ratee task performance and interpersonal factors on supervisor and peer performance ratings. *Journal of Applied Psychology, 80,* 168–177.

Brief, A. P., & Motowidlo, S. J. (1986). Prosocial organizational behaviors. *Academy of Management Review, 10,* 710–725.

Campbell, J. P. (1983). Some possible implications of "modeling" for the conceptualization of measurement. In F. Landy, S. Zedeck, & J. Cleveland (Eds.), *Performance measurement and theory* (pp. 271–298). Hillsdale, NJ: Erlbaum.

Campbell, J. P. (1990). Modeling the performance prediction problem in industrial and organizational psychology. In M. D. Dunnette & L. M. Hough (Eds.), *Handbook of industrial and organizational psychology* (Vol. 1, 2nd ed., pp. 687–732). Palo Alto, CA: Consulting Psychologists Press.

Campbell, J. P., Gasser, M. B., & Oswald, F. L. (1996). The substantive nature of job performance variability. In K. R. Murphy (Ed.), *Individual differences and behavior in organizations* (pp. 258–299). San Francisco: Jossey-Bass.

Campbell, J. P., McCloy, R. A., Oppler, S. H., & Sager, C. E. (1993). A theory of performance. In N. Schmitt & W. C. Borman (Eds.), *Personnel selection in organizations* (pp. 35–70). San Francisco: Jossey-Bass.

Dye, D. A., Reck, M., & McDaniel, M. A. (1993). The validity of job knowledge measures. *International Journal of Selection and Assessment, 30,* 153–157.

Ferris, G. R., Judge, T. A., Rowland, K. M., & Fitzgibbons, D. E. (1994). Subordinate influence and the performance evaluation process. *Organizational Behavior and Human Decision Processes, 58,* 101–135.

Frese, M., Kring, W., Soose, A., & Zempel, J. (1996). Personal initiative at work: Differences between East and West Germany. *Academy of Management Journal, 39,* 37–63.

George, J. M., & Brief, A. P. (1992). Feeling good—doing good: A conceptual analysis of the mood at work-organizational spontaneity relationship. *Psychological Bulletin, 112,* 310–329.

George, J. M., & Jones, G. R. (1997). Organizational spontaneity in context. *Human Performance, 10,* 153–170.

Hedge, J. W., & Borman, W. C. (1995). Changing conceptions and practices in performance appraisal. In A. Howard (Ed.), *The changing nature of work* (pp. 451–482). San Francisco: Jossey-Bass.

Hunter, J. E. (1983). A causal analysis of cognitive ability, job knowledge, job performance, and supervisor ratings. In F. Landy, S. Zedeck, & J. Cleveland (Eds.), *Performance measurement and theory* (pp. 257–266). Hillsdale, NJ: Erlbaum.

Janz, T. (1982). Initial comparisons of patterned behavior description interviews versus unstructured interviews. *Journal of Applied Psychology, 67,* 577–580.

Janz, T. (1989). The patterned behavior description interview: The best prophet of the future is the past. In R. W. Eder & G. R. Ferris (Eds.), *The employment interview: Theory, research, and practice* (pp. 158–168). Thousand Oaks, CA: Sage.

Latham, G. P. (1989). The reliability, validity, and practicality of the situational interview. In R. W. Eder & G. R. Ferris (Eds.), *The employment interview: Theory, research, and practice* (pp. 169–182). Thousand Oaks, CA: Sage.

Latham, G. P., Saari, L. M., Pursell, E. D., & Campion, M. A. (1980). The situational interview. *Journal of Applied Psychology, 65,* 422–431.

Latham, G. P., & Skarlicki, D. P. (1995). Criterion-related validity of the situational and patterned behavior description interviews with organizational citizenship behavior. *Human Performance, 8,* 67–80.

MacKenzie, S. B., Podsakoff, P. M., & Fetter, R. (1991). Organizational citizenship behavior and objective productivity as determinants of managerial evaluations of salespersons' performance. *Organizational Behavior and Human Decision Processes, 50,* 123–150.

McCrae, R. R., & Costa, P. T. (1996). Toward a new generation of personality theories: Theoretical contexts for the five-factor model. In J. S. Wiggins (Ed.), *The five-factor model of personality* (pp. 51–87). New York: Guilford Press.

Mero, N. P. (1994). *Contextual influences on the rating process: The effects of accountability and rating outcomes on performance rating quality.* Unpublished doctoral dissertation, University of Florida.

Mero, N. P., & Motowidlo, S. J. (1995). Effects of rater accountability on the accuracy and favorability of performance ratings. *Journal of Applied Psychology, 80,* 517–524.

Motowidlo, S. J. (1986). Information processing in personnel decisions. In K. M. Rowland & G. R. Ferris (Eds.), *Research in personnel and human resource management* (Vol. 4, pp. 1–44). Greenwich, CT: JAI Press.

Motowidlo, S. J., Borman, W. C., & Schmit, M. J. (1997). A theory of individual differences in task and contextual performance. *Human
Performance, 10,* 71–83.

Motowidlo, S. J., Carter, G. W., Dunnette, M. D., Tippins, N., Werner, S.,
Burnett, J. R., & Vaughan, M. J. (1992). Studies of the structured behavioral interview. *Journal of Applied Psychology, 77,* 571–587.

Motowidlo, S. J., Dunnette, M. D., & Carter, G. W. (1990). An alternative
selection procedure: The low-fidelity simulation. *Journal of Applied
Psychology, 75,* 640–647.

Motowidlo, S. J., & Tippins, N. (1993). Further studies of the low-fidelity
simulation in the form of a situational inventory. *Journal of Occupational and Organizational Psychology, 66,* 337–344.

Motowidlo, S. J., & Van Scotter, J. R. (1994). Evidence that task performance should be distinguished from contextual performance. *Journal of Applied Psychology, 79,* 475–480.

Murphy, K. R., & Cleveland, J. N. (1995). *Understanding performance appraisal.* Thousand Oaks, CA: Sage.

Organ, D. W. (1988). *Organizational citizenship behavior: The good soldier syndrome.* San Francisco: New Lexington Press.

Organ, D. W. (1997). Organizational citizenship behavior: It's construct
clean-up time. *Human Performance, 10,* 85–97.

Podsakoff, P. M., Ahearn, M., & MacKenzie, S. B. (1997). Organizational
citizenship behavior and the quantity and quality of work group performance. *Journal of Applied Psychology, 82,* 262–270.

Podsakoff, P. M., & MacKenzie, S. B. (1994). Organizational citizenship
behavior and sales unit effectiveness. *Journal of Marketing Research,
31,* 351–363.

Podsakoff, P. M., & MacKenzie, S. B. (1997). Impact of organizational citizenship behavior on organizational performance: A review and suggestions for future research. *Human Performance, 10,* 133–151.

Schmit, M. J., Motowidlo, S. J., De Groot, T., Cross, T., & Kiker, D. S.
(1996, April). *Explaining the relationship between personality and job performance.* Paper presented at the meeting of the Society for Industrial and Organizational Psychology, San Diego, CA.

Smith, C. A., Organ, D. W., & Near, J. P. (1983). Organizational citizenship behavior: Its nature and antecedents. *Journal of Applied Psychology, 68,* 653–663.

Speier, C., & Frese, M. (1997). Generalized self-efficacy as a mediator and
moderator between control and complexity at work and personal
initiative: A longitudinal field study in East Germany. *Human Performance, 10,* 171–192.

Stevens, M. J., & Campion, M. A. (1996). *Staffing work teams: Development and validation of a selection test for teamwork settings.* Unpublished manuscript.

Van Scotter, J. R., & Motowidlo, S. J. (1996). Evidence for two factors of contextual performance: Job dedication and interpersonal facilitation. *Journal of Applied Psychology, 81,* 525–531.

Walz, S. M., & Niehoff, B. P. (1996). Organizational citizenship behaviors and their effect on organizational effectiveness in limited-menu restaurants. In J. B. Keys & L. N. Dosier (Eds.), *Academy of Management best papers proceedings* (pp. 307–311).

Werner, J. M. (1994). Dimensions that make a difference: Examining the impact of in-role and extra-role behaviors on supervisory ratings. *Journal of Applied Psychology, 79,* 98–107.

CHAPTER 4

Contingent Employees
Individual and Organizational Considerations
Charles L. Hulin
Theresa M. Glomb

A view of the U.S. labor force as a monolithic, amorphous mass of career employees, each holding a full-time, permanent job for long periods of time, is not accurate. Such a view fails to consider the heterogeneity and differences in explicit or implicit employment contracts among the groups and subpopulations of organizational employees at work today. Part-time, temporary, contract, seasonal, or casual workers—collectively termed *contingent workers* for simplicity in this chapter—are becoming integral parts of the human resources of many organizations; these employees now represent approximately 25 percent of the employees in the United States, and their numbers are increasing (Conference Board, 1995). The contingent work industry appears to be a permanent and growing part of our industrial environment and its profit structure suggests that the industry has a sound financial basis. Figures 4.1 and 4.2 show the growth in numbers of these contingent workers in the United States

Note: The authors thank Magda Sawicka for her many hours tracking down data on the temporary work industry and compiling it into understandable form, and for her general assistance in the library search tasks necessary to prepare this chapter. We also acknowledge the insightful comments and suggestions of the editors of this volume, Daniel Ilgen and Elaine Pulakos, and the editor of the *Frontiers* Series, Sheldon Zedeck.

since the 1970s. Data on temporary workers since 1993, not shown in Figure 4.1, suggest an increasing rate of these workers in the U.S. workforce.

Contingent workers have become a factor that organizational researchers must deal with if we are to develop general theories of behavior and performance in organizations. The relevant dimensions along which contingent workers differ from permanent, full-time workers, and the importance of these differences, should be explored thoroughly before we generalize to this growing population. Excluding contingent workers from our empirical studies in work organizations represents a shortsighted approach to research addressing important questions about the U.S. workforce in the next millennium. Researchers and organizational managers must address the unique issues of job performance and the related job attitudes and behaviors of contingent workers. Redefining the meanings of our basic organizational constructs such as work,

Figure 4.1. Average Daily Number of Temporary Workers in the United States, 1970–1993.

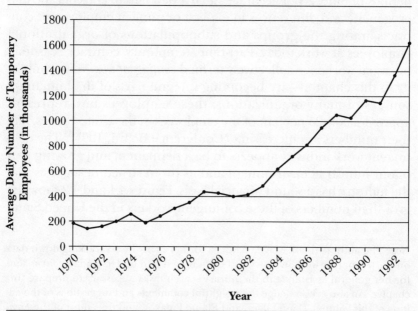

Source: Based on National Association of Temporary Services, 1994.

career, commitment, and even performance may be necessary to explain the job performance behaviors of these workers.

In this chapter we define performance broadly as the psychological and behavioral responses that influence employee performance and, ultimately, organizational effectiveness. In this definition we include counterproductive behaviors such as organizational withdrawal (Hanisch & Hulin, 1990, 1991) and such extra-role responses as prosocial and contextual performance behaviors (Borman & Motowidlo, 1993). This definition expands our focus to include organizational responses such as job satisfaction (Roznowski & Hulin, 1992) and organizational commitment, which have empirically demonstrated proximal and distal links to performance. Using these constructs as additional components of performance, the implications of contingent workers for organizational performance and the

**Figure 4.2. Part-Time Work Industry
in the United States, 1975–1995.**

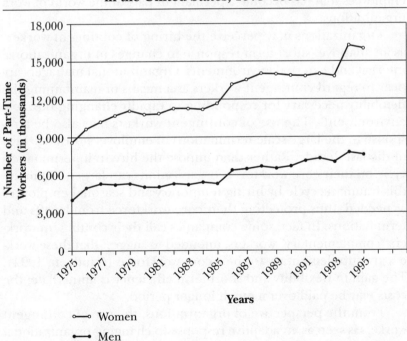

Source: U.S. Department of Labor, Bureau of Labor Statistics.

implications for human resource strategies, training programs, motivational practices, supervisory practices, and other personnel actions can be explored.

Changing Meanings of Work and Working Careers

Myriad changes in organizational environments have fundamentally affected the jobs and careers of individuals as well as the makeup and heterogeneity of aggregated workforces (Tilly, 1991). These changes and trends in workforces do not seem to have been anticipated by organizational scientists. The view of the coming millennium from the proximity of 1998 contrasts with the projections of what work was to become that were presented twenty-five years ago in *Work and Nonwork in the Year 2001,* a book edited by Dunnette (1973). None of the chapters in that book addressed in depth the issues being raised today by the reliance on temporary employees that has become a permanent part of the world of work organizations.

Organizations may perceive the hiring of contingent workers as an adaptive, short-term response to changes in organizations' internal and external environments. Organizational managers appear to regard contingent workers as a means of maintaining the flexibility necessary for responding to rapidly changing business environments. The use of contingent workers may also be a response to the large-scale terminations of employees (downsizing) of the last decade. Rather than impose the hire-train-termination cycle on their core workforce, organizations can largely eliminate this traumatic cycle by hiring temporary and seasonal employees as needed, thus protecting their core workforce from layoffs and terminations. In fact, some companies call their contingent workers "complementary" workers, intended to suggest that these workers are supplementary to their core workforce (Caudron, 1994). The gain in flexibility and short-term efficiency is immediate; the costs may be paid over a much longer period.

From the perspective of organizations, the use of contingent workers is seen as an adaptive response to changing organizational environments. From the perspective of individual employees, economic, social, and demographic changes as well as the changing demographics of the workforce have created a world of work that is more complex and less stable than it was twenty-five years ago. Although no one economic or demographic change is solely responsible for the changing nature of work or the paths of work careers, together they are causing structural unemployment and changes in the composition of aggregate workforces. Previously comfortable niches involving traditional full-time, permanent work are less available. Part-time, seasonal, and casual work, regarded in the past as safety nets for students or productive escapes for older individuals desiring to enter or reenter the workforce, are now likely to be part of workers' careers at times other than their student or geriatric years. Contingent work has become the nexus of employment for many blue collar workers, professionals, and other white collar workers. Individuals may combine two or more temporary or contract jobs into a means of financial support. Large-scale terminations of employees, plant closings and relocations, and organizational restructuring have created sizable pools of temporarily unemployed or permanently underemployed individuals who are faced with supporting themselves and their families while seeking (usually) full-time jobs similar to the ones that were restructured out of their work lives.

Retirement is another part of working careers that plays an employment role for organizations and individuals. Early retirement decisions, influenced by federal legislation and financially attractive buyouts, coupled with longer life expectancies, lead to a substantial number of trained and skilled employees who are spending more years in retirement. These individuals may desire, or need, to return to work on a temporary or part-time basis. Organizations may find their own retirees to be an excellent source of well-trained contingent employees. Retired workers' motivations for working may be substantially different from those of contingent workers who are working strictly for the additional income; they may also have motivations for working in common with other contingent workers.

These trends in the structure of the workforce and changes in the business environments of organizations suggest the need to expand our thinking about our workforce and the models and theories used to explain job performance and related behavioral constructs. We may have to adopt a more explicitly stochastic model of working careers and effective work behavior than we seem to have assumed up to now. Movements from full-time, permanent employment to temporary work to retirement and back to temporary or part-time work with occasional side trips into part-time, seasonal, or contract work are becoming more common career paths. With each job change, the possibility of different definitions of what constitutes an effective employee should be recognized. Understanding performance in these sequential work roles may require approaches different than those in use today for understanding the behaviors and decisions of full-time, permanent workers. These are empirical questions that need to be answered.

Conceptual Framework

We rely on dimensions that partially differentiate categories of workers to avoid problems of defining fuzzy sets or classifications of workers. Dimensions that appear relevant for defining this space are *expected hours of work per week, permanence of employment by hiring organization,* and *source of the employee* (that is, whether from inside or outside the organization). These dimensions define a theoretical space that we often implicitly and explicitly partition into regions and label as full-time, temporary, part-time, and casual employees as though the categories were nonoverlapping, distinct, and by themselves informative about the members in each employment classification. We avoid problems inherent in typologies or taxonomies of employees if we focus on the dimensions that generate the space rather than fixating on isolated regions or classifications of workers at the corners of the n-dimensional space of all organizational employees. Nevertheless, it is useful to indicate the general regions in this space where traditional classifications of workers may be approximately located.

Workers employed by an organization on a permanent basis, whose normal hours of work are sufficient so that both the organization and the employees regard the employment contract as representing full-time work, would be located in the lower rear right region of the space depicted in Figure 4.3. Normally these employees would be expected to work more than thirty hours per week, depending on the work shifts and their distribution across days of the week. Hours per week are fuzzy limits to this region, however, and are only part of the theoretically interesting defining properties of these workers' jobs.

Figure 4.3. Dimensions Defining the Space of Full-Time, Temporary, Casual, and Contract Workers.

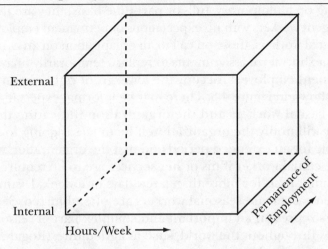

Workers employed on a more or less permanent basis where the number of hours worked per week are regarded by both the employer and the employee as constituting less than full-time employment would be those in the lower rear left region of the space shown in Figure 4.3. There may be an expectation of regular employment for a more-or-less fixed number of hours and shifts each week by both the organization and the employee. The expected number of hours worked each week is again a fuzzy limit, normally fewer than thirty. Expectations of permanent employment, and the source of the employees as from and remaining with the organization are the other defining characteristics of these part-time workers.

Temporary workers occupy the upper front region of the space in Figure 4.3. These workers may work full-time or less than full-time. They are normally external, temporary workers supplied by a temporary work firm that charges a fee for supplying them to the organization. These workers' contracts are normally with the temporary work firm rather than with the employing work organization. Temporary workers are often hired to replace permanent workers for a specific period. They may be hired to work on a specified project and their employment ceases when the project is completed. Both the temporary worker and the focal work organization recognize the expected duration of employment. If the temporary workers are retirees from the firm they are working for and are now working on a temporary, full- or part-time basis, they are internal contingent workers with no expectations of permanent employment.

Casual workers, those on call to an organization on an as-needed basis for short-term assignments to replace temporarily unavailable permanent employees, occupy the lower front right region of the space shown in Figure 4.3. There may be informal expectations between casual workers and the organization indicating that the worker will notify the organization if he or she is going to be unavailable for an extended period and that the organization will notify the casual worker if his or her services are to be required on a continuing basis for more than a few days or a week. Distinctions between casual and seasonal workers are often blurred. Seasonal workers represent an important and complex part of seasonal industries throughout the world, such as agriculture (Rogaly, 1996) or recreation and tourism.

The boundaries of these categories of workers are fuzzy. Further conceptual tussling with the defining characteristics of different classifications of employees or with demarcations among the regions of the space shown in Figure 4.3 may be of marginal usefulness. The movement by individuals across these dimensions through the course of their work life coupled with the fuzziness of the boundaries of many classifications of work and workers make research and policy on this problem both complex and timely. Arbitrary definitions imposed on the classifications or sets of workers for legal, legislative, or administrative purposes may or may not correspond to psychological or organizational realities; it is these latter relations that organizational researchers need to consider.

Empirical Research on Contingent Employees

Empirical investigations of part-time employees have accumulated since these workers were labeled the "missing persons in organizational research" (Rotchford & Roberts, 1982). The missing persons label is probably more applicable now to other types of contingent workers on which there is still little empirical work. Because the empirical research has been largely on the part-time work experience, the research discussed in this chapter will necessarily deal with part-time employees as imperfect representatives of the more diverse set of contingent workers. We emphasize, however, that we do not combine all these workers, thinking them homogeneous; there may be as much variance within groups of contingent workers as there is between contingent and full-time, traditional employees (McGinnis & Morrow, 1990; Feldman, 1990).

Research on part-time employees has been concerned largely with comparisons between part-time and full-time workers on demographics, job attitudes, and work behaviors. These variables are related indirectly to performance issues of contingent workers. Little research, however, has focused specifically on the job performance of these workers. Much of the existing research is not guided by strong theory; it provides few insights into why differences exist or develop among categories of employees and what the consequences of these differences might be. Theory has been used largely to support post hoc explanations of results rather than to guide systematic research. Recently, researchers have called for a more theoretical approach to investigating these issues (Feldman, 1990; McGinnis & Morrow, 1990)—a call that has been answered by emphasizing *social comparison theories* (Thibaut & Kelley, 1959; Adams, 1965), *discrepancy models* (Lawler, 1973), *expectancy theory* (Peak, 1955; Tolman, 1932; Vroom, 1964; Naylor, Pritchard, & Ilgen, 1980), and the *theory of partial inclusion* (Katz & Kahn, 1978).

Contingent workers' situations present researchers with unique methodological challenges that make research in this area difficult and sparse. Vecchio (1984) addressed the sample-specific confound in research on part-time and full-time workers, noting that previous studies have relied largely on homogenous samples that have limited variance on relevant constructs and limited generalizability. The temporary nature of many contingent workers makes data collection difficult and the integrity of the data uncertain. Both work attitudes and work performance measures are dynamic and require time in the organization to develop and stabilize; the trajectories by which contingent and noncontingent workers approach these stable levels of attitudes and performance may also differ. In addition, time and commitment by the organization are required to obtain the most relevant measures possible. Depending on managers' views of the importance of research on these employees, contingent workers may not be made available for research purposes.

Performance

The difficulties of conducting research on contingent workers, coupled with conceptual problems in defining the full range of behaviors and psychological responses directly and indirectly related to performance, make the lack of research on the performance of contingent workers understandable. Comparisons among employees are especially difficult if the jobs of contingent workers differ from those of full-time employees in terms of work tasks, work status, direct rewards and fringe benefits, and other critical job features. The covarying multivariate set of job characteristics may be jointly responsible for observed differences; the multivariate set must be disaggregated before causal status can be assigned to any one of the variables.

One perspective on the work performance of contingent employees suggests that in the short-term an organization may get more productivity per payroll dollar from a temporary worker than from a full-time employee because the temporary worker is often paid only for hours worked and may receive no fringe benefits. In contrast, a full-time employee is paid for time when things are slow; for sick days and holidays; when they are reassigned to routine tasks to keep them busy; when work tasks may not be as well defined as they are for temporary workers; and for behaviors that may be inefficient, such as attending meetings, socializing, or engaging in office politics. The finding by Cherrington (cited in Miller, 1983) that the average employee spends approximately 50 percent of his or her time in nonwork tasks makes this argument compelling. The Bureau of Labor Statistics reports that temporary workers produce the equivalent of two hours more per day than their permanent counterparts (Caudron, 1994). Counterarguments caution that these productivity improvements may not take into account the productivity losses that occur at the beginning of a temporary job, when employees are unfamiliar with the work duties at the company. They may not account for other counterproductive work behaviors such as work withdrawal behaviors, conflicts with full-time counterparts, and the lack of contextual performance and prosocial organizational behaviors (Borman & Motowidlo, 1993).

The employment contract that a contingent worker has with the employing organization may have implications for performance.

Psychological contracts between individuals and work organizations are likely to be different for contingent workers and noncontingent workers. For the temporary worker there are two psychological contracts: one with the temporary work firm and the other, more limited in scope, with the organization to which they have been dispatched. The psychological contract with the temporary work organization may be very simple. The temporary firm finds them assignments in work organizations and pays them. In return, they show up, on time and properly attired, when dispatched and execute the tasks to which they are assigned by the work organization. Their psychological contract with the work organization to which they have been assigned is also likely to be quite simple. "You tell me specifically what tasks you want done in what period and I will do them. Don't expect me to go beyond those tasks. I will not expect you to go beyond what is spelled out in the contract." For the contingent worker, the distinctions between the job and their broader role as an organizational member may be trivial (Ilgen & Hollenbeck, 1991).

Given these rudimentary employment and psychological contracts, contingent workers are likely to carry out their assigned work tasks with few modifications. Not every contingent worker employed by an organization will be a paragon of commitment to assigned work tasks, but their work behaviors will be more heavily influenced by explicit job definitions specifying assigned tasks than will the work behaviors of permanent, full-time employees. Task or job requirements may control more of their behavior in organizations than do the same requirements for noncontingent workers. We are hypothesizing that contingent workers will do the things assigned by their supervisor or required by the job; the costs are that they may do little else to contribute to organizational performance.

Psychological contracts between full-time, permanent workers and their primary work organization are likely to be more complex in terms of both what is expected from the worker and what is expected from the organization. Organizations may expect commitment beyond the simple execution of assigned tasks, including citizenship duties that are necessary for an organization to function smoothly but that cannot reasonably be codified and standardized (such as showing new employees how to do their jobs better, representing the organization to outsiders, and performing routine housekeeping). Individual employees may expect that organizations "owe" them for their loyalty and commitment to nonjob tasks. Such debts may be paid in a number of nonfinancial ways, such as advanced training courses or informal flextime arrangements.

Differences in psychological contracts between contingent and noncontingent workers, through the process of spelling out the required and expected tasks, indirectly specify the relevant performance dimensions of each group. If the psychological contract for contingent workers is mute with respect to any prosocial or pro-organizational behaviors, or indeed to any of the extra-job behaviors that contribute to the specification of the work role beyond the job, then those behaviors cannot be regarded as part of the performance space of these workers. If there are no expectations regarding extra effort during periods when projects are due, then supervisory evaluations of such extra efforts are not relevant to the performance or rewards for contingent workers. Although attendance on days and at times scheduled is part of the contract for both groups of workers, timely attendance by contingent workers is likely to receive much greater emphasis than does attendance by noncontingent workers. This latter dimension of performance may be the same for both groups, but the weighting assigned to it when generating an overall performance estimate should differ.

The likelihood that psychological contracts and performance dimensions differ in meaningful ways between these two groups of workers raises important questions about the extent to which the performance of the two groups of workers can be compared meaningfully. Issues of comparison present challenges for researchers and also nearly preclude organizations from entering into an equation performance losses or gains from employing contingent workers to calculate the costs and gains accruing from this human resource strategy. Researchers have had difficulty operationalizing employee performance when it has been defined broadly to include such indirect effects on organizational effectiveness as work and job withdrawal behaviors, organizational citizenship behaviors, and related behaviors. This may be due to a reluctance to include the often poorly estimated benefits of prosocial behaviors as well as the indirect costs of turnover, absenteeism, lateness, missing meetings, wandering around looking busy, and related withdrawal behaviors that seem to be consequences of job attitudes and work-role characteristics. If, however, these behaviors significantly influence the functioning of the organization, their inclusion in the performance assessments of one or both groups of workers is necessary to define the location of the groups in performance space. Narrow conceptualizations of work performance, attitudes, and related behaviors will hamper our research efforts. The lack of research on the performance of contingent employees may perhaps be supplemented by research on such relevant topics as job satisfaction, organizational withdrawal, and organizational commitment.

The differences between contingent and noncontingent workers discussed earlier suggest that typical work withdrawal behaviors (such as absence and tardiness) account for more variance in overall performance of contingent workers than in the performance of noncontingent workers. Several factors may contribute to this. First, contingent workers are often hired into jobs in which the required tasks cannot be put off; the jobs must be filled and the tasks must be done. Being absent—not showing up when dispatched to the work organization—or showing up late for the work assignment is critical. The temporary work firm may be evaluated largely on the basis of the contingent workers' reliability. If a temporary work firm dispatches janitors to a building at night or receptionists to an office during the day and those workers do not show up as scheduled, the temporary work firm itself is negatively evaluated and may lose valuable clients. As a result, the temporary work firm itself is likely to sanction (negatively) work withdrawal behaviors more than they may be sanctioned for permanent, full-time workers. Empirical research has established the existence of relationships between job attitudes and work and job withdrawal (Hanisch & Hulin, 1990, 1991; Hanisch, Hulin, & Roznowski, 1998; Judge, 1990). Given these empirically established relationships, the importance of job attitudes within samples of contingent workers becomes an important issue.

Job Attitudes

Research demonstrates that job satisfaction, while not directly related to job performance (Iaffaldano & Muchinsky, 1985), does influence other, more distal variables that are related to job performance, such as work and job withdrawal (Hanisch & Hulin,

1990, 1991; Hulin, 1991) and organizational commitment (O'Reilly & Chatman, 1986).

Empirical research on the job attitudes of contingent workers can be best described as inconsistent. Several research studies have suggested that, after controlling for demographics, part-time employees have lower satisfaction with work, benefits, and the job overall (Miller & Terborg, 1979); lower career satisfaction (Hall & Gordon, 1973); and less favorable coworker and pay satisfaction (Steffy & Jones, 1990). Other research reports that part-time workers have more favorable attitudes than their full-time counterparts with respect to factors such as the organizational structure, the organization's policies and reward system, the level of trust among organizational members, the distribution of power, and overall job satisfaction (Eberhardt & Shani, 1984). Still other research reports no significant differences between job satisfaction dimensions for part-time and full-time workers (Logan, O'Reilly, & Roberts, 1973; McGinnis & Morrow, 1990; Vecchio, 1984) or among workers with differing levels of "peripherality" (represented by the degree of contact between workers and employers, defined by the regularity of employment and the number of hours worked) after controlling for demographics (Hom, 1979).

The research just discussed is concerned primarily with differences between part-time and full-time workers. Other research has capitalized on variance among part-time workers and has compared subsets of these workers across relevant dimensions and work characteristics such as permanence (Gannon & Nothern, 1971; Feldman & Doerpinghaus, 1992) and regularity of part-time employment (Jackofsky & Peters, 1987), preferred work schedule (Lee & Johnson, 1990; Morrow, McElroy, & Elliot, 1994), and voluntariness of contingent employment (Ellingson, Gruys, & Sackett, 1997). The variability found among contingent employees underscores the importance of examining these workers as they are located along defining dimensions similar to those found in Figure 4.3 rather than as discrete categories of employees.

McGinnis and Morrow (1990) propose the following primarily methodological explanations for the discrepancies in job satisfaction between part-time and full-time workers. First, the studies that controlled for demographics did not control for a common set of demographic indicators. Similarly, a research study may or may not have controlled for part-time and full-time workers having the same work assignments, job benefits, autonomy, and other work characteristics. Few studies have looked at the preferred work status and characteristics of the employee. Finally, the studies used different measures of job attitudes.

In addition to these methodological problems and sampling variance across studies, there are theoretical reasons for some of the observed differences. Differing frames of reference may explain, for example, the more positive job attitudes of irregular, part-time workers (Jackofsky & Peters, 1987). Income from even irregular, part-time work, if the worker's frame of reference is anchored on no work (and no regular income), may be more positively evaluated than the regular income of full-time, permanent employees whose frames of reference may be anchored somewhat higher on the job and pay scales. Variability in work characteristics such as schedule preferences within the samples may be partially responsible for inconsistencies in past research by obscuring systematic differences (Lee & Johnson, 1990). There is a need to look beyond a simple dichotomous work status variable to potential moderators of relationships, or to use the dimensions presented in Figure 4.3 to account for differences. Some additional variables to consider may be shift preference (Jamal, 1981), reasons for working an alternative work schedule, the permanence of the work (Hom, 1979; Feldman & Doerpinghaus, 1992), and the desirability to contingent workers of job characteristics such as autonomy and other work outcomes.

Full-time employees may perceive job satisfaction components as intercorrelated, creating a more nearly homogenous construct, unlike part-time workers' affective responses (Logan et al., 1973). Part-time employees typically exclude promotion satisfaction as a component of overall satisfaction because it often is not relevant for their evaluation of a work-role. Feldman (1990) suggests that these different conceptualizations may be due to groups differentially weighting the facets of job satisfaction when determining overall job satisfaction and motivations to work. Young students may weigh pay satisfaction as primary, and retirees may feel that stimulation and coworker camaraderie are the primary facets of overall job satisfaction. The development, meaning, and consequences of job attitudes may be quite different for workers as they vary along the dimensions shown in Figure 4.3.

Theoretical Frameworks

Research on job satisfaction and other job attitudes comparing permanent, full-time, and contingent workers has been interpreted primarily within one of four theoretical frameworks: the *social comparison model* or one of its many variants (Thibaut & Kelley, 1959; Adams, 1965), the *discrepancy model* (Lawler, 1973), *expectancy theory* (Peak, 1955; Tolman, 1932; Vroom, 1964; Naylor, Pritchard, & Ilgen, 1980), and the model of *partial inclusion* (Katz & Kahn, 1978). Social comparison issues are concerned with examining the choice of *comparison other* by contingent workers. Part-time workers may compare themselves to the full-time workers in their organization, to other part-time workers in their organization, or to part-time workers in other part-time jobs. Each of these different comparisons might result in dramatically different affect toward the focal part-time job. Part-time workers are likely to use other part-time workers at the organization as their comparison other, but the longer the part-time worker is employed by an organization, the more likely it is that he or she will use full-time workers as comparison others (Miller & Terborg, 1979; Feldman & Doerpinghaus, 1992).

The discrepancy framework (Lawler, 1973) proposes that job satisfaction results from an equitable comparison between the amount of an outcome that the worker perceives *should* be received and the outcome that *is* achieved. Considerations of the source of the belief about what should be received from a job make this approach similar to social comparison theory, if the source of the beliefs about what should be received is a comparison other, or similar to frame of reference theory, if the source of beliefs about what should be received are based on other jobs that the focal worker has experienced or knows about. Perceptions of organizational outcomes that are "deserved" by individuals may vary across the regions of the space depicted in Figure 4.3. For example, some contingent workers may seek nothing more than a paycheck, giving little attention to achievement or esteem needs. Struggling artisans, for example, may seek income from their "day job" to support their creative endeavors—their "real" job. Other contingent workers may seek differing outcomes; retirees, for example, may desire social activity.

Expectancy theory (Peak, 1955; Tolman, 1932, Vroom, 1964; Naylor et al., 1980) offers another approach that could be used in our attempts to understand the work motivations and attitudes of contingent workers. Differing expectations regarding outcomes from the work environment can influence the motivation, performance, and attitudes of contingent workers. Research suggests that part-time and full-time workers assign different valences to work outcomes that, combined with expectations, may lead to differences in forces to perform acts required for effective performance. Assessments of the components of expectancy theory may generate insights into the motivations of contingent workers even if the combinatorial rules specified by expectancy theory do not generate accurate predictions. In one study, after controlling for demographics, employees who worked fewer hours per week assigned less importance to the intrinsic outcomes of being informed, making decisions, and doing the job well, and more importance to the extrinsic outcomes of pay and fringe benefits (Wakefield, Curry, Mueller, & Price, 1987). We could disagree with the classification of intrinsic and extrinsic outcomes, but this research does suggest the need to account for differences in importance and valence of work outcomes in our theories of organizational behavior of contingent workers. Theories that stress intrinsic rewards may not be as relevant to contingent employees who assign lower valence to this class of outcomes from their contingent jobs. Differences in expectations may explain the more favorable job attitudes of part-time workers reported in some studies (Eberhardt & Shani, 1984); contingent workers who do not expect, or assign importance to, certain outcomes are not dissatisfied when their jobs fail to provide these outcomes. Outcomes considered to be motivators of performance for full-time employees may not be relevant for contingent workers.

It is impossible to tell from these data whether the differences in valences that workers attached to common job outcomes antedated their becoming contingent. It is apparent, however, that the existing differences can be exploited in a way that may improve the fit between contingent and noncontingent workers and their jobs. If contingent jobs typically do not provide intrinsic satisfactions, and if contingent workers do not value these outcomes, their assignment to such jobs is reasonable. Katz and Kahn (1978) and Graen and Scandura (1987) have argued that good employees work toward, and are rewarded with, inclusion in the organization or supervisor's inner circle. If inclusion is an unlikely job outcome, then such jobs should be staffed with workers for whom inclusion is not a valued outcome. Note that in designing jobs and contracts in this way, we may be consigning many workers to being peripheral to the organization and excluding them from the traditional high-performer role. If this is what an organization is comfortable with, then the present situation may be acceptable. If it is not, then researchers and human resource managers must rethink their definitions of high or even acceptable performance levels.

The partial inclusion hypothesis of Katz and Kahn (1978) suggests that contingent workers may not be fully incorporated into the social system of the organization and therefore cannot be expected to behave in accordance with norms and other perceptions shared among other, more included workers. The degree of inclusion, rather than work status, may provide insights into worker differences; it may be more informative of differences within work status groups than of differences between status groups that can be accounted for by other variables. It may also be the case that contingent workers feel included, but in their temporary work firm or in their occupation rather than in their work organization. The degree to which job permanence, hours of work per week, and whether the employee came from a temporary work firm or from the employing organization can account for variance along the inclusion dimension is a potentially important research question (see Figure 4.3).

Organizational Withdrawal

Job satisfaction considerations are important links in a network of organizational constructs that are antecedents of performance-relevant behavior. Research on turnover of part-time employees suggests, however, that traditional predictors of turnover for full-time employees, such as job attitudes, expectation of alternatives, and even turnover intentions (Hulin, 1991), are ineffective in predicting turnover among part-time employees (Gannon & Nothern, 1971). Traditional variables may be similarly inefficient for predicting absenteeism in contingent workers. Peters, Jackofsky, and Salter (1981) found that for full-time employees job satisfaction and thoughts of quitting were significantly related to turnover. Expectation of alternatives, job search behaviors, and intentions to leave were marginally related to turnover. None of these variables significantly predicted turnover for the part-time employees. Conversely, whether an employee's primary life involvement was work or school was predictive of turnover for part-time but not full-time workers (Werbel, 1985). Miller, Katerberg, and Hulin (1979), however, were able to predict turnover (reenlistment decisions) up to twelve months in the future of part-time military employees (national guard members) with impressive validities using attitudes and intentions. In general, however, this line of research suggests that full-time employees may make decisions to quit their job on the basis of different considerations than their part-time counterparts. This lends support for the notion that part-time employees may have a different psychology of work (Rotchford & Roberts, 1982), and it suggests different attitude-behavior frameworks for contingent workers.

Peters and colleagues (1981) provide three plausible explanations for the differences in turnover predictors: (1) part-time workers are members of social systems that may be more important than their job, and they make decisions to quit based on social-system concerns; (2) many part-time workers take jobs with the intention of quitting within a few months or at a specified time regardless of the job attitudes they may develop; and (3) part-time workers' partial inclusion (Katz & Kahn, 1978) in the organizational system may lead to distinct behavioral responses to job attitudes and organizational commitment that are different from the responses of full-time employees.

Determining the appropriate criteria to use in studies of relations between job attitudes and job behaviors, especially organizational withdrawal behaviors, is crucial. Researchers (Thurstone, 1931; Hull, 1941; Doob, 1947; Campbell, 1963; Dulany, 1968; Wicker, 1969; Ryan, 1970; Fishbein & Ajzen, 1974, 1975) have argued that there are no theoretical reasons to expect *general* attitudes to be related to *specific* isolated behaviors. Two individuals may have identical attitudes toward an object but each may enact different behaviors toward the object. These sets of behaviors have but one thing in common: considered as a multivariate response, the enacted behaviors are equivalently favorable or unfavorable toward the object. Doob (1947) also noted that most definitions of the attitude construct refer to *patterns* of overt behaviors rather than to single overt behaviors; any single overt behavior can seldom be predicted from a knowledge of the attitude alone. Attitudes mediate a repertoire of overt behaviors (Hanisch, 1995; Hanisch et al., 1998). Drawing inferences about inconsistent results when the empirical studies assess only a single isolated behavior is premature.

Theoretical models of organizational withdrawal suggest that the empirical studies reviewed earlier that relate contingent worker status or attitudes of part-time and full-time workers to turnover or absenteeism have sampled an overly restrictive set of withdrawal behaviors. The behaviors that contingent workers enact in response to job dissatisfactions, stress, or aversive working conditions may be different from the behaviors enacted by permanent or full-time workers. Noncontingent workers, if dissatisfied, are likely to attempt to change the tasks they are required to do, to withdraw from their day-to-day tasks, to be absent or tardy, to leave early, to miss meetings, and so on, to make their work role less aversive or dissatisfying. Contingent workers may not have these options available to them and may engage in different, compensatory withdrawal behaviors but with similar negative consequences for performance. Contingent workers who hold negative job attitudes are likely to translate those attitudes into withdrawal behaviors of some kind (Hanisch, 1995). These withdrawal behaviors are likely to be counterproductive and negatively influence the performance of contingent workers. We need to rethink our set of behavioral responses and study what the behaviors might be that constitute a withdrawal construct for contingent workers.

Organizational Commitment and Organizational Support

Other cognitive responses by employees to their organizational work roles that have direct and indirect implications for work performance are organizational commitment and perceived organizational support. Organizational commitment, defined as a worker's identification with and involvement in the organization as a whole, includes cognitive evaluations and acceptance of organizational goals and values, and behavioral intentions such as willingness to exert effort on behalf of the organization, and the desire or intention to remain in the organization (Cook, Hepworth, Wall, & Warr, 1981; O'Reilly & Chatman, 1986). Organizational commitment is more global and possibly slower to develop than job satisfaction. Contingent employees' jobs are generally (but not always) temporary; these individuals may work fewer hours per week, and they may be external to the focal organization. It is likely that these partially included employees will feel less organizational commitment than noncontingent employees; however, research on this issue is limited. McGinnis and Morrow (1990) found that no significant additional variance in commitment is explained by work status. However, Tansky, Gallagher, and Wetzel (1997) suggest that the organizational commitment of part-time workers is influenced by perceptions of equity relative to full-time workers. Research has also suggested links between organizational commitment and job performance (Meyer et al., 1989) and between organizational withdrawal behaviors such as absenteeism and decisions to quit (Williams & Hazer, 1986; Farkas & Tetrick, 1989). If organizational commitment is influenced by permanence of work, hours worked per week, and externality to the employing organization, the performance of contingent workers may be directly or indirectly influenced. Attempts to understand the nature of the psychological contract that contingent workers have with an employing organization or with a temporary work agency may offer insights into their organizational commitment and performance-relevant behaviors.

Perceived organizational support represented by company policies about salary, training opportunities, and benefits has been shown to be related positively to organizational commitment (Shore & Wayne, 1993). Policies that have an impact on organizational support are generally less favorable for contingent workers than for permanent employees and have been shown to influence performance (Eisenberger, Fasolo, & Davis-La Mastro, 1990). The lack of perceived organizational support and organizational commitment of contingent laborers may have negative implications for performance behavior, again depending on how performance is defined.

Organizational Implications

Individual-level psychological phenomena relating to the job performance of contingent workers occur in an organizational context that has been challenged to adapt to the makeup of new workforces. The flexibility that contingent workers offer to work organizations and the short-term financial benefits of hiring them instead of permanent, full-time workers are seen by organizational managers as being substantial. They may also be a business necessity (for example, substitute teachers). Although the financial benefits of contingent labor may be their most apparent and discussed consequences due to the quantifiability and direct influence of such benefits on profits, there are other less tangible ways that a shift toward contingent workers influences organizational effectiveness and human resource strategy. The wage and salary benefits accrued to organizations may be partially or even fully offset by costs to human resource systems, supervisors, coworkers, and workgroups. These latter costs are paid in a different coin than the benefits; comparisons of benefits and costs are problematic, easily avoided, and even illusory if inappropriate comparisons are made. Comparisons between the direct personnel costs of contingent workers and those of permanent, full-time workers that ignore the myriad other behaviors in which workers engage that are related to individual and organizational effectiveness are likely to prove misleading. The likely differences in performance, broadly defined to include contextual performance and organizational withdrawal behaviors as well as direct performance, that will accrue constitute an organizational outcome in need of further exploration.

By increasing the use of contingent workers, organizations may limit their future options. Unless changes toward greater use of contingent workers are part of comprehensive human resource strategies, organizations that fill short-term needs with contingent workers are depleting their human capital; today's expedient solutions may become tomorrow's human resource problems. When economic conditions improve and create a tighter labor market, companies that rely heavily on a contingent workforce will be disadvantaged; many of their less committed, contingent workers will seek and secure permanent jobs elsewhere. Contingent workers do not become part of the pool from which supervisors are selected.

They are less likely to engage in prosocial behaviors for the good of the organization. They are unlikely to be able, or even to be asked, to carry out the informal training and indoctrination of new employees in an organization. All of these are necessary characteristics that contribute in direct ways (large pools of potential supervisors) and indirect ways (prosocial behaviors) to the effectiveness of a work organization.

The addition of contingent workers to the workforce mix has altered the recruitment and selection of employees by organizations. Some organizations may use temporary worker trial periods in place of formal recruitment and selection tools. The National Association of Temporary and Staffing Services reports that three-fourths of current temporary workers became temporary workers in the hope of finding a permanent position through a temporary assignment (Caudron, 1995). Carefully designed selection programs, backed by empirical research, with the goal of selecting the best workers from a qualified pool of applicants are being replaced with selection procedures by a temporary agency seeking to match organizational needs with employee capabilities. The initial screening is supplemented by evaluations of the contingent workers by supervisors, and by extrapolations from current observations to long-term behavioral predictions. Formal empirical evaluations of the effectiveness of these alternative selection strategies are lacking.

An organization that relies on a supply of trained contingent workers provided by a local temporary work firm is taking resources from its local environment. These trained contingent workers represent significant contributions by systems in the environment to the welfare of the organization. Such organizations do not invest in training these human resources—no one washes a rental car. If, instead, the organization relies on selecting permanent employees and providing training for them, through the selection-training-turnover process the organization adds resources to the local environment. Regardless of which strategy is followed by an organization, the organization will have an impact on the macro-environment of which it is a part. Decisions regarding the burden of training are preempted by decisions to rely on contingent workers whenever possible. Individuals who are not exposed to developmental training experiences are not being provided with opportunities to become part of a permanent labor pool in the organization and perhaps be promoted to supervisor positions. Continuing failure to provide significant training programs for a growing part of our workforce is related to economic issues on a broader social scale. Belous (1989) has proposed that by shifting toward using contingent workers, organizations may be creating a two-tiered wage and skill structure in the workforce (Martin & Peterson, 1987). The top tier is composed of white, male, core employees, while the bottom tier comprises females and minorities who are overrepresented in the contingent workforce. By not providing training, organizations may be furthering the economic disadvantage of these segments of society and not improving their employability, thus providing them with little opportunity to become a core employee. Research on the macro-effects of training decisions and performance, broadly defined and perhaps reconceptualized, of contingent workers is needed to determine the full range of outcomes for the individual, the organization, and society.

Supervision of contingent workers is complicated by differences, actual or perceived, between these workers and full-time, permanent employees. Contingent workers often report experiencing work conflicts with and resentment toward full-time workers because the contingent workers feel that they are treated like second-class citizens (Caudron, 1995). Motivating employees to work side-by-side but under different behavior-reward contingencies, expectancies, and instrumentalities may require a sensitivity to unique issues presented by these workers that is not generally included in the repertoire of supervisory skills. Supervisors, as well as organizations, may have to adopt a somewhat different approach to performance; to show up on scheduled days, to not interfere with the work process of coworkers, and to not engage in negative behaviors rather than engaging in positive ones may be the most realistic expectations that managers can have of contingent workers. If this is so, this level of performance needs to be rewarded.

The shift toward more group-based work structures that often accompanies increasing job complexity and automation of subsystems is likely to act as a multiplier on the effects of the changing compositions of organizations' workforces. Contingent workers may have difficulties fitting into these group settings where group coordination and communication are as important as each individual doing his or her specific job. In many situations (such as aviation or nuclear power plants), an expert crew is needed rather than a crew of experts. Familiarity with the group processes required by the workflow may be an unrecognized necessity for effective and safe performance for such crews.

In social systems that require interactions between full-time and contingent employees, inefficiencies and miscommunications that are detrimental to performance will occur. Dysfunctional incidents such as the following have been reported:

- Conflicts between full-time permanent and contingent workers
- Lack of communication
- Failure by full-time employees, who may feel threatened, to equip contingent workers with necessary information and resources
- Resentment by contingent workers who perceive a hierarchical structure and assume that full-time employees are receiving more favorable work tasks and work schedules and experiencing supervisor favoritism

Social and communication problems occur frequently enough in work groups staffed with full-time permanent employees. The frequency and severity of these problems may be exacerbated in groups that include contingent workers who are filling in temporarily.

The use of contingent workers has implications for the financial and legal considerations of human resource departments. The most obvious advantage of hiring contingent employees are the lower short-term labor costs that reflect the absence of fringe benefit payments. Employee benefits such as health care, pensions, and unemployment and workers' compensation insurance now make up approximately 28 percent of all labor expenses (Gerhart & Milkovich, 1992). The argument, however, that the use of contingent employees has direct financial advantages for an organization may be temporary. Trends in employment legislation suggest that organizations may soon be required to provide benefits for contingent workers under certain conditions. Currently, health care is offered by some temporary-employment agencies. High copayments and the requirement that employees must work a minimum number of hours every week to be eligible make it difficult for most temporary workers to take advantage of these benefits. There is a decided lack of "golden handcuffs" for contingent workers that chain many employees to jobs they would otherwise happily quit. The lack of these golden handcuffs is, again, paid for in a different coin by contingent workers and the employing organization.

Conclusion

The current level of usage of contingent workers and their rapidly increasing numbers in the U.S. workforce (see Figures 4.1 and 4.2) represent an adaptation by organizations and individual employees to a set of circumstances dictated by events in the economic environment, by technological developments, and by the general need for increased flexibility to meet rapidly changing demands and opportunities in the gradual move toward a global economy. As adaptive as contingent work may be for individuals and as adaptive as contingent workers may be for organizations, the trend toward greater reliance on contingent workers illustrates the first three laws of organizational structure and functioning (with an acknowledgment to Barry Commoner):

1. Everything is related to everything else in organizations.
2. There is no such thing as a free lunch.
3. The costs and the benefits of policies can never be validly compared; they are received and paid in different coins over different time spans.

We have discussed the implications of the use of contingent workers and contingent work from the perspective of organizations and individual workers. Where the benefits (such as flexibility and reduced direct labor costs) to organizations are obvious, we have tried to make these clear. Where the costs to organizations are obvious or less direct and more long term, we have also discussed these. Similarly, we have discussed parallel costs and benefits for individual workers. The complexities of evaluating contingent workers were highlighted earlier in the third law of organizational functioning: costs and benefits are not directly comparable. Benefits often occur immediately and costs are more long-term; occasionally these time lags are reversed and benefits are realized only well after the policies are implemented. These complex temporal asynchronies may result in problems in the future for both organizations and individual employees, well after the time when the bill for the costs can be renegotiated.

Complexity, however, should be no deterrent to well-designed research and policy evaluation programs. The presence of contingent workers in many organizations does not appear to be a temporary phenomenon. Human resource strategies regarding contingent employees, and policies regarding the nature of the psychological contract they have with the employing organization, need careful attention and research. Otherwise, the potential benefits and flexibility these employees offer will be dissipated by the likely deficits in organizational and individual performance. The collective effects on macro-societal issues of micro-organizational policies regarding the employment of contingent workers also need to become part of the agendas of organizations and public policy advisers.

References

Adams, J. S. (1965). Inequality in social exchange. In L. Berkowitz (Ed.), *Advances in experimental psychology* (Vol. 2). New York: Academic Press.

Belous, R. (1989). Contingent workers and equal employment opportunity. In B. Dennis (Ed.), *Industrial relations research association series: Proceedings of the forty-first annual meeting* (pp. 325–329). New York: Industrial Relations Research Association.

Borman, W. C., & Motowidlo, S. J. (1993). Expanding the criterion domain to include elements of contextual performance. In N. Schmitt & W. C. Borman (Eds.), *Personnel selection in organizations* (pp. 71–98). San Francisco: Jossey-Bass.

Campbell, D. T. (1963). Social attitudes and other behavioral dispositions. In S. Koch (Ed.), *Psychology: A study of a science.* New York: McGraw-Hill.

Caudron, S. (1994). Contingent workforce spurs HR planning. *Personnel Journal, 73,* 52–60.

Caudron, S. (1995). Are your temps doing their best? *Personnel Journal, 74,* 33–38.

Conference Board. (1995). Contingent workers. *HR Executive Review, 3*(2).

Cook, J. D., Hepworth, S. J., Wall, T. D., & Warr, P. B. (1981). *The experience of work.* New York: Academic Press.

Doob, L. W. (1947). The behavior of attitudes. *Psychological Review, 54,* 135–156.

Dulany, D. E. (1968). Awareness, rules and propositional control: A confrontation with behavior S-R theory. In D. Horton & T. Dixon (Eds.), *Verbal behavior and S-R theory* (pp. 340–387). Upper Saddle River, NJ: Prentice Hall.

Dunnette, M. D. (Ed.). (1973). *Work and nonwork in the year 2001.* Belmont, CA: Wadsworth.

Eberhardt, B. C., & Shani, A. B. (1984). The effects of full-time versus part-time employment status on attitudes toward specific organizational characteristics and overall job satisfaction. *Academy of Management Journal, 27,* 893–900.

Eisenberger, R., Fasolo, P., & Davis-La Mastro, V. (1990). Perceived organizational support and employee diligence, commitment and innovation. *Journal of Applied Psychology, 75,* 51–59.

Ellingson, J. E., Gruys, M. L., & Sackett, P. R. (1997, April). *Satisfaction and performance of voluntary and involuntary temporary employees.* Paper presented at the meeting of the Society of Industrial and Organizational Psychology, St. Louis, MO.

Farkas, A. J., & Tetrick, L. E. (1989). A three-wave longitudinal analysis of the causal ordering of satisfaction and commitment on turnover decisions. *Journal of Applied Psychology, 74,* 855–868.

Feldman, D. C. (1990). Reconceptualizing the nature and consequences of part-time work. *Academy of Management Review, 15,* 103–112.

Feldman, D. C., & Doerpinghaus, H. I. (1992). Patterns of part-time employment. *Journal of Vocational Behavior, 41,* 282–294.

Fishbein, M. F., & Ajzen, I. (1974). Attitudes toward objects as predictors of single and multiple behavioral criteria. *Psychological Bulletin, 81,* 59–74.

Fishbein, M. F., & Ajzen, I. (1975). *Beliefs, attitudes, intentions, and behavior.* Reading, MA: Addison-Wesley.

Gannon, M. J., & Nothern, J. C. (1971). A comparison of short-term and long-term part-time employees. *Personnel Psychology, 24,* 687–696.

Gerhart, B., & Milkovich, G. T. (1992). Employee compensation: Research and practice. In M. D. Dunnette & L. M. Hough (Eds.), *Handbook of industrial organizational psychology* (Vol. 3, 2nd ed., pp. 481–569). Palo Alto, CA: Consulting Psychologists Press.

Graen, G. B., & Scandura, T. A. (1987). Toward a psychology of dyadic organizing. In L. L. Cummings & B. M. Staw (Eds.), *Research in organizational behavior* (Vol. 9, pp. 175–208). Greenwich, CT: JAI Press.

Hall, D. T., & Gordon, F. E. (1973). Career choices of married women: Effects on conflict, role behavior, and satisfaction. *Journal of Applied Psychology, 58,* 42–48.

Hanisch, K. A. (1995). Behavioral families and multiple causes: Matching the complexity of responses to the complexity of antecedents. *Current Directions in Psychological Science, 4,* 156–162.

Hanisch, K. A., & Hulin, C. L. (1990). Job attitudes and organizational withdrawal: An examination of retirement and other voluntary withdrawal behaviors. *Journal of Vocational Behavior, 37,* 60–78.

Hanisch, K. A., & Hulin, C. L. (1991). General attitudes and organizational withdrawal: An evaluation of a causal model. *Journal of Vocational Behavior, 39,* 110–128.

Hanisch, K. A., Hulin, C. L., & Roznowski, M. A. (1998). The importance of individuals' repertoires of behaviors: The scientific appropriateness of studying multiple behaviors and general attitudes. *Journal of Organizational Behavior, 16,* 463–488.

Hom, P. W. (1979). Effects of job peripherality and personal characteristics on the job satisfaction of part-time workers. *Academy of Management Journal, 22,* 551–565.

Hulin, C. L. (1991). Adaptation, persistence, and commitment in organization. In M. D. Dunnette & L. M. Hough (Eds.), *Handbook of industrial and organizational psychology* (Vol. 2, 2nd ed., pp. 445–505). Palo Alto, CA: Consulting Psychologists Press.

Hull, C. L. (1941, October 24). *Fractional antedating goal reactions as pure stimulus tasks.* Paper delivered at a meeting of the Institute of Human Relations.

Iaffaldano, M. T., & Muchinsky, P. M. (1985). Job satisfaction and job performance: A meta-analysis. *Psychological Bulletin, 97,* 251–273.

Ilgen, D. R., & Hollenbeck, J. R. (1991). The structure of work: Job design and roles. In M. D. Dunnette & L. M. Hough (Eds.), *Handbook of industrial and organizational psychology* (Vol. 2, 2nd ed., pp. 165–207). Palo Alto, CA: Consulting Psychologists Press.

Jackofsky, E. F., & Peters, L. H. (1987). Part-time versus full-time employment status differences: A replication and extension. *Journal of Occupational Behavior, 8,* 1–9.

Jamal, M. (1981). Shift work related to job attitudes, social participation and withdrawal behavior: A study of nurses and industrial workers. *Personnel Psychology, 34,* 535–547.

Judge, T. A. (1990). *Job satisfaction as a reflection of disposition: Investigating the relationship and its effect on employee adaptive behaviors.* Unpublished doctoral dissertation, University of Illinois at Urbana-Champaign.

Katz, D., & Kahn, R. L. (1978). *The social psychology of organizations.* New York: Wiley.

Lawler, E. E., III. (1973). *Motivation in work organizations.* Pacific Grove, CA: Brooks/Cole.

Lee, T. W., & Johnson, D. R. (1990). The effects of work schedule and employment status on the organizational commitment and job satisfaction of full-versus part-time employees. *Journal of Vocational Behavior, 38,* 208–224.

Logan, N., O'Reilly, C. A., III, & Roberts, K. H. (1973). Job satisfaction among part-time and full-time employees. *Journal of Vocational Behavior, 3,* 33–41.

Martin, J. E., & Peterson, M. M. (1987). Two-tier wage structures: Implications for equity theory. *Academy of Management Journal, 30,* 297–315.

McGinnis, S. K., & Morrow, P. C. (1990). Job attitudes among full- and part-time employees. *Journal of Vocational Behavior, 36,* 82–96.

Meyer, J. P., Paunonen, S. V., Gellatly, I. R., Goffin, R. D., & Jackson, D. N. (1989). Organizational commitment and job performance: It's the nature of the commitment that counts. *Journal of Applied Psychology, 74,* 152–156.

Miller, H. E., Katerberg, R., & Hulin, C. L. (1979). Evaluation of the Mobley, Horner, and Hollingsworth model of employee turnover. *Journal of Applied Psychology, 64,* 509–517.

Miller, H. E., & Terborg, J. R. (1979). Job attitudes of part-time and full-time employees. *Journal of Applied Psychology, 64,* 380–386.

Miller, M. (1983). The "wild card" of business: How to manage the work ethic in the automated workplace. *Management Review, 72,* 8–12.

Morrow, P. C., McElroy, J. C., & Elliot, S. M. (1994). The effect of work status, schedule, and shift on work-related attitudes. *Journal of Vocational Behavior, 45,* 202–222.

National Association of Temporary Services. (1994, June 30). *Bulletin to management.* Washington, DC: Bureau of National Affairs.

Naylor, J. C., Pritchard, R. D., & Ilgen, D. R. (1980). *A theory of behavior in organizations.* New York: Academic Press.

O'Reilly, C. A., III, & Chatman, J. (1986). Organizational commitment and psychological attachment: The effects of compliance, identification, and internalization of prosocial behavior. *Journal of Applied Psychology, 71,* 492–499.

Peak, H. (1955). Attitude and motivation. In M. R. Jones (Ed.), *Nebraska symposium on motivation* (pp. 149–188). Lincoln: University of Nebraska Press.

Peters, L. H., Jackofsky, E. F., & Salter, J. R. (1981). Predicting turnover: A comparison of part-time and full-time employees. *Journal of Occupational Behavior, 2,* 89–98.

Rogaly, B. (1996). Agricultural growth and the structure of "casual" labor hiring in rural west Bengal. *Journal of Peasant Studies, 23,* 141–165.

Rotchford, N. L., & Roberts, K. H. (1982). Part-time workers as missing people in organizational research. *Academy of Management Review, 7,* 228–234.

Roznowski, M., & Hulin, C. L. (1992). The scientific merit of valid measures of general constructs with special reference to job satisfaction and job withdrawal. In C. J. Cranny, P. C. Smith, & E. G. Stone (Eds.), *Job satisfaction: How people feel about their jobs and how it affects their performance* (pp. 123–163). San Francisco: New Lexington Press.

Ryan, T. A. (1970). *Intentional behavior: An approach to human motivation.* New York: Ronald Press.

Shore, L. M., & Wayne, S. J. (1993). Commitment and employee behavior: Comparison of affective commitment and continuance commitment with perceived organizational support. *Journal of Applied Psychology, 78,* 774–780.

Steffy, B. D., & Jones, J. W. (1990). Differences between full-time and part-time employees in perceived role strain and work satisfaction. *Journal of Organizational Behavior, 11,* 321–329.

Tansky, J. W., Gallagher, D. G., & Wetzel, K. W. (1997). The effect of demographics, work status, and relative equity on organizational commitment: Looking among part-time workers. *Canadian Journal of Administrative Sciences, 14,* 315–326.

Thibaut, J. W., & Kelley, H. H. (1959). *The social psychology of groups.* New York: Wiley.

Thurstone, L. L. (1931). The measurement of social attitudes. *Journal of Abnormal and Social Psychology, 26,* 249–269.

Tilly, C. (1991). Reasons for the continuing growth of part-time employment. *Monthly Labor Review, 114,* 10–18.

Tolman, E. C. (1932). *Purposive behavior in animals and men.* New York: Appleton-Century-Crofts.

Vecchio, R. P. (1984). Demographic and attitudinal differences between part-time and full-time employees. *Journal of Occupational Behavior, 5,* 213–218.

Vroom, V. (1964). *Work and motivation.* New York: Wiley.

Wakefield, D. S., Curry, J. P., Mueller, C. W., & Price, J. L. (1987). Differences in the importance of work outcomes between full-time and part-time hospital employees. *Journal of Occupational Behavior, 8,* 25–35.

Werbel, J. D. (1985). The impact of primary life involvements on turnover: A comparison of part-time and full-time employees. *Journal of Occupational Behavior, 6,* 251–258.

Wicker, A. W. (1969). Attitudes vs. actions: The relationship of verbal and overt behavioral responses to attitude objects. *Journal of Social Issues, 25,* 41–78.

Williams, L. J., & Hazer, J. T. (1986). Antecedents and consequences of satisfaction and commitment in turnover models: A reanalysis using latent variable structural equation methods. *Journal of Applied Psychology, 71,* 219–231.

CHAPTER 5

Continuous Learning

Manuel London
Edward M. Mone

Continuous learning is an increasingly important element of performance in light of today's environmental and organizational trends. The performance dimensions of continuous learning reflect the processes of development planning, learning, and applying new knowledge and skills to changing organizational conditions. This chapter examines these emerging performance dimensions from the perspectives of learning processes and content, and from the perspectives of individual behaviors and organizational support. Moreover, it develops a framework for conceptualizing and assessing the performance processes and outcomes of continuous learning.

From the perspective of the individual, continuous learning is the process by which one acquires knowledge, skills, and abilities throughout one's career in reaction to, and in anticipation of, changing performance requirements. The term *continuous* implies a strong and ongoing awareness of the need for and value of learning. This learning may be training to do the current job better, developing one's skills in anticipation of tomorrow's job requirements, or retraining for different job or career opportunities inside and outside the organization. Continuous learning is the hallmark of the protean career—one that is managed by the person, not by the

Note: The authors would like to thank the editors and Henrik Holt Larsen of the Copenhagen Business School for their valuable comments on an earlier draft. They are also grateful to the editors for developing the section "Issues in Rewarding Learning."

organization. The term *protean career* was coined by Hall (1976; Hall & Mirvis, 1996) based on the Greek god Proteus, who could change shape as needed. Employees' own choices and search for self-fulfillment, not the path of jobs followed in one organization, are the integrating elements in their careers. Individuals may have multiple careers or job sequences in different firms or even different professions. People who are committed to continuous learning search for new information about themselves and about emerging performance requirements that suggests a learning gap. Moreover, they are willing to devote the time, energy, and financial resources to gain the education needed to close the gap and improve their performance. This commitment implies that their learning is planned and self-guided. Self-development activities include reading a book related to a needed skill, finding a mentor or role model, watching a skill-building videotape, or practicing new skills and behaviors (Holt, Noe, & Cavanaugh, 1996). Learning can also be the result of organic, incidental experiences. People with a continuous learning mentality think about what they have learned from daily activities or unusual events and try to apply that knowledge later.

From an organizational perspective, continuous learning is "an organizationwide concern, value, belief, and expectation that general knowledge acquisition and application is important" (Tracey, Tannenbaum, & Kavanagh, 1995, p. 245). Planning for and participating in development to prepare for anticipated future job requirements become performance dimensions in their own right in addition to applying learning to enhance performance outcomes today. The organization provides the resources and support that promote continuous learning for performance improvement and preparation to meet future performance requirements. These resources may come in the form of supervisor support, human resource policies and programs for development and performance assessment, or both. Developmental activities include training courses, seminars, computer-based programs, and experiential learning. Planned learning takes place on the job as well as in the classroom.

Continuous learning is important for defining and assessing individual and organizational performance. A person's ability or willingness to engage in continuous learning, to learn effectively, and to demonstrate performance improvement are elements of performance definition and assessment. Participation in continuous learning is a measurable dimension of performance in and of itself. Employees can set goals for development in relation to performance requirements, and they can be rewarded for their developmental accomplishments and incremental improvements in performance. Supervisors' support for their employees' continuous learning can be measured and rewarded. Moreover, employees can learn to evaluate their own performance gaps and needs for continuous learning. These self-management skills and behaviors are increasingly critical in times of corporate shifts to flexible organizational structures and project-based work.

Table 5.1 lists forces and processes that drive continuous learning, and Table 5.2 lists alternative modes of continuous learning and performance outcomes. These topics are discussed throughout the chapter. In the first section of the chapter we consider implications of continuous learning for defining and assessing performance. General trends in society and organizations have implications for continuous learning. This suggests the need to understand how individuals become continuous learners and how organizations foster continuous learning performance. Adult learning performance should be understood in the context of change. Also, the changing work environment raises issues and challenges for assessing and rewarding the development of skills needed in the future. In the second section, we consider implications for employee motivation and development. We examine how individuals develop insight into their performance and establish learning strategies based on a commitment to self-development. We include discussions of learning orientation, using and seeking performance feedback, responding to career barriers, and learning from experience. In the third section we consider how organizations support the development of self-insight and learning through performance assessment, development, and reward systems. We examine the roles of managers as coaches, developers, and change agents. We also address how to build a continuous learning culture within the organization with continuous learning behaviors evaluated as dimensions of performance. We conclude by considering issues for research and public and organizational policies that promote performance improvement through continuous learning.

Table 5.1. Forces and Processes for Continuous Learning.

Trends
Teams
Projects, not functions
New technology
Higher standards
Focus on tomorrow's skills
Multiple constituencies
Leader as facilitator, coach, and developer
Temporary and part-time workers

Adult Learning
Self-directed learning
Recognition of and freedom from taken-for-granted assumptions about oneself and the environment
Thinking about the relevance and content of problems, not just their solutions
Raising critical questions and debates

Career and Learning Motivation
Self-insight
Learning orientation
Self-management and feedback
The value of feedback
Feedback seeking
Using multiple sources of feedback
Responding to career barriers
Learning from experience

Support for Continuous Learning
The learning organization
Continuous learning cultures
Transfer-of-training climate
Giving feedback
Performance management
Focus on professionalism
Preparing for future jobs
Retraining displaced workers

Table 5.2. Continuous Learning Modes and Outcomes.

Alternative Learning Modes	Possible Learning Outcomes	Development-Related Performance Dimensions for Technical and/or Managerial Vitality
Self-paced	Sense of achievement and self-satisfaction	Anticipating learning to meet changing job requirements
Reading	Social contacts	Setting development goals
Internet	Professional development	Participating in learning activities
CD-ROM	Continuing education	Asking for feedback
Audiotapes and videos	Job performance improvement	Performing well on tests, work samples, or trials that demonstrate learning acquisition
Short courses (in-house, training institutes or colleges, correspondence courses)	Employment stability	Applying learning on the job
College courses	Advancement	Demonstrating performance improvement
College degree programs (full- or part-time)	New career direction	
	Personal growth	

Figure 5.1 presents a model of the key environmental, individual, and organizational components of continuous learning and their interrelationships. The model suggests that environmental trends and adult learning processes are forces that influence motivation to learn and contribute to a continuous learning culture. These are vital components to both individual and organizational performance in many of today's organizations. The more the organization supports continuous learning, the more the value of learning is salient to employees, which in turn enhances their motivation to participate in developmental activities. Motivation affects the decision to use alternative learning modes. Learning modes may be self-paced, computer-guided, or instructor-led. They may also be long-term, perhaps aimed at obtaining a new degree, or short-term, perhaps simply reading a recently published scientific paper, attending a professional conference, or taking a one-day course. The availability of different modes of learning depends in part on organizational support. When support is not available, motivated individuals can go outside the organization on their own for learning that matches their career goals. Participation in learning activities leads to one or more outcomes, such as improved job performance, maintaining competence in one's profession, advancement, or new career directions. Indeed, participation in continuous learning and attendant demonstration of incremental improvement in performance are becoming important dimensions for performance assessment in many organizations.

Implications of Continuous Learning for Defining and Assessing Performance

Continuous learning has potentially profound effects on the concepts of performance and performance measurement. As Hesketh and Neal note in Chapter Two of this volume, we need new ways to incorporate continuous learning into the concept and assessment of performance—essentially rewarding employees for learning that cannot be used today. Hesketh and Neal observe that in the past jobs were assumed to be relatively static, and once a job was mastered the employee continued to perform competently, assuming adequate levels of motivation. The rapid pace of change in job requirements due to organizational, competitive, and tech-

Figure 5.1. Processes and Support for Continuous Learning.

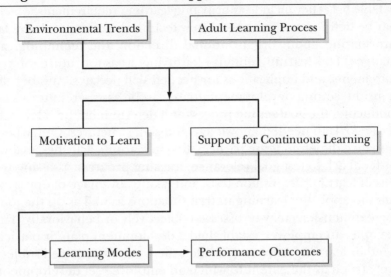

nological development means that employees must constantly show the capacity to engage in new learning as they cope with change. Learning and responsiveness to change, rather than absolute performance per se, become important. The performance assessment must focus on the employee's ability to keep relatively close to a moving target.

Development, then, becomes important in its own right, not just for its immediate effects on performance. Organizations must plan for, encourage, and reward development—preparing for tomorrow based on current available information and best judgments about organizational and technological directions. Rewards for development cannot wait for newly learned behaviors to be applied sometime in the future. The individual's development (that is, acquisition of knowledge and skills in preparation for anticipated future job requirements) must be measured and rewarded now. This implies the need for new performance dimensions that reflect technical or managerial vitality or both. These dimensions in turn may become criteria for selection and placement for future jobs and assignments. Past training success is likely to predict future training readiness and job success.

Examples of vitality-related performance dimensions are listed in Table 5.2. They include anticipating learning requirements, which may be defined as awareness of new technical demands relative to information about organizational direction and technological changes. This learning entails identifying areas for future job requirements, and implications for needed skill updates. Another dimension, setting development goals, can be assessed in terms of conducting the goal-setting process and determining the relevance of the goals to needed knowledge and skill structures. Other performance dimensions are participating in learning activities, asking for feedback to test goal relevance, tracking progress, assessing results of learning acquisition tests, and taking advantage of opportunities to apply the learning in trial situations as well as on the job. Some dimensions may be assessed objectively or behaviorally (for example, an employee established a development plan or participated in learning activities), while others may be assessed subjectively (such as the extent to which an employee set development goals, the extent to which the goals are likely to be important to the department, or the extent to which the goals were accomplished).

Changes in organizations and the environments in which they operate have demonstrated the importance of continuous learning to individual and organizational performance. Career opportunities and career patterns are changing. The thirty-year career with more or less continuous advancement or at least the guarantee of employment after reaching a career plateau has just about gone the way of the dinosaur. Although some people will have this experience, career patterns will be far more variable for many people. Each career move may necessitate acquiring new skills and knowledge. A pattern of searching the environment to determine skill needs, setting new career goals (possibly including career change), and embarking on a developmental program to meet these goals will likely be repeated three, four, or five times during a person's career (Hall & Mirvis, 1995).

In Chapter One of this book, Ilgen and Pulakos described major changes in how work is organized and accomplished. These changes have implications for changing performance dimensions related to continuous learning. Because of the trend toward process teams, individuals must learn how to contribute effectively to groups. Performance dimensions for leaders and team members include integrating newcomers, minimizing or overcoming process losses, developing alliances between groups, generating quality work outputs, and learning as a team. Group and team members will have to gain the skill of learning collectively. Groups need to move toward *synergistic learning,* in which team members jointly construct shared meanings and assumptions, which leads to members sharing their learning throughout the organization through their networks and contacts with others.

Continuous learning is needed to keep pace with never-ending advances in technology and associated changes in job requirements (Hesketh & Neal, Chapter Two, this volume). In addition, new technology is used for monitoring and tracking performance. Such technology helps employees and organizations to recognize performance gaps and identify areas for improvement. Increasing competition and higher quality expectations mean that customers drive performance standards, so employees, teams, and organizations need to learn how to be better attuned to the competitive environment. Employees need to prepare for tomorrow today. Performance therefore is not only based on past behavior. Individuals need to identify skill gaps and learn how to integrate this information into a learning plan. They need to recognize areas in which they should improve their current performance, to keep up with advances in their profession, and to anticipate how changes elsewhere in the firm and the industry may affect work demands and skill requirements. Individuals must learn how to integrate feedback from multiple sources, how to balance diverse and increased demands, and how to resolve role conflict and ambiguity. Managers must learn how to be facilitators, coaches, mentors, developers, and resource providers (Schwarz, 1994). To gain flexibility and reduce costs, organizations are relying increasingly on part-time and temporary employees. If people want part-time or temporary job opportunities, they will need to create their own development plan, invest their own time and resources, locate learning opportunities, participate in them, and then find ways to apply what they have learned.

The changing nature of organizations and the associated importance of continuous learning suggest that learning and responsiveness to change become important rather than absolute performance per se. This has implications for how performance is defined. The ability to learn and to deal with change must be incorporated into the definition of performance and how it is measured. Also, employees must show incremental performance improvement relative to the speed with which skill requirements are changing. Organizations must learn how to anticipate changing skill requirements and to recognize that skills vary in their difficulty and learning time. Moreover, they need to realize that performance change may not be immediate but will vary according to how long it takes to acquire a skill. So, for instance, employees may be able to learn some skills quickly, such as communication for improved customer relationships. Other skills, however, such as learning a new computer system, are more difficult because of the complexity of the skill and the level of the individual's ability. As a result, the organization's expectations for improved performance need to be tempered by the combination of skill difficulty, individual ability, and learning time.

Adult Learning as Performance Process and Outcome

Not only do today's workers need new skills, such as being able to utilize technology and work in teams, but they also need to rethink or reframe how they view their work and organizations. Because organizations must revitalize in order to compete in the global marketplace, individuals now find themselves in horizontal corporations ("The horizontal corporation," 1993), boundaryless organizations (Ashkenas, Ulrich, Jick, & Kerr, 1995), reengineered corporations (Hammer & Champy, 1993), and learning organizations (Senge, 1990).

Having the capacity both to acquire new skills and to reconceptualize how they think about work and organizations will be a constant demand on the workers of the future. Consequently, we use a broad definition of learning that takes into account the importance of recognizing the need for change. Adult learning "is the way in which individuals or groups acquire, interpret, reorganize, change or assimilate a related cluster of information, skills and feelings. It is also the primary way in which people construct meaning in their personal and shared organizational lives" (Marsick, 1987, p. 4). This definition suggests that learning occurs at the individual and group levels. It further suggests that learning involves acquiring skills and knowledge, as well as reorganizing or reframing knowledge and socially constructing new perspectives. This latter point is significant in that many of the workplace changes or organization interventions described by Ilgen and Pulakos in Chapter One require more than just new skills. They also call for cognitive and behavioral changes. Individuals must recognize and accept that work will be done differently, and they must acquire and apply new knowledge and skills to be successful contributors to the new work environment.

Self-Directed Learning

The principal vehicle for continuous learning may be self-directed learning. The concept was introduced by Knowles (1975) to practitioners more than twenty years ago, but it remains "one of those amorphous terms that occurs in adult education literature but that lacks precise definition" (Jarvis, 1992, p. 130). It has been researched as a goal, as a learning process, and as a learner characteristic (Candy, 1991; Cranton, 1996). Self-directed learning becomes a performance dimension in and of itself. That is, organizations must select and reward employees for being self-learners.

Support for self-directed learning as a strategy for engaging in continuous learning, however, will meet with resistance from at least three sources (Long, 1994). Resistance at the organizational level involves overcoming a history of fostering dependent approaches to learning. Roles tend to be prescribed for trainers and facilitators that limit learner initiative and suggest practices that emphasize recall, repetition, and memorization. As a result, self-directed learning initiatives are perceived to affect the traditional way of doing things. There may be resistance from trainers and facilitators who tend to prefer the familiar approaches and adhere to the traditional model of platform instruction. In addition, self-directed learning shifts the locus of control from the instructor to the learner, affecting the trainer's role as expert. Finally, employees, too, may resist the self-directed approach to learning. Their paradigm about learning is based on their experiences in elementary, high school, and perhaps college, where didactic instruction was the norm. Such instruction required little thinking on the part of the learner and rewarded a passive approach to learning. Resistance may also emerge because of fear—workers may not understand what the concept entails. In addition, engaging in self-directed learning requires a sense of competence and belief in oneself. Emotional resistance may stem from lack of a sense of self-efficacy (Long, 1994, p. 15).

Given that organizations expect and provide resources to enable employees to be self-directed learners, organizations should promote emancipatory learning—freeing workers from the assumptions they hold about themselves, their jobs, careers, and institutions that are no longer valid as we move into the twenty-first century (Mezirow, 1991). Techniques to do this include critical questioning and dialogue, critical incident exercises, role-plays, critical debates, and crisis-decision simulations (Brookfield, 1987), and using multiple techniques to engage in different learning domains. Rewarding self-directed learning will call attention to its importance in the organization and encourage employees to model their behaviors after those of self-directed learners.

Issues in Rewarding Learning

A basic question is what improved or increased skills are worth to an organization. Some organizations pay higher salaries to people with more skills. Employees earn salary increments or bonuses as they acquire additional skills. These employees are worth more to the organization because they can be asked to do different tasks as needed. In some industries, however, there is a trend toward deskilling. For instance, hospitals often prefer to have low-paid, low-skilled workers do specialized tasks such as drawing blood and taking temperatures, rather than have highly paid professionals, such as nurses, do these tasks. The low-skilled workers can be taught some additional skills that may earn them small increments in salary. Although the hospital still needs nurses, fewer of them are necessary because many of the tasks they have traditionally performed do not require the sophisticated skills in which they have been trained. Of course, unions and associations representing professionals, such as nurses, argue that highly trained professionals are worth their salaries even if some of the tasks they perform do not require all their skills.

Other issues arise in relation to employees learning skills that are not needed immediately. Such learning has a potentially important implication for performance assessment—that is, how should performance be assessed when learning is accomplished that is not relevant for today's job but is expected to be necessary in an anticipated job or to meet a future organizational need? Because proficiency in these skills will not be able to be evaluated (because the skills are not currently used), formal skill-proficiency testing could replace performance ratings in these cases. Behavioral exercises and cases might be used to assess future strategic skills. Such exercises may not be practical, however, in terms of their costs of development and administration.

A related issue is the extent to which the organization should reward employees for learning that may or may not be transferred effectively to the job. That is, an employee can attend a training course and be certified, but if the skill or content knowledge is not required today, then it is not clear that the employee can or will be motivated to use that new skill effectively on the job when it is required in the future. This may be true even if the employee passes a proficiency test that shows that he or she possesses the skill. The challenge for the organization is to reward and promote the development of future skills without ending up simply rewarding attendance in training programs.

Overall, organizations that support continuous learning in order to prepare employees for the future will need to invest in analyses that identify skills that are likely to be needed in the future, and in training in and assessment of these skills. This will be a dynamic process in that the anticipated skill needs will change periodically. In some cases, just-in-time training is the solution. This is training provided just prior to or just when it is needed. It will be necessary to keep a constant eye on changing skill requirements, and the organization will have to be fast to develop or purchase the needed training. Some skills, however (such as managing in an international environment), may take a long time to develop, and their need may not materialize to the extent or in the way anticipated. This becomes a cost of doing business in a dynamic environment. Individuals who learn skills that are not needed directly or immediately may find other ways to use those skills.

Another issue is how to keep skills current that may not be used on the job today but that may be strategic skills to possess for the future. An example is the way the military tries to maintain pilot and airborne (parachuting) skills when individuals go through career cycles in the Pentagon or other desk jobs. The military provides pay incentives for keeping up the skills with periodic days out of the office and in the field.

In general, if the principle vehicle for continuous learning is self-determination, the organization may not provide the direction and support for learning that employees have been led to expect. Nevertheless, the organization will select and reward people who are self-directed learners. These are the individuals who are able to maintain their skills at the level needed by the organization. The organization will periodically survey employees for the skills resident in the organization, assess and reward the acquisition of new skills, and evaluate and reward improvement in job performance.

Implications of Continuous Learning for Employee Motivation and Development

This section examines how individuals' learning orientation and motivation affect awareness of performance improvement needs and participation in continuous learning. We consider how employees develop insight about their performance and how they take action to seek feedback, respond to career barriers, and generally learn from experience.

Learning Orientation

Learning orientation affects the nature of learning goals and stems from people's beliefs about whether their abilities are fixed or changeable (Dweck, 1986; Holt et al., 1996). People who believe that their abilities are fixed are likely to set performance goals that lead others to value their competence, while those who believe that their abilities can be changed over time are likely to set learning goals that will increase their competence rather than impress others (Dweck & Legget, 1988). People who have a strong learning orientation pursue learning and self-development, keep up-to-date on professional and technical developments, and stay informed about industry practices and new developments (Holt et al., 1996).

Learning attitudes, perceptions of developmental needs, and understanding the benefits of training affect participation in developmental activities (Noe & Wilk, 1993). Learning attitudes include the motivation to learn and the motivation to use the knowledge and skills learned (Noe, 1986). Learning motivation is higher for employees who are aware of their developmental needs and who agree with the organization's assessment of their developmental needs. It is also higher for those who have experienced the positive effects of training in the past (Holt et al., 1996).

Performance Motivation and Insight

The components of career motivation may explain an individual's desire to participate in continuous learning activities. Generally, motivation consists of three components: the spark that initiates behavior (insight), the sense of direction and purpose (identity), and the will to persist even in the face of barriers (resilience) (London, 1983, 1985; London & Mone, 1987; Noe, Noe, & Buchhuber, 1990). All three components are essential for continuous learning. Here we concentrate on insight—that is, recognizing the learning gaps between current abilities, knowledge, and skills, and the abilities, knowledge, and skills needed now or in the future. To be motivated to learn, employees have to perceive a weakness in their self-concept and develop the notion that overcoming the weakness and building new strengths are necessary for extrinsic reasons (for example, "I can make more money" or "I can keep the job I have") or intrinsic reasons ("I enjoy learning" or "I get a sense of achievement from learning and applying new skills"). More specifically, insight is the ability to be realistic about oneself and one's career and to put these perceptions to use in establishing goals. Insight is enhanced when the situation provides a process for goal setting and ways to achieve those goals (such as career paths). Insight develops through information processing as employees receive information about their competency, possible job opportunities and career directions, and feedback about their performance in comparison to standards or expectations.

Using Performance Feedback

Insight formation entails receiving information about ourselves or others, integrating and reconciling that information with other information, discounting and discarding data, interpreting the information, and adding meaning (London, 1994, 1995a; Felson, 1985; Jussim, 1991). The nature of feedback affects insight formation. For example, we give more importance to objective feedback than to interpersonal or subjective feedback, unless the objective information is deemed unreliable (Jussim et al., 1992). We tend to ignore, avoid, or resist feedback that is personal and potentially linked to our self-concept, compared to feedback that deals specifically with task behaviors (Kluger & De Nisi, 1996). Once performance feedback is perceived, we interpret it in relation to our current beliefs about our abilities and performance (De Nisi, Cafferty, & Meglino, 1984). Information that is consistent with the image we already have of ourselves is accepted automatically (Beach, 1990; Mitchell & Beach, 1990). Inconsistent information, if not ignored or denied, may cause us to reinterpret the information or alter our self-concept. We tend to process information mindfully when decisions are problematic in some way or when we are forced or obligated to deal with the information, as we might be when we have to review performance information with our supervisor (Fiske & Neuberg, 1990; Fiske, Neuberg, Beattie, & Milberg, 1987; Kulik & Ambrose, 1993). So, favorable feedback tends to be processed mindlessly, while negative or mixed feedback tends to be processed mindfully because it commands attention (Fiske, 1993; Dunegan, 1993, 1995).

We learn and gain insights about ourselves when information cannot be processed automatically but must be deliberately categorized and a reason established for its occurrence. Self-insight comes when we attribute the reason to ourselves. People who accept feedback and attribute the cause to themselves are likely to set meaningful, realistic goals that have the potential of improving their performance (Taylor, Fisher, & Ilgen, 1984). Feedback is valuable for a number of reasons: it enhances learning, keeps goal-directed behavior on target, increases motivation to set higher goals, increases employees' abilities to detect errors on their own, increases the amount of power and control employees feel, and when positive, heightens employees' sense of achievement and internal motivation (see literature reviews by Ilgen, Fisher, & Taylor,

1979; Larson, 1984; and London, 1988, 1996). It contributes to increased self-awareness and willingness to engage in self-assessment (London, 1995b). The benefits of feedback, however, depend on its being delivered in a constructive (that is, clear, specific, and non-threatening) manner.

Seeking Performance Feedback

Seeking self-knowledge is a prerequisite for and motivator of growth and improvement, and it is critical for self-regulation (Ashford & Tsui, 1991). People seek feedback to obtain useful information, protect their ego or self-esteem, and control how they appear to others (Ashford & Cummings, 1983; Levy, Albright, Cawley, & Williams, 1995; Morrison & Bies, 1991). People seek feedback by monitoring the environment or by active inquiry (Ashford & Cummings, 1983).

Despite the potential value of feedback, seeking it is risky because it might be negative and call attention to one's weaknesses (Fedor, Rensvold, & Adams, 1992). Employees who need performance feedback the most (because they are performing poorly) are the least likely to seek it (Karl & Kopf, 1993). When they do, they try to minimize the negative feedback and protect their self-esteem (Larson, 1988). The result is that they are not likely to receive helpful feedback. This is frustrating for the supervisor who is responsible for giving feedback (Baron, 1988). (This dilemma probably generalizes to the need for training and learning—those who need it the most are not necessarily motivated to seek it.)

Overall, people who seek feedback, especially unfavorable feedback, are able to increase the accuracy of their self-understanding (Ashford & Tsui, 1991). The extent to which people seek feedback depends on several individual characteristics. Employees who have a high need for achievement and self-esteem choose sources who are highly expert and with whom they have a high-quality relationship (Vancouver & Morrison, 1995). Employees who have high performance expectations for themselves choose sources who can provide valued rewards. People who have low self-esteem and self-efficacy tend not to seek feedback from anyone. In addition, feedback seeking is a function of the perceived privacy of the feedback-seeking context. People are more likely to seek feedback when they believe that others will not know about it (for example, if the feedback is computerized) (Levy et al., 1995). Individuals have less desire for feedback after they become aware that the feedback is public, because they are concerned about how they will appear to others.

Using Multiple Sources of Performance Feedback

Performance feedback can promote continuous learning. The individual must be open to feedback, however. An increasingly popular technique for giving managers feedback is multisource ratings (Dunnette, 1993; Tornow, 1993). Often used specifically to provide managers with information that might help direct their development, this method recognizes the increased complexity of the managerial role and the value of having input from multiple constituencies (Bernardin & Beatty, 1987; London, Wohlers, & Gallagher, 1990). Often known as 360-degree feedback, multisource ratings ask subordinates, peers, a supervisor, the managers themselves, and sometimes customers for ratings on a set of items that reflect important elements of performance in the organization. London and Smither (1995) have suggested that the way people develop self-insight explains how they respond to multisource feedback. Employees compare feedback from others to their self-perceptions. Employees who have a favorable self-image, seek feedback, and are sensitive to others' views of them are more likely to compare feedback to their self-perceptions and make judgments about performance gaps. The tendency to make these comparisons is more likely when performance standards are clear and when the feedback process and content are important to organizational operations. Changes in self-awareness and self-image lead to changes in goals and skill development, and ultimately to improved performance.

Ratings from multiple sources may provide inconsistent information. Therefore, managers who receive this feedback have considerably more information to interpret and integrate than do those who receive feedback from only their supervisor. Hence, managers receiving multisource feedback can easily ignore or discount inconsistent information, automatically categorize results that match their self-image, and not profit from the feedback. Advice from a counselor (who could be the supervisor) or a set of guidelines presented in a workshop may help people to process the information mindfully, to evaluate the meaning of the ratings from the raters' perspectives, and to set goals for improvement.

Multisource feedback programs should incorporate methods for enhancing ratees' accountability for providing meaningful (that is, accurate and complete) information and raters' accountability for using the feedback. Raters' accountability may be enhanced by involving them in the process of creating the survey items and working with ratees to interpret the feedback reports. Ratees' accountability may be increased when they share the feedback reports with others and use them to establish development plans (London, Smither, & Adsit, 1996). Organizations that require managers to use survey feedback results for developmental planning increase the likelihood that these managers will share the feedback reports with raters, prepare a written developmental plan, and target skills for improvement (Holt et al., 1996).

Responding to Career Barriers

The way people process information about career barriers may affect their receptivity to continuous learning when it is most needed. A career barrier is an unfavorable event. It may be negative feedback, job loss, being passed over for a promotion, or losing a mentor, to name a few examples. A career barrier may be viewed objectively as an event. The impact of the event, however, may depend on how the individual interprets it. So how people respond to career barriers influences the extent to which they develop constructive or, alternatively, dysfunctional coping strategies. Some barriers are devastating but arise slowly, almost imperceptibly, and may not have strong emotional effects. By the time the individual recognizes the barrier, there is no time to start a continuous learning strategy, unless the individual has been in a continuous learning mode all along. Sudden, traumatic career barriers, such as job loss, may provide little warning. As a result, they offer the individual little or no opportunity to gain control and overcome the barrier.

The more traumatic the career barrier, the more likely it is to result in strong emotions (such as humiliation, depression, sadness, disappointment, apathy, hurt, anger, or fear) and in mindful cognitive processes for evaluating the situation (that is, determining why the barrier arose, how much control the individual has, and possible coping strategies) (George & Brief, 1995; Kanfer, 1990; London, 1997; Pekrun & Frese, 1992). Emotions can block mindful cognitive processing and the individual's openness to learning, or they can create biased cognitive processing (such as blaming others) that also prevents learning. Conversely, some emotions can energize the individual to maintain an optimistic, fighting attitude to overcome the barrier. People who are resilient (that is, who have high self-esteem and are more aware of how the environment affects them) and who have external support are likely to turn a career barrier into a learning opportunity. People who are vulnerable (and so seek information only for self-affirmation) or who lack support develop defensive explanations for the barrier and ineffective or possibly destructive coping responses. These individuals use self-protection mechanisms, such as denial and withdrawal, to avoid the situation (Wohlers & London, 1989). They may even handicap themselves in some way to avoid having to deal directly with the career barrier (such as saying, "I'm too old to learn").

Learning from Experience

Learning from experience is a continuous process. Some people learn readily from experience, others do not. People who learn from experience tend to be curious about how people and things work, accept responsibility for learning and change, and seek and use feedback (McCall, Lombardo, & Morrison, 1988). Learning from experience often entails dealing with failure in some form. Learning from hardships is more difficult than learning from other types of experiences. McCall and colleagues found that executives who learned from setbacks "were forced to confront the truth about themselves. They were forced to recognize that they had flaws and that these flaws made a difference" (p. 97). They could not continue to do well in their careers until they learned how to reduce their deficiencies. Executives who learned from business mistakes recognized the importance of persistence even when the odds for success seemed low. They learned to correct weaknesses where possible and to live with other weaknesses by compensating for them. For example, executives who knew they were inattentive to detail could hire staff who were good at detail. Those who were poor speakers could plan short speeches, use professional graphics, and share presentations (McCauley, Lombardo, & Usher, 1989).

The components of career motivation (resilience, insight, and identity) indicate that motivation is multidimensional. People need insight into themselves and the environment. They need the will to seek and clarify performance feedback from relevant sources. They also need to develop and implement plans. Although learning occurs during the normal course of events, it becomes especially difficult for those facing career barriers or other hardships. To be effective in a continuous learning environment, individuals need to be self-learners. This means they need to be autonomous, adaptable, and resilient in the face of change and career barriers. Such abilities have implications for personnel selection and development.

Organizational Support for Continuous Learning

So far we have considered implications of continuous learning for performance assessment and reward, and individuals' motivation to learn about and improve their own performance. We now examine in more depth organizational support for performance improvement and readiness.

Learning Organizations and Continuous Learning Cultures

Learning organizations are institutions that grow and develop over time, and they are institutions in which individuals grow and develop over time. The people in them embody and foster the concepts of continuous learning and performance improvement. By definition, learning organizations are capable of adapting to changes in the external environment by practicing continuous renewal of their structures and practices (Wishart, Elam, & Robey, 1996). This renewal occurs through ongoing experimentation and innovation, through intense team processes across hierarchical groups, and through networking (via computer, in person, or both). Learning organizations are good at acquiring information, storing it, and retrieving it selectively to identify appropriate courses of action. Performance improvement in learning organizations has the following characteristics:

- A shared vision among organization members as the focus and energy for learning, and as a benchmark against which to compare current reality and future programs
- Self-examination
- Radical new structures and learning teams (such as special multifunctional teams or "skunk works" that transcend bureaucracies and daily organizational functioning) used as vehicles for transferring learning
- External alliances for generating a steady flow of new ideas

In learning organizations, support for continuous learning is evident in the policies that emphasize employee development, and in the organization's values and norms that encourage quality improvement, innovation, and competitiveness. "A continuous learning culture encourages and promotes the acquisition, application, and sharing of knowledge, behaviors, and skills from a variety of sources. Continuous learning may be encouraged through supervisor and peer support for learning, diverse and challenging task assignments, and organizational systems and structures that facilitate efforts to be progressive, innovative, and competitive" (Tracey et al., 1995, p. 241). Further, Tracey and colleagues outlined four components of a continuous learning work environment, building on Dubin (1990), Noe and Ford (1992), and Rosow, Zager, and Casner-Lotto (1988):

1. Knowledge and skill acquisition are essential responsibilities of every employee's job, so jobs must be designed to be challenging enough to promote personal development. Learning is integrated into all the jobs in the firm. Everybody understands and accepts this.
2. Knowledge and skill acquisition are supported by social interaction and work relationships. An interactive work environment gives employees an understanding of each other's tasks and how they are interrelated. Teamwork within units and cooperative alliances between units are encouraged.
3. Formal systems reinforce achievement and offer chances for personal development. The organization provides employees with the resources and opportunities they need to acquire and apply valuable knowledge and skills. Policies inform organization members about the importance of continuous learning.

4. Innovation and competition are expected and rewarded. Employees ascribe to the highest performance standards, and they expect as much from one another. Concurrently, the organization strives to be the best in its industry.

As a result of these four attributes, employees in a continuous learning environment share perceptions and expectations that learning is an essential part of the way the organization or institution does business. "These perceptions and expectations constitute an organizational value or belief and are influenced by a variety of factors, including challenging jobs; supportive social, reward, and development systems; and an innovative and competitive work setting" (Tracey et al., 1995, p. 241). As such, continuous learning becomes part of the organization's culture.

The work environment influences the extent to which newly trained employees are able to apply the skills they have learned. A study of 505 supermarket managers from fifty-two stores found that support for the specific skills learned and, more generally, an environment that supports continuous learning improved the transfer of supervisory skills from training to the job (Tracey et al., 1995). Employees who reported more environmental support were viewed by the supervisors as having changed their behavior in accordance with the goals of the course.

Transfer-of-Training Climate

Tracey, Tannenbaum, and Kavanagh, (1995) distinguished between *continuous learning culture* and *transfer-of-training climate*. The former is a general concept reflecting the overall organizational atmosphere (social support, innovation, and standards of excellence for continuous learning). The latter, while also important to the support of continuous learning, is a specific concept reflecting characteristics of the organizational environment that support and reinforce applying on the job what was learned in training. These characteristics are reminders for trainees to use the training after they return to the job. A study of 102 management trainees and their supervisors as well as 297 managerial coworkers in 102 restaurants from a large chain of fast-food franchises found that coworkers' perceptions of transfer climate in the restaurants were related to posttraining behavior of the trainees (Rouiller & Goldstein, 1993). (Managerial coworkers rated transfer climate, and supervisors and subordinates rated the trainees' behaviors several weeks after the arrival of the management trainee.) Two aspects of transfer-of-training climate—situational cues and consequences—were equally important predictors of learning transfer. An example of a situational cue is a goal set by the supervisor for the employee to use a newly learned skill. An example of a consequence is a supervisor's giving the subordinate positive feedback and public recognition for using the learned skill. Tracey and colleagues' research (1995) found that both transfer-of-training climate and continuous learning culture are important to the transfer of training of experienced employees who attend training and then return to work.

Giving Feedback

As suggested earlier, performance feedback can be important for insight about oneself, for setting goals for continuous learning, and for evaluating goal accomplishment (Atwater & Yammarino, 1997; Locke & Latham, 1990). In general, supervisors dislike giving negative feedback as much as subordinates dislike getting it. Supervisors even feel uncomfortable giving positive feedback. They are more inclined to give feedback when the task is important, when the supervisor depends on the subordinates for task accomplishment, when the supervisor believes that performance feedback would have a positive effect on subordinates, and when the norm or role expectation in the organization is that supervisors give feedback (London, 1995a; Larson, 1984). Baron (1988) distinguished between constructive and destructive feedback. Constructive feedback is specific and considerate, and makes fair and accurate causal attributions. Destructive feedback is general, inconsiderate, and threatening, and makes unfair and inaccurate causal attributions (for example, blaming poor performance on the individual's incompetence).

Performance Management

Organizational programs support continuous learning by establishing directions for development (that is, determining what employees need to know given the current and emerging business environment) and by providing the resources for employee assessment (sometimes self-assessment) and training. (See London & Mone, 1994, for detailed descriptions of comprehensive programs that support continuous learning.) These processes begin with a future job analysis to identify dimensions of leadership and management that are of growing importance given the changing environment and the changing nature of work. Human resource development specialists do this analysis by conducting interviews with executives and managers in and outside the organization. Performance dimensions are defined and refined with ongoing input from executives. The final set of dimensions are the basis for developing an integrated human performance system that includes recruitment and selection, training for new and current employees, job placement and movement opportunities, appraisal and feedback processes, and reward systems. A communications package is developed to describe the model to employees, as well to explain its implications for management systems, describe the available training, and make clear the responsibility to learn and apply the elements of the model. The managers, with the support of their supervisors, are responsible for self-assessment and learning new skills. This is an evolving process. Once designed, it needs to be revised and repackaged to meet changing conditions.

Another type of organizational continuous learning program encourages employees to enhance their professionalism and maintain performance excellence in their area of expertise. The design of this type of program begins with benchmark analyses to determine best professional practices in other firms that can be used as guidelines. Generally, the professionals work together, often with a consultant, to establish standards, expected areas of competence and knowledge, and criteria for excellence. Courses and job experiences may be specified as part of a mastery path to certification and continued development. A professionalism model lists and describes core competencies and specialty areas and suggests ways to learn and measure them. The same language and processes could be applied to other areas of professional development such as marketing, accounting, operations management, and information systems.

Preparing for Future Jobs

Continuous learning is a means of enhancing employees' value to the firm in their current jobs or, when downsizing occurs, for other positions, and as a result increases employees' employability. If employees need to be displaced, it is hoped that they will be able to find other employment because they have up-to-date skills and knowledge that are needed by other enterprises. At Intel, the manufacturer of computer chips, employees are given opportunities for skills training and financial rewards for skill acquisition. This gives the organization flexibility in being able to move employees to new areas or outplace employees when necessary. As a result, the company is a choice employer that attracts and retains talented individuals.

An example of a joint union-management effort to support training in preparation for possible employee dislocations is the Alliance for Employee Growth and Development. Supported financially by AT&T and the Communications Workers of America, the alliance funds training programs requested by employees at local sites. The employees determine the type of training they want based on information about skills needed by the company and in the outside job market. Examples of supported programs are tuition for computer training given at local community colleges and training centers set up at the plant for customized training programs.

Government, university, and business partnerships for training may help support continuous learning at small organizations. For instance, in some states, such as New York, government matching funds are provided to businesses that need training for economic expansion. Businesses work with engineering schools to establish areas for potential business expansion. Money from the business is matched with government funds to ensure that employees have the skills and knowledge they need to contribute to the firm's growth.

Job loss, of course, is a major career barrier (Leana & Feldman, 1992). As discussed earlier, the trauma and emotions associated with job loss make establishing a constructive coping strategy difficult. Workers who come from organizations with continuous learning cultures will have a leg up on those who do not. They may find reemployment immediately, or they may be psychologically open to retraining that will increase their job opportunities. Workers who do not have this background may resist retraining and be subject to the negative effects of depression, anger, and loss.

A number of programs have been established to help displaced workers overcome dysfunctional emotions and learn constructive ways of coping. The learning may focus on job search skills or on acquiring new technical skills and knowledge. Such programs are often joint efforts of government funding agencies (for instance, programs stemming from legislation for displaced workers in the defense industry), colleges and universities, and local businesses that have job openings for interns as well as employees. (See London, 1995a, for a detailed description of such programs.)

In summary, the concept of a learning organization suggests that individual and organization development are mutually supportive and synergistic. Individuals learn as organizational systems that support learning are adopted and a continuous learning culture evolves. Also, the organization develops a continuous learning culture as individuals take responsibility for their learning, seek learning opportunities, and apply their newly acquired knowledge and skills. Some organizations work hard to establish cultures that encourage continuous learning as an essential component of performance. Such organizations not only provide training but also reward the use of new skills and knowledge on the job. Giving feedback is an important part of this culture. Performance excellence programs show employees how to improve their performance relative to today's organizational goals. Special professional development may be available for technical specialists to maintain the organization's competitiveness. Moreover, organizations recognize that they cannot be content with meeting today's challenges. They have to act now to ensure that employees have the skills and knowledge that will be needed tomorrow.

Conclusion and Directions for Research and Practice

The changing nature of work imposes increased demands for training in specific skills (technical and human resource). The pace of change indicates the need for continuous, and often transformational, learning to maintain and enhance performance. People must be attuned to their own developmental needs, and organizations must provide the enabling resources, including training and rewards for learning. Researchers should therefore develop a better understanding of how people process information; interpret events, such as career barriers and negative performance feedback; and develop constructive coping strategies that include learning. Research is also needed to understand how these cognitive processes and coping strategies contribute to team and organization development as members learn about one another's expectations, competencies, and behaviors, leading to more effective teamwork and flexible organizational processes and structures.

Organizations establish continuous learning cultures that support and reward employee education and development. Continuous learning becomes part of everyone's job performance. For workers who have lost their jobs, joint ventures between businesses, universities, and government agencies can promote learning and prepare individuals for successful reemployment. To make all this happen, human resource development practitioners need to keep pace with changing directions of the business, new work structures, and advances in continuous learning systems. They must also understand how adults learn as individuals and in groups, and they must be able to facilitate self-directed learning.

Despite the importance of continuous learning to organizational change and to employees' competence to perform at needed levels, training is not a panacea or the single solution to employment security and performance enhancement. It must be accompanied by other human resource efforts (such as selection, appraisal, feedback, and reward systems) and a variety of developmental mechanisms and opportunities for learning (such as job movement, analysis of successes and failures, participation in simulations, and observation). These modes of learning should take advantage of technological advancements (such as CD-ROMs, personal computers, and videos) that make information and learning accessible and cost-effective. Research should determine the effects of various programs that support continuous learning and performance management. In particular, research should establish how the components of a human performance system (such as cycles of goal setting, development, feedback, further development, and performance changes) can be designed to work together most effectively. This research could test support mechanisms for continuous learning as it tests goal setting, evaluation of performance improvement, and performance feedback and reinforcement. This raises challenges for the measurement of learning over time, for assessing continuous learning as an important dimension of performance in and of itself, and for establishing criteria for levels of performance improvement as learning takes place.

Organizations and individuals will need to overcome barriers to continuous learning. These barriers may reside in the individual's resistance to learning. People need to be awakened to changing organizational demands, and they need to perceive that learning is feasible and rewarded. Organizations need to invest resources in continuous learning. This means giving continuous learning more than lip service. In part it means expecting employees to make continuous learning a part of their jobs and expecting supervisors to be coaches and developers. Supervisors must view employee development as part of the work group's output. Learning must have demonstrable value at present or in the near future. New learning needs to be reinforced in order for the training to transfer to the job. Researchers must face the challenges of investigating how individuals learn, measuring learning, and assessing its effects on behavioral change and performance. They must also study how groups and organizations develop as their members learn.

Education is costly, and our society is not ready to provide education for all comers at any cost. Some universities are downsizing along with corporations. Large organizations with deep pockets in high-tech areas recognize the importance of continuous learning and provide training to many of their employees. Employees in smaller organizations may be left to fend for themselves, although such organizations can be very intensive and effective learning environments. Moreover, there is an increasing disparity among different types of jobs—between those that require sophisticated knowledge and those that require few skills. The solutions lie in concerted efforts at the local level—often partnerships between educational institutions, government agencies, and business—to support economic growth through human resource development. Evaluation research is needed to determine the value of these programs from the individual, organizational, and societal perspectives.

People and organizations need to be accountable for continuous learning just as they should be accountable for other elements of performance. That is, they need to accept and meet their responsibilities and justify their actions. Organizations must also provide employees with timely and accurate performance feedback, and information about organizational changes and job expectations. Supervisors need to be trained in how to provide this information. Also, researchers and organizations should support the development and application of resources that employees need to use this information for their continuous learning. Continuous learning should be incorporated into job requirements, and be a basis for setting development and performance goals and for evaluating accomplishment of those goals.

The overarching concept in assessing continuous learning as a set of performance dimensions is job or performance vitality—vitality in technical and managerial skills, in abilities, and in knowledge areas. Readiness to learn may be another component of continuous learning for performance assessment. Readiness may have both ability (knows how to learn) and motivational (wants to learn) elements. As such, performance reviews and discussions will need to assess dimensions of continuous learning performance, such as those listed in Table 5.2, and organizational policies and programs will need to provide the resources that support continuous learning cultures.

References

Ashford, S. J., & Cummings, L. L. (1983). Feedback as an individual resource: Personal strategies of creating information. *Organizational Behavior and Human Performance, 32,* 370–398.

Ashford, S. J., & Tsui, A. S. (1991). Self-regulation for managerial effectiveness: The role of active feedback seeking. *Academy of Management Journal, 34*(2), 251–280.

Ashkenas, R., Ulrich, D., Jick, T., & Kerr, S. (1995). *The boundaryless organization: Breaking the chains of organizational structure.* San Francisco: Jossey-Bass.

Atwater, L. E., & Yammarino, F. J. (1997). Self-other agreement: A review and model. In G. R. Ferris (Ed.), *Research in personnel and human resources management* (Vol. 5, pp. 121–174). Greenwich, CT: JAI Press.

Baron, R. A. (1988). Negative effects of destructive criticism: Impact on conflict, self-efficacy, and task performance. *Journal of Applied Psychology, 73,* 199–207.

Beach, L. R. (1990). *Image theory: Decision making in personal and organizational contexts.* New York: Wiley.

Bernardin, H. J., & Beatty, R. W. (1987). Can subordinate appraisals enhance managerial productivity? *Sloan Management Review, 28*(4), 63–73.

Brookfield, S. D. (1987). *Developing critical thinkers: Challenging adults to explore alternative ways of thinking and acting.* San Francisco: Jossey-Bass.

Candy, P. C. (1991). *Self-direction for lifelong learning: A comprehensive guide to theory and practice.* San Francisco: Jossey-Bass.

Cranton, P. (1996). *Professional development as transformative learning: New perspectives for teachers of adults.* San Francisco. Jossey-Bass.

De Nisi, A. S., Cafferty, T. P., & Meglino, B. M. (1984). A cognitive view of the performance appraisal process: A model and research propositions. *Organizational Behavior and Human Performance, 33,* 360–396.

Dubin, S. S. (1990). Maintaining competence through updating. In S. L. Willis & S. S. Dubin (Eds.), *Maintaining professional competence* (pp. 9–43). San Francisco: Jossey-Bass.

Dunegan, K. J. (1993). Framing, cognitive modes, and image theory: Toward an understanding of a glass half full. *Journal of Applied Psychology, 78,* 491–503.

Dunegan, K. J. (1995). Image theory: Testing the role of image compatibility in progress decisions. *Organizational Behavior and Human Decision Processes, 62,* 79–86.

Dunnette, M. D. (1993). My hammer or your hammer. *Human Resource Management, 32,* 373–384.

Dweck, C. S. (1986). Motivational processes affecting learning. *American Psychologist, 41,* 1040–1048.

Dweck, C. S., & Legget, E. L. (1988). A social-cognitive approach to motivation and personality. *Psychological Review, 95,* 256–273.

Fedor, D. B., Rensvold, R. B., & Adams, S. M. (1992). An investigation of factors expected to affect feedback seeking: A longitudinal field study. *Personnel Psychology, 45,* 779–805.

Felson, R. B. (1985). Reflected appraisal and the development of self. *Social Psychology Quarterly, 48,* 71–78.

Fiske, S. T. (1993). Controlling other people: The impact of power on stereotyping. *American Psychologist, 48,* 621–628.

Fiske, S. T., & Neuberg, S. L. (1990). A continuum of impression formation, from category-based to individuating processes: Influences of information and motivation on attention and interpretation. In. L. Berkowitz (Ed.), *Advances in experimental and social psychology* (Vol. 23, pp. 1–74). San Diego, CA: Academic Press.

Fiske, S. T., Neuberg, S. L., Beattie, A. E., & Milberg, S. J. (1987). Category-based and attribute reactions of some information conditions of stereotyping and individuating processes. *Journal of Experimental and Social Psychology, 23,* 399–427.

George, J. M., & Brief, A. P. (1995). *Motivational agendas in the workplace: The effects of feelings on focus of attention and work motivation.* Tulane Working Papers Series. New Orleans: A. B. Freeman School of Business, Tulane University.

Hall, D. T. (1976). *Careers in organizations.* Glenview, IL: Scott, Foresman.

Hall, D. T., & Mirvis, P. H. (1995). Careers as lifelong learning. In A. Howard (Ed.), *The changing nature of work* (pp. 323–362). San Francisco: Jossey-Bass.

Hall, D. T., & Mirvis, P. H. (1996). The new protean career: Psychological success and the path with a heart. In D. T. Hall (Ed.), *The career is dead—long live the career: A relational approach to careers* (pp. 15–45). San Francisco: Jossey-Bass.

Hammer, M., & Champy, J. (1993). *Reengineering the corporation.* New York: HarperCollins.

Holt, K., Noe, R. A., & Cavanaugh, M. (1996). Managers' developmental responses to 360-degree feedback. Paper presented at the annual meeting of the Society for Industrial and Organizational Psychology, San Diego, CA.

The horizontal corporation (1993, December 20). *Business Week,* pp. 76–81.

Ilgen, D. R., Fisher, C. D., & Taylor, M. S. (1979). Consequences of individual feedback on behavior in organizations. *Journal of Applied Psychology, 64,* 349–371.

Jarvis, P. (1992). *Paradoxes of learning: On becoming an individual in society.* San Francisco: Jossey-Bass.

Jussim, L. (1991). Social perception and social reality: A reflection-construction model. *Psychological Review, 98,* 54–73.

Jussim, L., Soffin, S., Brown, R., Levy, J., & Kohlhepp, K. (1992). Understanding reactions to feedback by integrating ideas from symbolic interactionism and cognitive evaluation theory. *Journal of Personality and Social Psychology, 62*(3), 402–421.

Kanfer, R. (1990). Motivation theory and industrial/organizational psychology. In M. D. Dunnette & L. M. Hough (Eds.), *Handbook of industrial and organizational psychology* (Vol. 1, 2nd ed., pp. 75–170). Palo Alto, CA: Consulting Psychologists Press.

Karl, K. A., & Kopf, J. M. (1993, August). Will individuals who need to improve their performance the most volunteer to receive videotaped feedback? Presented at the annual meeting of the Academy of Management, Atlanta, GA.

Kluger, A. N., & De Nisi, A. (1996). The effects of feedback interventions on performance: A historical review, a meta-analysis, and a preliminary feedback intervention theory. *Psychological Bulletin, 119,* 254–284.

Knowles, M. S. (1975). *Self-directed learning.* River Grove, IL: Follett.

Kulik, C. T., & Ambrose, M. L. (1993). Category-based and feature-based processes in performance appraisal: Integrating visual and computerized sources of performance data. *Journal of Applied Psychology, 78,* 821–830.

Larson, J. R., Jr. (1984). The performance feedback process: A preliminary model. *Organizational Behavior and Human Performance, 33,* 42–76.

Larson, J. R., Jr. (1988). The dynamic interplay between employees' feedback-seeking strategies and supervisors' delivery of performance feedback. *Academy of Management Review, 14,* 408–422.

Leana, C. R., & Feldman, D. C. (1992). *Coping with job loss: How individuals, organizations, and communities respond to layoffs.* San Francisco: New Lexington Press.

Levy, P. E., Albright, M. D., Cawley, B. D., & Williams, J. R. (1995). Situational and individual determinants of feedback seeking: A closer look at the process. *Organizational Behavior and Human Decision Processes, 62,* 23–37.

Locke, E. A., & Latham, G. P. (1990). *A theory of goal setting and task performance.* Upper Saddle River, NJ: Prentice Hall.

London, M. (1983). Toward a theory of career motivation. *Academy of Management Review, 8,* 620–630.

London, M. (1985). *Developing managers: A guide to motivating and preparing people for successful managerial careers.* San Francisco: Jossey-Bass.

London, M. (1988). *Change agents: New roles and innovation strategies for human resource professionals.* San Francisco: Jossey-Bass.

London, M. (1994). Interpersonal insight in organizations: Cognitive models for human resource development. *Human Resource Management Review, 4,* 311–332.

London, M. (1995a). Giving feedback: Source-centered antecedents and consequences of constructive and destructive feedback. *Human Resource Management Review, 3,* 159–188.

London, M. (1995b). *Self and interpersonal insight: How people learn about themselves and others in organizations.* New York: Oxford University Press.

London, M. (1996). *Job feedback: Giving, seeking, and using feedback for performance improvement.* Hillsdale, NJ: Erlbaum.

London, M. (1997). Overcoming career barriers: A model of cognitive and emotional processes for realistic appraisal and constructive coping. *Journal of Career Development, 24,* 25–38.

London, M., & Mone, E. M. (1987). *Career management and survival in the workplace: Helping employees make tough career decisions, stay motivated, and reduce career stress.* San Francisco: Jossey-Bass.

London, M., & Mone, E. M. (1994). Managing marginal performance in an organization striving for excellence. In A. K. Lorman (Ed.), *Human dilemmas in work organizations: Strategies for resolution.* New York: Guilford Press.

London, M., & Smither, J. W. (1995). Can multisource feedback change self-awareness and behavior? Theoretical applications and directions for research. *Personnel Psychology, 48,* 803–840.

London, M., Smither, J. W., & Adsit, D. J. (1996). A framework for the effective use of multisource feedback. Paper presented at the annual meeting of the Society for Industrial and Organizational Psychology, San Diego, CA.

London, M., Wohlers, A. J., & Gallagher, P. (1990). 360-degree feedback surveys: A source of feedback to guide management development. *Journal of Management Development, 9,* 17–31.

Long, H. B. (1994). Resources related to overcoming resistance to self-direction in learning. In R. Hiemestra & R. G. Brockett (Eds.), *Overcoming resistance to self-direction in adult learning.* San Francisco: Jossey-Bass.

Marsick, V. J. (Ed.) (1987). *Learning in the workplace.* London: Croom Helm.

McCall, M. W., Jr., Lombardo, M. M., & Morrison, A. M. (1988). *The lessons of experience: How successful executives develop on the job.* San Francisco: New Lexington Press.

McCauley, C. D., Lombardo, M. M., & Usher, C. J. (1989). Diagnosing management development needs: An instrument based on how managers develop. *Journal of Management, 15,* 389–403.

Mezirow, J. (1991). *Transformative dimensions of adult learning.* San Francisco: Jossey-Bass.

Mitchell, T. R., & Beach, L. R. (1990). ". . . Do I love thee? Let me count. . . ." Toward an understanding of intuitive and automatic decision making. *Organizational Behavior and Human Decision Processes, 47,* 1–20.

Morrison, E. W., & Bies, R. J. (1991). Impression management and the feedback-seeking process: A literature review and research agenda. *Academy of Management Review, 16,* 522–541.

Noe, R. A. (1986). Training attributes and attitudes: Neglected influences of training effectiveness. *Academy of Management Review, 11,* 736–749.

Noe, R. A., & Ford, J. K. (1992). Emerging issues and new directions for training research. In G. R. Ferris & K. M. Rowland (Eds.), *Research in personnel and human resource management* (Vol. 10, pp. 345–384). Greenwich, CT: JAI Press.

Noe, R. A., Noe, A. W., & Buchhaber, J. A. (1990). Correlates of career motivation. *Journal of Vocational Behavior, 37,* 340–356.

Noe, R. A., & Wilk, S. L. (1993). Investigation of the factors that influence employees' participation in development activities. *Journal of Applied Psychology, 78,* 291–302.

Pekrun, R., & Frese, M. (1992). Emotions in work and achievement. In C. L. Cooper & I. T. Robertson (Eds.), *International review of industrial and organizational psychology* (Vol. 7). New York: Wiley.

Rosow, J. M., Zager, R., & Casner-Lotto, J. (Eds.). (1988). *Training—the competitive edge: Introducing new technology into the workplace.* San Francisco: Jossey-Bass.

Rouiller, J. Z., & Goldstein, I. L. (1993). The relationship between organizational transfer climate and positive transfer of training. *Human Resource Development Quarterly, 4,* 377–390.

Schwarz, R. M. (1994). *The skilled facilitator: Practical wisdom for developing effective groups.* San Francisco: Jossey-Bass.

Senge, P. M. (1990). *The fifth discipline: The art and practice of the learning organization.* New York: Doubleday.

Tornow, W. W. (1993). Perceptions or reality: Is multiperspective measurement a means or an end? *Human Resource Management, 32,* 221–230.

Tracey, J. B., Tannenbaum, S. I., & Kavanagh, M. J. (1995). Applying trained skills on the job: The importance of the work environment. *Journal of Applied Psychology, 80,* 239–252.

Vancouver, J. B., & Morrison, E. W. (1995). Feedback inquiry: The effect of source attributes and individual differences. *Organizational Behavior and Human Decision Processes, 62,* 276–285.

Wishart, N. A., Elam, J. J., & Robey, D. (1996). Redrawing the portrait of a learning organization: Inside Knight-Ridder, Inc. *Academy of Management Executive, 10,* 7–20.

Wohlers, A. J., & London, M. (1989). Ratings of managerial characteristics: Evaluation difficulty, co-worker agreement, and self-awareness. *Personnel Psychology, 42,* 235–260.

CHAPTER 6

Customer-Driven Employee Performance

David E. Bowen
David A. Waldman

Customers have become a significant factor in how employee performance is defined and assessed in many firms. Performance refers to behavior associated with the accomplishment of expected, specified, or formal role requirements on the part of individual organizational members (Campbell, 1990). Increasingly, customer expectations have become the standard by which these role requirements are defined and by which supporting behaviors are identified. Both practitioners and academics alike face the challenge of making sense of the meaning and implications of customer-driven employee performance.

The shift to customer-driven employee performance certainly is an about face for most human resource management (HRM) professionals. As Schneider (1994) has noted, HRM has tended to follow an industrial revolution–oriented model that focuses on performance relative to internally set and internally relevant standards. Effectiveness criteria used to assess HRM practices are typically dominated by internally defined employee standards such as attendance and the number of products made or sold. HRM practices are seldom validated against externally defined standards such as marketplace customers' perceptions of quality. Indeed, a recent article on market-focused HRM began by stating that the term itself would sound like an oxymoron to many practitioners and researchers (Bowen, 1996).

Customer-driven performance is still a relatively novel thought for academics, as well. Management theory has been criticized for ignoring the role of customers in organizations (see, for example, Peters & Waterman, 1982)—and that criticism is still largely valid today. The word *customer* only rarely appears in journal articles, management textbook indices, or session titles at academic conferences. The absence of customer-driven research may be explained by Danet's observation (1981) that organizational theorists view organizations from the top down (management's perspective) or from the inside looking around (employees' perspective) but rarely from the outside in (the customer's perspective). Not surprisingly, the academic literature has not dealt extensively with the meaning and implications of customer-driven employee performance.

Overview

In this chapter we explore the meaning of customer-driven employee performance and its implications for HRM, in the context of two major changes of the last decade that have helped to instill a customer orientation in many organizations: the quality revolution and the growth of services.

The Quality Revolution

It is now well known that during the late 1970s and 1980s, many businesses in the United States began to lose ground to global competitors. This was due largely to these competitors' adhering to higher quality standards than U.S. companies for such products as automobiles and electronics. As U.S. consumers became increasingly quality conscious, corporate America's competitive edge dulled further.

Dean and Evans (1994) chronicle how America "woke up to quality" during the 1980s. In 1984, the U.S. government designated October as National Quality Month. In 1987, Congress established the Malcolm Baldrige National Quality Award. This spurred the advancement of the Total Quality Management (TQM) movement, which initially was most prominent in the manufacturing sector but is now frequently practiced in the service sector as well (Schonberger, 1992). The foremost principle of TQM is customer focus

(Dean & Bowen, 1994). The guiding philosophy behind the quality revolution, as it has taken hold in various initiatives in diverse organizational settings, is that the central objective of quality improvement is to satisfy customers.

The Growth of Services

By 1993, the service sector represented 78 percent of total U.S. employment and 73 percent of the gross domestic product; studies of the fastest growing careers in the U.S. economy typically focus on service opportunities (Zeithaml & Bitner, 1996). It is difficult to ignore the role of customers in service settings (such as restaurant diners and hospital patients) because they are often physically present within the organization's boundaries, even coproducing the services they consume (such as bussing their own tables; Bowen & Schneider, 1988). Thus employee performance in service-oriented businesses is quite literally customer-driven. It involves, for example, frequent face-to-face encounters with customers, which leads to "emotional display rules" (Ashforth & Humphrey, 1993; Hochschild, 1979, 1982; Rafaeli & Sutton, 1987) being a role requirement. Additionally, the intangibility of many services (such as consulting or entertaining) also makes the measurement of work quality dependent on customers' perceptions, because conformance to physical specifications as a quality measure is less possible with services than with manufactured goods (Bowen & Schneider, 1988; Reeves & Bednar, 1994). The service sector offers established, useful models of how customer-driven employee performance is conceptualized and reinforced through staffing, reward systems, and development (Dean & Bowen, 1994). Both in practice and in the research literature, services have taken the issue of customer-driven employee performance seriously.

We suggest that the quality revolution and the growth of services have spawned a customer-driven orientation within many organizations. The majority of this chapter develops the implications of being customer-driven for how employee performance is conceptualized. We then describe how these new views of customer-driven employee performance might affect staffing, personnel actions (such as reward systems), and development. We close with some research issues and a discussion of practitioner issues involved in customer-driven employee performance.

Origins and Implications of a Customer-Driven Orientation

Table 6.1 displays the factors that gave rise to the customer-driven orientation, namely the quality revolution and services. The services factor is further broken down into the three characteristics that numerous researchers have suggested are key to understanding the nature of the interface between the service firm and the customer (see Bowen & Schneider, 1988). In the middle column of the table we list the implications of these factors for reconceptualizing employee performance. That is, a customer-driven work environment suggests unique role requirements and associated behaviors for employees. In turn, this uniquely defined customer-driven view of employee performance has implications for staffing, personnel actions, and development.

Quality Revolution Implications

By 1991, *Business Week* was calling quality "a global revolution affecting every facet of the business. For the 1990s and far beyond, quality must remain the priority for business" (Dean & Evans, 1994). One facet of business clearly affected was the definition of "good" employee performance.

Reconceptualization of Employee Performance

In the 1980s, definitions of quality work shifted from conforming to internal specifications to meeting or exceeding customers' expectations (Reeves & Bednar, 1994). Relatedly, although there are different interpretations of TQM content, almost everyone would agree that customer focus is one of TQM's core principles (see, for example, Dean & Bowen, 1994; Hackman & Wageman, 1995). The basic rationale of TQM is the belief that customer satisfaction is the most important requirement for long-term organizational success. Management practices that support the principle of customer focus include promoting direct contact with customers, collecting information about customers' expectations, sharing this information widely throughout the organization, and using customer data to set employee performance standards and to provide employees with performance feedback.

Table 6.1. Origins and Implications of a Customer-Driven Orientation.

Causal Factors	Implications for Reconceptualization of Employee Performance	Some Implications for HRM
Quality Revolution	Customer-focused role requirements (both internal and external customers)	Hiring based on customer-oriented abilities and values
		360-degree appraisal processes
		Group-based appraisals and rewards
	Difficult to specify concrete performance standards	Avoid folly of rewarding A while hoping for B
Growth of Services Characterized by Intangibility	Both the outcome of employee behavior and employee behavior itself influence customer perceptions of quality	Behaviorally anchor, for employees, dimensions of service quality as perceived by internal/external customers
	Pace of work may be highly variable	Hire for organization, not just the job; cross-train
Simultaneous Production and Consumption	Employees in face-to-face service encounters simultaneously fill both operations and marketing roles	Use personality testing to assess service orientation
	Employee attitudes, mood, and emotions "show" to customers	Clarify emotional display rules via training in "rites of integration"
	Employee dress is job-related	Validate HRM practices against external criteria
	Customers may be a target of organizational citizenship behaviors (OCBs)	Assess HRM effectiveness against employee perceptions of fairness
Customer Coproduction	Supervise customers as "partial employees"	Train employees in how to manage customer behavior
	Negotiate competing attempts (from management, customers, frontline employees) to control service encounters	Manage stress arising from role conflict, such as job rotation between high and low customer-contact positions

TQM proponents have argued that traditional Western conceptualizations of employee performance have not assumed enough of a systems perspective. The systems perspective defines an organization as a network of interacting units and processes intended to realize some purpose (Ashforth, 1992; Katz & Kahn, 1978). The systems perspective can provide important insights into the determinants of performance.

TQM has spawned a debate into whether person factors or system factors are primarily responsible for work performance (see Dobbins, Cardy, & Carson, 1991; Cardy & Carson, 1996; Waldman, 1994a, 1994b). Person factors are differences between individuals in ability or motivation that have been shown to account for substantial variance in work performance (Campbell, 1990; Hunter & Hunter, 1984). Deming (1986, 1993) took a broad perspective on what constitutes a performance system. Processes both exogenous and endogenous to the system that can affect employee performance have previously been viewed as including a range of interpersonal, organizational, and technical factors (Blumberg & Pringle, 1982; Peters, O'Connor, & Eulberg, 1985; Waldman, 1994b). These factors are largely out of the control of lower-level employees. TQM views employee performance as being influenced more by system factors than by person factors.

This system's view of the determinants of employee performance suggests that management, as the system's architect, is ultimately more responsible for customer satisfaction than any individual employee working in the system. This conceptualization of employee performance also suggests that approaches to performance appraisal should take system factors into account.

TQM proponents have also argued that an organization should not be conceived as a closed, self-contained system but rather as *open,* including for example, both suppliers and customers. Consequently, the TQM philosophy becomes aligned with the notion of boundaryless organization (Ashkenas, Ulrich, Jick, & Kerr, 1995).

An interesting critical analysis of TQM's open systems claims was offered by Sitkin, Sutcliffe, and Schroeder (1994). They argued that most traditional approaches to TQM maintain a largely closed-system perspective with regard to addressing customer concerns such as work design, and that performance is driven by internal specifications. They labeled this approach "total quality control," which they claimed only moderately allowed for customer involvement and understanding. Here traditional conceptualizations of employee performance still largely hold true. In contrast, "total quality learning" more clearly depicts an open systems perspective, involving permeable organizational boundaries that allow for quantum leaps in customer involvement, understanding, and innovation.

External Versus Internal Customers

The quality movement and TQM highlighted a distinction between external and internal customers. The former is most obvious, representing the clients or customers of an organization's products or services. The notion of internal customer is a bit more complex. Internal customers could represent coworkers who in a team environment should serve each other's work-related needs in a supportive and cooperative manner. The same notion applies to functions viewing other functions as their customers. Moreover, this view of the internal customer leads to a reconceptualization of manufacturing work as service work: "*manufacturing can be seen as a set of interrelated services,* not only between the company and the ultimate consumer, but within the organization. Manufacturing is a customer of product design; assembly is a customer of manufacturing; sales is a customer of packaging and distribution. If quality is meeting and exceeding customer expectations, then manufacturing takes on a new meaning, far beyond product orientation. . . . The Baldrige Award criteria . . . do not distinguish between manufacturing and service, even though awards are given in both categories" (Dean & Evans, 1994, p. 11, emphasis added).

Lower-level employees can also be considered the customers of managers. That is, the manager is responsible for providing resources, development, and support for employees within the manager's span of control. In addition, both the manager and a work unit's employees are responsible for meeting the expectations of external customers either directly or indirectly, by first satisfying the expectations of internal customer groups who are closer in the value chain to the final product or service ultimately provided to external customers. In sum, an assumption of TQM is that failure to meet the needs of internal customers will likely affect external customers. Employees thus need to view themselves as customers of some employees and as suppliers to others.

Advantages and Disadvantages of Customer Focus

A customer focus in the definition of work performance has both advantages and disadvantages. An obvious advantage is that organizations are realizing that in an increasingly competitive marketplace, performance must be targeted toward external customers simply to ensure organizational survival. Performance may conform perfectly to internally set standards, such as standards set by one's supervisor. If those standards fail to meet customer needs, however, overall organizational performance will suffer. The advantage of customer-defined role requirements is stated well by Lawler (1996):

> Perhaps the simplest way of expressing how control works in the new logic is to say that it is better to have a customer and the external market controlling an individual's performance than to use a set of bureaucratic rules, procedures, and a supervisor for control. In order to move control into the hands of the market or customer, the entire organization has to be structured so that employees can get feedback from customers about their performance and their responses to customer needs. This can guide performance in ways that a supervisor or a system cannot duplicate, because the customer—not some person or system that is acting as a proxy for the customer—is the ultimate arbiter of success. The customer is more likely to point employees in the right direction and to prompt change as the customer and the competitive environment change.

A disadvantage of customer focus is that it may lead to measurement difficulties because customer satisfaction is inherently subjective. This is particularly true in the case of intangible services, as we detail later. In contrast, internally based conformance to specifications facilitates more precise or objective measurement. Furthermore, aggregation issues can pose challenges for the conceptualization of *individual* performance (Reeves & Bednar, 1994). For example, Ghorpade and Chen (1995) posed the example of a waiter serving food in a restaurant. Customer satisfaction in this situation is the result of a large number of variables, including the quality of food supplies, the skill of the cooks, the behavior of personnel (including the waiter), and the physical atmosphere. In short, satisfaction is brought into alignment by a host of factors and individuals, only one of which is the waiter. Moreover, a problem in one system-based area (such as quality of food supplies) could be inaccurately attributed to another area (such as the waiter). In such a case, to reward or punish any one person for customer satisfaction or its lack might be inaccurate and unfair.

This example highlights the teamwork principle of TQM. A number of writers have suggested that this principle implies cooperative efforts on the part of workers and management to work together to attain outcomes (such as customer satisfaction) and solve performance problems (Prince, 1994; Waldman, 1994a). In other words, performance is defined not only in terms of individual contributions but also in terms of the extent to which individuals contribute to cooperative team efforts.

Implications for Human Resource Management

The customer focus of the quality revolution, and the TQM movement that followed, has not fully permeated management practice, such as HRM, to the extent seemingly called for by a customer focus imperative. As Lengnick-Hall (1996) and Sitkin, Sutcliffe, and Schroeder (1994) observed, many quality management initiatives have a rather limited view of potential customer involvement in the TQM process. Lengnick-Hall adds that although it is now possible to find the importance of the customer mentioned in organizational theory, very little is offered on how "to translate customer orientation words into customer orientation deeds. Most ideas concerning customers remain more narrow in scope than other elements of quality enhancement programs" (p. 795). In what follows, we describe how reconceptualizing employee performance in a customer-driven context requires its own unique, complementary approaches to human resource management.

Customer focus has direct implications for employee selection and training. Traditionally, both selection and training have been geared toward the job and its specific technical and cognitive skill requirements. Bowen, Ledford, and Nathan (1991) presented a model of hiring for person-organization fit that focused on the selection of individuals across jobs who fit not only specific job requirements but also the culture and strategies of the overall organization. Customer-based abilities and values represent one category of selection and training criteria that would seem to cut across jobs in a customer-focused firm. The time is right for more validation research on the use of customer-oriented selection devices (forms, situational tests, and so forth). To the extent that customer-based abilities transcend the predictive potential of more general cognitive abilities, an added benefit of such research could be the identification of selection procedures with less adverse impact on minority groups.

Customer focus holds perhaps even greater implications for performance management and appraisal processes. Three hundred and sixty–degree appraisals have gained much attention in recent years as organizations have attempted to expand feedback communication channels (Tornow, 1993). Such forms of appraisal provide an alternative to traditional top-down sources of feedback and appraisal, which increasingly appear to be inconsistent with ongoing developments in management thought and practice. For example, with their focus on whether subordinates meet the expectations of supervisors, traditional top-down appraisals enact essentially the opposite of TQM's principle of customer focus.

The 360-degree appraisal process can be viewed in terms of customer-supplier relationships, a common aspect of the TQM customer focus principle. A customer can be viewed as an individual, either internal or external to the organization, who uses the services or raw materials provided by another individual or individuals, who is the supplier. In such appraisal the customer is the source of feedback on the extent to which the supplier has fulfilled expectations and needs. The supplier becomes the receiver or recipient of the appraisal. When viewed in this framework, it is logical for peers or coworkers to receive feedback from one another (peer appraisal), for managers to receive feedback from subordinates (upward appraisal), for employees in one unit to receive feedback from internal customers in another work unit, and for employees in various work units to receive feedback from external customers. The use of multiple raters can offer a more complete assessment of the many person and system factors that may affect any one individual's performance in meeting internal or external customer expectations.

Some measurement issues arise that pertain to the latter two scenarios, specifically with regard to aggregation. For example, in the case of external customer ratings, as was evident with the previously described restaurant waiter example, it may not be possible to attain reliable customer appraisals for a particular employee. As another example, customers of bank branches tend to be served by different tellers at different times, not by the same teller all of the time. External customer appraisals in this situation might make more sense if the customer feedback is given to an entire group of tellers (London & Beatty, 1993).

The logic that it takes a group of employees, not just one individual's performance, to satisfy a customer suggests that customer-driven appraisals and reward systems should be group-based (Hackman & Wageman, 1995; Prince, 1994). Individual efforts in organizations must increasingly be integrated into a total group effort and output. This idea lead Gabris, Mitchell, and McLemore (1985) to conclude that the natural unit of analysis for appraisal in many organizations should be the group rather than the individual. This would appear to be particularly true of quality-driven organizations in which customer focus, the systems perspective, and the importance of teamwork are valued.

We say much more about these customer-focused HRM implications as we now turn to the nature of customer-driven work in a service environment.

Service Implications

In the "moment of truth" between service employees and customers, both internal and external, the nature of employee performance is shaped by three defining characteristics of service (Bowen & Schneider, 1988). We describe each of these, and their implications for reconceptualizing employee performance and designing HRM practices.

Intangibility

Services are much less tangible than physical goods or products (Levitt, 1981). This is particularly true as services travel the continuum from consumer services, such as fast food, to professional services, such as education and health care. Intangibility emphasizes that the consumer *experience* is as important as, or more important than, the consumer good; thus the quality of the interaction between employee and customer is critical (Bowen & Schneider, 1988). Shostack (1977) notes that because of intangibility, more than one version of reality may be found in a service market: "The reality of a service varies according to the mind of the beholder"(p. 42).

Implications for Reconceptualizing Employee Performance

The focus on the consumer experience rather than on a consumer good is the reason that Gronroos (1990) identifies two dimensions of service quality that matter to customers. One is technical quality, or the actual outcome of the service encounter, such as a prepared meal or legal advice from an attorney. The other is functional quality, or how the outcome was delivered, such as the interpersonal style of the service provider. The more intangible the service is, the more diverse will be the assessments of technical quality across customers. Moreover, the more intangible the service is, such as financial advice or customer service support of a complex product, the more customers will rely on the service provider's displayed behavior in assessing the quality of service overall (Bowen & Schneider, 1988). This is because as customers' uncertainty about how to assess service task accomplishment increases, their reliance on employee behaviors as quality cues also increases. Although this is particularly true of the more intangible services, research across services generally indicates that customers' assessments of employee courtesy and competence are significantly correlated (Parasuraman, Zeithaml, & Berry, 1988; Schneider & Bowen, 1985).

The potential variance in customer perceptions of the same service experience (beauty is in the eye of the beholder) poses challenges in defining standards, for both behaviors and outcomes, for customer-driven employee performance. First, given the difficulties in defining and measuring the intangible aspects of service, the use of goal setting to guide service employee behavior becomes very difficult (Mills, Chase, & Margilies, 1983). Second, Shostack's point (1997) about multiple versions of service reality makes sampling a critical issue with customer surveys (*Which* customers' expectations should drive employee performance?). This variance also raises the issue of how meaningful it is to aggregate customer perceptions.

Implications for HRM

To deal with the challenge of specifying concrete performance standards for service quality, organizations often resort to the counting of tangibles, such as number of customers served per day, as criteria of effectiveness. These countables may fail, however, to capture the more intangible service aspects, such as empathy, that customers value. In other words, service settings may be particularly prone to commit the "folly of rewarding A while hoping for B" (Kerr, 1975). Management may hope that employees will be warm and friendly (B) but actually reward employees only for speed (A).

To avoid this folly yet still set concrete standards for employees, firms need to anchor the intangibles in behavior. The form such anchoring could assume is illustrated by how Parasuraman, Zeithaml, and Berry (1985) have identified the ten determinants of service quality identified by customers, as shown in Table 6.2. The table reveals that customers pay attention to a wide array of evidence in assessing service quality.

Parasuraman, Zeithaml, and Berry (1985) specified the determinants in behavioral terms, permitting the development of behaviorally anchored or behavioral observation scales. This helps "tangibilize" the intangible meaning of *quality service* to both external and internal customers. Such behavior-based descriptions of service can then indicate what skills, knowledge, and abilities should be screened in selection, the content of training programs, behaviors for which standards must be specified, and the behavioral bases for performance-contingent rewards. The critical ingredient is to capture the customer's voice in the HRM mix. The HRM staff may need to work closely with the market research staff to ensure that the specification of desired behaviors is customer driven, not just internally driven.

Simultaneous Production and Consumption

In services, there are typically no middlemen or intermediate distribution linkages between production and consumption. Service operations frequently involve direct, face-to-face interactions between the customer and employee to complete the transaction (Chase, 1978; Czepiel, Solomon, & Surprenant, 1985; Fuchs, 1968; Mills & Margulies, 1980), which gives rise to mutual influence occurring

Table 6.2. Determinants of Service Quality.

Reliability involves consistency of performance and dependability. It means that the firm performs the service right the first time. It also means that the firm honors its promises. Specifically, it involves:

- Accuracy in billing
- Keeping records current
- Performing the service at the designated time

Responsiveness concerns the willingness or readiness of employees to provide service. It involves the timeliness of service:

- Mailing a transaction slip immediately
- Calling the customer back quickly
- Giving prompt service (e.g., setting up appointments quickly)

Competence means possession of the required skills and knowledge to perform the service. It involves:

- Knowledge and skill of the contact personnel
- Knowledge and skill of operational support personnel
- Research capability of the organization (e.g., a securities brokerage firm)

Access involves approachability and ease of contact. It means:

- The service is easily accessible by telephone (lines are not busy and they don't put you on hold)
- Waiting time to receive service (e.g., at a bank) is not extensive
- Convenient hours of operation
- Convenient location of service facility

Courtesy involves politeness, respect, consideration, and friendliness of contact personnel (including receptionists, telephone operators, etc.). It includes:

- Consideration for the customer's property (e.g., no muddy shoes on the carpet)
- Clean and neat appearance of public contact personnel

Communication means keeping customers informed in language they can understand and listening to them. It may mean that the company has to adjust its language for different customers—increasing the level

Table 6.2. Determinants of Service Quality *(continued).*

---

of sophistication with a well-educated customer and speaking simply and plainly with a novice. It involves:

- Explaining the service itself
- Explaining how much the service will cost
- Explaining the trade-offs between service and cost
- Assuring the consumer that a problem will be handled

Credibility involves trustworthiness, believability, honesty. It involves having the customer's best interests at heart. Contributing to credibility are:

- Company name
- Company reputation
- Personal characteristics of the contact personnel
- The degree of hard sell involved in interactions with the customer

Security is the freedom from danger, risk, or doubt. It involves:

- Physical safety (Will I get mugged at the automatic teller machine?)
- Financial security (Does the company know where my stock certificate is?)
- Confidentiality (Are my dealings with the company private?)

Understanding/knowing the customer involves making the effort to understand the customer's needs. It involves:

- Learning the customer's specific requirements
- Providing individualized attention
- Recognizing the regular customer

Tangibles include the physical evidence of the service:

- Physical facilities
- Appearance of personnel
- Tools or equipment used to provide the service
- Physical representations of the service, such as a plastic credit card or a bank statement
- Making customers comfortable in the service facility.

Source: Parasuraman, Zeithaml, and Berry (1985). Used by permission of the American Marketing Association.

between customer and employee (Mills, Hall, Leidecker, & Margulies,1983; Schneider, Parkington, & Buxton, 1980).

Implications for Reconceptualizing Employee Performance

This principle leads to the flow of work in a service context being highly variable and difficult in terms of balancing the supply and demand sides of the service operation (Sasser, 1976). Services cannot be inventoried, so demand peaks cannot be managed by simply taking goods off a shelf (Berry, 1980). This complicates staffing, because staffing in relation to demand is less predictable than staffing in relation to the pace of the assembly line (Chase, 1978). Moreover, we believe that most models of employee motivation, job design, occupational stress, and HRM practices have evolved based on a view of work in which workflow is far more uniform than is typical of customer-driven work situations.

Face-to-face contact with customers results in individual employees performing multifunctional tasks. Service workers tend to be minifactories unto themselves because they not only help produce the output but they are simultaneously involved in selling it (Sasser, 1976). Service employees in service encounters are said to function as a "service trinity" (Lovelock, 1981): they help run the service operation, market the service, and are equated by customers with the service.

Because these employees perform in front of the customer, thereby both producing and marketing, a number of employee attributes become performance-related that may not be as job-related for employees who are not visible to customers.

• *Employee attitudes.* In customer contact service positions, the job-relevant behaviors of employees (such as being courteous to customers) may be more closely related to attitudes than are performance behaviors in other, less service-oriented settings (Wiley, 1996). Employee attitudes can spill over onto customers. There is now a substantial body of research establishing the correlation between employee attitudes and customer data (customer attitudes, switching behavior, and even profitability; for reviews, see Schneider & Bowen, 1993; Wiley, 1996). In brief, many studies show a positive relationship between what employees report about their experiences as employees and what customers report about their experiences as service consumers.

A consistent result in research in this area is that customers report that they obtain higher service quality when the employees who service them report that they are satisfied at work (see the reviews cited in the preceding paragraph). Consequently, the dispositional approach to understanding job satisfaction (Judge, 1992) is very relevant for customer contact service positions. A number of studies have made the case that individuals' basic predispositions to being happy in life are generally predictive of their subsequent job satisfaction (Pulakos & Schmitt, 1983; Staw & Ross, 1985).

An implication of this phenomenon for the employee-customer linkage is that it is better to hire more upbeat and happy people because their subsequent job satisfaction correlates with customer perceptions of service quality. At the same time, the dispositional perspective claims that job satisfaction is only *partly* determined by employees' basic predisposition. The rest of the variance is explained via the influence of workplace conditions. The overarching point, though, is that regardless of whether one subscribes to a dispositional or situational perspective on the antecedents of employee job satisfaction, linkage research indicates that customer satisfaction may be a consequence of such satisfaction. (Whether this relationship is causal or only correlational is discussed later.) That is, there is a customer-driven rationale for the importance of having satisfied employees.

Finally, this line of thinking also suggests that the job satisfaction–job performance controversy is conceptualized and resolved differently in a service context than in a product context. In brief, the correlation between job satisfaction and job performance may be higher in services, particularly if customer attitudes are the performance criteria (Bowen, 1991).

• *Emotional labor.* Service employees in customer-contact positions must perform what Hochschild (1983) has termed "emotional labor." In her book *The Managed Heart: The Commercialization of Human Feeling,* she describes how flight attendants, for example, must act pleasant and courteous toward passengers continuously— on every flight, every day, in every service encounter—even if they are actually feeling miserable themselves.

Hochschild (1979, 1983) described the concept of emotional labor as the act of expressing socially desired emotions during service transactions. Her work on emotions is consistent with that of others (such as Rafaeli & Sutton, 1987, 1989; Van Maanen & Kunda, 1989) who suggest that the manner in which employees display their feelings has a strong impact on the quality of service transactions. Ashforth and Humphrey (1993), who define emotional labor as the act of displaying appropriate emotion, note that it can be considered a form of impression management. They focus on the critical role of emotional labor in customer-contact functions, for transactions involving both external and internal customers.

• *Mood at work.* The emotions perspective on employee performance invites an examination of how the mood of service employees at work may have different antecedents and consequences compared to their job satisfaction. Recall that the studies mentioned earlier of the relationship between employee data and customer data used job satisfaction as the employee attitude of interest. George (1989) has argued that job satisfaction is conceptually distinct from one's mood at work. Although job satisfaction has both affective and cognitive components, typical measures of job satisfaction focus more on cognition (Brief & Robertson, 1989). In contrast, mood at work refers to affective states that are present on the job; mood reflects affect *at* work rather than affect about work (George & Brief, 1992). Employee mood at work might spill over onto customers even more than job satisfaction, particularly when job satisfaction is assessed primarily as a cognition. This outcome is even implied by the title of George and Brief's article, "Feeling Good—Doing Good."

• *Employee dress.* Rafaeli and Pratt (1993) have developed a theoretical framework based on the core proposition that the different attributes of organizational dress are meaning-laden symbols. For example, wearing a uniform enhances employee compliance with prescribed role requirements, influences the organization's image in the eyes of outsiders, and delineates members from nonmembers. Rafaeli and Pratt note that delineation is especially crucial in service settings where the interaction between members and nonmembers is critical to production. In all, employee dress is one aspect of the "servicescape" (Bitner, 1992) that customers assess in forming their perceptions of service quality.

• Finally, a number of researchers have recently developed the idea of viewing customers as targets of organizational citizenship behaviors (OCBs), in addition to the more studied targets—peers, subordinates, and supervisors (Blancero, Johnson, & Lakshman, 1996; Bowen & Folger, 1994). The reasoning here is that the categories of OCBs—altruism, courtesy, sportsmanship, conscientiousness, and civic virtue (Organ, 1988)—have a strong service-oriented flavor. They are regarded as extra-role behaviors—as outside of formal role requirements. Furthermore, OCBs may be more strongly associated with customer perceptions of the quality of service delivery than more easily quantifiable in-role behavioral requirements such as number of sales calls made or number of customer service calls handled (Blancero et al., 1996). Overall, employees' displaying *discretionary* effort may be the sign of truly effective service providers (such as Federal Express). This is particularly true when the employee's behavior is visible to the customer.

In a TQM context, it may be difficult to separate work performance from OCBs. For example, Bushe (1988) described a total quality culture in terms of norms, values, and reward procedures that emphasize holistic behavior oriented toward cooperation with fellow organizational members. Work performance in such an environment would tend to be defined broadly to include accomplishing tasks and taking initiative beyond expectations, as well as sharing information with and helping coworkers (that is, internal customers) and external customers. Moorman and Blakely (1993) included such behaviors under the rubric of OCB. Yet in a TQM context these behaviors might be both expected and formally rewarded (Blackburn & Rosen, 1993; Bushe, 1988). More is said about OCBs and customer-driven performance in a later section of this chapter.

Implications for HRM

The difficulty in coordinating supply and demand that arises from variable workflow argues in favor of hiring for the organization, not just for the job (Bowen et al., 1991). That is, employees should have the abilities or aptitudes to match a cluster of jobs, not just one specific job. Obviously cross-training would also support this multitasking approach. More broadly, good overall person-organization fit, including the fit of personal needs and traits with organizational culture, may be particularly important in service work. Fit is positively associated with employee satisfaction (Rounds, Dawis, & Lofquist, 1987) which, as we have stated, correlates with customer satisfaction.

Selecting employees on the basis of personality characteristics seems called for in this context, given the range of person attributes that are apparent to customers. Earlier we mentioned the desirability of hiring upbeat people. More specifically, the real goal should be advances in personality testing to determine service orientation. In this area, promising work has been done by Robert Hogan and his colleagues at Hogan Assessment in Tulsa, Oklahoma (Hogan, Hogan, & Busch, 1989). Hogan's measure of service orientation as an aspect of personality is defined as follows:

Willingness to treat coworkers and customers with courtesy, consideration, and respect

Perceptiveness regarding customer needs

Ability to communicate accurately and pleasantly

He found significant statistical relationships between how five samples of service workers (such as nurses and bank tellers) were rated on the job and their service orientation scores on the personality test.

Emotional Display Rules

Relative to emotional labor, organizations differ in their norms for expressed emotions by their members (Hochschild, 1983; Rafaeli & Sutton, 1987). These norms have been labeled "feeling rules" (Hochschild, 1983) or, perhaps more commonly, "display rules" (Ashforth & Humphrey, 1993; Ekman, 1973; Rafaeli & Sutton, 1987). Display rules indicate the contextually appropriate ways in which emotion is to be displayed. Van Maanen and Kunda (1989) assert that the more emotional work is performed in a role, the more rules occupants are responsible for following.

Employees can be trained in emotional display rules as one component of an organization's enactment of rites of integration, which Siehl, Bowen, and Pearson (1992) have suggested are a useful way to conceptualize and manage the service encounter. Rites of integration have been defined as planned social interactions that consolidate various forms of cultural artifacts (language, displayed emotions, gestures, ritualized behavior, symbols, and the physical setting) with the objective of achieving a temporary sense of closeness between potentially divergent subsystems, such as managers and employees (Trice & Beyer, 1984), or between service providers and customers (Siehl, Bowen, & Pearson, 1992).

Different rites of integration can be designed to produce the different levels of psychological closeness that customers expect in various types of service encounters. For example, customers in convenience stores do not expect psychological closeness (Sutton & Rafaeli, 1988), and the appropriate rites of integration there would consist of emotional displays that were pleasant, low empathy, and even-tempered, as well as ritualized behaviors and gestures that were not very animated, and impersonal symbols. In contrast, customers value a sense of psychological closeness with therapists and doctors, for example. Rites of integration here include emotional displays of compassion and sympathy; ritualized behavior of personal talk, eye contact, and facial expressiveness; and personal symbols. In sum, rites of integration can be an approach by which employees display emotion on the job in contextually appropriate ways.

Validating HRM Practices Against External Criteria Using the Linkage Research Methodology

HRM practices such as hiring and training should be validated against not only employee outcomes like job satisfaction but also against customer criteria such as their perceptions of service quality. This validation approach makes it possible to document which HRM practices are the most strongly correlated with dimensions of service quality (such as the dimensions of customer perceptions from Parasuraman, Zeithaml, & Berry, 1985). Studies that assess HRM in this way have shown that there are indeed practices that correlate significantly with customer criteria, but also that there are HRM practices that do not (Schneider & Bowen, 1993). The point is that each HRM staff group needs to determine which of its own practices are critical success factors in satisfying its external customers.

Assessing HRM Effectiveness from a Users' Reactions Perspective

This approach would mean that HRM would add internal customer satisfaction as a consideration to the list of technical criteria used to assess the effectiveness of HRM practices. In addition to HRM's traditional focus on psychometric properties (such as reliability), inferences (such as validity), and financial benefits, the user reactions perspective takes into account the manner in which an HRM practice is perceived by its consumer (Cardy & Dobbins,

1994). A key issue within this perspective is fairness—whether users feel that practices in selection, performance appraisal, and so on are fair. For example, research in this area has found that the job relatedness of the selection procedure influenced how applicants perceived procedural and distributive fairness, as well as influencing their job performance once they were hired (Gilliland, 1994).

The fairness of HRM practices, as perceived by internal customers, may influence service quality, as perceived by external customers. Bowen, Gilliland, and Folger (in press) proposed a framework in which employee perceptions of fairness are associated with employee OCBs, which in turn are associated with the dimensions of service quality we presented in Table 6.1. Relatedly, Blancero and colleagues (1996) have suggested that when customer-contact employees feel that the organization has violated the psychological contract, employees withhold customer service OCBs.

Customer Coproduction

Customers of services act not only as consumers but also as producers. For example, the quality of a doctor's diagnosis and prescription is partly dependent upon patients describing their illness correctly, diners bussing their own tables in fast-food restaurants, and dental patients operating their own suction devices; and there are even self-service alternatives, such as automatic teller machines. As Gersuny and Rosengren (1973) observed, the economic market and division of labor is more clear with respect to goods than it is for services. The involvement of customers as producers has led to their being labeled "partial employees" of the organization (Mills et al., 1983; Mills & Morris, 1986) and to the view that customers are part of the service firm's human resources (Bowen, 1986).

Implications for Reconceptualizing Employee Performance

Again, customers cannot only receive what an organization produces and delivers, they can also directly and indirectly influence the firm's operations and outcomes (Lengnick-Hall, 1996). In manufacturing settings, coproduction is avoidable; in services, particularly professional and human services, avoidance often is not possible (Gersuny & Rosengren, 1973; Lengnick-Hall, 1996). The more customers are coproducers, the more influence they will have on the quality of work outcomes that supervisors and customers may still tend to attribute primarily to employee performance.

Customer presence and coproduction create a potential contest for the control of the service encounter among management, customer-contact employees, and customers' sometimes competing expectations (Bateson, 1985). A number of attributes of the service environment give the upper hand in this contest to the customer (Rafaeli, 1989):

Physical proximity. In most convenience stores, twenty-five inches separate a cashier and a customer, eighty inches separate two cashiers, and management is far removed.

The amount of time that customers and cashiers spend together. Cashiers spend 78 percent of their time interacting with customers and only 13 percent of their time interacting with management.

The amount and immediacy of feedback that customers provide. Customers share thoughts about items in the store, shopping and cooking tips, and how they feel both about the cashier personally and about the reputation of the store.

The crucial role that cashiers attribute to customers. Cashiers understand that customers are responsible for the store's, and their own, economic survival.

The dysfunctional consequences of not resolving this contest for control are clear. Research in banks, for example, has shown that when tellers prefer to deal flexibly with customers but believe that management wants them to deal with customers in inflexible, bureaucratic ways, then tellers report feelings of stress, and customers rate service quality more poorly (Parkington & Schneider, 1979).

Another unique role requirement for service employees is that they are responsible for supervising customers as partial employees. They must coach, and work with, those customers who are involved in coproduction (Schneider & Bowen, 1995). That is, customers who are involved in coproducing service have role requirements to fulfill themselves, and they may need frontline employees to provide guidance and support as they do so.

Implications for HRM

Frontline employees require training in how to manage customers as partial employees, which is different from merely meeting their expectations as consumers. A necessary first step is for management and the front line to conduct essentially a job analysis of the customer's coproduction role. That is, they must clearly state what behaviors are critical for customers to display in fulfilling their coproduction roles. Then, as Bowen (1986) has described, to perform their coproduction role well customers must possess the three determining attributes of individual-level performance (Vroom, 1964), also required of employees:

Role clarity: they must understand what behaviors are expected of them in their role as producers.

Ability: they must possess the skills necessary to perform the expected behaviors.

Motivation: they must see that performing these behaviors is instrumental to obtaining the intrinsic or extrinsic rewards they value.

Whether partial employees are customers bussing their own table in a restaurant or consumers responsible for coproducing the servicing of capital equipment, frontline service employees must oversee whether these people have the necessary role clarity, ability, and motivation. This can entail providing new customers with a realistic service preview (Bowen, 1986; Mills & Morris, 1986), selecting as the firm's target market only certain customers who have the necessary coproduction abilities and aptitudes (market segmentation), and offering price discounts to coproducing customers.

Managing the stress of customer-contact jobs can yield important outcomes both for employees and for customers. These employees must simultaneously meet the demands of both the business and the customer. There are two objectives of stress management unique to employees in these positions: first, management must communicate openly with frontline employees to reach a shared agreement on the orientation toward customers (recall the research indicating the negative consequences of role ambiguity for both employees and customers).

Second, management must ensure that frontline employees have the resources necessary to satisfy customers in the service encounter. The literature on occupational stress has long emphasized that perceived lack of control over what occurs to one on the job is stressful (Matteson & Ivancevich, 1982). When employees deal with customers face-to-face, or over the phone, and do not have the resources or freedom to meet their expectations, they experience absence of control. Relatedly, a recent study found that the strongest correlation of service employee job satisfaction was their perception that they have the capability to satisfy the customer (Heskett et al., 1994).

Even when frontline employees have the necessary resources to serve the customer, they might still need time away from the "emotional labor" of customer contact. One tactic that can be used is to provide employees who typically work in high-customer-contact positions with minisabbaticals during which they might work in low-customer-contact, back-office positions.

Research Issues in Customer-Driven Employee Performance

There are several research issues that are particularly relevant in the study of customer-driven employee performance:

• *Applications of linkage research are needed to better understand the requirements and consequences of customer-driven employee performance.* Linkage research involves integrating and correlating data collected from employees with data in other key organizational databases. The purpose of linkage research is to identify those elements of the work environment—as described by employees—that correlate with or link to critically important organizational outcomes such as customer satisfaction and business performance (Wiley, 1996).

Linkage research that collects data from different sources (such as employees, customers, shareholders, and the community) faces some significant problems when attempting to integrate the information. The following problems face both scholars and practitioners doing this type of research in organizations, as described by Schiemann (1996) and other authors.

1. *Data from these different sources have historically been owned by different functions,* such as human resources, marketing, and finance.

These different functions are often reluctant to share information that has been their source of power and the evidence of what, if any, value-added they return to the firm. Obviously firms with a strong TQM orientation will suffer less from this problem.

2. *Different research methods, scalings, or both have been used by those collecting data from different stakeholders.* Industrial psychologists may have collected employee satisfaction data using five-point Likert scales administered through on-site surveys. In contrast, market researchers have often used seven- or ten-point scales to assess customer satisfaction, and so-called trade-off formats to assess the importance customers place on different product and service attributes. It is not always a simple matter to compare data collected by these different approaches.

3. *Data from different sources are typically used by various members of the organization for different purposes.* Data on employee attitudes and values often have their own follow-up processes either in place or implied so that top and middle management can develop initiatives for improving employee satisfaction and productivity. This data collection effort and follow-up typically involve a majority of the organization and require senior management commitment. In contrast, data collection by market researchers typically involves fewer decision makers and conclusions, and initiatives based on the data often affect fewer employees.

4. *There may be tension over the relative credibility and strategic relevance of "hard" versus "soft" measures.* Profit data from finance may be viewed by senior management as more objective and consequential than perceptual data on employee and customer satisfaction. A solution to this problem is the "balanced scorecard" approach (Kaplan & Norton, 1992, 1996). This approach advocates setting objectives and measuring performance with four distinct objectives:

Learning and growth: assessing the characteristics of the people, the organizational infrastructure, and whether they support long-term success

Internal: evaluating key internal processes

Customer: determining customer needs and satisfaction

Financial: appraising the ultimate results that business provides its shareholders

5. *There may be confusion over correlation versus causation.* Linkage research results typically lend themselves only to interpretations of association. There is, however, the implicit assumption that changes in employee data lead to changes in customer data, such as customer retention. To examine this, Schneider, White, and Paul (1998) used structural equation modeling to test the causal direction between employee perceptions and customer perceptions. Their results showed that the path coefficients running from employee to customer over time were essentially identical to the path coefficients running from customer perceptions to employee perceptions.

These results support Bowen's call (1991) for more research on how customer attitudes and behavior spill over to employees, in turn affecting their work attitudes and behaviors. Examples of prior work on this causal direction include Ouchi's study (1977) of how department store customers impose their will on store clerks and Rafaeli's work (1989) on how shoppers try to control the behavior of fast-food clerks.

6. *More research is needed on what determines the pattern of relationships among desired outcomes.* There is often an assumption that all good things go together, for example, that gains in employee satisfaction are associated with gains in customer satisfaction and profitability. Yet Moeller and Schneider (1986) presented data that showed that favorable employee attitudes were positively correlated with profitability in an eye care chain, but employee attitudes and perceptions of customer service quality were uncorrelated, and perceptions of customer service quality were also unrelated to profitability. In a study of a retail store chain, Wiley (1991) found that while employee and customer satisfaction were positively correlated, unit business performance (measured by net income) was not related to employee satisfaction and, in fact, was negatively correlated with measures of customer satisfaction. In studies of an insurance company and a telephone company that were implementing self-managing teams, Ledford and colleagues (1996) found that employee perceptions of quality of working life, employee productivity, and customer perceptions of customer service were uncorrelated. Indeed, meta-analytic research may now be necessary to summarize relationships among employee and customer measures. As well, research is needed to find the conditions under which different relationships among outcomes hold. One variable

that is likely to be important in this regard is time—for example, how long must a firm be customer-driven before it sees positive returns?

• *Aside from linkage research, more research is needed on how customer data actually get used, or don't get used, by organizational decision makers.* At a recent conference on service quality, presenters from GTE expressed the view that although the hardware and software for collecting customer data had increased the quantity and even quality of information over the years, organizational decision makers were still putting little of that information to use. They suggested that customer data are overcollected and underutilized. Schneider and Bowen (1995) also observed that many businesses monitor customers' perceptions of quality and customer satisfaction as if those data were useful in and of themselves. They encourage firms to monitor quality for improvement, not for the sake of the data.

• *Research is needed on how best to implement customer-driven HRM practices.* There is a need to develop valid selection measures that tap into the types of customer and team skills that we have considered here. To date, the lion's share of selection validation research has been devoted to evaluating cognitive abilities (see Hunter & Hunter, 1984). Can customer and team skills be assessed in a way that avoids social desirability and is valid? Are there appropriate surrogate measures involving biographical or personality information? The answers to these questions pose exciting challenges for selection researchers.

We encourage research to determine what factors are associated with employees' and managers' acceptance of 360-degree appraisal practices that include data from internal and external customers. Research has shown that managers often neglect or refuse to carry out appraisals, largely because they do not accept the process as having value (Fried, Tiegs, & Bellamy, 1992). Bretz, Milkovich, and Read (1992) noted that, unlike researchers, managers tend to define validity and accuracy in terms of acceptability to organizational members, including themselves. Consequently, issues such as reactions to and preferences for appraisal methods become paramount. This may be even more true for 360-degree appraisals, compared to traditional managerial appraisal, because the former can be threatening and is typically conducted anonymously. That is, acceptability is critical because providers of 360-degree appraisals, or internal and external customers, may fear retribution, and it is impossible to trace whether specific individuals have completed 360-degree appraisals. We define *acceptability* as either the willingness to provide input data (in the case of customers) or (in the case of recipients) to receive and utilize 360-degree data.

What factors can affect the acceptability of 360-degree appraisals? In line with the foregoing discussion, one likely factor is the extent of a firm's adoption of the TQM philosophy. Other factors may also come into play, especially those associated with perceived procedural and distributive fairness (Greenberg, 1986). For example, 360-degree appraisals may be considered more fair, and hence acceptable, if recipients have the autonomy and training and the organizational resources necessary to satisfy customers (internal and external). In addition, recipients are likely to be more accepting of the process if the customers being asked to provide appraisals are competent to do so—that is, are familiar with the recipients' work and job demands and are willing and able to provide accurate ratings. In sum, although some work has been completed regarding acceptability (such as Antonioni, 1994; Barclay & Harland, 1995; Waldman & Bowen, 1998), more research is needed to address this important issue facing the implementation of 360-degree appraisal processes.

Managerial Issues in Customer-Driven Employee Performance: From Individual to Organizational Performance

Although the theme of this book is individual employee performance, we want to close by emphasizing that customer-driven performance must be an organizational imperative if customers are to be satisfied. All individuals, across levels and functions, must perform well together—seamlessly—in order to produce goods and services that meet customer expectations. For example, remember our earlier point that the HRM and market research staffs will need to cooperate in designing HRM practices based on customer-defined behavioral anchors of service quality. The seamless organization is a compelling consequence of a shift in focus from internally driven performance standards associated with meeting the requirements of a job to externally driven performance standards associated with meeting the expectations of customers. A single individual can perform a job well, but it takes the entire organization to satisfy customers.

This organizational-level perspective on customer-driven performance has been expressed in two ways that deserve mention. First, customer-driven organizations must create an overall organizational climate in order for service to be successful in meeting customers' expectations (Schneider, 1990). Climate is determined by the messages that employees of organizations obtain from the policies and practices under which they work and the kinds of behaviors they feel are rewarded, supported, and expected. Thus, in a climate for service, the imperative of meeting customers' expectations is the unifying theme of all these policies, practices, and desired behaviors.

All the HRM implications we have discussed can be viewed not just as influencing individual employee performance but also as creating and reinforcing a climate for service. A case in point is our earlier mention of hiring for the organization, not just for the job. Within this organizational perspective, HRM should derive its profile of the appropriate employee characteristics based not only on a job analysis but also on an organizational analysis (Bowen et al., 1991). The latter analysis should attempt to specify the type of organization (such as customer-driven) to which employees are, it is hoped, being well matched.

Second, organizations must formulate a business strategy to focus on specific customer segments—or falter. This is the theme of Treacy and Wiersema (1995), who advise firms to choose their customers, narrow their focus, and dominate their market. Research by Nayyar (1992) has also demonstrated that a focus on specific customer segments yields high success. The next generation of thinking may be mass customization, which is a business strategy that competes on multiple market segments of one (Pine, Victor, & Boynton, 1993).

Market segmentation identifies which customers should drive employee performance. For example, is it always correct that the customer is always right when expressing dissatisfaction? The only dissatisfied customers who are always right are customers who are targeted by the business strategy. The customer who is not right—not right for the business—is one who is not a target customer and finds that the quality is poor. Not retaining that customer may actually make sense; the organization might even be wise to "fire" such a customer.

Strategically defined market segments can also help resolve the issue we raised earlier about the possible high variance in customers' perceptions of a firm's service quality. This variance might signal that the firm has not clearly defined its service concept for the marketplace, that it has failed to match its service concept to a specified market segment, or both. There may be some customers who are dissatisfied with not receiving a type of service that the organization never intended to provide.

The HRM implications of this thinking is that firms should implement *market-segmented* HRM (Schneider, 1994; Bowen, 1996). Rather than pursuing generic HRM best practices, the firm should hire people who fit the firm's market segment, train people to meet the expectations of the firm's customers, and reward employees so that the market segment they want to dominate has satisfied customers. These are the customers who should drive employee performance throughout the organization. For example, Southwest Airlines views its competitive advantage as being a fast and fun carrier, so it tries to hire people who are fast and fun, and then trains and rewards them for being that way. Moreover, all other organizational practices, such as choice of aircraft and facilities, are also designed to execute this segmented strategy. Relatedly, Bowen and Lawler (1992a, 1995) have advocated a contingency approach to empowering service employees that argues that for some market segments—such as high-volume, low-cost services—empowerment may not in fact be sound practice. Market-segmented HRM fits neatly with the contingency and configurational perspectives on HRM that have received considerable attention in the literature recently (Delery & Doty, 1996).

In sum, we have offered numerous insights on the customer orientation that has arisen from the quality revolution and growth of services. Employee performance standards that are only internally driven and defined will be less and less a characteristic of effective organizations. Our discussion of the meaning of customer-driven employee performance can hopefully inform the design of HRM practices that will satisfy both employees and customers.

References

Antonioni, D. (1994). The effects of feedback accountability on upward appraisal ratings. *Personnel Psychology, 47,* 349–356.

Ashforth, B. E. (1992). The perceived inequality of systems. *Administration and Society, 24,* 375–408.

Ashforth, B. E., & Humphrey, R. H. (1993). Emotional labor in service roles: The influence of identity. *Academy of Management Review, 18,* 88–115.

Ashkenas, R., Ulrich, D., Jick, T., & Kerr, S. (1995). *The boundaryless organization: Breaking the chain of organizational structure.* San Francisco: Jossey-Bass.

Barclay, I. H., & Harland, L. K. (1995). Peer performance appraisals: The impact of rater competence, rater location, and rating correctability on fairness perceptions. *Group and Organization Management, 20,* 39–60.

Bateson, J.E.G. (1985). Perceived control and the service encounter. In J. A. Czepiel & C. F. Surprenant (Eds.), *The service encounter* (pp. 67–82). San Francisco: New Lexington Press.

Berry, L. L. (1980, May-June). Service marketing is different. *Business,* pp. 24–29.

Bitner, M. J. (1992). Servicescapes. *Journal of Marketing, 56,* 57–71.

Blackburn, R., & Rosen, B. (1993). Total quality and human resources management: Lessons learned from Baldrige Award–winning companies. *Academy of Management Executive, 7*(3), 49–66.

Blancero, D., Johnson, S. A., & Lakshman. (1996). Psychological contracts and fairness: The effects of violations on customer service behavior. *Journal of Market-Focused Management, 1*(1), 49–64.

Blumberg, M., & Pringle, C. C. (1982). The missing opportunity in organizational research: Some implications for a theory of work performance. *Academy of Management Review, 7,* 560–569.

Bowen, D. E. (1986). Managing customers as human resources. *Human Resource Management, 25,* 371–384.

Bowen, D. E. (1991). Interdisciplinary study of service: Some progress, some prospects. *Journal of Business Research, 20,* 71–79.

Bowen, D. E. (1996). Market-focused HRM in service organizations: Satisfying internal and external customers. *Journal of Market-Focused Management, 1*(1), 31–47.

Bowen, D. E., & Folger, R. (1994, April). The meaning and measurement of fairness in service exchange. Presentation at the Society for Industrial and Organizational Psychology, Nashville, TN.

Bowen, D. E., Gilliland, S. W., & Folger, R. (in press). HRM and service fairness: How being fair to employees spills over on to customers. *Organizational Dynamics.*

Bowen, D. E., & Lawler, E. E., III. (1992a). The empowerment of service workers: What, why, how, and when. *Sloan Management Review, 33*(3), 31–39.

Bowen, D. E., & Lawler, E. E., III. (1992b). Total quality-oriented human resources management. *Organizational Dynamics, 20,* 29–41.

Bowen, D. E., & Lawler, E. E., III. (1995). Empowering service employees. *Sloan Management Review, 36*(3), 73–84.

Bowen, D. E., Ledford, G. E., Jr., & Nathan, B. R. (1991). Hiring for the organization, not the job. *Academy of Management Executive, 5*(4), 35–51.

Bowen, D. E., & Schneider, B. (1988). Services marketing and management: Implications for organizational behavior. In B. M. Staw & L. L. Cummings (Eds.), *Research in organizational behavior* (Vol. 10). Greenwich, CT: JAI Press.

Bretz, R. D., Jr., Milkovich, G. T., & Read, W. (1992). The current state of performance appraisal research and practice: Concerns, directions, and implications. *Journal of Management, 18,* 321–352.

Brief, A. P., & Robertson, L. (1989). Job attitude organization: An exploratory study. *Journal of Applied Social Psychology, 19,* 717–727.

Bushe, G. R. (1988). Cultural contradictions of statistical process control in American manufacturing organizations. *Journal of Management, 14,* 19–31.

Campbell, J. P. (1990). Modeling the performance prediction problem in industrial and organizational psychology. In M. D. Dunnette & L. M. Hough (Eds.), *Handbook of industrial and organizational psychology* (Vol. 1, 2nd ed., pp. 687–732). Palo Alto, CA: Consulting Psychologists Press.

Cardy, R. L., & Carson, K. P. (1996). Total quality and the abandonment of performance appraisal: Taking a good thing too far? *Journal of Quality Management, 1,* 193–206.

Cardy, R. L., & Dobbins, G. (1994). Validity versus user reactions in selection: Where to draw the line? *Human Resources Division News, 18*(1), 9–10.

Chase, R. B. (1978). Where does the customer fit in a service operation? *Harvard Business Review, 56*(2), 137–142.

Czepiel, J. A., Solomon, M. R., & Surprenant, C. (Eds.). (1985). *The service encounter.* Lexington, MA: Heath.

Danet, B. (1981). Client-organization relationships. In P. C. Nystrom & W. H. Starback (Eds.), *Handbook of organization design.* New York: Oxford University Press.

Dean, J. W., Jr., & Bowen, D. E. (1994). Management theory and total quality: Improving research and practice through theory development. *Academy of Management Review, 19*(3), 392–418.

Dean, J. W., Jr., & Evans, J. R. (1994). *Total quality: Management, organization and strategy.* St. Paul: West.

Delery, J. E., & Doty, D. H. (1996). Modes of theorizing in strategic human resource management: Tests of universalistic, contingency, and configurational performance predictions. *Academy of Management Journal, 39,* 802–835.

Deming, W. E. (1986). *Out of the crisis.* Cambridge: Massachusetts Institute of Technology, Center for Advanced Engineering Study.

Deming, W. E. (1993). *The new economics for industry, government, education.* Cambridge: Massachusetts Institute of Technology, Center for Advanced Engineering Study.

Dobbins, G. H., Cardy, R. L., & Carson, K. P. (1991). Examining fundamental assumptions: A contrast of person and system approaches to human resource management. *Research in Personnel and Human Resources Management, 3,* 1–38.

Ekman, P. (1973). Cross-culture studies of facial expression. In P. Ekman (Ed.), *Darwin and facial expression: A century of research in review* (pp. 169–222). New York: Academic Press.

Fried, Y., Tiegs, R. B., & Bellamy, A. R. (1992). Personal and interpersonal predictors of supervisors' avoidance of evaluating subordinates. *Journal of Applied Psychology, 77,* 462–468.

Fuchs, V. R. (1968). *The service economy.* New York: National Bureau of Economic Research.

Gabris, G. T., Mitchell, K., & McLemore, R. (1985). Rewarding individual and team productivity: The Biloxi merit bonus plan. *Public Personnel Management, 14,* 231–244.

George, J. M. (1989). Mood and absence. *Journal of Applied Psychology, 75,* 107–116.

George, J. M., & Brief, A. P. (1992). Feeling good—doing good: A conceptual analysis of the mood-at-work–organizational spontaneity relationship. *Psychological Bulletin, 112*(2), 310–329.

Gersuny, C., & Rosengren, W. R. (1973). *The service society.* Cambridge, MA: Shenkman.

Ghorpade, J., & Chen, M. M. (1995). Creating quality-driven performance appraisal systems. *Academy of Management Executive, 9*(1), 32–41.

Gilliland, S. W. (1994). Effects of procedural and distributive justice in reactions to a selection system. *Journal of Applied Psychology, 79*(5), 691–701.

Greenberg, J. (1986). Determinants of perceived fairness of performance evaluations. *Journal of Applied Psychology, 71,* 340–342.

Gronroos, C. (1990). *Service management and marketing: Managing the moment of truth in service competition.* San Francisco: New Lexington Press.

Hackman, J. R., & Wageman, R.(1995). Total quality management: Empirical, conceptual, and practical issues. *Administrative Science Quarterly, 40,* 309–342.

Heskett, J. L., Jones, T. O., Loveman, G. W., Sasser, E., & Schlesinger, L. A. (1994). Putting the service profit chain to work. *Harvard Business Review, 72*(2), 164–174.

Hochschild, A. R. (1979). Emotion work, feeling rules, and social structure. *American Journal of Sociology, 50,* 242–252.

Hochschild, A. R. (1983). *The managed heart: The commercialization of human feeling.* Berkeley: University of California Press.

Hogan, R. T., Hogan, J., & Busch, A. (1984). How to measure service orientation. *Journal of Applied Psychology, 69,* 167–173.

Hunter, J. E., & Hunter, R. F. (1984). Validity and utility of alternate predictors of job performance. *Psychological Bulletin, 96,* 72–98.

Judge, T. A. (1992). The dispositional perspective in human resources research. In G. R. Ferris & K. M. Rowland (Eds.), *Research in personnel and human resources management* (Vol. 10). Greenwich, CT: JAI Press.

Kaplan, R. S., & Norton, D. P. (1992). The balanced scorecard: Measures that drive performance. *Harvard Business Review, 70*(1), 71–79.

Kaplan, R. S., & Norton, D. P. (1996). *The balanced scorecard: Translating strategy into action.* Boston: Harvard Business School Press.

Katz, D., & Kahn, R. L. (1978). *The social psychology of organizations* (2nd ed.). New York: Wiley.

Kerr, S. (1975). On the folly of rewarding A while hoping for B. *Academy of Management Journal, 18,* 769–783.

Lawler, E. E., III. (1996). *From the ground up: Six principles for building the new logic organization.* San Francisco: Jossey-Bass.

Ledford, G. E., Jr. (1996). Assessing team-based work interventions.

Lengnick-Hall, C. A. (1996). Customer contribution to quality: A different view of the customer-oriented firm. *Academy of Management Review, 21,* 791–824.

Levitt, T. (1981). Marketing intangible products and product intangibles. *Harvard Business Review, 59*(2), 94–102.

London, M., & Beatty, R. W. (1993). 360-degree feedback as competitive advantage. *Human Resource Management, 32,* 353–372.

Lovelock, C. H. (1981). Why marketing management needs to be different for services. In J. H. Donnelly & W. R. George (Eds.), *Marketing of services.* Chicago: American Marketing Association.

Matteson, M. T., & Ivancevich, J. M. (1982). *Management job stress and health.* New York: Free Press.

Mills, P. K., Chase, R. B., & Margulies, N. (1983). Motivating the client/employee system as a service production strategy. *Academy of Management Review, 8,* 301–310.

Mills, P. K., Hall, J. K., Leidecker, J. K., & Margulies, N. (1983). Flexiform: A model for professional service organizations. *Academy of Management Review, 8,* 118–131.

Mills, P. K., & Margulies, N. (1980). Toward a core typology of service organizations. *Academy of Management Review, 5,* 255–265.

Mills, P. K., & Morris, J. H. (1986). Clients as "partial employees" of service organizations: Role development in client participation. *Academy of Management Review, 11,* 726–735.

Moeller, A., & Schneider, B. (1986). Climate for service and the bottom line. In M. Venkateson, D. M. Schmalonese, & C. Marshall (Eds.), *Creativity and the bottom-line.* Chicago: American Marketing Association.

Moorman, R. H., & Blakely, G. L. (1993). *Individualism-collectivism as an individual difference predictor of organizational citizenship behavior.* Paper presented at the annual meeting of the Academy of Management, Atlanta.

Nayyar, P. A. (1992). Performance effects of three foci in service firms. *Academy of Management Journal, 35,* 985–1009.

Organ, D. W. (1988). *Organizational citizenship behavior: The good soldier syndrome.* San Francisco: New Lexington Press.

Ouchi, W. (1977). The relationship between organizational structure and organizational control. *Administrative Science Quarterly, 22.*

Parasuraman, A., Zeithaml, V. A., & Berry, L. L. (1985). A conceptual model of service quality and its implications for future research. *Journal of Marketing, 49,* 41–50.

Parasuraman, A., Zeithaml, V. A., & Berry, L. L. (1988). SERVQUAL: A multiple item scale for measuring consumer perceptions of service quality. *Journal of Retailing,* 12–40.

Parkington, J. J., & Schneider, B. (1979). Some correlates of experienced job stress: A boundary-role study. *Academy of Management Journal, 22,* 270–281.

Peters, L. H., O'Connor, E. J., & Eulberg, I. R. (1985). Situational constraints: Sources, consequences, and future considerations. *Research in Personnel and Human Resources Management, 3,* 79–114.

Peters, T. J., & Waterman, R. H., Jr. (1982). *In search of excellence: Lessons from America's best-run companies.* New York: HarperCollins.

Pine, B. J., Victor, B., & Boynton, A. C. (1993). Making mass customization work. *Harvard Business Review, 71*(2), 108–119.

Prince, B. (1994). Performance appraisal and reward practices for total quality organizations. *Quality Management Journal, 1*(2), 36–46.

Pulakos, E. D., & Schmitt, N. (1983). A longitudinal study of a valence model approach for the prediction of job satisfaction of new employees. *Journal of Applied Psychology, 68,* 307–312.

Rafaeli, A. (1989). When cashiers meet customers. An analysis of the role of supermarket cashiers. *Academy of Management Journal, 32,* 245–273.

Rafaeli, A., & Pratt, M. G. (1993). Tailored meanings: On the meaning and impact of organizational dress. *Academy of Management Review, 18,* 32–55.

Rafaeli, A., & Sutton, R. I. (1987). The expression of emotion as part of the work role. *Academy of Management Review, 12,* 23–37.

Rafaeli, A., & Sutton, R. I. (1989). The expression of emotion in organization life. In B. M. Staw & L. L. Cummings (Eds.), *Research in Organizational Behavior* (Vol. 11, pp. 1–42). Greenwich, CT: JAI Press.

Reeves, C. A., & Bednar, D. A. (1994). Defining quality: Alternatives and implications. *Academy of Management Review, 19*(3), 419–445.

Rounds, J. B., Dawis, R. V., & Lofquist, L. H. (1987). Measurement of person-environment fit and prediction of satisfaction in the theory of work adjustment. *Journal of Vocational Behavior, 31,* 297–318.

Sasser, E. (1976). Match supply and demand in service industries. *Harvard Business Review, 56*(2), 133–148.

Schiemann, W. A. (1996). Driving change through surveys: Aligning employees, customers, and other key stakeholders. In A. I. Kraut (Ed.), *Organizational surveys: Tools for assessment and change* (pp. 88–116). San Francisco: Jossey-Bass.

Schneider, B. (1990). The climate for service: An application of the climate construct. In B. Schneider (Ed.), *Organizational climate and culture.* San Francisco: Jossey-Bass.

Schneider, B. (1994). HRM: A service perspective—toward a customer-focused HRM. *International Journal of Service Industry Management, 5,* 64–76.

Schneider, B., & Bowen, D. E. (1985). Employee and customer perceptions of service in banks: Replication and extension. *Journal of Applied Psychology, 20,* 423–433.

Schneider, B., & Bowen, D. E. (1993). The service organization: Human resource management is crucial. *Organizational Dynamics, 21,* 39–52.

Schneider, B., & Bowen, D. E. (1995). *Winning the service game.* Boston: Harvard Business School Press.

Schneider, B., Parkington, J. J., & Buxton, V. M. (1980). Employee and customer perceptions of service in banks. *Administrative Science Quarterly, 25,* 252–267.

Schneider, B., White, S. M., & Paul, M. C. (1998). Linking service climate and customer perceptions of service quality: Test of a causal model. *Journal of Applied Psychology, 83*(2), 150–163.

Schonberger, R. J. (1992). Total quality management cuts a broad swath—through manufacturing and beyond. *Organizational Dynamics, 20*(4), 16–28.

Shostack, G. L. (1977). Banks sell services—not things. *Bankers Magazine, 32,* 40–45.

Siehl, C., Bowen, D. E., & Pearson, C. M. (1992). Service encounters as rites of integration: An information-processing model. *Organization Science, 3,* 537–555.

Sitkin, S. B., Sutcliffe, K. M., & Schroeder, R. G. (1994). Distinguishing control from learning in total quality management: A contingency perspective. *Academy of Management Review, 19,* 537–564.

Staw, B. M., & Ross, J. (1985). Stability in the midst of change: A dispositional approach to job attitudes. *Journal of Applied Psychology, 70,* 469–480.

Sutton, R. I., & Rafaeli, A. (1988). Untangling the relationship between displaced emotions and organizational sales: The case of convenience stores. *Academy of Management Journal, 31,* 461–487.

Tornow, W. W. (1993). Introduction to special issue on 360-degree feedback. *Human Resource Management, 32,* 221–230.

Treacy, M., & Wiersema, F. (1993). Customer intimacy and other value disciplines. *Harvard Business Review, 71*(2), 84–93.

Trice, H. M., & Beyer, J. M. (1984). Studying organizational cultures through rites and ceremonials. *Academy of Management Review, 9,* 653–669.

Van Maanan, D. J., & Kunda, G. (1989). Real feelings: Emotional expression and organizational culture. In B. M. Staw & L. L. Cummings (Eds.), *Research in organizational behavior* (Vol. 11, pp. 43–103). Greenwich, CT: JAI Press.

Vroom, V. (1964). *Work and motivation.* New York: Wiley.

Waldman, D. A. (1994a). The contributions of total quality management to a theory of work performance. *Academy of Management Review, 19,* 510–536.

Waldman, D. A. (1994b). Designing performance management systems for total quality implementation. *Journal of Organizational Change Management, 7*(2), 31–44.

Waldman, D. A., & Bowen, D. E. (1998). The acceptability of 360-degree appraisals: A customer-supplier relationship perspective. *Human Resource Management, 37*(2), 117–130.

Wiley, J. W. (1991). Customer satisfaction: A supportive work environment and its financial cost. *Human Resource Planning, 14,* 117–128.

Wiley, J. W. (1996). Linking survey results to customer satisfaction and business performance. In A. I. Kraut (Ed.), *Organizational surveys: Tools for assessment and change* (pp. 88–116). San Francisco: Jossey-Bass.

Zeithaml, V. A., & Bitner, M. J. (1996). *Services marketing.* New York: McGraw-Hill.

CHAPTER 7

Leadership and the Changing Nature of Performance

Robert G. Lord
Wendy Gradwohl Smith

How well a nation, army, university, business, or any other organization performs is often attributed to its leaders. Although the leader's influence is often overestimated, there is no doubt that leaders do have impacts on performance across multiple levels, from the individual to the work group to the organization (Day & Lord, 1988). Leaders not only have a crucial role in influencing performance through both direct and indirect means, but they also help to define what is and is not effective performance.

In this chapter we argue that the relation between leadership and performance is likely to increase because of the changes discussed by other authors of this book, while at the same time exercising effective leadership may become more difficult. For example, increased diversity in experience and technical training will reduce the degree to which organizational members share common performance standards. Concurrently, greater ethnic, racial, and gender diversity will increase the potential tensions among team members due to less homogeneous values and beliefs. Increased diversity will also create multiple, and often conflicting, subordinate expectations of leaders. Thus, increased diversity creates greater need for leaders to define performance and manage group conflict effectively, while at the same time it makes it more difficult for leaders to be perceived as such by group members with different leadership expectations.

As with increased diversity, many of the other changes noted by authors in this book also have dual effects—they increase the degree to which performance depends on effective leadership, while at the same time substantially altering traditional leadership processes. It is our belief that the net effect of such changes is to alter leadership processes in organizations fundamentally, requiring that leadership be reconceptualized so that its relationship to performance can be fully appreciated. Thus we begin by focusing on the construct of leadership itself, reconceptualizing it as an emergent social process. This conceptual model of leadership, which we develop in detail in the first half of the chapter, will then serve as the basis for the second half of the chapter, which discusses the impacts that leadership can have on performance.

Several chapters in this book indicate that the changing nature of work and the changing demographics of the workforce will create new leadership demands. Table 7.1 summarizes some of the important trends noted by other authors of this volume that will affect the relationship of leadership to performance. Considering these trends led us to several conclusions that have motivated our reconceptualization of leadership as an emergent social process. First, we expect that these trends will shift the origin of leadership activities in organizations from hierarchical, job-based loci to reciprocal, employee-based loci. Second, we argue that the changes shown in Table 7.1 are likely to reduce substitutes for leadership (Kerr, 1977; Kerr & Jermier, 1978), and therefore to increase the need for effective leadership if high levels of performance are to be achieved. Third, we also expect that leaders will have to address many issues that affect performance through indirect means. For example, effective leadership will be increasingly concerned with two issues that only indirectly affect performance—establishing organizational identities and promoting continuous learning within the context of ongoing task and organizational demands. Fourth, we stress that future leaders need to understand how their activities fit within the cognitive-affective-social systems of followers. We then develop a framework to promote such understanding. Finally, we show how the framework can be used to identify some of the challenges that will confront future leaders, and we suggest potentially effective ways to enhance performance.

Table 7.1. Summary of Trends in the Workforce.

Issue	In the Past	Current Trend	Relevant Chapter
1. Work organization	Map job onto employee Relative ease in identifying KSAOs	Map job onto team More or different KSAOs and greater difficulty identifying KSAOs	9
2. Design of jobs	Stable jobs Common elements of jobs shared among a number of people	Less stable jobs Common elements of jobs shared among fewer people	2
3. Technology	Relative ease in identifying individual and technological contributions to performance Little performance monitoring using technology	Confounding individual and technological contributions to performance Greater performance monitoring using technology	3
4. Control of performance	Internal sources used for performance standards	External sources used for performance standards	7
5. Meaning of performance	Performance defined by past behavior One cultural view of good performance	Performance defined by future behavior, continuous learning Different cultural views of good performance	6
6. Leadership and supervision	Traditional leadership and supervision	Leadership that emphasizes skill development, teams, and identities	8
7. Part-time and temporary workers	Minimal concern for commitment to organization, learning, and development due to the stability and structure of jobs	Greater concern for commitment to organization, learning, and development due to the instability and team-based nature of jobs	5

Our focus in this chapter is mainly on leadership in face-to-face, dyadic superior-subordinate relations. Certainly leadership at executive levels is important for explaining organizational performance (see Lord & Maher, 1991; Day & Lord, 1988), and leadership can be thought of in connection with group levels (Lord & Engle, 1996; Manz, 1986; Manz & Sims, 1980, 1987) or organizational levels (Schein, 1992). Similarly, the effects of many workforce trends such as diversity and globalization can be analyzed at the group level (Jackson, Stone, & Alvarez, 1993) or at the organizational level (Gioia & Thomas, 1996). We focus, however, on dyadic levels in order to develop and apply a more coherent theoretical perspective for relating leadership to performance.

Definition and Reconceptualization of Leadership

To assess the effects of the changes noted in Table 7.1 on leadership processes, one needs a clear definition and conceptualization of leadership. Most of the prior work on leadership shares a common set of assumptions that see leaders as being important causal agents who are held accountable for the outcomes of their subordinates, work teams, or organizations. Leaders are also seen as important sources of organizational structures and strategies (Katz & Kahn, 1978), identities (Gioia & Thomas, 1996), culture (Schein, 1992), and coordination through a formal chain of command. Most critically, leadership is seen as resulting from qualities of a specific individual (traits, behavior, insight, assertiveness, and so forth).

Though it is consistent in seeing leaders as important origins of organizational processes, this traditional view led to a variety of leadership definitions. Leadership has been defined in terms of traits (Mann, 1959), behavior (Schriesheim & Kerr, 1974; Bass & Avolio, 1989), role development or clarification (House, 1971; Graen & Scandura, 1987), social influence (Hollander & Offermann, 1990), and social perceptions (Lord & Maher, 1991), to name a few. Our approach is to define leadership as *a social perception, grounded in social-cognitive psychological theory, that produces an influence increment for the perceived leader* (Katz & Kahn, 1978). Leadership activities, then, would be defined as activities that increase attributions of leadership, either directly, such as by impression management activities, or indirectly, by changing task outcomes or fulfilling group or organizational requirements. Thus our approach can include most of the aspects of leadership that are reflected in these various definitions.

As shown in Figure 7.1, social perceptions and behavior are explainable in terms of more fundamental cognitive and affective processes that unfold in a context of increasingly diverse jobs, people, cultures, markets, and nations. Most of the issues we address involve both cognitive and affective elements as reflected in social processes. These factors in turn affect organizational outcomes and individual performance. Though the cognitive and affective components in Figure 7.1 are separated for clarity of presentation, the dotted line connecting them represents the interdependence of these two processes.

Leadership occurs through these basic, ongoing, psychological processes, rather than being a separate entity or process. For example, rather than seeing charismatic or transformational lead-

Figure 7.1. Model of the Leadership Process.

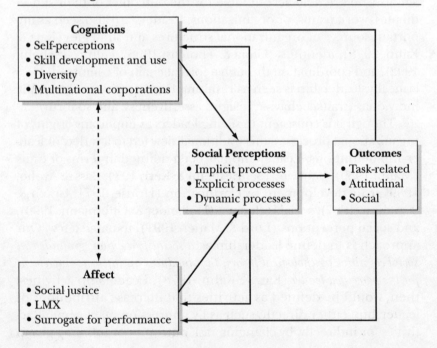

ership as something unique to a specific individual, we see it as an outcome of ongoing social interaction between leaders and followers that is explainable in terms of underlying social and cognitive theory. In other words, leadership is an emergent process that results from the interaction of the elements shown in Figure 7.1 rather than being an exogenous process that would be represented as a separate box associated with leader characteristics. Thus we suggest that the locus of leadership is not in a single person or organizational position but rather in a confluence of factors that flow together over time, people, and tasks.

We emphasize social perceptions in Figure 7.1 because the leadership aspects of traits or behaviors are derived from their interpretation by others. Thus a core element of leadership is "the process of being perceived by others as a leader" (Lord & Maher, 1991, p. 11). This perception allows leaders to exert more influence on group processes or individual cognitions (Hollander & Offermann, 1990), but it is also the consequence of past activities, associated outcomes, and the way they are interpreted in a specific context by specific individuals. Changing any of these elements can substantially alter leadership processes. For example, Hall, Workman, and Marchioro (1998) found that the relationship of target characteristics (androgyny) to attributions of leadership depended on the gender of the target as well as on the group task. Perceiver characteristics, such as being schematic in leadership domains, also affect leadership perceptions (Smith, Brown, Lord, & Engle, 1998). In addition, Meindl, Ehrlich, and Dukerich (1985) found that the leadership construct is more salient and more likely to be used to make sense of extreme rather than moderate performance (either very good or very bad performance), illustrating the importance of historical context for leadership perceptions. Thus leadership is a situated social perception (Chartrand & Bargh, 1996), with the accessibility of this construct for perceivers depending on situational cues, perceiver schemas, and target characteristics and behavior.

Locus of Organizational Leadership

If leadership perception processes can change depending on the nature of the task, the schematicism of perceivers, or the extremity of performance, then the locus of leadership is not solely in a particular leader or a set of leadership qualities but rather in the sensemaking processes engendered by a variety of variables (Chartrand & Bargh, 1996; Hall & Lord, 1995; Meindl, 1995). This perspective clearly conflicts with more traditional views, which see the source of leadership as being primarily within the characteristics of individuals. As contextual factors become increasingly important in defining leadership, future leaders will need to develop more complex and context-dependent leadership skills. Diversity in employees will create multiple views (implicit theories) of effective leadership, as will cultural variability (Gerstner & Day, 1994; O'Connell, Lord, & O'Connell, 1990) and different group identities (Hains, Hogg, & Duck, 1997). The ability of future leaders to understand and adjust to such differences will likely influence their effectiveness. Thus factors such as self-monitoring ability (Snyder, 1979) and cognitive complexity may be increasingly important characteristics for future leaders.

Although leadership perceptions result from the sense-making processes of others, it should also be stressed that leaders use the perceptual capital created by such perceptions to influence a variety of additional sense-making processes that occur in organizations. One particularly critical issue, which is the focus of this book, is the definition of performance. Effective employees often do more than fulfill the demands of their focal task or formal role (Motowidlo & Schmit, Chapter Three, this volume; Organ, 1988). Leaders can be a critical factor in expanding accepted definitions of performance to include such factors as citizenship behaviors and contextual performance. They can also emphasize factors such as employee skill development as being important aspects of employee performance. Moreover, as well as expanding the definition of effective performance, leaders can help shape views on what factors (such as diligence) determine effective performance and what are unacceptable means of achieving high performance because of conflict with an organization's culture or moral values.

Increased Need for Effective Leadership

Conceptualizing leadership as an emergent, contextually dependent process suggests that in the future it may be a more variable process. Yet we expect that the *need* for effective leadership will actually increase. As discussed in the following section, many of the changes noted in Table 7.1 suggest that common substitutes for leadership will be less prevalent in future work situations. Thus a critical challenge for future leaders may well be to compensate for changes in organizations, tasks, and workers, even though the social complexity created by such changes makes it more difficult for leaders to provide the type of "influence increment" (Katz & Kahn, 1978) normally expected of effective leaders. In addition, rather than compensating through increasing task- or relationship-oriented behaviors, future leaders may have to adopt more indirect approaches (Day & Lord, 1988) that attempt to change subordinate cognitive structures, group functioning, or contextual variables.

Substitutes for Leadership

This section reviews one of the classic leadership theories, the substitutes-for-leadership theory, developed by Kerr (1977) and Kerr and Jermier (1978). This theory depicts effective leadership as one of several factors that can promote high levels of subordinate performance. We discuss the applicability of Kerr and Jermier's theory in light of the trends identified in Table 7.1. Further, in Table 7.2, we try to show how changes that reduce substitutes can be responded to in two very different ways as leaders attempt to maintain high levels of performance. *Direct responses* are traditional, leader-centered responses such as increasing task- or relationship-oriented leadership behaviors. Here we essentially apply the logic of Kerr and Jermier's theory in reverse, suggesting that where future trends reduce leadership substitutes, leaders can respond by increasing the type of behavior associated with that substitute. *Indirect responses* involve changing processes in subordinates, groups, organizations, or tasks that can also substitute for leadership behavior. These approaches are indirect because the leader is operating through some other mechanism to address critical needs. Indirect responses are often distributed over time or people, rather than being focused in some specific leader action. Often the specific context will determine whether direct or indirect leadership approaches are more effective in producing high performance.

Table 7.2. Reasons for and Direct and Indirect Responses to Reduced Substitutes for Leadership.

Source of Substitute	Reason*	Direct Response	Indirect Response
Subordinate Characteristics			
1. Ability, experience, training, or knowledge	1, 2, 5, 6	Mentoring, job assignments, feedback processes	Encouraging continuous learning through value activation and activating possible selves
2. Need for independence	1, 6	Encouraging feedback-seeking	Controlling cognition and understanding affective responses
Task Characteristics			
3. Unambiguous and routine	1, 2, 6	Encouraging feedback-seeking	Managing meaning by developing relevant cognitive structures
4. Methodologically invariant	1, 2, 6	Providing empowerment and supportive leadership	
5. Providing accomplishment feedback	3, 4, 5, 6	Integrating multiple views of performance	
Organizational Characteristics			
6. Formalized plans, goals, and responsibility	1, 2, 4, 5, 6, 7		Activating values and identities consistent with organization
7. Inflexible rules and procedures	1, 2, 4, 5, 6, 7		Activating values consistent with organization
8. Cohesive work groups	6, 7		Building collective identities that include demographically and culturally diverse groups
9. Spatial distance between superior and subordinate	1, 2, 4, 5, 6	Building up self-esteem and self-efficacy	

*Refer to Table 7.1.

The substitutes-for-leadership theory posits that several individual, task, and organizational characteristics could make leadership behaviors useless or unnecessary to produce effective subordinate performance (Kerr, 1977; Kerr & Jermier, 1978). Past research (for example, Howell & Dorfman, 1981) has provided mixed results as to the validity of the theory; yet a recent meta-analysis has shown that substitutes explain more variance in work outcomes than do leadership behaviors (Podsakoff, MacKenzie, & Bommer, 1996). For example, Podsakoff and colleagues found that substitutes for leadership explained 20.2 percent of the variance across ten criterion variables (such as organizational commitment, satisfaction, and role conflict), almost three times the variance that leader behaviors explained. The substitute variables had a greater effect than leadership behavior on all of the criterion variables in the meta-analysis, except for in-role performance; for in-role performance, leader behaviors had a stronger relationship to performance than any of the substitutes for leadership.

These findings do not lessen the importance of leadership in organizations, however. Podsakoff, MacKenzie, and Bommer (1996) explain that leaders affect subordinate and organizational outcomes by direct means (that is, by leader behaviors) and by indirect means (by constructing the work environment). Leaders therefore help create these substitutes for leadership within the organization. Other research makes a similar point, arguing that there are many indirect means by which leaders can affect work unit or organizational performance (Day & Lord, 1988; Lord & Maher, 1991). For example, indirect activities of leaders may change the processes in subordinates that generate behavior rather than directly influencing behavior. That is, leaders may change cognitive structures such as values, identities, possible selves, and self-efficacy, which in turn have profound effects on subordinate behavior. The following coverage of changes in subordinate, task, and organizational characteristics ties Table 7.1 trends to both direct and indirect leadership responses.

Subordinate Characteristics

A subordinate's ability, experience, training, knowledge, and need for independence can act as substitutes for leadership. The way work is now being organized, the design of jobs, and the meaning of performance, however, reduce the role of substitutes for leadership as a means to influence subordinate performance. Jobs have become more complex and unstable; they are requiring more or different knowledge, skills, and abilities (Table 7.1, point 1), and fewer people are sharing the same job elements (point 2). Because of these work trends, highly specialized workers may find it difficult to adjust to new and varied task demands. Also, performance is becoming increasingly defined by continuous learning or self-directed learning rather than relying on past training and experience (point 5). Leaders may provide the motivation and the mechanisms for subordinates to apply their specific skills to the job, as well as the encouragement needed for continuous learning to meet changing job demands (point 6).

Because many jobs are moving to team-based rather than individual-based work (point 1), a subordinate's need for independence may actually be a drawback. This change brings forth many initial problems, such as interpersonal conflicts, role ambiguity, task ambiguity, and so on. Team leaders are likely to reduce and eliminate some of the social and task problems that are less prevalent in individual-based work (point 6). Leaders may enable their subordinates to control cognitions and to understand affective responses that influence perceptions and subsequently affect performance.

Task Characteristics

The structure of job tasks is another substitute for leadership. Three types of structured tasks (unambiguous and routine tasks, methodologically invariant tasks, and tasks that provide feedback) serve as leadership replacements in the work setting. These types of structured tasks are becoming less common, however. First, because jobs are becoming less stable (Table 7.1, point 2) and involve more team-based work (point 1), job tasks are more likely to be ambiguous and nonroutine. The role of the leader is not necessarily to control the team, but rather to provide techniques for managing meaning (Gioia, Thomas, Clark, & Chittipeddi, 1994) and knowledge that lead to effective solutions and performance (point 6).

Second, methodologically invariant tasks are ones in which there is a high degree of control due to standardization, mechanization, or serial interdependence (Kerr & Jermier, 1978). As mentioned earlier, team-based work (point 1), less stable jobs, and fewer common job elements between people (point 2) lead to an environment in which workers have less individual control. In this case, the leader may need to exert supportive leadership (such as support for self-worth) and empowerment (such as negotiating latitude in decision making) to increase subordinate perceptions of control, which can have favorable effects on performance and satisfaction (Keller & Dansereau, 1995).

Third, tasks that provide their own feedback on accomplishments would reduce the need for a leader to give performance feedback. Yet several new factors complicate the feedback process. For example, technological advances have made it more difficult to separate individual performance from technological contributions (point 3), which interferes with immediate, clear, and accurate feedback. (See Hesketh & Neal, Chapter Two, this volume, for a discussion of ways to separate the individual and technology components of performance.) Also, performance standards have begun to incorporate multiple contingencies. Current trends show that both external and internal clients' definitions of performance are important (point 4). (See Bowen & Waldman, Chapter Six, this volume, for a discussion of customer-driven employee performance.) Different cultural views of good performance can also hinder the feedback process (point 5). Conflicting cultural definitions of performance standards can make it challenging for workers to know exactly how well or how poorly they are doing. Leaders are therefore necessary to provide the appropriate feedback, which integrates the performance standards of multiple constituencies (point 6).

One particularly important substitute involves the ability of teams to exert self-leadership through self-observation, goal setting, and self-rewards (Neck, Stewart, & Manz, 1996). In such cases, teams essentially set up control systems that manage their own activities. Manz and Sims (1980) see the self-management construct as another substitute for leadership; we believe, however, that leaders need to socialize acceptance of organizational values and identities for self-leadership to contribute to organizational objectives. We would argue that this involves indirect leadership.

Organizational Characteristics

Several characteristics of the organization can serve as substitutes for leadership. Organizations with a high degree of formalization and inflexibility, with closely knit work groups, and with spatial distance between supervisor and subordinate may not require the same level of leadership as other organizations with similar performance levels. Formalization and inflexibility within organizations provide clear direction for the organization as well as for the workers. Specific goals, plans, responsibilities, rules, and procedures provide a highly structured environment for workers. Yet, as noted in Table 7.1, team-based work (point 1), the instability and complexity of jobs (point 2), and the changing meaning of performance standards (points 4 and 5) make it harder for modern workers to translate formal goals and inflexible procedures into appropriate action. Effective management of organizational identities (Dutton, Dukerich, & Harquail, 1994; Gioia & Thomas, 1996) is one indirect means to address these problems.

The increase in the number of part-time, temporary, and work-at-home employees creates another concern for organizations (point 7). These workers may perceive less organizational support and have less organizational commitment than full-time workers. (See Hulin & Glomb, Chapter Four, this volume, for a discussion of contingent employees.) The leader, therefore, can increase perceptions of organizational support by taking an active role in the socialization process, explaining policies and procedures, and helping workers see the link between organizational policies and appropriate actions (point 6). One way in which leaders may do this is by activating values within subordinates that are consistent with organizational culture. Another way that leaders may tie organizational policies to actions is by changing the individual- or group-level processing structures and dynamics that generate behavior (Lord & Engle, 1996).

Closely knit, cohesive work groups may be hindered by the existence of part-time and temporary workers (point 7). Also, a more diverse workforce may influence work group cohesiveness, which can affect organizational outcomes. For example, research (such as O'Reilly, Caldwell, & Barnett, 1989) suggests that individuals in heterogeneous and less socially integrated groups experience greater turnover. Therefore, the leader's responsibility may be to provide a sense of cohesiveness and structure through affective and cognitive means (point 6). Leaders may do this by activating collective identities that make the "we" perspective more salient (Brewer & Gardner, 1996).

Spatial distance between superiors and subordinates increases the amount of autonomy, independence, and reliance on one's own skills and abilities on behalf of the subordinate. When, however, tasks are varied and nonroutine, require new or underutilized skills and abilities (points 1 and 2), and do not provide clear feedback on performance (points 4 and 5), leadership is crucial. Instead of superiors and subordinates being physically close, it may be more important for the leader to promote psychological closeness through activating knowledge structures and identities that build up self-esteem and self-efficacy (Eden, 1992) within the worker (point 6).

In short, as shown in Table 7.1, there are many trends that should make substitutes less prevalent for future leaders. These trends, however, will not necessarily return us to a situation in which increasing task- or relationship-oriented leadership activities (Schriesheim & Kerr, 1974) are the most appropriate response to ensure high performance. Nor can these trends be addressed merely by advocating the most currently popular leadership style—transformational leadership behavior (Bass & Avolio, 1989). Where direct leadership approaches are required, the need is likely to be for flexibility (Hall et al., 1998) rather than for a particular type of leadership. For many trends, however, more indirect types of leadership may be more appropriate responses.

Potential Problems in Influencing Subordinate Performance

To summarize our argument, we have asserted that leadership should be reconceptualized as an emergent social process, that the locus of leadership will shift away from supervisors to broader networks of individuals, that the need for effective leadership will increase due to reduced substitutes for leadership, and that many important leadership activities will involve indirect rather than direct leadership.

These trends present several problems for leaders. First, changing aspects of subordinates that generate behavior (such as schemas or possible selves) is much more difficult than changing behavior, because the former is much less salient, less observable, and will change more slowly than behaviors (Argyris, 1976). Second, the effect of such changes on important organizational processes (motivation, learning, performance) is also less observable and therefore harder to evaluate. Many of the cognitive and affective structures involved may operate automatically and are normally outside of conscious awareness for both subordinates and supervisors. Consequently, recognizing the need for change or determining whether change has occurred may be more difficult. A third problem is that because both the activities and the outcomes of such changes are distributed over time, their causal impact is difficult to evaluate (Lord & Maher, 1991). Leaders who emphasize such indirect means to produce effective subordinates may not be seen by others as exhibiting leadership as it is typically defined. Thus it is less likely that they will be seen as effective leaders, which in turn limits their potential influence on subordinates (see, for example, Hollander & Offermann, 1990). Fourth, these perceptual issues are compounded in more diverse workforces, where gender, racial, ethnic, and cultural differences may produce varied ideas of what effective leaders should be like. A further complication is that demographic diversity in leaders will increase the variability in leadership styles (Eagly & Johnson, 1990).

In short, future leaders must be concerned with two critical issues: What things should they do to produce more effective subordinates, and how will they get subordinates to accept such influence from individuals who use less directive, assertive leadership styles? Our answer to both questions involves a deeper understanding of the cognitive-affective-social processes identified in Figure 7.1. Many of the factors that facilitate subordinate motivation and development (such as perceptions of social justice, identification with leaders, and positive affective relations) may also serve as a basis to legitimize a leader and increase his or her potential influence.

Using the Model to Affect Subordinate Performance

We turn now to a closer examination of the model shown in Figure 7.1 and its potential use in responding to changes that will confront future leaders. In the following sections we discuss each major component of the model, focusing on its value to leaders as

it suggests ways to affect subordinate performance while also enhancing subordinates' perceptions of leaders.

Cognitions and Performance

The cognitive construct in our model encompasses many different
topics and processes, but one critical factor in determining subordinate performance is their beliefs about their own capabilities.
Performance is often limited as much by beliefs about what we can
do than by our actual ability.

Self-Perceptions and Performance

Bandura (1991) has extensively studied the role of self-efficacy in
regulating goals and performance, and Eden's work on leadership
(1992) shows that leaders' expectations regarding subordinate capabilities significantly affect performance. The point we want to
stress here, however, is that such "self-views" of subordinates do not
exist in isolation but instead are parts of more aggregate cognitive
structures concerned with self-identities. We begin with a brief ex-
planation of self-identities and then illustrate how influencing self-
identities is one means by which leaders can have a profound
impact on subordinate performance.

As with roles, we have multiple self-identities; all of them may
not be activated at the same time, however. In fact, Martindale
(1980, 1981) suggests that activation of one self-identity may inhibit
the activation of other self-identities. Self-identities are chosen on
the basis of our values and needs (Carver & Scheier, 1981, 1990;
Cropanzano, James, & Citera, 1993) and based on social processes
that often involve organizational leaders (Freiberg & Lord, 1996).
Self-identities serve to direct our actions toward attaining a specific
goal. For example, if one sees oneself as a high-performing employee, this self-identity can lead to many specific task goals. These
goals in turn produce explicit and implicit self-regulatory processes
(Austin & Vancouver, 1996; Klein, 1989; Lord & Levy, 1994) that
keep performance on these tasks above the standards implied by
one's self-identity.

Self-identities are also important to consider because they constrain future possible selves, which are one's beliefs and expectations
for future behavior (Markus & Nurius, 1986; Markus & Ruvolo,

1989). Future possible selves provide the motivation toward new growth in creating other self-identities. For example, individuals who see their future possible selves as leaders may be more likely to seek out leadership positions or activities than individuals who do not see their future possible selves as leaders.

Self-identities and future possible selves are reciprocally related, and both influence current work and social activities, as well as their interpretation. An implication of this perspective is that leaders can influence their subordinates' social experiences by providing them with tasks and encouragement that develop self-schema within particular domains and, in turn, activate self-identities that will motivate individuals toward goal accomplishment. Because the meaning of work is becoming more heterogeneous due to less identification with jobs or organizations (such as with part-time and temporary workers), leaders cannot rely on motivating employees at the task level. Instead, one alternative strategy to motivate employees toward performance is to activate a higher level construct that encompasses multiple tasks. According to Cropanzano and colleagues (1993), this is one function of self-identities.

While development of higher level identities may first seem like a daunting task for leaders, we suggest that it is often a normal outcome of high-quality leader-subordinate interactions. Bauer and Green (1996) have suggested that the development of leader-member exchange is based on a three-level trust cycle in which leaders first develop expectations that subordinates will perform effectively (the cognitive level); then, based on these expectations, they delegate key tasks to subordinates (the behavioral level); and finally, they develop positive affective bonds when this trust is confirmed (the emotional level). Such processes have self-assessment and self-verification value to subordinates, particularly new employees, who may be uncertain about their organizational identity or their worth to a particular work group. Over time such trust cycles may lead subordinates to identify with leaders or other in-group members, providing a social basis for one's organizational identity (Freiberg & Lord, 1996). If this cycle is repeated with multiple tasks, as is likely for effective and dedicated employees who have high-quality exchange relationships, multiple tasks and competencies would become organized in terms of this self-identity as a trusted, competent, liked, and perhaps privileged work group member.

Linking multiple work tasks to self-identities has both short-run and long-run consequences. In the short run, increased job satisfaction, self-worth, self-esteem, and sense of ownership are likely. An important long-run consequence is that future possible selves are affected. Activating the appropriate self-identity can encourage a person to reconceptualize their beliefs and expectations about the self and may spark a new desire for learning and skill development in a particular area. These individuals may also be more persistent in the face of failure. Individuals who perform tasks that are not linked to an activated self-identity are more likely to become discouraged and quit in the face of temporary failure (Lips, 1995).

Skill Development and Use and Performance

An important trend in modern organizations is that effective performance is becoming increasingly dependent on what workers know. Terms such as *knowledge workers* and practices such as "pay for skills" reflect such changes. These trends make the use and development of knowledge critical determinants of performance. Similarly, managing development and use of knowledge is an increasingly important requirement of effective leadership.

Future pressures to manage skill development effectively are likely to come from a variety of sources: competitive advantages are likely to be increasingly dependent on utilizing advanced technologies, major growth in the labor force is likely to come from less skilled workers (Jackson et al., 1993), and technology-based training approaches (such as Web sites and computer-based software) will be used to control costs of training programs and make them more convenient for workers. Coupled with these trends are recent advances in our understanding of skill development and application (Anderson, 1987; Van Lehn, 1996). This research shows that the highest levels of skill require extensive, domain-specific practice involving thousands of hours. Skills are very domain specific, and training procedures that speed training may not enhance retention or generalization from training to job situations (Schmidt & Bjork, 1992). These findings suggest that technological fixes are not going to supplant on-the-job learning as a means of skill development. Thus most learning will occur in the same situations as task performance, and learning will be intermixed with performance. Leaders must therefore structure work situations to facilitate both learning and performance. To address the dual and sometimes conflicting requirements of effective task performance and continued learning, leaders must allow subordinates the freedom to experiment and learn from errors (Frese & Zapf, 1994), and they should encourage mastery rather than performance-learning orientations where high degrees of context-specific skill are required.

Appropriate use of existing skills is likely to be another critical issue in achieving high levels of performance. Needed skills for a work group may be distributed more widely over subordinates as demographic diversity increases heterogeneity in skills. Matching employee skills to task requirements then becomes both more critical to gaining the benefits of heterogeneity (Jackson et al., 1993) and more difficult as tasks become more diverse and short-term. This issue is also likely to be affectively charged because subordinate self-enhancement motivations (Banaji & Prentice, 1994) are likely to bias subordinate's self-assessment of their own skills. Limited feedback-seeking, particularly by more experienced workers (Ashford, 1989), may also limit self-assessment in critical skill areas, although stressing mastery rather than performance goals may enhance feedback-seeking (Van de Walle & Cummings, 1997). Further, to the extent that critical skills are unequally distributed across demographically diverse groups (gender, race, ethnicity, and particularly age), task assignments based on skill levels may be misperceived as reflecting various demographic biases or lack of procedural justice. Leaders need to be aware, then, that task assignment is an affective as well as a cognitive issue that has impacts on self-identities and skill development, as well as on short-term performance.

Diversity and Performance

One critical aspect of cognitive structures is the extent to which they are shared among members of a work group or team. Differences in task-related schemas (such as problem spaces and mental maps) can be a critical source of communication and coordination problems that limit group or team performance. Yet such differences in schemas can also increase the heterogeneity of resources available to a group, potentially increasing performance. Differences in more general schemas, such as self-identities or stereotypes, can have a broader impact on performance through their effects on social and motivational processes.

According to Markus (1977), cognitive schemas develop from experience. Individuals, with different demographic and cultural backgrounds are likely to have very different schemas, which they automatically apply to simplify work situations. One might therefore expect that the increasing trend toward diverse work groups would create a critical challenge for future leaders who must maintain high levels of performance in spite of the heterogeneity in cognitive schemas among their workers.

Maintaining high performance among diverse work groups is complicated by the fact that the effects of diversity can occur at multiple levels of aggregation. Research indicates that heterogeneous organizations, work groups, or units show greater incidence of turnover (Jackson et al., 1991; McCain, O'Reilly, & Pfeffer, 1983; Pfeffer & O'Reilly, 1987; Wagner, Pfeffer, & O'Reilly, 1984) are less socially integrated (O'Reilly et al., 1989) and communicate less often (Zenger & Lawrence, 1989) than homogeneous groups. At the cross-level of analysis, Tsui, Egan, and O'Reilly (1992) found that sexually and racially heterogenous groups were negatively related to individual psychological commitment and intent to stay with the organization, and positively related to absenteeism. At the dyad level, Tsui and O'Reilly (1989) found that differences between the supervisor and subordinate in sex, race, education level, and job tenure had significant influences on outcome variables (such as performance ratings, liking, role ambiguity, and role conflict). And at the individual level, individuals who are dissimilar from organizational members are more likely to leave (Jackson et al., 1991; O'Reilly et al., 1989; Wagner et al., 1984).

Such difficulties may reflect a number of interrelated processes associated with diversity. On a superficial level, they may merely reflect difficulties in communication and interpretation of situations stemming from different experiences and backgrounds. In such cases, leaders can improve performance by facilitating communication and by creating common understanding and shared problem spaces (Lord, 1976). Socialization processes and immersion in a common organizational culture also will, in time, help to overcome such negative aspects of heterogeneity by creating shared cognitive schemas.

The negative effects of diversity may also stem from the effects of various prejudices associated with ethnic, racial, or gender differences. Prejudice is often based on stereotypes, which are automatically activated (Brewer, 1989; Fiske & Neuberg, 1990; Devine, 1989; Greenwald & Banaji, 1995) and serve to simplify information processing (Macrae, Milne, & Bodenhausen, 1994). These processes allow individuals to rely on information in cognitive categories rather than integrating new information with existing beliefs (Hamilton & Sherman, 1994). Thus, biased perceptions (Banaji & Greenwald, 1995), self-limiting and self-fulfilling behaviors (Heilman, 1983), and prejudice (Devine, 1989) may all result from cognitive structures that simplify information processing for perceivers.

Demographically indexed cognitive structures may also be a basis for collective identities (Brewer & Gardner, 1996), which creates an additional consequence of increased diversity. For example, social identities (Banaji & Prentice, 1994; Turner, Oakes, Haslam, & McGarty, 1994) often depend on demographic similarity. As diversity increases among workers within an organization, different social identities are likely to exist (such as whites versus blacks). These social identities can lead to biases in favor of the in-group and against the out-group (Billig & Tajfel, 1973; Tajfel, 1970; Tajfel, Flament, Billig, & Bundy, 1971). One means to address this issue is to change the level of aggregation at which the self is defined. Brewer and Gardner (1996) note that the self can be defined at three levels of aggregation: group (collective), interpersonal (relational), or individual (personal). Leaders may be effective at changing the level of aggregation at which individuals view themselves or with which they identify; moving to a relational or personal level of aggregation may negate potential in-group and out-group biases. Also, expanding the social identification process to a much higher level (such as organizational versus work group) may lead to bias against other organizations, which serves as healthy competition, rather than out-groups being within the organization.

In sum, many social-cognitive processes associated with diversity can substantially affect individual and group processes, thereby limiting individual and group performance. Future leaders must take several actions to avoid these detrimental effects of diversity. They must be especially mindful of processes such as categorization and stereotyping and social-cultural identification in order to promote appropriate change (Di Tomaso & Hooijberg, 1996). Diversity also requires the leader to play an active role in changing mental structures such as stereotypes or categories, social identities (Di Tomaso & Hooijberg, 1996), and self-schemas so that self-limiting behaviors are eliminated. The leader may be required to help workers develop or revise categories and stereotypes to maximize rather than limit other people's performance.

To ensure high levels of performance, leaders must not only manage social-cognitive processes within diverse workgroups, but they must also provide motivation that is appropriate for each individual's gender, age, ethnicity or race, and culture. For example, offering rewards that benefit the group rather than the individual may be more appropriate for individuals of cultures that emphasize collectivism rather than individualism (see Kitayama, Markus, Matsumoto, & Norasakkunkit, 1997; Markus & Kitayama, 1991).

Performance in Multinational Corporations

The problems in managing diversity that we have just discussed are compounded in multinational corporations, where managers and subordinates often come from different cultures. Here, not only may cognitive differences be more extreme than already discussed, but they may also be reinforced by very different cultural values, different past work experiences, and different scripts and categories (Shaw, 1990). As a consequence, social processes will require more controlled processing because familiar categories and scripts often do not fit social stimuli or situations. This cognitive strain is often accompanied by affective strain associated with uncertainty, unfulfilled expectations, and different views of procedural justice.

Leaders in multinational corporations must be sensitive to and adjust to such differences to sustain high levels of performance. Leaders operating within a foreign culture may face the most severe challenge because the leadership skills they have developed through experience may not generalize to new cultures with different leadership prototypes (Gerstner & Day, 1994; O'Connell et al., 1990). Leaders who are operating in their home country but who have expatriate subordinates face different problems. Here leadership activities may need to be tailored to expectations of particular individuals, yet leaders must also recognize the need to be perceived as being fair to all groups of workers. One potential solution to such problems that is advocated by Graen (1997) is to select and train "transculturals" as leaders. Transculturals are individuals who can transcend cultural differences and bring together individuals from diverse backgrounds.

Cultural differences may be particularly important in considering the indirect leadership activities stressed in this chapter. For example, a leader might attempt to engage the self-identity of subordinates as a means to motivate an individual. Markus and Kitayama (1991), however, note that Western and Asian cultures have very different construals of the self, others, and the relation of oneself to others. Western cultures stress an *independent* view of the self that involves attending to the self, awareness of differences from others, and asserting the self; Asian cultures, in contrast, emphasize an *interdependent* view based on fitting in with others and creating harmonious interdependence with them. These very different self systems will create a very different basis for social interactions and emergent leadership processes. For example, an interdependent view of self would make fulfilling other group members' needs, desires, and goals much more important than would an independent-self view in fostering leadership perceptions. Explanations for causality in interdependent as compared to independent self-construals would be more likely to be in group rather than individual processes (reducing the credit given to leaders), and feedback processes may have very different functions. Social comparisons and reflected appraisals are likely to be more critical for developing an independent self-view, whereas relations with others may be more critical to interdependent self-views. Understanding the implications of such differences for individual and team performance will be an increasingly important challenge for future leaders.

Affect and Performance

The model in Figure 7.1 emphasizes affective as well as cognitive factors associated with leadership. Affect can have many effects on social processes, but we think that three affective issues are particularly important for understanding the impacts that social processes can have on both job performance and leadership perceptions: social justice, employee identification with leaders, and affect as a surrogate for performance.

Social Justice and Performance

Social justice perceptions have many important effects on organizational outcomes, and they can be viewed as pertaining to both distributive and procedural issues (Greenberg, 1987). If future organizations are characterized by more diversity, less standard jobs, more temporary jobs, more frequent changes, multinational work sites, and altered compensation principles such as pay for skills, social justice concerns may be particularly important for leaders to manage effectively. Greenberg's work (1987, 1988, 1990) shows that perceptions of social justice can have impacts on motivational determinants of job performance. Social justice also affects subordinates' perceptions of and identification with leaders (Tyler, 1997). Maintaining high levels of perceived leadership allows leaders to have greater influence over many potential determinants of performance. Because this latter consequence of social justice has not been thoroughly considered in the leadership literature, we focus on it here.

Tyler and Lind (1992) note that procedural justice may be more critical to establishing authority- or legitimacy-based relationships because it is seen as enduring, whereas outcomes associated with distributive justice are one-time events. Tyler and Lind stress that people are sensitive to procedural issues because they symbolize the value of an individual to their group. People also look to groups for information on worth or self-identity (Turner et al., 1994), which is conveyed by information regarding their position in a group. Such relational issues are likely to be particularly important to future workers who will have to function in a more fragmented, heterogenous, and short-term work context.

Perceptions of procedural justice are closely tied to how leaders behave and are perceived by others. On the basis of Tyler and Lind's relational model (1992, p. 159), we expect that leaders can establish perceptions of procedural justice by focusing on three issues: trust, standing, and neutrality. *Trust* is engendered by conveying concern for both the needs and the views of other employees. With a more diverse workforce, leaders must be sensitive to the varied needs and views of potential employees. *Standing* depends on interactional factors such as politeness, respecting the dignity of others, and recognizing their rights. *Neutrality* is based on an absence of bias or prejudice, on honesty, and on fact-based as opposed to opinion-based decision making. Diversity issues, openness, and decision-making style may thus have important procedural justice implications for future leaders attempting to establish neutrality.

Our suggestion, then, is that future leaders will need to pay particular attention to these procedural justice issues as a means of establishing an employee's value in a group, which then legitimizes the leader's authority and, in turn, engenders voluntary compliance on the part of employees (Tyler, 1997). Influence based on legitimacy may be particularly important when workers are at different sites than their superiors, or when they work at home or at different hours than their supervisors. In such cases, direct monitoring of behavior (Komaki, 1986) may not be possible for leaders. Procedural justice issues may also be critical in developing a basis for identification with a leader, an additional affectively related issue that is critical for developing future leaders.

Leader-Member Exchange and Performance

It is widely recognized that an important component of management activity is the establishment and maintenance of organizational paradigms through symbolic activities (Gioia et al., 1994; Pfeffer, 1981). Equally important are the symbolic activities of leaders that help establish collective identities (Banaji & Prentice, 1994; Dutton et al., 1994; Gioia & Thomas, 1996; Turner et al., 1994). Identities vary in level of aggregation from *personal identities,* which are self-categorizations based on perceived similarities and differences with other individuals, to *social identities,* which are based on perceived similarities and differences with groups or social categories (Banaji & Prentice, 1994; Brewer & Gardner, 1996). Freiberg and Lord (1996) suggest that a leader's symbolic activities can engage either the personal or the social identities of subordinates, having very different consequences in a number of areas. For example, they suggest that transactional leaders emphasize personal identities and instrumental exchanges. Such leadership increases the salience of distributive justice issues. In contrast, transformational leadership is much more likely to engage social self-identities by emphasizing membership in common groups and enhancing the importance of procedural justice concerns. Thus the symbolic activities of leaders can alter subordinates' working self-identities

(Markus & Wurf, 1987) and the basis for evaluating social justice. For example, in a review of several studies, Tyler (1997) reports that when individuals identify with leaders or adopt collective identities, relational justice issues become more important relative to instrumental justice concerns.

We suspect that future leaders need to be aware of these different possibilities, to understand whether their organizational context or their personal style is oriented toward engaging the personal or social identities of followers, as well as whether personal or social identities are most salient for subordinates. Mismatches in terms of type of identity emphasized (such as leaders emphasizing personal identities when organizations or individuals stress social identities) may be one critical source of low performance, poor communication, and low levels of leader-member exchange. Such mismatches are particularly likely when leaders come from different cultures than subordinates or organizations, because Western cultures tend to emphasize personal identities but Eastern cultures stress social and collective identities (Kitayama et al., 1997).

Many of the trends identified in Table 7.1 (such as diversity, temporary work, home-based work, shorter careers) will make social identities harder to establish in work situations, while other trends (such as greater team orientation and increasingly frequent change) may make social identities critical for effective organizational functioning. As well as having impacts on performance, "identity management" by leaders would also have important affective consequences for workers, because self-identities are ubiquitous and affectively oriented processing structures (Banaji & Prentice, 1994; Markus & Wurf, 1987). Thus we believe that leaders of the future need to move beyond concerns with issues such as whether their behavior style is transformational or transactional, and pay more attention to how it is symbolically interpreted by followers. Symbolic interpretation in turn depends on which aspects of follower identities are salient and which aspects are engaged by a leader's activities (Cropanzano et al., 1993). Together, subordinates' identities and leaders' activities activate the processing structures and dynamics that generate behavior. Thus they are fundamental determinants of performance.

Affect as a Surrogate for Performance

Research on leader-member exchange shows that early affective reactions predict the subsequent quality of exchanges (Liden, Wayne, & Stilwell, 1993). The importance of affect stems from two factors. First, affect may be a surrogate for performance evaluation. Social perceptions always have a substantial affective component, which is often less dependent on attentional resources than more symbolically based cognitions are (Srull & Wyer, 1989). Typically, perceivers form on-line affective evaluations of others and may use these general affective summaries as surrogates for performance assessments (Robbins & De Nisi, 1994). Thus performance information may have its effect on leader-member exchange quality through the affective reactions (liking) of dyadic partners (Wayne & Ferris, 1990). This view is also consistent with the previously described trust cycle (Bauer & Green, 1996) involving high performance expectations, delegation, and affective reactions.

Affect is also important because it may result from engaging the self-identity of followers. Many studies show that perceived similarity is positively associated with liking and leader-member exchange quality (Engle & Lord, 1997; Liden et al., 1993; Pulakos & Wexley, 1983; Turban & Jones, 1988; Turban, Jones, & Rozelle, 1990). One plausible interpretation of such findings is that perceived similarity leads individuals to identify with the other dyadic member and produces an affective reaction that directly affects social relationships (Greenwald & Banaji, 1995; Tyler, 1997). This process is particularly likely for individuals who see themselves as high performers and on this basis may see themselves as being similar to other high-performing individuals in a work group.

We suspect that leaders (or followers) are not very sensitive to whether affective reactions stem from prior performance levels or from other factors such as perceived similarity. Given the pervasive effects of perceived similarity on social relations and the expected diversity in future workforces, leaders need to be especially sensitive to this potential basis for affective bonds and its potential to influence the nature of leader-member exchanges. To be seen as procedurally just and to be fair to dissimilar employees, future leaders need to be particularly careful to include dissimilar others in in-groups. They also need to differentiate between affective reactions that are based on organizational performance of subordinates and affective reactions based on job-irrelevant demographic characteristics.

Social Processes and Performance

Performance in work groups is often seen as being determined by the group's technology, the distribution of resources among group members (group composition), and the interpersonal processes involved in transforming individual abilities into work outcomes. A critical determinant of performance is whether social processes create "process losses" or "process gains" (Steiner, 1972). The model of leadership in Figure 7.1 places social perceptions as the critical mediator linking affect and cognitions to outcomes such as performance, because we see social perceptions as an important source of process gains or losses, and also because leadership is a social perception process. Effectively managing social perceptions is particularly challenging to leaders because perceptions can have both an implicit and an explicit basis, and because implicit processes may be ignored due to their lower salience. Effects of social processes can also be compounded over time through dynamic processes.

Implicit Processes

Social perception can be largely an implicit process when the individual being perceived is a close match to schemas that are highly available to perceivers. Such implicit processes are particularly important in work situations because they are not disrupted by the cognitive load produced by work tasks. Further, many processes that are typically considered to be explicit and effortful can also be accomplished implicitly. For example, with little careful analysis, attributions may be made to salient sources such as people rather than situations (Lord, 1995; Taylor & Fiske, 1978); as discussed earlier, performance evaluations may be automatically incorporated into evaluative reactions to others (Robbins & De Nisi, 1994); leadership perceptions may be based on a relatively automatic matching of target characteristics and behaviors to categories held by perceivers (Lord & Maher, 1991); and impression management may be an inherent aspect of most social interactions that occurs with or without awareness (Schlenker & Weigold, 1992). Much of what people know about these aspects of social behavior may also have been learned implicitly (Seger, 1994).

Because such processes are implicit, their operation and consequences are likely to be misunderstood. For example, stereotypes (Greenwald & Banaji, 1995), implicit leadership theories (Rush, Thomas, & Lord, 1977), misattribution of causes to actors rather than situations (Gilbert & Malone, 1995), on-line evaluative impression formation (Srull & Wyer, 1989), and image management (Schlenker & Weigold, 1992) may all have effects on social processes that people deny have occurred or that they explain with more rational, effortful processing. We expect that understanding and managing such processes is likely to be particularly challenging to future leaders.

Explicit Processes

Explicit social processes, in contrast, often are consciously regulated or are the focus of explicit organizational policy or training procedures. For example, when outcomes are negative or unexpected, such as when an employee performs poorly, we may think very carefully about potential causes (Wong & Weiner, 1981). Formal performance appraisal may be supported by interventions such as frame-of-reference training. Similarly, we may pay explicit attention to extreme affective reactions that we experience, and we may consciously attempt to manage the affective reactions of others by many impression-management techniques.

Though such explicit social processing is common, it is not likely to be typical. Because explicit processes are better encoded, however, and therefore more easily retrieved than implicit processes, they are likely to be overrepresented in organizational members' understanding of social processes. Our point, then, is simply that commonsense interpretations of social processes, though not wrong, reflect an unrepresentative sampling of social processes. Consequently, interventions based on these commonsense interpretations are not likely to be effective as bases for altering leadership or subordinate performance processes. Our approach to this problem has been to try to broaden the perspective applied to leadership as a means to suggest alternatives that may be more effective in addressing the challenges that are likely to confront future leaders.

Dynamic Processes

Although implicit and explicit processes can be viewed separately, in reality they interrelate over time. An important aspect of the model shown in Figure 7.1 that we have avoided until now is the effects of time. Time can be incorporated into mathematical models of social processes (Nowak & Lewenstein, 1994) and leadership perceptions (Hanges et al., 1997), but for our purposes it is sufficient to distinguish between short-term and long-term effects. Short-term effects can be roughly equated with salient expectations held in working memory. Directive, task-oriented leadership behaviors typically have short-term effects. Long-terms effects occur by the aggregations of these short-term effects into cognitive structures such as schemas.

Short-term effects are easier to conceptualize and assess empirically, but many social processes may have dramatic effects only when cumulated over time. For example, biases against females as leaders have been well documented (such as Eagly & Karau, 1992) and may stem in part from the closer correspondence of leadership prototypes to typical male characteristics than to typical female characteristics (Goktepe & Schneider, 1989; Hall et al., 1998; Heilman, Block, Martell, & Simon, 1989; Lord, De Vader, & Alliger, 1986; Mann, 1959). Yet these effects are typically small when one adopts a short-run perspective. For example, Barrett and Morris (1993) note that gender typically explains between 1 and 5 percent of the variance in performance ratings. When long-run, cumulative effects are considered, however, the consequences of this gender-based leadership bias are quite different. Martell, Lane, and Emrich (1996) show that when a constant bias is applied using a tournament model for managerial promotion, the underrepresentation of female managers may be quite large, even when beginning with an equal number of male and female managers. The researchers' simulation indicates that a gender-based bias that explains only 5 percent of the variance in performance ratings accumulates through successive cycles of promotions to fill only 29 percent of the very top-level management positions with women; alternatively, a 1 percent bias yields women in 35 percent of these top-level positions (fifty of these positions were filled by women when no bias existed). Thus small biases, when cumulated through successive promotion decisions, may yield practically important effects.

Small-group research yields very similar findings. For example, in an experimental study of groups with the same number of males and females, Hall and colleagues (1998) found that gender bias explained less than 7 percent of the variance in leadership ratings, producing female emergent leaders in only 29 percent of the groups; biases explaining only 1 percent of the variance in ratings still resulted in only 32 percent of the emergent leaders being female. These results are strikingly similar to Martell and colleagues' simulation (1996).

Though we chose gender because it was a convenient example, the points we make hold for race, age, ethnicity, and other individual differences. That is, small implicit biases may cumulate over successive interactions to produce very large differences in explicit processes such as promotion or selection rates for the individuals in disadvantaged groups. Given the projected diversity in future workforces, such effects are likely to be particularly important both in creating fair employment practices and in maximizing the contribution to performance of various individual abilities.

Outcomes

Our proposed leadership model depicts an interchange of cognitive and affective factors that directly influence social perceptions and indirectly affect outcomes. As previously stated, leaders affect organizational outcomes through direct and indirect means (Day & Lord, 1988; Lord & Maher, 1991). In this section we discuss the leader's role as a change agent in subordinates' performance given the current work trends.

Task-Related Outcomes

Leaders can influence subordinates' performance through feedback, skill development, and motivation. The current work trends, however, show that feedback, skill development, and motivation may be particularly difficult for future leaders to provide. Informal feedback or formal performance evaluations have become increasingly complex for several reasons. Work that is performed within teams or off-site (such as at home) may be hard to evaluate, and separating individual contributions from a team effort or having little opportunity to monitor performance may make the evaluation process difficult for leaders. Thus, the traditional performance appraisal model in which supervisor evaluates subordinate may need revision. (See Chapter Three of this volume, by Motowidlo & Schmit, for a discussion of this issue.) Instead, a more professional evaluation model, one that uses more diverse feedback sources, such as team members and clients, may be necessary, but it may be complicated by the diversity issues noted earlier. Further, as Motowidlo and Schmit also note, leaders may need to increase attention to contextual performance as well as task performance because contextual performance is needed to support the rapidly changing technical core of future organizations.

Subordinate skill development has become more demanding for similar reasons. Subordinates may experience fewer mentorships as they become more physically isolated from their leaders. Also, the quality of these mentorships may be affected by diversity issues. For example, attitude and demographic similarities (such as level of education) between the subordinate and supervisor can affect the quality of leader-member relations (Basu & Green, 1995). The quality of exchange, in turn, has been positively linked with outcomes such as subordinate career progress (Wakabayashi & Graen, 1984; Wakabayashi, Graen, Graen, & Graen, 1988), subordinate decision influence (Scandura, Graen, & Novak, 1986), work opportunities such as boundary spanning and decision-making liaison activities (Dansereau, Graen, & Haga, 1975; Graen & Cashman, 1975; Liden & Graen, 1980), and performance and job satisfaction (Graen, Novak, & Sommerkamp, 1982). These positive effects of high-quality exchange relationships encourage and develop subordinates' skills. Yet they may be limited by diversity effects and by physical separation of leaders and subordinates.

Several potential responses are available to leaders. First, leaders may work particularly hard to establish effective training and mentoring relations in spite of the limitations just discussed. Second, they may emphasize higher-level constructs such as values and identities (Cropanzano et al., 1993; Lord & Engle, 1996) and let subordinates or groups manage their own learning, as with self-leading groups (Neck et al., 1996). The leader's role then is to activate appropriate self-identities that provide links to personal projects, goals, and specific tasks and skills (Cropanzano et al., 1993). Subordinates who are able to build paths from identities to specific performance standards to specific skill requirements are more likely to recognize skill deficiencies and direct their own learning in acquiring needed skills. Third, leaders must adopt new roles as facilitators, coaches, and developers rather than as monitors and directors of performance (London & Mone, Chapter Five, this volume). Such "facilitative leaders" share information needed for effective decisions, and stress common interests and understanding of values and assumptions that underlie behavior. (See Chapter Five for a more complete description of facilitative leadership.) Fourth, organizations are beginning to emphasize technology-based self-directed learning and skill development to supplement or replace formal training and mentorships. Leaders can provide resources and encourage these innovative approaches to learning, but they should also recognize that these approaches may be most appropriate for a select group of employees (Du Bois, Brown, Smith, & Lord, 1996; London & Mone, Chapter Five, this volume).

Finally, because of a variety of work changes, motivation may be even more of a challenge than in the past. Traditional leadership emphasizes factors such as monitoring (Komaki, 1986), goal setting (Latham & Locke, 1991), clarification of paths to goals (House, 1971), and control of rewards as means to motivate subordinates. Many factors, however, make such approaches less appropriate for future work situations. For example, teams may substitute for leaders (Neck et al., 1996), performance may be difficult to evaluate due to task complexity and variety, appropriate paths to goals may be better known to workers than to leaders, and work may occur in situations that cannot be monitored by leaders (such as part-time or at-home work). In such situations, the indirect approaches to motivation that we have already discussed may be more appropriate.

Attitudinal Outcomes

Leader behavior is also related to nontask or attitudinal outcomes such as job satisfaction (Smith, Organ, & Near, 1983), organizational citizenship behaviors (Podsakoff, MacKenzie, Moorman, & Fetter, 1990), and organizational commitment (Glisson & Durick, 1988). Job satisfaction, organizational citizenship behaviors, and organizational commitment are important because they have been positively linked to job performance (MacKenzie, Podsakoff, & Fetter, 1993;

Meyer et al., 1989; Ostroff, 1992; Petty, McGee, & Cavender, 1984), although causal processes may involve complex mediators and other distal variables (see Hulin & Glomb, Chapter Four, this volume). Job satisfaction also has been found to affect organizational citizenship behaviors (Kemery, Bedeian, & Zacur, 1996), which have been defined as positive, discretionary acts that are not formal requirements of one's job (Organ, 1988), and which have been positively linked with organizational commitment (Mathieu, 1991; Mathieu & Zajac, 1990).

Leaders can influence these nontask outcomes both directly and indirectly. For example, transactional leadership has been found to influence directly the occurrence of organizational citizenship behaviors, whereas transformational leadership, which operates through employee trust, has a mediated effect on organizational citizenship behaviors (Podsakoff et al., 1990). If leaders are successful in providing task and relational support, as identified in the earlier discussion of substitutes for leadership (see Table 7.2), then direct leader behaviors should increase the amount of subordinate job satisfaction, organizational citizenship behaviors, and organizational commitment. Conversely, indirect behaviors such as changing values and activating self-identities can have more long-term effects on these nontask outcomes. Leaders may change subordinate's values so that they are more aligned with organizational values. By doing so, appropriate self-identities should be activated that allow the subordinate to function efficiently and effectively, which in turn should increase job satisfaction and organizational commitment.

Social Outcomes

There are several social outcomes from the process we have outlined that are important for setting the stage for future performance. Processes such as leader-member exchange and self-identities can play an integral role in the development of the worker in future contexts. As discussed earlier, leaders need to be aware of their relationship with subordinates (leader-member exchange) so that leaders are able to include dissimilar individuals in in-groups. Otherwise, leaders may be perceived as procedurally unjust and experience less influence over dissimilar subordinates. Because leader-member exchange relationships can have powerful implications for outcomes such as organizational commitment (Duchon, Green, & Taber, 1986), turnover (Graen, Liden, & Hoel, 1982; Vecchio & Godbel, 1984) and performance (Graen, Novak, & Sommerkamp, 1982; Liden & Graen, 1980), leaders must be especially aware of how they treat and are perceived by each subordinate.

As emphasized throughout this chapter, leaders may have the largest impact on subordinate performance by activating self-identities. According to Brewer and Gardner (1996), people form personal, relational, and collective selves. The *personal self* is the unique individual as defined through comparisons to others. When the personal self is salient, transactional relations are likely and issues such as distributive justice and self-enhancement may be paramount. The *relational self* is dependent on interpersonal relations, and may be particularly important in dyadic leader-member relations or transformational leadership activities. The *collective self* identifies with certain groups and self-defines by comparison to group prototypes. It is critical for developing group-based identities, which may be needed for work teams to function effectively, but it can also be a source of divisiveness where demographic heterogeneity exists. Thus, differing bases of self-representation can foster qualitatively different social relations that have quite different consequences for individual, dyadic, and group-level performance.

Leaders can align social and work processes by emphasizing the appropriate basis of self-representation. For example, subordinates who have worked independently in a job are likely to activate the "personal self" in most situations. However, where hierarchical leadership is appropriate or many diverse social roles exist, the "relational self" may be a critical basis for social processes. If jobs shift to more team-based work, the "collective self" may be more appropriate and contribute positively to team identification and performance. Such self-oriented leadership must also consider the constraints created by demographic and cultural diversity and by social justice concerns, which we discussed previously.

Conclusion

To be effective, leaders will need to address a number of specific issues. Table 7.3 summarizes key issues that leaders should keep in mind in considering how to respond to the potential changes identified in this book. Such issues become particularly important as definitions of effective performance are expanded to include organizational citizenship behaviors (Organ, 1988) and employee skill development. They also suggest that an expanded definition of leadership is needed. Future leaders may function more as catalysts for cognitive, affective, and social determinants of performance than as direct regulators of employee performance.

Both the model we developed and the issues we covered suggest that leadership in the future will be a more complex, multiperson, emergent social process. Yet effective leadership will be an even more critical factor in influencing individual and group performance. The model in Figure 7.1 emphasizes that leadership emerges from the interaction, over time, of affective and cognitive factors. Similarly, cognitive and affective factors combine over time to affect performance through social perceptions. Performance and leadership are also reciprocally related over time in that being perceived as a leader affords greater influence and capacity to affect subordinate performance, yet subordinates' successful past

**Table 7.3. Key Issues for Leaders
to Consider in Managing Work Trends.**

Issue	Topics Needing Attention
Automatic/implicit processes	Stereotyping and categorization, attribution bias, implicit leadership theories
Effects of engaging identities and possible selves	Motivation, developing personal projects and goals, skill development
Demographic diversity	Less cohesive work groups, heterogenous skills, identity confusion, communication difficulties
Affect process and leadership	LMX, trust, liking, social justice, self-enhancement motivation
Consequences of more complex and more varied tasks	Need for continuous learning, importance of multisource feedback, procedural fairness in matching skills to task demands

performance is a critical determinant of leadership perceptions (Lord & Maher, 1991) as well as affective and cognitive processes (Staw, 1975).

We expect that this complexity will create some identifiable qualities that are needed for future leaders to be successful. First, future leaders will need a dual orientation on task performance and subordinate development. They will also need to focus on affective as well as cognitive factors in the work situation. Hence, a strong interpersonal orientation, a characteristic more closely associated with females than with males, is one requirement of successful future leaders. Second, leaders need to focus on indirect, employee-centered means as well as direct, task-centered means to achieve high performance. These factors suggest that successful future leaders will be less concerned with personal power and self-promotion, and more concerned with the welfare of others. Because indirect means to influence performance may take longer to have effects and be harder to evaluate than direct means, future leaders should also have a long-run rather than a short-run orientation. These factors are more clearly associated with collective rather than personal identities, and Asian rather than Western cultures. Third, because of the complexities required for dual orientations, effective future leaders are likely to need high intellectual ability and high working memory capacity to manage cognitive load. Fourth, managing subordinate performance will require behavioral flexibility and sensitivity to increasing diversity among subordinates. Finally, to understand and appropriately respond to changes in the way work is performed and the way effective performance is defined, leaders need the capacity to look beyond surface issues such as subordinate (or leader) behavior and focus on more enduring factors that generate employee goals and behavior or that define acceptable performance to subordinates.

Identifying such qualities implies that achieving effective leadership and high levels of performance is primarily a selection or training issue for future organizations. Our depiction of leadership as an emergent social process, however, implies that it is not just a leader-centered process. Leadership is an interaction between leaders and followers (Hall & Lord, 1995), not merely a quality of leaders. Thus the qualities of emergent leaders also depend on how leadership is defined by group, organizational, or national cultures (Pawar &

Eastman, 1997). Consequently, effective future leadership also requires change in the collective leadership prototypes that underlie leadership categorization. Cultural change at multiple levels will also be required to allow leaders with different qualities to emerge and lead. Without such change, the greater variety of leadership resources provided by the increased diversity of future organizations may not be effectively used, and we may find that future leaders are much the same as current leaders. If this occurs, the potential to achieve higher levels of performance as well as more satisfying future organizations will be missed.

References

Anderson, J. R. (1987). Skill acquisition: Compilation of weak-method problem solutions. *Psychological Review, 94,* 192–210.

Argyris, C. (1976). *Increasing leadership effectiveness.* New York: Wiley.

Ashford, S. J. (1989). Self-assessment in organizations: A literature review and integrative model. In L. L. Cummings & B. M. Staw (Eds.), *Research in organizational behavior* (Vol. 11, pp. 133–174). Greenwich, CT: JAI Press.

Austin, J. T., & Vancouver, J. B. (1996). Goal constructs in psychology: Structure, process and context. *Psychological Bulletin, 120,* 338–375.

Banaji, M. R., & Greenwald, A. G. (1995). Implicit gender stereotyping in judgments of fame. *Journal of Personality and Social Psychology, 68,* 181–198.

Banaji, M. R., & Prentice, D. A. (1994). The self in social contexts. *Annual Review of Psychology, 45,* 297–332.

Bandura, A. (1991). Social cognitive theory of self-regulation. *Organizational Behavior and Human Decision Processes, 50,* 248–287.

Barrett, G. V., & Morris, S. B. (1993). The American Psychological Association's amicus curiae brief in *Price Waterhouse* v. *Hopkins. Law and Human Behavior, 17,* 201–215.

Bass, B. M., & Avolio, B. J. (1989). Potential biases in leadership measures: How prototypes, leniency, and general satisfaction relate to ratings and rankings of transformational and transactional leadership constructs. *Educational and Psychological Measurement, 49,* 509–527.

Basu, R., & Green, S. G. (1995). Subordinate performance, leader-subordinate compatibility, and exchange quality in leader-member dyads: A field study. *Journal of Applied Social Psychology, 25,* 77–92.

Bauer, T. N., & Green, S. G. (1996). Development of leader-member exchange: A longitudinal test. *Academy of Management Journal, 39,* 1538–1567.

Billig, M. G., & Tajfel, H. (1973). Social categorization and similarity in intergroup behavior. *European Journal of Social Psychology, 3,* 27–51.

Brewer, M. B. (1989). A dual-process model of impression formation. In R. S. Wyer & T. K. Srull (Eds.), *Advances in social cognition* (Vol. 1, pp. 1–36). Hillsdale, NJ: Erlbaum.

Brewer, M. B., & Gardner, W. (1996). Who is this "we"? Levels of collective identity and self representations. *Journal of Personality and Social Psychology, 71,* 83–93.

Carver, C. S., & Scheier, M. F. (1981). *Action and self-regulation: A control-theory approach to human behavior.* New York: Springer-Verlag.

Carver, C. S., & Scheier, M. F. (1990). Origins and functions of positive and negative affect: A control process view. *Psychological Review, 97,* 19–35.

Chartrand, T. L., & Bargh, J. A. (1996). Automatic activation of impression formation and memorization goals: Nonconscious goal priming reproduces effects of explicit task instructions. *Journal of Personality and Social Psychology, 71,* 464–478.

Cropanzano, R., James, K., & Citera, M. (1993). A goal hierarchy model of personality, motivation, and leadership. In L. L. Cummings & B. M. Staw (Eds.), *Research in organizational behavior* (Vol. 15, pp. 267–322). Greenwich, CT: JAI Press.

Dansereau, F., Graen, G. B., & Haga, W. (1975). A vertical dyad linkage approach to leadership in formal organizations. *Organizational Behavior and Human Performance, 13,* 46–78.

Day, D. V., & Lord, R. G. (1988). Executive leadership and organizational performance: Suggestions for a new theory and methodology. *Journal of Management, 14,* 111–122.

Devine, P. G. (1989). Stereotypes and prejudice: Their automatic and controlled components. *Journal of Personality and Social Psychology, 56,* 5–18.

Di Tomaso, N., & Hooijberg, R. (1996). Diversity and the demands of leadership. *Leadership Quarterly, 7,* 163–187.

Du Bois, D., Brown, D., Smith, W. G., & Lord, R. G. (1996). *The determinants of self-directed learning and its outcomes.* Unpublished manuscript.

Duchon, D., Green, S. G., & Taber, T. D. (1986). Vertical dyad linkages: A longitudinal assessment of antecedents, measures, and consequences. *Journal of Applied Psychology, 71,* 56–60.

Dutton, J. E., Dukerich, J. M., & Harquail, C. V. (1994). Organizational images and member identification. *Administrative Science Quarterly, 39,* 239–263.

Eagly, A. H., & Johnson, B. T. (1990). Gender and leadership style: A meta-analysis. *Psychological Bulletin, 108,* 233–256.

Eagly, A. H., & Karau, S. J. (1992). Gender and the emergence of leaders: A meta-analysis. *Journal of Personality and Social Psychology, 60,* 685–710.

Eden, D. (1992). Leadership and expectations: Pygmalion effects and other self-fulfilling prophecies in organizations. *Leadership Quarterly, 3,* 271–305.

Engle, E. M., & Lord, R. G. (1997). Implicit theories, self-schema, and leader-member exchange. *Academy of Management Journal, 40,* 988–1010.

Fiske, S. T., & Neuberg, S. L. (1990). A continuum of impression formation, from category-based to individuating processes: Influences of information and motivation on attention and interpretation. In M. P. Zanna (Ed.), *Advances in experimental social psychology* (Vol. 23, pp. 1–74). New York: Academic Press.

Freiberg, S. M., & Lord, R. G. (1996, July). *Understanding the dynamics of leadership: The interaction of self-concepts in the leader/follower relationship.* Paper presented at the Eighth Annual Convention of the American Psychological Society, San Francisco.

Frese, M., & Zapf, D. (1994). Action as the core of work psychology: A German approach. In M. D. Dunnette, L. M. Hough, & H. C. Triandis (Ed.), *Handbook of industrial and organizational psychology* (Vol. 4, 2nd ed., pp. 271–340). Palo Alto, CA: Consulting Psychologist Press.

Gerstner, C. R., & Day, D. V. (1994). Cross-cultural comparison of leadership prototypes. *Leadership Quarterly, 5,* 121–134.

Gilbert, D. T., & Malone, P. S. (1995). The correspondence bias. *Psychological Bulletin, 117,* 21–38.

Gioia, D. A., & Thomas, J. B. (1996). Identity, image, and issue interpretation: Sensemaking during strategic change in academia. *Administrative Science Quarterly, 41,* 370–403.

Gioia, D. A., Thomas, J. B., Clark, S. M., & Chittipeddi, K. (1994). Symbolism and strategic change in academia: The dynamics of sensemaking and influence. *Organization Science, 5,* 363–383.

Glisson, C., & Durick, M. (1988). Predictors of job satisfaction and organizational commitment in human service organizations. *Administrative Science Quarterly, 33,* 61–81.

Goktepe, J. R., & Schneider, C. E. (1989). Role of sex, gender roles, and attraction in predicting emergent leaders. *Journal of Applied Psychology, 74,* 165–167.

Graen, G. B. (1997). *Global leadership in century XXI: Challenges and implications for development.* Unpublished manuscript.

Graen, G. B., & Cashman, J. (1975). A role-making model of leadership in formal organizations: A development approach. In J. G. Hunt & L. L. Larson (Eds.), *Leadership frontiers* (pp. 143–166). Kent, OH: Kent State University Press.

Graen, G. B., Liden, R. C., & Hoel, F. (1982). The role of leadership in the employee withdrawal process. *Journal of Applied Psychology, 67,* 868–872.

Graen, G. B., Novak, M. A., & Sommerkamp, P. (1982). The effects of leader-member exchange and job design on productivity and satisfaction: Testing a dual attachment model. *Organizational Behavior and Human Performance, 30,* 109–131.

Graen, G. B., & Scandura, T. A. (1987). Toward a psychology of dyadic organizing. In B. M. Staw & L. L. Cummings (Eds.), *Research in organizational behavior* (Vol. 9, pp. 175–208). Greenwich, CT: JAI Press.

Greenberg, J. (1987). A taxonomy of organizational justice theories. *Academy of Management Review, 12,* 9–22.

Greenberg, J. (1988). Equity and workplace status: A field experiment. *Journal of Applied Psychology, 73,* 606–613.

Greenberg, J. (1990). Employee theft as a reaction to underpayment inequity: The hidden cost of pay cuts. *Journal of Applied Psychology, 75,* 561–568.

Greenwald, A. G., & Banaji, M. R. (1995). Implicit social cognition: Attitudes, self-esteem, and stereotypes. *Psychological Review, 102,* 4–27.

Hains, S. C., Hogg, M. A., & Duck, J. M. (1997). Self-categorization and leadership: Effects of group prototypicality and leader stereotypicality. *Personality and Social Psychology Bulletin, 23,* 1087–1099.

Hall, R. J., & Lord, R. G. (1995). Multi-level information-processing explanations of followers' leadership perceptions. *Leadership Quarterly, 6,* 265–287.

Hall, R. J., Workman, J. W., & Marchioro, C. A. (1998). Sex, task and behavioral flexibility effects on leadership perceptions. *Organizational Behavior and Human Decision Processes, 74,* 1–32.

Hamilton, D. L., & Sherman, J. W. (1994). Stereotypes. In R. S. Wyer & T. K. Srull (Eds.), *Handbook of social cognition* (Vol. 2, pp. 1–68). Hillsdale, NJ: Erlbaum.

Hanges, P., Lord, R. G., Day, D., Sipe, W., Smith, W. G., & Brown, D. (1998). *Leadership and gender bias: Dynamic measures and nonlinear modeling.* Manuscript submitted for publication.

Heilman, M. E. (1983). Sex bias in work settings: The lack of fit model. In L. L. Cummings & B. M. Staw (Eds.), *Research in organizational behavior* (Vol. 5, pp. 269–298). Greenwich, CT: JAI Press.

Heilman, M. E., Block, C. J., Martell, R. F., & Simon, M. C. (1989). Has anything changed? Current characterizations of men, women, and managers. *Journal of Applied Psychology, 74,* 935–942.

Hollander, E. P., & Offermann, L. R. (1990). Power and leadership in organizations: Relationships in transition. *American Psychologist, 45,* 179–189.

House, R. J. (1071). A path goal theory of leader effectiveness. *Administrative Science Quarterly, 16,* 321–338.

Howell, J. P., & Dorfman, P. W. (1981). Substitutes for leadership: Test of a construct. *Academy of Management Journal, 24,* 714–728.

Jackson, S. E., Brett, J. F., Sessa, V. I., Cooper, D. M., Julin, J. A., & Peyronnin, K. (1991). Some differences make a difference: Individual dissimilarity and group heterogeneity as correlates of recruitment, promotions and turnover. *Journal of Applied Psychology, 76,* 675–689.

Jackson, S. E., Stone, V. K., & Alvarez, E. B. (1993). Socialization amidst diversity: The impact of demographics on work team oldtimers and newcomers. In L. L. Cummings & B. M. Staw (Eds.), *Research in organizational behavior* (Vol. 15, pp. 45–110). Greenwich, CT: JAI Press.

Katz, D., & Kahn, R. L. (1978). *The social psychology of organizations* (2nd ed.). New York: Wiley.

Keller, T., & Dansereau, F. (1995). Leadership and empowerment: A social exchange perspective. *Human Relations, 48,* 127–146.

Kemery, E. R., Bedeian, A. G., & Zacur, S. R. (1996). Expectancy-based job cognitions and job affect as predictors of organizational citizenship behaviors. *Journal of Applied Social Psychology, 26,* 635–651.

Kerr, S. (1977). Substitutes for leadership: Some implications for organizational design. *Organization and Administrative Sciences, 8,* 135–403.

Kerr, S., & Jermier, J. M. (1978). Substitutes for leadership: Their meaning and measurement. *Organizational Behavior and Human Performance, 22,* 375–403.

Kitayama, S., Markus, H. R., Matsumoto, H., & Norasakkunkit, V. (1997). Individual and collective processes in the construction of the self: Self-enhancement in the United States and self-criticism in Japan. *Journal of Personality and Social Psychology, 72,* 1245–1267.

Klein, H. J. (1989). An integrated control theory model of work motivation. *Academy of Management Review, 14,* 150–172.

Komaki, J. L. (1986). Toward effective supervision. *Journal of Applied Psychology, 71,* 270–279.

Latham, G. P., & Locke, E. A. (1991). Self-regulation through goal setting. *Organizational Behavior and Human Decision Processes, 50,* 212–247.

Liden, R. C., & Graen, G. B. (1980). Generalizability of the vertical dyad linkage model of leadership. *Academy of Management Journal, 23,* 451–465.

Liden, R. C., Wayne, S. J., & Stilwell, D. (1993). A longitudinal study of the early development of leader-member exchanges. *Journal of Applied Psychology, 78,* 662–674.

Lips, H. M. (1995). Through the lens of mathematical/scientific self-schemas: Images of students' current and possible selves. *Journal of Applied Social Psychology, 25,* 1671–1699.

Lord, R. G. (1976). Group performance as a function of leadership behavior and task structure: Toward an explanatory theory. *Organizational Behavior and Human Performance, 17,* 76–96.

Lord, R. G. (1995). An alternative perspective on attribution theory. In M. J. Martinko (Ed.), *Attribution theory: An organizational perspective* (pp. 333–350). Delray Beach, FL: St. Lucis Press.

Lord, R. G., De Vader, C., & Alliger, G. (1986). A meta-analysis of the relation between personality traits and leadership perceptions: An application of validity generalization procedures. *Journal of Applied Psychology, 71,* 402–410.

Lord, R. G., & Engle, E. M. (1996). Leadership, teams, and culture change: Changing processing structures and dynamics. In M. E. Beyerlein, D. A. Johnson, & S. T. Beyerlein (Eds.), *Advances in interdisciplinary studies of work teams* (Vol. 3, pp. 211–238). Greenwich, CT: JAI Press.

Lord, R. G., & Levy, P. E. (1994). Moving from cognition to action: A control theory perspective. *Applied Psychology, 43,* 335–367.

Lord, R. G., & Maher, K. J. (1991). *Leadership and information processing: Linking perceptions and performance.* New York: Routledge.

MacKenzie, S. B., Podsakoff, P. M., & Fetter, R. (1993). The impact of organizational citizenship behavior on evaluations of salesperson performance. *Journal of Marketing, 57,* 70–80.

Macrae, C. N., Milne, A. B., & Bodenhausen, G. V. (1994). Stereotypes as energy-saving devices: A peek inside the cognitive toolbox. *Journal of Personality and Social Psychology, 66,* 37–47.

Mann, R. D. (1959). A review of the relationships between personality and performance in small groups. *Psychological Bulletin, 56,* 241–270.

Manz, C. C. (1986). Self-leadership: Toward an expanded theory of self-influence processes in organizations. *Academy of Management Review, 11,* 585–600.

Manz, C. C., & Sims, H. P., Jr. (1980). Self-management as a substitute for leadership: A social learning theory perspective. *Academy of Management Review, 5,* 361–367.

Manz, C. C., & Sims, H. P., Jr. (1987). Leading workers to lead themselves: The external leadership of self-managing work teams. *Administrative Science Quarterly, 32,* 106–129.

Markus, H. R. (1977). Self-schema and processing information about the self. *Journal of Personality and Social Psychology, 35,* 63–78.

Markus, H. R., & Kitayama, S. (1991). Culture and the self: Implications for cognition, emotion, and motivation. *Psychological Review, 98,* 224–253.

Markus, H. R., & Nurius, P. (1986). Possible selves. *American Psychologist, 41,* 954–969.

Markus, H. R., & Ruvolo, A. (1989). Possible selves: Personalized representations of goals. In L. A. Pervin (Ed.), *Goal concepts in personality and social psychology* (pp. 211–241). Hillsdale, NJ: Erlbaum.

Markus, H. R., & Wurf, E. (1987). The dynamic self-concept: A social psychological perspective. *Annual Review of Psychology, 38,* 299–337.

Martell, R. F., Lane, D. M., & Emrich, C. E. (1996). Male-female differences: A computer simulation. *American Psychologist, 51,* 157–158.

Martindale, C. C. (1980). Subselves: The internal representations of situational and personal dispositions. In L. Wheeler (Ed.), *Review of personality and social psychology* (Vol.1, pp. 193–218). Thousand Oaks, CA: Sage.

Martindale, C. C. (1981). *Cognition and consciousness.* Homewood, IL: Dorsey.

Mathieu, J. E. (1991). A cross-level nonrecursive model of the antecedents of organizational commitment and satisfaction. *Journal of Applied Psychology, 76,* 607–618.

Mathieu, J. E., & Zajac, D. M. (1990). A review and meta-analysis of the antecedents, correlates, and consequences of organizational commitment. *Psychological Bulletin, 108,* 171–194.

McCain, B. E., O'Reilly, C. A., III, & Pfeffer, J. (1983). The effects of departmental demography on turnover: The case of a university. *Academy of Management Journal, 25,* 626–641.

Meindl, J. R. (1995). The romance of leadership as a follower-centric theory: A social constructionist approach. *Leadership Quarterly, 6,* 329–341.

Meindl, J. R., Ehrlich, S. B., & Dukerich, J. M. (1985). The romance of leadership. *Administrative Science Quarterly, 30,* 78–102.

Meyer, J. P., Paunonen, S. V., Gellatly, I. R., Goffin, R. D., & Jackson, D. N. (1989). Organizational commitment and job performance: It's the nature of the commitment that counts. *Journal of Applied Psychology, 74,* 152–156.

Neck, C. P., Stewart, G. L., & Manz, C. C. (1996). Self-leadership within self-leading teams: Toward an optimal equilibrium. In M. E. Beyerlein, D. A. Johnson, & S. T. Beyerlein (Eds.), *Advances in interdisciplinary studies of work teams* (Vol. 3, pp. 43–66). Greenwich, CT: JAI Press.

Nowak, A., & Lewenstein, M. (1994). Dynamical systems: A tool for so-cial psychology? In R. R. Vallacher & A. Nowak (Eds.), *Dynamical systems in social psychology* (pp. 17–53). San Diego, CA: Academic Press.

O'Connell, M. S., Lord, R. G., & O'Connell, M. K. (1990, August). *An empirical comparison of Japanese and American leadership prototypes: Implications for overseas assignment of managers.* Paper presented at the Academy of Management Convention, San Francisco.

O'Reilly, C. A., III, Caldwell, D. F., & Barnett, W. P. (1989). Work group demography, social integration, and turnover. *Administrative Science Quarterly, 34,* 21–37.

Organ, D. W. (1988). *Organizational citizenship behavior: The good soldier syndrome.* San Francisco: New Lexington Press.

Ostroff, C. (1992). The relationship between satisfaction, attitudes, and performance: An organizational-level analysis. *Journal of Applied Psychology, 77,* 963–974.

Pawar, B. S., & Eastman, K. (1997). The nature and implications of contextual influences on transformational leadership: A conceptual examination. *Academy of Management Review, 22,* 80–109.

Petty, M. M., McGee, G. W., & Cavender, J. W. (1984). A meta-analysis of the relationships between individual job satisfaction and individual performance. *Academy of Management Review, 9,* 712–721.

Pfeffer, J. (1981). Management as symbolic action: The creation and maintenance of organizational paradigms. In L. L. Cummings & B. M. Staw (Eds.), *Research in organizational behavior* (Vol. 3, pp. 1–53). Greenwich, CT: JAI Press.

Pfeffer, J., & O'Reilly, C. A., III. (1987). Hospital demography and turnover among nurses. *Industrial Relations, 26,* 158–173.

Podsakoff, P. M., MacKenzie, S. B., & Bommer, W. H. (1996). Meta-analysis of the relationships between Kerr and Jermier's substitutes for leadership and employee job attitudes, role perceptions, and performance. *Journal of Applied Psychology, 81,* 380–399.

Podsakoff, P. M., MacKenzie, S. B., Moorman, R. H., & Fetter, R. (1990). Transformational leader behaviors and their effects on followers' trust in leader, satisfaction, and organizational citizenship behaviors. *Leadership Quarterly, 1,* 107–142.

Pulakos, E. D., & Wexley, K. N. (1983). The relationship among perceptual similarity, sex, and performance ratings in manager-subordinate dyads. *Academy of Management Journal, 26,* 129–139.

Robbins, T. L., & De Nisi, A. S. (1994). A closer look at interpersonal affect as a distinct influence on cognitive processing in performance evaluations. *Journal of Applied Psychology, 79,* 341–353.

Rush, M. C., Thomas, J. C., & Lord, R. G. (1977). Implicit leadership theory: A potential threat to the internal validity of leader behavior questionnaires. *Organizational Behavior and Human Performance, 20,* 93–110.

Scandura, T. A., Graen, G. B., & Novak, M. A. (1986). When managers decide not to decide autocratically: An investigation of leader-member exchange and decision influence. *Journal of Applied Psychology, 71,* 579–584.

Schein, E. H. (1992). *Organizational culture and leadership* (2nd ed.). San Francisco: Jossey-Bass.

Schlenker, B. R., & Weigold, M. F. (1992). Interpersonal processes involving impression regulation and management. In M. R. Rosenzweig & L. W. Porter (Eds.), *Annual review of psychology* (Vol. 43, pp. 133–168). Palo Alto, CA: Annual Reviews.

Schmidt, R. A., & Bjork, R. A. (1992). New conceptualizations of practice: Common principles in three paradigms suggest new concepts for training. *Psychological Science, 3,* 207–216.

Schriesheim, C. A., & Kerr, S. (1974). Psychometric properties of the Ohio State leadership scales. *Psychological Bulletin, 81,* 756–765.

Seger, C. A. (1994). Implicit learning. *Psychological Bulletin, 115,* 163–195.

Shaw, J. B. (1990). A cognitive categorization model for the study of intercultural management. *Academy of Management Review, 15,* 626–645.

Smith, C. A., Organ, D. W., & Near, J. P. (1983). Organizational citizenship behavior: Its nature and antecedents. *Journal of Applied Psychology, 68,* 653–663.

Smith, W. G., Brown, D., Lord, R. G., & Engle, E. M. (1998). *Leadership self-schemas and their effect on leader impressions.* Manuscript submitted for publication.

Snyder, M. (1979). Self-monitoring processes. In L. Berkowitz (Ed.), *Advances in experimental social psychology* (Vol. 12, pp. 86–128). New York: Academic Press.

Srull, T. K., & Wyer, R. G., Jr. (1989). Person memory and judgment. *Psychological Review, 96,* 58–83.

Staw, B. M. (1975). Attributions of the "causes" of performance: A general alternative interpretation of non-sectional research on organizations. *Organizational Behavior and Human Performance, 13,* 414–432.

Steiner, I. D. (1972). *Group processes and productivity.* New York: Academic Press.

Tajfel, H. (1970). Experiments in intergroup discrimination. *Scientific American, 223,* 96–102.

Tajfel, H., Flament, C., Billig, M. G., & Bundy, R. F. (1971). Social categorization and intergroup behavior. *European Journal of Social Psychology, 1,* 149–177.

Taylor, S. E., & Fiske, S. T. (1978). Salience, attention, and attribution: Top of the head phenomena. In L. Berkowitz (Ed.), *Advances in experimental social psychology* (Vol. 11, pp. 250–289). New York: Academic Press.

Tsui, A. S., Egan, T. D., & O'Reilly, C. A., III. (1992). Being different: Relational demography and organizational attachment. *Administrative Science Quarterly, 37,* 549–579.

Tsui, A. S., & O'Reilly, C. A., III. (1989). Beyond simple demographic effects: The importance of relational demography in superior-subordinate dyads. *Academy of Management Journal, 32,* 402–423.

Turban, D. B., & Jones, A. P. (1988). Supervisor-subordinate similarity: Types, effects, and mechanisms. *Journal of Applied Psychology, 73,* 228–234.

Turban, D. B., Jones, A. P., & Rozelle, R. M. (1990). Influences of supervisor liking of a subordinate and the reward context on the treatment and evaluation of that subordinate. *Motivation and Emotion, 14,* 215–233.

Turner, J. C., Oakes, P. J., Haslam, S. A., & McGarty, C. (1994). Self and collective: Cognition and social context. *Personality and Social Psychology Bulletin, 20,* 454–463.

Tyler, T. R. (1997). The psychology of legitimacy: A relational perspective on voluntary deference to authorities. *Personality and Social Psychology Review, 1,* 323–345.

Tyler, T. R., & Lind, E. A. (1992). A relational model of authority in groups. In R. Zanna (Ed.), *Advances in experimental social psychology* (Vol. 25, pp. 115–191). New York: Academic Press.

Van de Walle, D., & Cummings, L. L. (1997). A test of the influence of goal orientation on the feedback-seeking process. *Journal of Applied Psychology, 82,* 390–400.

Van Lehn, K. (1996). Cognitive skill acquisition. In J. T. Spence, J. M. Darley, & D. J. Foss (Eds.), *Annual review of psychology* (Vol. 47, pp. 513–539). Palo Alto, CA: Annual Reviews.

Vecchio, R. P., & Godbel, B. C. (1984). The vertical dyad linkage model of leadership: Problems and prospects. *Organizational Behavior and Human Performance, 34,* 5–20.

Wagner, W. G., Pfeffer, J., & O'Reilly, C. A., III. (1984). Organizational demography and turnover in top-management groups. *Administrative Science Quarterly, 29,* 74–92.

Wakabayashi, M., & Graen, G. B. (1984). The Japanese career progress study: A seven-year follow up. *Journal of Applied Psychology, 69,* 603–614.

Wakabayashi, M., Graen, G. B., Graen, M., & Graen, M. (1988). Japanese management progress: Mobility into middle management. *Journal of Applied Psychology, 73*, 217 227.

Wayne, S. J., & Ferris, G. R. (1990). Influence tactics, affect, and exchange quality in supervisor-subordinate interactions: A laboratory experiment and field study. *Journal of Applied Psychology, 75*, 487–499.

Wong, P.T.P., & Weiner, B. (1981). When people ask "why" questions, and the heuristic of attributional search. *Journal of Personality and Social Psychology, 40*, 650–663.

Zenger, T. R., & Lawrence, B. S. (1989). Organizational demography: The differential effects of age and tenure distributions on technical communication. *Academy of Management Journal, 32*, 353–376.

Developing Adaptive Teams

A Theory of Compilation and Performance Across Levels and Time

Steve W. J. Kozlowski
Stanley M. Gully
Earl R. Nason
Eleanor M. Smith

The nature of work is changing. There is an explosion of interest in work teams, which are increasingly used as the basic building blocks of organizations. Although there are many forces behind this fundamental reconfiguration of work from individuals to teams, prominent among them is the increasing rate of change, its unpredictability, and its pervasiveness. More than a quarter of a century ago, Terreberry (1968) predicted increasing turbulence in organizational environments and asserted that adaptability would become increasingly central to organizational effectiveness. That future is here today. The demands that organizations must satisfy

Note: We wish to thank Eduardo Salas and Janis A. Cannon-Bowers for their energy, ideas, and stimulation of our work on teams. Our appreciation to J. Kevin Ford for his thoughtful insights, and to Christina J. Burch and Matthew R. Smith for their help during the early stages of this work. We also acknowledge the helpful comments of the volume and series editors. The views expressed in this chapter are the sole responsibility of the authors.

are dynamic. Rising expectations create a need for continuous improvement in product and process. Rapidly shifting contingencies, both internal and external, create a need for adaptability. How do we ensure that teams are capable of meeting these performance demands for continuous improvement and adaptability?

Human performance is a complex phenomenon incorporating both process and outcome aspects (Campbell, Gasser, & Oswald, 1996). Human resource management (HRM) activities often focus primary attention on a conceptualization of performance in terms of outcomes. The goal of establishing the quality of interventions (such as validating selection or evaluating training) drives a need for summary indicators that attempt to capture the sum total of a performance process over time. Although this view of performance is necessary, it is important to avoid reifying outcomes as though they *were* performance. They are simply one approach for capturing aspects of a complex phenomenon.

Process-oriented approaches focus on the knowledge, attitudes, and behavior that yield performance outcomes. Efforts to conceptualize team performance focus primarily on these processes (Fleishman & Zaccaro, 1992; McIntyre & Salas, 1995). Yet efforts to assess team performance often push us back to a retrospective, static, summary outcome orientation. If we wish to understand performance and its improvement, we must focus on processes of learning and skill acquisition, which ultimately yield performance. The changing nature of work, the need for constant improvement and adaptability, necessitates a more dynamic, process-oriented perspective on team performance. Knowledge, skills, and performance are not static; they build developmentally with experience: *what teams know, how they learn it, and the performance of which they are capable changes over time.* Developmental approaches are not well represented in our literature. We believe that it is essential to build theory with a more dynamic conceptualization of team performance and its compilation—a theory that integrates development and performance.

We make three assumptions that are relevant to the theory we construct.

• *First, we take a broad view of team effectiveness—one that incorporates a dynamic model of learning and performance.* We regard adaptability and continuous improvement as performance capabilities that are critical long-term characteristics of team effectiveness. In the short term, changing external contingencies require rapid shifts in role requirements across team members. Individuals and the team must be capable of adapting performance to meet these changing demands. In the long term, the push toward continuous learning and improvement requires incremental enhancement of team processes and outcomes. We assume that the process of team development builds these performance capabilities and must be considered an integral aspect of team effectiveness (Hackman, 1987, 1990).

The emphasis on continuous improvement and adaptability as distal performance capabilities necessitates consideration of the underlying knowledge and skills that compile with experience. Over time, different content domains, processes, and outcomes are the focus of attention as knowledge, skills, and performance incrementally improve. Consider the nature of expert performance. We know that differences between novices and experts are not merely a matter of degree; they are also a matter of kind. As novices make the transition to being experts, they progress through a series of learning stages during which their knowledge and skills compile into qualitatively different forms—from declarative to procedural to strategic (Anderson, 1987; Ford & Kraiger, 1995). This blurs the distinction between learning and skill acquisition as a process, and performance as an outcome. Expert performance is developmentally dynamic, and entwined in the learning process.

Teams progress through a similar process of knowledge and skill compilation, but one that entails different focal levels—individual, dyad, and team—as well as time. One way to disentangle learning and performance in this conceptualization is to distinguish the *content* that is the focus of learning, the *process* by which knowledge and skills are acquired, and the cognitive, behavioral, and affective *outcomes* that serve as indicators of performance capability. Thus the acquisition of knowledge and skills, and the performance that they enable, are distinguishable but entwined. It is equally important to recognize that these specifications are not static; content, processes, and outcomes change over time.

Thus the key conceptual dimensions of our theory incorporate (1) temporal development, (2) shifts in focal level, and (3) shifts in attention to different content, processes, and outcomes. We conceptualize team compilation as a developmental process that proceeds across levels and time. Knowledge, skills, and performance capabilities build successively across levels during compilation. Individuals compile from an initial self-focus (How do I perform my task?) to a dyadic focus (Who do I work with to accomplish tasks?) to a team focus (How do we coordinate, adapt, and accomplish team tasks?). A critical issue concerns learning and performance capabilities that facilitate developmental transitions. Our framework specifies the content, processes, and outcomes that are relevant at different levels and at different points in the compilation process.

• *Second, as the organizing unit of work shifts from individuals to teams, it is critical that we maintain a clear understanding of the nature of individual contributions to team effectiveness.* It is axiomatic that teams do not behave, individuals do. We believe, however, that approaches that focus on identifying the knowledge, skills, and abilities (KSAs) that an individual should possess in a team context can provide only a limited gain in our understanding of team effectiveness. Such approaches, which focus solely on the individual level, neglect the interaction and coordination that are so central and distinctive in teams. At the other extreme, approaches that focus solely on the team level are also limited. Individuals are the fundamental theoretical unit of teams, but teams are not just the sum of the individual parts. Treating teams as additive aggregates of individuals neglects this essential fact. Thus we assume that a model of team effectiveness should disentangle performance contributions that cut across different levels—individual, dyad, and team (Kozlowski & Salas, 1997).

• *Third, the kind of adaptive performance that is required of teams necessitates skill development that occurs in the performance context.* In other words, our model assumes that learning, development, and performance are embedded in the workplace. The increasing penetration and integration of advanced technology systems into the workplace, and the resulting need to continually upgrade skills, creates an opportunity to reconfigure the focus of team training systems from the classroom to the workplace (Kozlowski, 1998). Advanced systems increasingly offer the potential to incorporate on-line performance monitoring, feedback, and evaluation operating in real time. This potential will increasingly allow us to treat performance as process rather than as retrospective outcome. We acknowledge the ethical dilemma posed by this prospect if misused, although we believe that the dilemma can be resolved by recognizing the difference between process feedback for the purpose of learning and skill development, and outcome feedback for the purpose of reward or reprimand. It is the latter that raises ethical concerns, whereas the former is of great benefit for learning and performance enhancement. In the not-distant future, systems will be able to monitor performance and provide tailored developmental feedback. With an appropriate student model—one that is sensitive to dynamic performance requirements across levels and time—such systems will make training and learning integral aspects of everyday job performance. In our view, the future holds great promise for an integration of development and performance through new and powerful training technologies.

In summary, the changing nature of work necessitates more integrative thinking about team development, performance, and effectiveness. We regard team effectiveness in the long term as a product of the developmental process; learning that underlies development provides the foundation for performance effectiveness. Team effectiveness models generally assume that formative development has been accomplished, and they place primary theoretical emphasis on accounting for variations in team outcomes. Our approach makes development an integral aspect of team performance and effectiveness.

The purpose of this chapter is to build a normative theory of team compilation. We begin by specifying team performance demands, limitations in existing models of team development, and three theoretical dimensions that guide our model. We then build a theoretical framework to address these issues. Our model specifies critical developmental phases and transitions, shifts in the focal level of compilation and the content process, and outcomes that comprise the focus of learning and performance at different levels and times in the compilation process.

Theoretical Issues in Team Compilation

Team Performance Demands: Implications for Development

The terms *group* and *team* are often used interchangeably, although some researchers distinguish them with respect to differences in contexts, tasks, and interdependence requirements (Salas, Dickinson,

Converse, & Tannenbaum, 1992). For our purposes, the primary issue is not the terms per se, which we will use interchangeably, but the underlying factors that distinguish different types of work groups or teams. We regard these factors as anchoring the ends of a complexity continuum that distinguishes simple from complex work groups and teams. Teams are defined as two or more individuals who socially interact, have one or more common goals, exist to perform task-relevant functions, exhibit workflow interdependencies, and are embedded in an organizational context (Argote & McGrath, 1993; Hackman, 1992; Hollenbeck, Ilgen, Sego, & Major, 1995; Kozlowski et al., 1996a; Salas et al., 1992). Differences in performance contexts and demands at the ends of the complexity continuum are summarized in Table 8.1.

Many, if not most, work teams are in performance contexts toward the complex end of the continuum. This context is exemplified by task forces; by strategy, cross-functional, and production teams; by surgical staffs, aircrews, and control teams—what some refer to as action teams (Sundstrom, De Meuse, & Futrell, 1990). The task is often highly structured but dynamic; goals are common but task requirements are specialized; roles are differentiated, with coordinated patterns of workflow interdependence specified by task requirements; and expertise is distributed across the individuals who constitute the team. In these situations, effectiveness hinges on the ability of team members to integrate their individual performances to meet temporally paced coordination demands, and to adapt that coordinated interdependence to dynamic situational demands. Team performance is not merely a pooled aggregate, or the individual actions of a team leader; it is the result of an adaptive network of linkages among tasks, roles, and goals at the individual and team levels (Kozlowski et al., 1996a; Kozlowski, Gully, Salas, & Cannon-Bowers, 1996b). Thus, team performance is a combination of individual and team-level contributions that unfold over time. Performance is a critical concern for work teams.

The other end of the continuum, represented by clinical, therapy, and other consensus-oriented groups (such as committees, councils, and juries) is less complex (Tuckman, 1965). These groups are characterized by a highly ambiguous context: an unstructured, internally oriented, and static task; a common goal but unspecified roles; the absence of explicit task interaction and coordination demands; and very little roughly equivalent prior task experience. Group tasks of this type make few demands for specific interactions among team members. The performance of these groups is typically regarded as a simple additive or averaged aggregate of individual contributions. Social interaction is the critical concern.

Representative group development models are summarized in Table 8.2. Although there are some minor variations, most models are remarkably parallel with respect to the descriptive stages and the focus on interpersonal processes and outcomes. They address

Table 8.1. Continuum of Team Performance Contexts and Demands.

	Simple Teams	Complex Teams
Task	• Unstructured • Internally oriented • Static	• Structured • Externally driven • Dynamic
Goals	• Common • Individual contribution unspecified • Fixed	• Common • Individual contribution specified • Shifting
Roles	• Unspecified • Common • Equivalent knowledge and skill	• Specified • Differentiated • Specialized knowledge and skill
Process Emphasis	• Social roles • Social interaction • Conflict, norm formation	• Task roles • Task interaction • Performance coordination
Performance Demands	• Make an additive (pooled) or averaged contribution to group product	• Coordinate individual performance in real time • Adapt to changing contingencies • Continuously improve over time

Table 8.2. Summary of Group and Team Development Models.

Source	Developmental Stages				
	Early Formation ------→		Development ------→		Disbandment
Bion (1961)	Dependency	Fight/Flight	Pairing	Work	
Caple (1978)	Orientation	Conflict	Integration	Achievement	Order
Francis & Young (1979)	Testing	Infighting	Getting Organized	Mature Closeness	
Gibb (1964)	Acceptance	Data Flow	Goals and Norms	Control	
Hill & Gruner (1973)	Orientation	Exploration		Production	
Kormanski & Mozenter (1987)	Awareness	Conflict	Cooperation	Productivity	Separation
Modlin & Faris (1956)	Structuralism	Unrest	Change	Integration	
Tuckman (1965)	Forming	Storming	Norming	Performing	
Tuckman & Jensen (1977)	Forming	Storming	Norming	Performing	Adjourning
Whittaker (1970)	(Preaffiliation)	Power and Control	Intimacy	Differentiation	Separation
Yalom (1970)	Orientation	Conflict	Intimacy		Termination

Notes: There are some variations in the basic developmental framework across the models. Whittaker (1970) considers a preaffiliation stage. Other models incorporate a stage to represent decomposition (Kormanski & Mozenter, 1987; Tuckman & Jensen, 1977; Yalom, 1970), or later aspects of the life cycle (Caple, 1978).

Two models of work group development (not shown in the table) represent more significant departures. Gersick's two-stage "punctuated equilibrium" model (1988) posits (1) an immediate pattern of activity as it focuses on task completion. Note that the constraints of a single project objective and limited time may limit the applicability of the punctuated equilibrium model to ad hoc or temporary terms. Morgan and colleagues (1986) use a nine-stage model that integrates Tuckman and Gersick, essentially repeating Tuckman's four stages both before and after the punctuated equilibrium, and then adding a disbanding stage.

In spite of these variations, most models of group development are remarkably parallel with respect to the descriptive stages. In addition, there is a stream of research that is not of direct interest here that takes a more microfocus on the developmental stages relevant to group problem solving (Bales & Strodtbeck, 1951) and other group functions (such as production, well-being, and support; McGrath, 1990).

unstructured contexts with minimal performance demands (Bettenhausen, 1991; Gully, in press; Levine & Moreland, 1990). This characteristic has several implications that limit the utility of most existing models to aiding an understanding of the development of knowledge and performance capabilities for work teams. We address these implications in the form of three theoretical dimensions that are incorporated in our model of team compilation.

Dimensions of Team Compilation

We focus on the complex end of the continuum to address neglected issues relating to task environments, structures, and developmental processes of work teams. A primary focus of our theory is to specify the compilation of knowledge, skill, and performance capabilities of adaptive teams. We use three theoretical dimensions as the underpinnings for our approach: (1) developmental process and transition points; (2) focal levels of primary processes—individual, dyadic, and team networks—and the performance implications of task interdependencies for compilation to the team level; and (3) specification of content, processes, and outcomes at different levels and transition points in the compilation process. The theoretical structure of the framework is illustrated in Figure 8.1.

Developmental Continuum and Transition Points

The temporal unfolding that occurs during the evolution of a team is a central feature of developmental models. Effective teams are not created full-blown and mature; they form, establish regulatory mechanisms, and evolve through a series of recognizable changes over time. Most models of team development are characterized by discontinuities that represent different stages of development. Stage models have been criticized for assuming that all groups proceed through the same experiential sequence with no provision for variations (Sundstrom et al., 1990), and because they are assumed to specify significant discontinuities at fixed periods of development (Bettenhausen, 1991; Gersick, 1988).

We conceptualize the process as a more continuous series of phases, with partial overlap at transitions. Discontinuities occur at the transitions, but the shifts are not necessarily abrupt. Characterization of team compilation as a sequence of modal phases and

Figure 8.1. Team Compilation: Development, Performance, and Effectiveness Across Levels and Time.

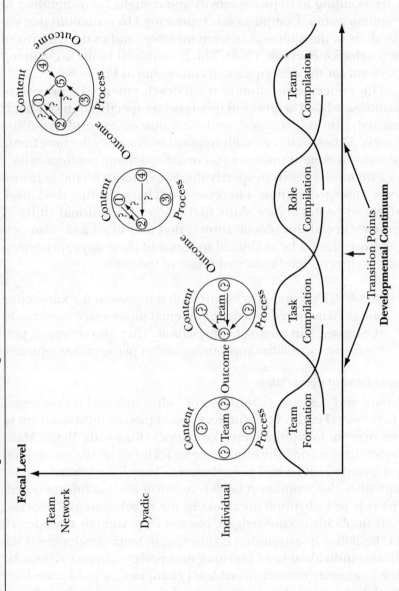

transition points is a necessary theoretical abstraction—a reasonable way to represent compilation. From this perspective, the developmental dimension may be represented as a waveform, with peaks corresponding to in-phase activity and troughs corresponding to transition points. Compilation is represented by transitions that signify shifts in the attention of team members and in the patterns of their behavior (Gersick, 1988). This is illustrated by the overlapping waveform for the developmental continuum in Figure 8.1.

Our conceptualization of team development as a process of learning and skill acquisition incorporates specification of what is learned, how it is learned, and what outcomes result from the process. Although it is virtually impossible to specify the time frame for stage-to-stage transitions (there are too many contingencies), a useful model needs to specify the outcomes that enable transitions. This specification is necessary for characterizing the knowledge and performance skills that trigger transitional shifts. A consequence of this specification is that individual and team performance should be evaluated in terms of their appropriateness for the current developmental phase of the team.

Proposition 1: Outcome specifications that represent the knowledge and skills acquired in a developmental phase *enable transition* to the subsequent phase of compilation. They also represent performance capabilities appropriate at that phase of development.

Focal Level of Compilation

Groups and teams are composed of individuals and yet represent a higher-level entity. By definition, group models must confront issues relevant to multiple levels of analysis (Rousseau, 1985). Many models have skirted the levels issue by focusing on the group level and ignoring individual contributions. They have tended to conceptualize the group as relatively uniform and undifferentiated. The role of individual members in the developmental process, while implicitly acknowledged, has not been directly considered. Yet the skill acquisition that is inherent in team development implicates individual-level learning and performance; we must be able to identify the individual-level changes that yield team-level capabilities. Thus the specification of the means by which lower-level units *compile* into the higher-level entity must be explicitly addressed by theory. This is represented by the shifts in focal level shown in Figure 8.1 that occur as the team evolves.

Neglect of the linkage among levels during team evolution is due to a limited conceptualization of team performance contexts. Teams at the complex end of the continuum typically face an external situation that drives performance requirements for the team. The external situation is dynamic and responsive to team actions. The difficulty and tempo of team tasks may cycle quite dramatically. In addition, teams at the complex end of the continuum are often staffed by specialists with differential role requirements. In these performance contexts, interactions among team members are dictated by task-based interdependencies among roles, and by the necessity to coordinate and pace individual responses. Individual and team performance are represented by the configuration of role linkages and by the task contingencies that determine the linkages. Team members must have an opportunity to explore and learn these role linkages—a process that is necessarily developmental and that builds capabilities across successively higher focal levels (Kozlowski et al., 1996a). It is this linkage of knowledge and performance skills across levels that contributes to team adaptability and continuous improvement—long-term indicators of team effectiveness. Distinguishing among levels and characterizing how individuals, dyads, and teams are distinct and yet related in the collective are essential.

Proposition 2a: Knowledge and skills compile across successively higher-level units—individual, dyad, and team network—as a central aspect of the team development process. This compilation process, which links knowledge and performance capabilities across different levels, is central to long-term team effectiveness.

Task or workflow interdependence must be addressed as an integral aspect of the levels theme, because it determines the nature of the linkage across levels. Interdependence is the structure of workflow relations across team members. It determines the links among roles and the coordination and pacing requirements that link roles together into the team. Mathematical models of interdependence tend to focus on aggregates (Shiflett, 1979; Steiner,

1972), whereas a workflow conceptualization allows individuals within the team to be distinguished.

Pooled interdependence exists when each member makes discrete, additive contributions to the group task. No specific pattern of task interaction is required, and there are no demands to coordinate individual task contributions. This characterizes the simple end of the team continuum. Sequential interdependence exists when each member makes discrete contributions to the whole task in a fixed, serial order. Under this form of interdependence, a unidirectional pattern of workflow interaction is specified that also adds demands for simple coordination and pacing requirements. Reciprocal interdependence exists when members make discrete, serial contributions to team tasks that are bidirectional so that the outputs of one are inputs for another and vice versa. Intensive interdependence exists when workflows are simultaneous and parallel, as well as reciprocal, serial, and pooled. This characterizes interdependence at the complex end of the continuum, and necessitates coordination by feedback and mutual adjustment among team members *as tasks are performed* (Thompson, 1967; Van de Ven, Delbecq, & Koenig, 1976). It places emphasis on the process aspects of team performance.

Members of complex teams possess specific functional roles with corresponding task responsibilities that are not duplicated in other roles, and they possess expertise in the form of specific knowledge, skills, and abilities associated with the functional role. Such tasks require coordinated interactions, that is, task-driven exchanges of information or behavior that are synchronous in time and space (Kozlowski et al., 1996a; McGrath, 1990). Also, such tasks necessitate adaptive workflows to meet unfolding task demands. Thus, as the complexity of task interdependence increases, the emphasis on underlying skills that enable coordination increases as well. For example, demands made by sequential workflows with their stable input-output relations and fixed pacing are much less challenging than the demands made by intensive workflows, where input-output relations and pacing may vary over task cycles. It is with respect to these more complex forms of interdependence that the compilation of knowledge and performance capabilities is most relevant.

Proposition 2b: Teams based on more complex forms of workflow interdependence have performance demands for synchronous coordination and adaptation that must be developed in the performance context as a key aspect of the compilation process.

Considering both issues together—levels of analysis and workflow interdependencies—we believe that it is necessary to characterize the compilation process as incorporating a shift in the focal level of the units of theoretical interest over time—from individuals to linked dyads to an interdependent team. In other words, knowledge, skills, and performance capabilities compile across successively higher levels over time. Moreover, to articulate the implications of complex task interdependencies, it is necessary to adopt a conceptualization of the team that captures adaptive changes in workflow. Complex teams are not systems of uniform interaction and exchange. Rather, they represent sets of task-relevant relations (links) among roles (nodes). Externally driven task demands determine the appropriate configuration of nodes and links that constitute the workflow at any given point in time, with the sequence, timing, and pacing of activation across the nodes and links representing coordination.

In this view, the team is not simply an aggregate or uniform entity at a higher level of analysis; rather, it is an adaptive network. It can be conceptualized as a series of network configurations (linked to task requirements) that map relations (links) among roles (nodes). Thus different network patterns correspond to different externally determined task contingencies. An ideal process of team compilation is predicated on members comprehending these patterns of role exchange and the relation of the network patterns to tasks and situations. This knowledge and skill provide a basis for team adaptability. That is, it enables individuals, dyads, and teams to reconfigure their workflows and modify their performance to satisfy short- and long-term demands for change. We regard adaptive performance as the culmination of team compilation, and the foundation for long-term team effectiveness (Kozlowski, 1998; Smith, Ford, & Kozlowski, 1997).

One form of long-term team adaptability is concerned with the ability of the team to improve internal team processes continually by reconfiguring the network to satisfy appropriate criteria (such as efficiency, effectiveness, or member preference). Another form of adaptability is concerned with the ability of the team to revise or reconfigure the network to meet immediate internal or external contingencies. By exploring alternative network configurations, the workflow may be modified to accomplish the task under shifting demands. This form of adaptability is useful for addressing emergent external situations or internal blockages or failures. Team members must be able to explore transaction alternatives to develop these adaptive performance skills.

Our model describes how this conceptualization of the team as an adaptive network compiles across focal levels over time. Shifts in the pattern of interactions among team members as they learn more complex interdependencies are represented by the development of the network structure shown in Figure 8.1. As team members make transitions from a collection of unconnected and self-focused individuals to interacting dyads to adaptive team networks, they increasingly exhibit more attention to the roles of other members and to their interdependence within the team. Their capability to manage coordinated workflows through dyadic and networked links yields team adaptive performance.

Proposition 2c: More complex workflow interdependencies necessitate greater emphasis on flexible role development in the later phases of team compilation. The focus of knowledge and performance skills is on role-to-role dyadic interdependencies and exploration of team-level role networks. This enables individuals, dyads, and teams to modify workflows to meet short-term demands for performance adaptability and long-term demands for continuous improvement.

Content, Processes, and Outcomes

Most group and team development models have neglected content, processes, and outcomes that are relevant to work team performance because of their focus on simple contexts. The lack of structure and performance demands means that a considerable amount of effort must be devoted to establishing some means to guide interactions as the group attempts to accomplish its goal. It is thus appropriate that most models focus on the formation of social structure to guide behavior. The *content* of these models focuses on the quality of interpersonal relations, the creation of group norms, and social status distinctions (Bettenhausen, 1991; Levine & Moreland, 1990). The *processes* are concerned with negotiation, power, and coalition formation and the factors relevant to them, such as group demographic composition or minority influence. *Outcomes* generally attempt to capture the implications of interactional relations by considering such factors as conflict, cohesion, and consensus.

Although these factors are relevant, as they likely aid the development of task-relevant skills, this conceptualization of content, processes, and outcomes is limited in its ability to help us understand work team performance. When roles are differentiated by task requirements, as opposed to social attraction and status, additional factors are implicated. Moreover, a broader conceptualization of team interdependence necessitates recognition that different content, processes, and outcomes become relevant at different points along the developmental continuum. Knowledge and performance expectations, and the focal level at which they apply, are dynamic over time. Our model identifies cognitive, behavioral, and affective outcomes at the transition points that facilitate movement to the next focal level of compilation, as illustrated in Figure 8.1.

Proposition 3: Each phase of team development implicates a specific focal level, primary learning process, and particular content domain relevant to compilation. Outcomes at each phase are indicators of knowledge, skill achievement, and performance capability that signal transitional readiness. It is the integration of these elements that structures and regulates team compilation as a process encompassing development, performance, and effectiveness.

The Team Compilation Model

Model Overview

Our model characterizes team compilation as a process that proceeds across levels and time. It specifies content, processes, and outcomes that are relevant at different focal levels and at different points along the developmental continuum. It is formulated around a sequence of phases as members make the transition from individual focus to dyadic focus to team-level focus. We envision the phases as a series of modal representations of compilation. Each phase is characterized by a particular level of focus, a primary learning process and content domain, and a set of knowledge and performance outcomes that trigger compilation to the next level and phase.

We have drawn upon diverse literatures to specify the content, process, and outcomes in the model, including socialization, skill acquisition, role development, team performance and effectiveness, and social networks. Each literature is distinct due to its attention to a single focal level. Socialization and skill acquisition focus on individual learning. Role theory is focused on dyadic processes of role creation, negotiation, and routinization. Social network theory provides a means to link the individual within the team as a whole. When considered alone, each literature is limited in its contribution. When linked together, however, by consideration of levels, time, and transitions, the literatures provide an integrated foundation for the theory. Table 8.3 illustrates the focal level, content, process, and outcomes associated with each phase of the model.

At initial formation, the team is really no more than a collection of individuals; it is a team in name only. During phase one, *team formation,* individuals seek information to reduce ambiguity about interpersonal issues that will govern the team. They also begin to seek information about the basic nature of the team, its purpose, and their place in it, although as yet no common understanding exists among team members regarding perceptions, affect, and behavior.

Once an interpersonal foundation is established, the team moves to phase two, *task compilation.* There is still an individual focus as team members try to demonstrate their task competency. For an interdependent team, some task knowledge, by definition, must be linked to the activities of other team members (role information). We presume, however, that attention to links with other members of the team is limited during this initial task-learning phase. Individual team members are most concerned about what they need from other team members, and are less concerned

Table 8.3. Content, Process, and Outcomes of Team Compilation Across Levels and Time.

	Phase 1	Phase 2	Phase 3	Phase 4
Focal Level	Individual	Individual	Dyadic	Team
Content Domain	Social knowledge	Task knowledge	Role knowledge	Network knowledge
Primary Process	*Socialization* • Information seeking • Leaders as mentors/models • Self-disclosure	*Skill acquisition* • Social learning • Experimentation/practice • Information provision, modeling, persuasion	*Role negotiation* • Role episodes • Horizontal negotiations • Repeated dyadic interactions	*Network repertoire* • Explore transaction alternatives • Diagnose/evaluate • Modify network • Add to repertoire
Cognitive, Affective, and Behavioral Outcomes	*Interpersonal knowledge* • Skills/abilities • Personalities • Attitudes and values *Team orientation* • Commitment to goals • Shared climate perceptions • Norms	*Task mastery* • Competence • Performance strategies • Prioritize tasks *Self-regulation* • Monitor performance • Goal setting • Self-efficacy • Resilience to failures and ambiguity	*Role identification* • Role sets • Activity pacing • Response coordination • Boundaries of responsibility *Role routinization* • Streamlined communications • Implicit coordination • Personalized interactions • Reduced role conflict	*Continuous improvement* • Mutual performance monitoring • Team load balancing • Mutual error detection *Team adaptability* • Network selection • Network invention • Coordination maintenance

with what they need to do for others. Basic task competencies are established (task mastery), and team members begin to monitor and regulate performance on their individual tasks (self-regulation).

Phase three, *role compilation*, elaborates dyadic relationships. Having established basic task knowledge, team members begin to probe their dyadic links with others. They enact horizontal role linkages that are necessary to accomplish particular team tasks. Team members come to understand how their task outputs and pacing affect those with whom they directly interact. Team members focus not only on what they need but also on what they need to do to help others. The model suggests that this is when we first begin to see the coordinated interactions that are the hallmark of team effectiveness.

After the initial establishment of routine patterns of interaction, team performance becomes more streamlined and efficient. Team members then begin to attend to the networks of role linkages that connect individuals to the team. This is illustrated by transition to phase four, *team compilation*. The focal level is the entire team. Team members learn how to improve their network of roles continuously to deal with routine, normative situations. The team also develops regulatory skills that enable performance to be adapted to changing situations both internal and external to the team.

Compilation Phases and Transitions: Content, Processes, and Outcomes

Phase 1: Team Formation

At initial formation, the team is a loose collection of individuals. Socialization research identifies how individuals "make sense" and deal with the uncertainty of new work environments (Louis, 1980). They are initially self-focused as they attempt to understand the new setting and its constraints. Social uncertainty is very high because the members lack knowledge of one another. In addition, the nature of the team, its goals, and the fit of individuals within it are not established. Thus initial team formation represents a phase of high ambiguity and self-awareness.

Research suggests that newcomers have difficulty addressing performance demands before social ambiguity is resolved. During entry, newcomers seek social knowledge relevant to understanding interpersonal relationships. They also acquire knowledge about the group, such as its goals, climate, and group norms (Feldman, 1981). The primary ways that newcomers acquire information are inquiry, observation, and exploration (Ostroff & Kozlowski, 1992). In addition, information provision is an important aspect of socialization, with leaders and other influential team members sharing information and serving as mentors and models. The leader can communicate information about team goals and norms, and assist in the development of shared perceptions among team members (Kozlowski et al., 1996a). Thus key outcomes during initial formation that enable transition to task performance are knowledge about social relationships and an orientation to the team as a whole.

Interpersonal Knowledge. Interpersonal knowledge of other team members is essential to structuring interactions. Team members' understanding of one another sets the pattern and tone of communication. Individuals must coordinate with teammates who have unique skills and abilities, personalities, and attitudes. The acquisition of interpersonal knowledge during initial team formation leads to improved task performance later in the developmental process (Gabarro, 1990).

Learning about other team members and resolving interpersonal issues must be settled before individuals will devote attention to work tasks (Katz, 1980). Feldman (1981) found that new employees were not able to elicit task information from their coworkers until the new employees were trusted. Moreover, individuals do not respond to the challenging aspects of their tasks with high performance (Kozlowski & Hults, 1986) or positive affect (Katz, 1978) until interpersonal issues are resolved. Attempts to define social relationships focus on reducing the uncertainty of interpersonal interaction (getting to know each other) and determining what behavior will be accepted. Members interact and observe one another, seeking to construct a schema for interpreting their social environment.

The development of interpersonal knowledge can be facilitated by providing opportunities for team members to interact and self-disclose. Self-disclosure of member attributes reduces the possibility of conflicts among team members as they learn to handle the unique abilities, personalities, and attitudes in the team. Mitchell

(1986) reported that team members' disclosure of internal frames of reference regarding work orientation, past experiences and backgrounds, and job attitudes led to improved working relationships immediately and over time. Interventions such as T-group training and team building are designed to hasten the self-disclosure. The goals of T-group training include accurately sensing the reactions of other team members to one's behavior, and accurately perceiving the behavior of other team members (Berger & Berger, 1972). Team building can also establish a facilitative emotional climate (Cooper & Mangham, 1971) and accelerate socialization of the team (Christen, 1987). The acquisition of interpersonal knowledge facilitates the development of effective social relationships among team members. In addition to interpersonal knowledge, team members also need to develop a common understanding of the team, its purpose, and its requirements.

Team Orientation. The development of a team orientation requires information on team goals, expectancies for task behaviors, and interaction norms. This knowledge allows team members to see how their individual roles and goals align with team goals, and provides a basis for the development of shared perceptions among team members (Nieva, Fleishman, & Rieck, 1978; Zander, 1982). Team members seek information about what the team is trying to accomplish (goals), about what it is like to be a part of this team (team climate), and about what behavior is acceptable (norms). This information is sought by asking the leader, communicating with peers, and observing what is rewarded. Mentors, leaders, and other influential members can create a strong team orientation by explicitly providing this information or by modeling appropriate behavior (Major & Kozlowski, 1997; Ostroff & Kozlowski, 1993).

A team orientation among team members develops members' attachment and commitment to team goals. As individuals accept the importance of team goals, they are increasingly willing to defer their individual fulfillment to achieve the objectives of the team. For this to occur, team members must share information regarding team goals, norms, procedures, and their purposes (Morgan et al., 1986; Nieva et al., 1978). By the end of the first phase of team development, team members should develop an understanding of team purpose that provides the foundation for an increasing commitment to team goals and for future team performance.

Climate perceptions are formed early during the integration of team members. Leaders are implicated as shapers of consensual climate perceptions (Kozlowski & Doherty, 1989; Major, Kozlowski, Chao, & Gardner, 1995). Because events can be interpreted in a variety of ways, individualized interpretations can lead to disorganized responses. A consensual climate provides a shared interpretation of events (Kozlowski & Hattrup, 1992) that yields improved team performance (Gersick & Hackman, 1990; Morgan et al., 1986). Consensus should increase over the life cycle of the team, indicating convergence of perceptions about the team and its environment.

The formation of team norms is another aspect of team orientation. Leaders are influential mentors and models in norm formation, which occurs early in development and quite quickly. Norms are tacit expectations governing person-to-person interaction (Allen, 1987). Newcomers are most ready to accept norms early in socialization (Moreland & Levine, 1988). For example, Ginnett (1987) found that captains of aircrews set norms in the first few moments of team formation that influenced behavior for the remainder of the team's life. In addition, team members who shift to a greater reliance on leaders show improved adjustment to their work roles over time (Ostroff & Kozlowski, 1992).

Performance Implications. Phase 1 is devoted to the development of individual-level knowledge and skills. Individuals must first acquire interpersonal knowledge about their teammates and an orientation to the team before they can attend to their task performance. Interpersonal knowledge includes their teammates' skills and abilities, personalities, and attitudes. Individuals must also develop a team orientation, including a commitment to team goals, climate perceptions, and behavioral norms. Although these outcomes do not represent performance capabilities per se, they must be resolved to enable a transition to the task compilation phase.

Phase 2: Task Compilation

After establishing social space and learning the nature of the team, its purpose, and their place in it, team members shift attention to focus on individual task performance. Prior to team formation, team members may have had training or experience in their specialized area. Team members are often at various levels of task proficiency, yet all must achieve competence, because individual task proficiency is necessary for effective team performance (Salas et al., 1992). In addition, it is within the team context that members learn how to perform in a dynamic, real-time setting. Although individuals coordinate with the activities of others, team members are primarily self-focused on their individual task performance during this phase.

Individual proficiency differentiates more and less effective teams (Glickman et al., 1987; Tziner & Eden, 1985). Individual performance is an outcome of skill acquisition, which involves social and self-regulated learning (Bandura, 1977b, 1991). According to social learning theory, individuals acquire skills through an iterative process of observing others and modeling their behaviors. This includes information seeking, vicarious observation of others' behavior, and experimenting and practicing individual tasks. With experience they begin to proceduralize and automatize their skills. Declarative knowledge compiles into task routines that yield more fluid and less error-prone performance (Anderson, 1987). Task routines also allow team members to devote more attention to monitoring, evaluating, and regulating performance. During this second phase of team compilation, team members develop individual outcomes of task mastery and self-regulation skills.

Task Mastery. Task mastery refers to the development of individual task proficiency. It includes the development of task routines, priorities, and strategies. The team performance literature indicates that individual task proficiency is a necessary but insufficient condition for team performance (Salas et al., 1992). Research also suggests that individuals must first achieve task mastery before they can focus attention on team performance (Klaus & Glaser, 1970).

To master tasks and develop performance strategies, individuals must focus both on *how to* perform their tasks and on *how well* they are performing them. Team members acquire this information by asking leaders, instructors, or experienced teammates; by monitoring the behavior of others (Morrison, 1993); or by experimenting on their own (Ostroff & Kozlowski, 1992; Smith & Kozlowski, 1994). Task mastery can be facilitated by providing process feedback during early skill acquisition. By establishing an environment of open information exchange, influential team members can also model the acceptability of asking questions and accepting critical feedback. In addition, observing competent models allows team members to learn performance strategies (Bandura, 1982). Modeling may be especially important for learning performance strategies, because this information may not be available from a new team member's past experiences (Gist & Mitchell, 1992).

Experimentation and practice are critical for task mastery. Ford, Quiñones, Sego, and Sorra (1992) found that trained skills often are not transferred because they are not practiced on the job. This has implications when individuals must practice in a team setting, where the nature of the team task creates differential practice opportunities. All team members need equivalent opportunities to practice to ensure that they master their skills. Leaders can serve a special role as coach and guide to facilitate skill acquisition for all members by ensuring equivalent practice experiences (Kozlowski et al., 1996b).

Moreover, without opportunities to make and learn from mistakes, team members may attempt to achieve errorless performance without actually learning the underlying skills needed for long-term effectiveness. Fedor, Rensvold, and Adams (1992) suggest that individuals who are performing well may be lulled into a false sense of security regarding their performance. They may be less likely to seek feedback, although task performance during later phases of team development may require that they adapt their strategies or procedures.

Individual performance and adaptability can be enhanced through a sequence of mastery experiences. Attention to superficial aspects of the task can be minimized by defining learning goals and by leading members through a sequence of experiences with the objective of exploring increasingly complex skills. These mastery experiences provide an opportunity to explore task contingencies, make errors, and receive diagnostic feedback relevant to the learning objectives. Research demonstrates that mastery experiences build a deeper comprehension of the task, and the capability to adapt that knowledge to improve performance in novel situations (Kozlowski et al., 1995; Kozlowski et al., 1996c).

Self-Regulation. As team members master their individual tasks, they are able to devote greater attention to the motivational processes directing their individual performance. Self-regulation is the process of guiding goal-directed activities over time and

across changing circumstances (Karoly, 1993). Three primary subfunctions in the self-regulatory process are self-monitoring, self-judg-
ment, and self-reaction (Bandura, 1991). First, team members begin
to monitor their task performance with reference to a goal. Self-
observation provides information for setting appropriate goals and
for evaluating progress towards their attainment. Self-observation
leads to a judgmental process where behavior is compared to personal goals. Finally, these performance judgments lead to self-reac-
tions that provide the mechanism for the regulation of action. When
there are negative discrepancies between performance and personal
standards, the resulting dissatisfaction motivates corrective changes
in behavior. Thus self-regulation is central to learning, motivation,
and performance.

Self-efficacy affects all three subfunctions of the self-regulatory
process. It is defined as an individual's confidence or expectation
that he or she can successfully perform (Bandura, 1977b). Self-
efficacy affects which aspects of performance a team member will
monitor, the goals that individuals set for themselves, and their
level of goal commitment (Bandura, 1991; Locke, Frederick, Lee,
& Bobko, 1984). It also determines how a team member will cope
in an uncertain or difficult situation and how long they will persist
in that situation (Bandura, 1977a).

Self-efficacy is developed through processes such as mastery experiences, exposure to models and other vicarious experiences,
and verbal persuasion, with mastery experiences being the most
influential source of information (Bandura, 1982). When team
members perform their tasks well, self-efficacy is heightened; when
they repeatedly fail, self-efficacy expectations are lowered. This is
especially true early in skill acquisition. Thus initial assignments
should be less difficult, to allow team members to experience success at their tasks. If over time tasks increase in difficulty and team
members set progressively harder goals for successful performance,
they will be able to diagnose and learn from their mistakes more
effectively. Such sequenced mastery experiences have been shown
to increase self-efficacy and to provide performance resilience
under more complex and demanding task conditions (Kozlowski
et al., 1995, 1996c).

Mastery experiences yield task familiarity, information concerning the adequacy of individual KSAs, and performance strate-

gies utilizing these KSAs. Modeling also provides information about the adequacy of KSAs (Gist & Mitchell, 1992). When individuals observe other team members successfully performing a task, their own efficacy expectations are increased (Bandura, 1982). Verbal persuasion may be used to convince team members that they possess the capabilities necessary to successfully perform tasks. For example, encouraging performance feedback increases self-efficacy, which is accompanied by an increase in performance (Tuckman & Sexton, 1991). Conversely, if negative feedback is communicated destructively, self-efficacy will be lowered (Baron, 1988). Thus leaders and others can help to build the self-efficacy of team members by providing encouraging, constructive feedback. As team members gain task experience, prior performance has a diminishing influence on subsequent performance, while self-regulatory factors exert an increasing influence on future performance.

Performance Implications. Phase 2 is devoted to the acquisition of individual task knowledge and performance skills. Individuals acquire the knowledge and skills that enable task mastery. They can demonstrate basic task proficiency, apply task strategies, and establish task priorities. They also acquire self-regulatory skills, enabling them to set appropriate goals, monitor performance, and make adjustments to meet the goals. Self-regulatory skills also build task-specific self-efficacy, which provides resilience to task challenges, ambiguity, and failure. This resilience is particularly important in a team context where coordination requirements will increase opportunities for performance failures. Mastery of individual tasks and the development of strong self-regulatory skills and self-efficacy enable another developmental shift. At this point, team members are capable of making the transition to focus on dyadic workflow interdependencies and role-related performance.

Phase 3: Role Compilation

Although the performance requirements of team members are defined by their individual tasks, the team context also imposes coordination responsibilities. This necessitates that dyads have a mutual understanding of their linked input-output transactions. Developing this understanding requires team members to shift their attention from individual task mastery to the mutual performance expectations that stem from task-based dyadic relations, that is, to the linked input-output transactions that define coordinated interdependence.

During phase three, team members learn to coordinate their performance with other team members, answering such questions as, "With whom must I interact to complete tasks?" and "How do I balance the requirements others place on me with my own task requirements?" The process in this phase is based on role theory (Katz & Kahn, 1978), which describes dyadic role negotiation and definition. We synthesize content and outcomes of this role development process using the team performance literature. The content of phase three is the role knowledge necessary to perform in a team context. The primary outcomes during role compilation are role identification and routinization.

Role Identification. When team members move beyond a focus on individual performance, they confront the boundaries of their responsibility. They learn how the team context affects their performance—specifically, *who* they interact with to perform their tasks, *what* the content is of dyadic input-output transactions, and *when* they perform acts to ensure coordination is maintained across the team. The process by which team members identify the who, what, and when of performance requirements is based on our adaptation of Katz and Kahn's dyadic model of role development (1978). During role development, team members send role expectations, receive expectations, and respond with role behavior. The entire cycle forms a role episode. As role episodes are repeated over time, the sender's expectations and the receiver's behavior are modified as they iteratively negotiate a dyadic relationship (Graen & Scandura, 1987; Seers, 1989).

Applications of role theory often emphasize unidirectional role development whereby roles are imposed. Compilation of role relationships in a team context, however, suggests a shift from an asymmetric process to a mutual process of role negotiation. We emphasize negotiation for two primary reasons. First, role imposition does not address interdependence requirements among team members. Because team members form a dyadic relationship with each role-set member, conflicting demands among them must be negotiated. Members must compromise, which emphasizes the negotiated nature of team member roles. A second context feature that leads to a greater emphasis on role negotiation is the focus on horizontal rather than vertical dyadic relations. Although it is important to recognize that other relationships exist (such as vertical relationships in hierarchical teams), the relations of importance are horizontal because exchanges among team members are essential to performance. Successful negotiation of expected behavior in horizontal dyads enables the *coordinated* behavior on which team performance depends.

The result of horizontal member exchange (HMX) (Nason, 1995) is the acquisition of specific role knowledge about the dyadic *input-output transactions* dictated by task interdependencies. The first question that team members must resolve is the who of dyadic interactions. Who requires outputs from me and from whom do I require inputs? For any team task, each role has an associated role set composed of the members with whom direct interaction is required. In turn, a team member may be a part of the role sets of many different team members. As a whole, the role sets for a team capture the information about from whom inputs are required and to whom outputs must be provided. The variety and typicality of the situations to which team members are exposed determines who is included in each member's role sets. Different team tasks require individuals to coordinate with different team members, thus creating a number of different possible role sets, each appropriate for a particular situation and team task. Over repeated performance episodes, team members learn the role sets defined by the commonly performed team tasks. These are the team members' normative role sets.

The second role identification question that team members must answer is, What is the content of the role expectations of other team members? Team members determine the boundaries of their responsibilities. These responsibilities are the task-specific behavioral expectations that role-set members transmit to the focal member. During role compilation, team members negotiate their boundaries of responsibility. The resulting negotiated roles will likely contain more behaviors than each member anticipated being "part of my job," and fewer behaviors than role-set members desire.

The third role identification question concerns when to perform role behaviors. This is central to team coordination and performance. Coordination and pacing requirements spring from the demands of team tasks, with greater interdependence increasing the need to learn about coordination and pacing. Over repeated task episodes, team members learn to sequence and time their role behaviors with the members of their normative role sets (Gabarro, 1990). Team members learn two categories of role behavior that yield performance (Fleishman & Zaccaro, 1992). First, they learn the *activity pacing* or tempo of team activities, and how to pace their own activities to fit. Second, they learn *response coordination,* which is the sequence and timing of performance required by the team task.

Learning the who, what, and when of role responsibilities as a set defines the outcome of role identification. When these issues are resolved, team members have determined the members of their role sets for a set of normative team tasks, they have negotiated specific task-based behavioral requirements with the members of those normative role sets, and they have determined the pacing, sequencing, and timing requirements for those behaviors. These outcomes enable team members to coordinate their performance with members of their role sets.

Role Routinization. In addition to learning the basic who, what, and when of role expectations, team members personalize their dyadic relations. They learn how task-relevant personal characteristics affect input-output transactions. In other words, they learn how to tailor their task interactions to fit the individual differences of their teammates. Team members personalize their dyadic relationships based on the abilities, tendencies, and preferences of dyad members. Thus, under the role routinization outcome, members refine coordination mechanisms and enhance dyadic performance links.

Theory suggests that team members must learn one another's personal characteristics to coordinate their actions and function effectively as a team. Knowledge of another's personality, needs, and performance capabilities enables task-relevant behaviors to be predicted (Cannon-Bowers, Salas, & Converse, 1993; Kleinman & Serfaty, 1989). We propose that team members will share interpersonal knowledge not uniformly but rather in a manner compatible with their role relationships. Team members whose roles require them to interact will develop shared interpersonal knowledge to personalize their interactions. Team members who do not interact during task performance may share the social interpersonal knowledge gained in phase one, but they will not share the task-based interpersonal knowledge developed during phase three.

Gabarro's analysis (1990) of the dimensions along which working relationships develop provides some insight into the ways in which dyadic task-based relationships are personalized and refined. Over repeated task-based interactions, communication expands from a sole reliance on verbal channels to the use of nonverbal channels as well. Team members learn each other's nonverbal language. They also learn to substitute shorthand forms of communication for longer, more explicit messages. Shorthand communication requires a dyad to have a common understanding of the expanded meaning of a condensed communication. Over time, dyads may also establish unique norms.

Performance Implications. During role compilation, team members focus attention on dyadic linkages required for coordination and performance. The primary content of phase three is the role knowledge for direct dyadic relationships. The role identification outcome entails the who, what, and when of role expectations. Members establish role sets based on the tasks the team frequently performs; they negotiate boundaries of responsibility; and they learn to pace, sequence, and time their performance behavior. The role routinization outcome includes the unique knowledge that team members use to further refine and personalize dyadic interactions. Over the course of repeated role episodes, members negotiate personalized relationships to fit the task-relevant characteristics of their role set.

Role compilation in phase three provides the foundation for team adaptive performance that is the focus of phase four. Because dyads establish the input-output linkages that define coordinated workflows, they must have the freedom to specify their role-to-role performance expectations. Moreover, excessive emphasis on team performance outcomes in a traditional sense (that is, productivity) will divert attention from this role development process. Such an emphasis may retard the acquisition of important capabilities that are essential for team effectiveness (Kozlowski et al., 1996a; Kozlowski et al., 1996b).

Phase 4: Team Compilation

The task-based dyadic links that compile in phase three are the foundation for understanding team performance as a network of roles. In phase four, team members broaden their dyadic view to include more distal, indirect role linkages. They begin to see the team as sets of alternative role networks linked by task interdependencies. They begin to understand the effects of central roles and critical paths on performance, and to explore transaction alternatives that can ameliorate overloads, blockages, and miscoordination. This understanding is important; research suggests that knowledge regarding team member roles and interdependencies is a crucial aspect of team performance (Cream, Eggemeier, & Klein, 1978; Roth, Hritz, & Lewis, 1984).

The process in this phase is based on social network theory. Networks comprise a set of nodes connected by links that represent relationships among the nodes (Brass, 1995). In our model, the nodes represent roles or positions, and the links signify workflow transactions. These transactions must be coordinated in the sense that coordination refers to synchronous transactions across links in the network. In our conceptualization, patterns of links and nodes are activated from moment to moment to meet required input-output transactions. The general tempo of the workflow represents activity pacing, and the sequence of activation across roles refers to response coordination (Fleishman & Zaccaro, 1992; Nieva et al., 1978). This conceptualization extends traditional perspectives of networks. Network theory typically focuses on social relations as opposed to task links, and tends to view networks as static. We conceptualize team networks as dynamic and evolving. Teams can develop multiple network configurations to address different external contingencies and to refine internal processes. This ability to improve network functioning continually in the long term, and to adapt it in the short term, is central to team performance.

Routine tasks foster the development of normative team networks. In the long term, teams can continually improve performance by exploring alternative configurations and making incremental changes that refine role networks. A refined network enables members to engage in mutual performance monitoring, to balance workloads, and to develop mechanisms for error detection. These capabilities are important aspects of team performance (Fleishman & Zacarro, 1992; Morgan et al., 1986; Shiflett, Eisner, Price, & Schemmer, 1982).

Teams also encounter tasks that are novel or emergent. Nonroutine tasks require adaptation of the network to meet dynamic task demands, another critical aspect of team performance (Boguslaw & Porter, 1962). The external situation determines team tasks, and task interdependencies create specific network configurations. Thus, when the team encounters a novel situation or the situation changes in some unexpected way, tasks performed by the team and the corresponding network may need to change. Adaptive performance is predicated on a repertoire of networks. Although repertoires develop through exploration over time, the process of team adaptability requires a short-term cycle of "on-line" selection or creation, evaluation, and modification of the network to fit the task. Teams learn to fit networks to meet external situational demands, to modify networks to deal with internal problems, and to maintain coordination under dynamic or stressful conditions. Essentially teams develop the capability to self-regulate performance—adapting to meet shifting contingencies.

As teams explore transaction alternatives in an effort to improve and adapt, they must consider key network characteristics that are implicated in effectiveness. Roles in a network can vary in centrality. Central roles have many direct links with other team members and are at the nexus of workflows. Critical paths are links that are frequently used or that carry important information. Overloads on central roles and bottlenecks in critical paths will hinder team performance, and are likely focal points for network refinement. Moreover, errors or failures in central roles or along critical paths may cascade throughout the network, making central roles and critical paths targets for performance monitoring and error detection. It also makes them targets for new transaction alternatives that circumvent overloads and blockages. As teams learn how critical paths, central roles, and transactions affect performance, they can incrementally refine normative configurations and develop alternative networks. In our model these are critical performance capabilities, and the culmination of team compilation.

Continuous Improvement. Training, technological or structural constraints, and tradition, among other factors, facilitate the development of normative networks. The basis for incremental refinement of normative networks is the exploration of transaction alternatives. Transaction alternatives are optional workflows through which input-output exchanges can be accomplished. Team members may build new links, perform new roles, take on role responsibilities previously relegated to another member, discard or bypass roles, or dissolve links between roles. Each of these modifications is a transaction alternative. Changes in transaction patterns need to be compatible across all affected roles, implicating role negotiation on a large scale. By evaluating modified networks on such criteria as efficiency, quality, or member satisfaction, gradual improvements in team performance can be realized.

Teams that explore, modify, and refine networks can more effectively balance workloads and reduce the likelihood of bottlenecks. Alternative configurations can facilitate mutual performance monitoring and error detection, which can reduce the likelihood that mistakes will cascade throughout the network. Teams can improve the operation of a network by refining and synchronizing the tempo and pacing of activities. Thus continuous improvement of the team network focuses on three aspects of team performance: workload balancing, performance monitoring, and error detection.

Workload balancing adjusts member resources to fit task requirements across all roles in the network (Shifflet, Eisner, Price, & Schemmer, 1982). It is critical because team members must be sensitive to the combined effects of multiple roles on another member. A single member interacting with a central role at a particular time will not overload that role. However, ten members interacting with a central role at the same time will overload it. One option distributes the work of the central role among other members. Another option lowers the tempo so that the central role has more time to process information. The team can also sequence the workflow, giving the central role time to process each piece separately. These examples demonstrate how a team can refine the network by balancing the workload.

Mutual performance monitoring provides information used in "feedforward" and feedback mechanisms (Cooper, Shiflett, Korotkin, & Fleishman, 1984; Fleishman & Zaccaro, 1992) that contribute to team performance (Morgan et al., 1986). It yields error detection at the point of origin, correcting errors before they cascade throughout the network. Errors can propagate throughout the network if they are sent to a central role or along a critical path. Error propagation can be reduced or eliminated through mutual performance monitoring, error detection, and feedback (Boguslaw & Porter, 1962; Denson, 1981; Glickman et al., 1987; Morgan et al., 1986; Volpe, Cannon-Bowers, Salas, & Spector, 1996). As team members continuously refine and improve their networks for routine tasks, they also create the foundation for team adaptability.

Team Adaptability. Teams must learn to be adaptive in response to novel task demands (Boguslaw & Porter, 1962). Nonroutine tasks may emerge from changes in the external situation or from internal contingencies, such as equipment failures or the loss of a key member. Novel tasks require new network solutions. Adaptability is the capability of the team to maintain coordinated interdependence and performance by selecting an appropriate network from its repertoire or by inventing a new configuration. Thus adaptability refers to a metamorphic shift in the team network in the short-term to deal with the performance demands of a nonroutine task.

Team adaptability is facilitated by a network repertoire. Although the process of building a repertoire occurs through network refinement, team adaptability requires rapid selection, evaluation, and modification as contingencies emerge. The team must quickly determine an appropriate configuration. The fit of the network must then be evaluated. Modifications may need to be made. In the event that no configuration meets the task demands, a new network must be invented. New networks will be based on knowledge that team members have acquired through the exploration of transaction alternatives. This conceptualization indicates three key outcomes underlying team adaptability for nonroutine tasks: network selection, network invention, and coordination maintenance.

Network selection involves the ability of team members to simultaneously and rapidly select an appropriate network from their repertoire. Teams with a shared understanding of the contingencies that connect different networks to team tasks will be better able to synchronously select an appropriate configuration (Kozlowski et al., 1996a; Zalesny, Salas, & Prince, 1995). Such shared perceptions or team mental models can facilitate implicit coordination and yield rapid responses (Cannon-Bowers et al., 1993; Orasanu, 1990). Team experience, training, and guidance by the team leader can facilitate the sharing of knowledge about which team network is appropriate for what task situation (Kozlowski et al., 1996b). Adaptive teams will have created a repertoire of networks for different situations as well as corresponding indicators that signify when a switch in configuration must occur.

Network invention involves the ability of team members to create new networks rapidly. All teams may occasionally encounter problems for which they have had limited experience or training. Such problems may include, but are not limited to, unexpected loss of a critical member, changes in workflow such that key roles or paths become overwhelmed, or technology failures. When faced with such problems, the team must quickly modify its configuration. New roles must be defined and new links must be established. Teams that have explored transaction alternatives will be better able to modify networks on-line than teams that have not engaged in exploration.

Coordination maintenance is the ability to maintain coordination and pacing to meet the ebb and flow of novel task demands (Fleishman & Zacarro, 1992). Teams must be able to synchronize the pacing and sequence of activities to avoid bottlenecks and overloads. This form of adaptability can be enhanced by exploring and testing the fit of different pacing and coordination sequences to novel task situations, and by understanding when and how tempos are relevant. Team coordination is facilitated when members understand when to choose alternative configurations, and how the pacing and coordination varies within a given configuration.

When teams explore alternative networks, they will have a wider repertoire of configurations from which to choose when tasks change. They will be more likely to adapt their performance. Teams that have not explored alternatives will have few network configurations from which to choose. They will find it difficult to modify transaction alternatives quickly or efficiently, and will be less likely to adapt. When faced with nonroutine tasks, teams low on adaptability will tend to persist in habitual patterns that may significantly hinder performance (Gersick & Hackman, 1990). In contrast, adaptive teams will be more capable of adjusting to emergent situations, bypassing central role overloads, and smoothing bottlenecks to maintain links along critical paths.

Performance Implications. For teams to exhibit continuous improvement and to develop adaptive performance capabilities, team members must share an understanding of the team as a flexible network of role linkages. Networks describe the patterns of workflow interdependence among roles and specify the nature of coordinated interactions among members. In the long term, teams can incrementally refine networks for routine tasks by exploring transaction alternatives. This process also provides a foundation for adaptability by creating a repertoire of different networks. Non-routine tasks call for the rapid selection of a network from the repertoire, or the invention of new networks. Teams must be able to adjust team-member tasks, task boundaries, and task responsibilities as the situation requires. The exploration of alternative networks and coordination sequences in relation to different tasks will yield a team in which performance is constantly improving and adaptive in the face of dynamic contingencies.

Discussion

Conceptualizing Team Performance

Our effort to understand team performance through team development may seem counterintuitive. As a point of contrast, it is useful to consider the assumptions of the more conventional perspective. That approach assumes that teams are up and running, that everyone has the appropriate skills. Thus the primary focus is to specify performance requirements, preferably in measurable form. If the conventional approach of identifying KSAs is used, the primary unit will be the individual. This assumes, of course, that performance is static over time, exists primarily at the individual level and is under individual control, and yields tangible outcomes. Although there are many useful purposes to which this approach may be applied, it does not extend theoretical understanding of team performance in light of the changing nature of work.

The Changing Nature of Work

We began this chapter by considering three issues in the changing nature of work, highlighting their implications for our theory of team compilation. First, the increased emphasis on flexibility and adaptability necessitates a developmental perspective of job and role requirements and their evolution over time. Static models are ill-suited for task contexts that cycle performance demands in the short-term and evolve requirements in the long-term. We need to integrate learning processes, as the foundation for adaptability and continuous improvement, with performance outcomes. Second, as organizations increasingly structure work design around teams, it is critical that we have a clear understanding of the contributions that individuals make to team performance. We need models that enable us to decompose the individual-level components of team-level performance. Third, the increasing diffusion of advanced technology systems into every corner of the workplace, and the necessity to upgrade skills continually, creates an opportunity to shift the focus of training systems from the classroom to the workplace. It is becoming possible to design technology systems with the capability to monitor responses and to provide tailored developmental feedback to the performer so that training and learning are integral aspects of everyday job performance. We need theory to guide the application of these emerging technological capabilities; theory that regards learning as a foundation for and integral aspect of performance; and models that specify learning requirements and mechanisms and the resulting knowledge and performance capabilities. We believe that a strong effort to understand team development is the best way to elaborate the underpinnings of team effectiveness.

Team Compilation

These issues provide a point of departure for our model. The theory assumes that team development provides the foundation for the knowledge and skill acquisition that are essential for team performance and long-term effectiveness. The theory conceptualizes team compilation as a process that proceeds across levels and time. Team performance compiles across levels from a loose set of self-focused individuals to linked dyads to an adaptive and continuously improving team network. It specifies content, processes, and outcomes that are relevant at different focal levels and at different phases across the developmental continuum. That is, it indicates what needs to be learned, how it is learned, and what performance capabilities result at a particular level at that point in the compilation process. Thus the model defines the developmental phases and transitions that occur as individual, dyads, and team acquire the capability to adapt and continually improve. It is in this regard that the model contributes to our understanding of team performance as a dynamic interplay of process and outcome, with team effectiveness as a long-term product of this developmental process.

Theory Elaboration, Boundary Conditions, and Performance Implications

Our model is focused, as opposed to all encompassing, to enable testing and evaluation (Goodman, 1986). It is constrained by several boundary conditions to allow presentation of the central conceptual factors and rationale. At this point it is useful to highlight these boundary conditions, to suggest elaborations of the base model to address them, and to draw implications for performance.

New Teams

The model assumes the formation of new teams. It does so to allow us to outline fully the logic of compilation across levels and time. We acknowledge, however, that many teams have a long history, with the continual transition out of old members and the socialization of new members. Transitions of this sort are not explicit in the model. We regard these personnel transitions as instances of individual socialization in the team context, not as team-level phenomena per se. There are models that address individual socialization (Moreland & Levine, 1989) and group socialization (Anderson & Thomas, 1995). In addition, there are several models that address process mechanisms and outcomes of newcomer socialization (such as Chao et al., 1994; Morrison, 1993; Ostroff & Kozlowski, 1992). These models are consistent with our model, particularly during phase 1 and phase 2. From a performance perspective, existing teams exert pressure on the newcomer to conform to their performance standards, with relatively less accommodation exerted by the newcomer. Team performance is enhanced to the extent that the newcomer is successfully socialized into the team.

Organizational Context

Organizational culture and climate provide an embedding context, and set constraints on team compilation and performance (Kozlowski & Salas, 1997). While we acknowledge this impact, it is not a primary focus of our model. Rather, we focus on more critical local contextual characteristics—on technology and structure represented in team workflows. The local context is more important, pervasive, and salient (Argote & McGrath, 1993). It is in the local context that interventions designed to improve team compilation and performance will have the greatest effect.

Leaders

Our purpose in this chapter has been to map compilation and performance that are relevant to the team as a self-regulating entity. Leaders, however, can be important facilitators of this process. They are instrumental during formation (phase 1) and skill acquisition (phase 2). And although they are not explicitly addressed in the model, leaders can play a central role in facilitating role negotiation in phase 3 and in network exploration in phase 4. We have addressed the leader role in team development and performance from both theoretical and application perspectives in other work that is consistent with the present model (Kozlowski et al., 1996a; Kozlowski et al., 1996b). Leaders can exert considerable leverage on the performance improvement that is inherent in the compilation process.

Unidirectional Compilation

The model describes compilation as a one-way process and does not explicitly consider factors that might shift the team back to earlier developmental phases and focal levels. For example, replacement of the leader in a hierarchical team or the turnover of a significant mass in an ongoing team would undermine performance and necessitate a new cycle of compilation. We expect that compilation and the process of regaining performance would be faster when enough existing members remain to absorb new members and when the new leader does not attempt to reshape the team. Conversely, new members may bond together and reject existing norms, performance standards, and role expectations. This would likely result in polarization, coalition formation, and a protracted struggle for dominance, with negative effects on performance. A considerable literature addresses these processes (Bettenhausen, 1991; Levine & Moreland, 1990), providing guidance on conflict and its management. Our model implies that significant replacement should be accompanied by an effort to compile a new team and new performance expectations—that is, synthesis of the new and old, as opposed to an accommodation of new members to existing norms and expectations.

Phases and Time Frames

We did not delve into variability of these temporal considerations, although their variability is inherent in our theory. Emphasis on both of these factors is expected to be determined by characteristics of the team performance context. Earlier phases of the model are more relevant for teams with simpler forms of interdependence. Outcome specifications for phase 2 constitute the primary performance requirements for the simplest teams. Somewhat more complex teams also incorporate outcome specifications for phase 3. In effect, simple workflow interdependencies represent task systems that are at the individual (pooled coordination) or dyadic (sequential coordination) focal levels. Performance inherent in more complex workflow interdependencies (that is, reciprocal and team coordination) necessitates greater emphasis on phases at the dyadic and team network focal levels. That is, complex teams necessitate further compilation to yield performance that meets the requirements for phase 4. Thus phase emphasis and duration are expected to be contingent on the complexity of workflow interdependence.

Team Termination

The model makes no explicit assumption about the lifespan for team compilation and performance. It concludes its description of the compilation process with the idea that teams can continually improve performance for normative tasks and can develop adaptive capabilities for emergent tasks. We do not assume that an intact team will continue to refine these outcomes endlessly, although the point at which learning and performance asymptote is an open question. The literature indicates that low turnover and high tenure are associated with performance decrements at the individual and team levels. Teams may reduce attention to continuous improvement and team adaptability over time, adopting habitual routines that reduce mutual monitoring and coordination requirements (Gersick & Hackman, 1990). Research indicates that increasing job tenure moderates (that is, reduces) the relationship between task complexity and individual affect (Katz, 1978) and performance (Kozlowski & Hults, 1986). Similarly, project teams evidence lower productivity (Katz, 1982) and creativity with increasing group longevity. In practice this may not be a critical factor in that one can anticipate some degree of personnel turbulence in the long term. It also suggests, however, that compilation should be continuously monitored in the longer term to detect and diagnose the onset of developmental stasis. It may be advisable to inject new members into an ongoing team periodically to disrupt routines and force a recompilation process. This may provide a means to inject new life into old teams. The appropriate combination of new members and time frames to accomplish this recompilation, however, are theoretically elusive.

Practical Implications for Enhancing Team Performance

Staffing

One obvious implication of our theory is that individuals need to possess abilities relevant to their position requirements. There is nothing startling about this implication; it is the bedrock assumption of industrial and organizational psychology models of person-job fit. This base implication, however, is focused on the individual level and does not consider the broader context for team performance. Several recent efforts have considered the implications of the team context. Reviews have endeavored to determine the effects of team composition (Jackson, May, & Whitney, 1995; Moreland & Levine, 1992), to establish individual-level KSA requirements for teamwork (Stevens & Campion, 1994), to define the performance context (Borman & Motowidlo, 1993), and to derive the dimensions of team performance (Fleishman & Zacarro, 1992; McIntyre & Salas, 1995).

Less obvious implications from the current model are derived from individual differences potentially relevant to (1) team-level continuous improvement and adaptability and (2) the compilation of skills across levels. Individual differences that reference ability, personality, and learning and motivation are relevant. For example, one means to improve team performance is to identify individual differences that facilitate the role negotiation processes that are central in phase 3 and the network exploration processes that are central in phase 4. Research suggests that role negotiation processes, represented by positive HMX relationships, are facilitated by perceived similarity in abilities, attitudes, and perceptions (Nason,

1995). Attitudes and perceptions are more malleable to experience, whereas abilities are regarded as stable. Indeed, because ability affects role performance, and because role performance affects the development of HMX, ability may be critical in role negotiation. This suggests that it may be desirable to constrain the range of team-member ability to make it more similar across the team (Tziner & Eden, 1985), assuming, of course, that ability levels match job requirements. Nason (1995) reported that perceived ability affected HMX, and that HMX affected perceptual convergence, communication, coordination, and team performance.

The personality trait of collectivism may also be a useful individual difference for facilitating dyadic exchange. Driskell and Salas (1992) reported that dyads composed of high collectivism pairs were more cooperative and collaborative, and communicated more than mixed dyads or dyads composed of high individualism pairs. Thus team tasks that necessitate role negotiation, reciprocal coordination, and mutual adjustment are likely to have enhanced performance when team members' personalities are consonant with the compilation process and performance requirements.

Finally, emerging research provides evidence that individual learning and performance orientation traits have important implications for learning, motivation, and performance. Individuals high on learning orientation approach situations with an exploratory attitude, and endeavor to master the knowledge and skills needed to succeed. They regard ability as malleable and they self-reference performance improvements. In contrast, performance-oriented individuals are outcome focused. They see ability as fixed, and they reference effectiveness to an external goal or the performance of others (Dweck, 1986). Research has shown that learning-oriented individuals learn faster and are more adaptable in new and difficult situations (Kozlowski et al., 1995). It may thus be desirable to select learning-oriented individuals to staff complex teams where adaptive performance is an important aspect of effectiveness.

Training and Development
One implication of our framework is the need to recognize that conventional views of training as special experiences removed from the work context will be increasingly limited. We need to integrate

training into the work setting, to make it a regular aspect of everyday work experience. This will necessitate a reconceptualization of training systems in organizations (Kozlowski, 1998). As we endeavor to push training into the workplace, there are two likely leverage points. One is the use of training strategies to enhance adaptive performance; the other is the incorporation of training capabilities or tools into work technology systems.

In regard to the first leverage point—the use of new training strategies—Smith, Ford, and Kozlowski (1997) reviewed a variety of training interventions that were intended to provoke active learning. By improving deep comprehension, knowledge structure, and self-regulatory and metacognitive skills, these techniques enhance knowledge and skills that yield adaptive performance. They include advance organizers, analogies, guided discovery, error-based training, metacognitive instruction, learner control, and sequenced mastery goals, among others. Research suggests that these interventions have been generally effective. A key practical advantage of these training strategies is that they have the potential to be easily integrated into existing training environments and work settings.

In regard to the second leverage point—incorporating training capabilities into work technology—the increasing penetration of technology into the workplace offers the potential to build training capabilities into the design of the team task system. Discussion of this potential to measure performance on-line is often limited to intrusive evaluative measurement and its ethical implications. We agree that this is a trap to be avoided. Technical improvements, however, in monitoring and artificial intelligence will eventually allow each team member to have a real-time, "intelligent" tutor that monitors performance, compares it to a model of performance compilation, and provides process feedback to guide learning (Salas et al., 1996). This developmental use of technology has many positive benefits. We are still a ways away from implementing these systems; considerable improvements in artificially intelligent "expert" and "student" models are required. The construction of intelligent tutoring systems is dependent on clearly articulated models of knowledge and skill development at the individual, dyadic, and team levels. Our model of compilation and performance may serve as a point of departure for such efforts.

Performance

Skill compilation is a central feature of the model. There are two key implications, both of which relate to the three themes in the underlying theory. One implication is the need to recognize that the content of performance outcomes shifts over time. In effect, this is akin to the notion of dynamic criteria, where the relationship between predictors and criteria weakens over time as other factors increasingly account for "performance," conceptualized as a static global criterion. Rather than focusing on changes on the predictor side, the compilation model identifies knowledge, skill, and performance capabilities at different points in the developmental process.

The composition of team performance changes with compilation. In phase 1, performance is not the relevant focus. Rather, individuals must have opportunities to resolve social ambiguity and to bond to the team as an entity. Without this foundation, individuals will have difficulty focusing on performance. In phase 2, individuals focus on task proficiency. They need to achieve competency, and until they do they will have difficulty attending to the interdependencies inherent in team performance. In phase 3, dyads define roles, establish boundaries, and set performance expectations that govern coordinated interactions. This is the foundation for team performance. Team members must have an opportunity to define performance standards within the confines of team objectives. In phase 4, teams explore alternative roles and network structures for accomplishing team goals. Teams must be provided with opportunities to compile these skills. That means that the imposition of performance outcome goals too early in the process can inhibit or retard the acquisition of critical skills. It also means that the imposition of team structure and performance routines, with little opportunity for teams to explore alternatives, can inhibit continuous improvement and adaptive performance. Teams must have time to develop, and the freedom to self-regulate and self-manage.

A second implication of compilation as a central feature of the model has to do with focal levels and workflow interdependencies. Pooled tasks, which predominate in simple teams, are essentially independent. Such team situations should be conceptualized at the individual level, which should serve as the basis for performance assessment, feedback, and rewards. Most work teams are complex. Their team tasks are founded on individual-level behavior and performance but have outcomes at the team level that transcend simple additive models of aggregation. For complex teams, coordination between dyads and across the team network is central to team performance. This suggests that performance assessment, feedback, and rewards must address both the individual within the team (the team as the context for individual-level behavior) and the team as a whole. Frankly, research is very limited with respect to this issue. At the risk of overgeneralizing, it seems clear that both individual and team-level goals and feedback are critical to the performance of complex teams (Gully, 1997; Mitchell & Silver, 1990; Pritchard et al., 1988). Thus, as organizations increasingly move toward team-based work designs, systems for assessment, feedback, and rewards will need to be developed that move beyond the individual-level focus that is still so ubiquitous in our field.

Conclusion

The world of work is changing. This change is forcing a fundamental reevaluation of the ways that industrial and organizational psychology solves basic problems concerning selection, training, and performance management. The field's conceptual frameworks, methods, and tools have served our needs in these areas quite well. They are best suited, however, for a world of work that is characterized by stable, well-defined jobs that can be decoupled from their context. That is the work world of the past. The field needs theories, methods, and tools that recognize jobs as dynamic, emergent, and embedded in team and organizational contexts.

Our response to this challenge has been to construct a theory that conceptualizes team performance as the result of a compilation process proceeding across levels and time. Team performance is not static; it is dynamic and evolutionary. Thus our efforts to understand performance in teams must reflect change over time, must account for different performance requirements at different stages of compilation, and must be considered simultaneously at the individual, dyadic, and team levels. We are hopeful that this theory makes a small contribution in our movement toward understanding work in the twenty-first century.

References

Allen, R. (1987). Group norms: Their influence on training. In R. Craig (Ed.), *Training and development handbook: A guide to human resource development* (pp. 180–194). New York: McGraw-Hill.

Anderson, J. R. (1987). Skill acquisition: Compilation of weak-method problem solutions. *Psychological Review, 94,* 192–210.

Anderson, N., & Thomas, H.D.C. (1995). Work group socialization. In M. West (Ed.), *Handbook of work groups* (pp. 423–450). New York: Wiley.

Argote, L., & McGrath, J. E. (1993). Group processes in organizations: Continuity and change. In C. L. Cooper & I. T. Robertson (Eds.), *International review of industrial and organizational psychology* (Vol. 8, pp. 333–389). New York: Wiley.

Bales, R. F., & Strodtbeck, F. L. (1951). Phases in group problem solving. *Journal of Abnormal and Social Psychology, 46,* 485–495.

Bandura, A. (1977a). Self-efficacy: Towards a unifying theory of behavioral change. *Psychological Review, 84,* 191–215.

Bandura, A. (1977b). *Social learning theory.* Upper Saddle River, NJ: Prentice Hall.

Bandura, A. (1982). Self-efficacy mechanism in human agency. *American Psychologist, 37,* 122–147.

Bandura, A. (1991). Social cognitive theory of self-regulation. *Organizational Behavior and Human Decision Processes, 50,* 248–287.

Baron, R. A. (1988). Negative effects of destructive criticism: Impact on conflict, self-efficacy, and task performance. *Journal of Applied Psychology, 73,* 199–207.

Berger, M., & Berger, P. (Eds.). (1972). *Group training techniques.* New York: Halsted Press.

Bettenhausen, K. (1991). Five years of groups research: What we have learned and what needs to be addressed. *Journal of Management, 17,* 345–381.

Bion, W. R. (1961). *Experiences in groups.* New York: Basic Books.

Boguslaw, R., & Porter, E. H. (1962). Team functions and training. In R. M. Gagne (Ed.), *Psychological principles in system development* (pp. 387–416). New York: Holt, Rinehart and Winston.

Borman, W. C., & Motowidlo, S. J. (1993). Expanding the criterion domain to include elements of contextual performance. In N. Schmitt & W. C. Borman (Eds.), *Personnel selection in organizations* (pp. 71–98). San Francisco: Jossey-Bass.

Brass, D. J. (1995). A social network perspective on human resources management. In G. R. Ferris (Ed.), *Research in personnel and human resources management* (Vol. 13, pp. 39–79). Greenwich, CT: JAI Press.

Campbell, J. P., Gasser, M. B., & Oswald, F. L. (1996). The substantive nature of job performance variability. In K. R. Murphy (Ed.), *Individual differences and behavior in organizations* (pp. 258–299). San Francisco: Jossey-Bass.

Cannon-Bowers, J. A., Salas, E., & Converse, S. A. (1993). Shared mental models in expert team decision making. In N. J. Castellan Jr. (Ed.), *Individual and group decision making* (pp. 221–246). Hillsdale, NJ: Erlbaum.

Caple, R. B. (1978). The sequential stages of group development. *Small Group Behavior, 9,* 470–476.

Chao, G. T., O'Leary-Kelly, A. M., Wolf, S., Klein, H. J., & Gardner, P. D. (1994). Organizational socialization: Its content and consequences. *Journal of Applied Psychology, 79,* 730–743.

Christen, J. (1987). Team building. In R. Craig (Ed.), *Training and development handbook: A guide to human resource development* (pp. 443–455). New York: McGraw-Hill.

Cooper, C., & Mangham, I. (1971). *T-groups: A survey of research.* New York: Wiley-Interscience.

Cooper, M., Shiflett, S., Korotkin, A. L., & Fleishman, E. A. (1984). *Command and control teams: Techniques for assessing team performance* (ARRO Final Report). Washington, DC: Advanced Research Resources Organization.

Cream, B. W., Eggemeier, F. T., & Klein, G. A. (1978). A strategy for the development of training devices. *Human Factors, 20,* 145–158.

Denson, R. W. (1981). *Team training: Literature review and annotated bibliography.* (Tech. Rep. AFHRL-TR-80–40). Wright-Patterson Air Force Base, OH: Logistics and Technical Training Division, Air Force Human Resources Laboratory.

Driskell, J. E., & Salas, E. (1992). Collective behavior and team performance. *Human Factors, 34,* 277–288.

Dweck, C. S. (1986). Motivational processes affecting learning. *American Psychologist, 41,* 1040–1048.

Fedor, D. B., Rensvold, R. B., & Adams, S. M. (1992). An investigation of factors expected to affect feedback seeking: A longitudinal field study. *Personnel Psychology, 45,* 779–805.

Feldman, D. C. (1981). The multiple socialization of organizational members. *Academy of Management Review, 6,* 309–318.

Fleishman, E. A., & Zaccaro, S. J. (1992). Toward a taxonomy of team performance functions. In R. W. Swezey & E. Salas (Eds.), *Teams: Their training and performance* (pp. 31–56). Norwood, NJ: Ablex.

Ford, J. K., & Kraiger, K. (1995). The application of cognitive constructs and principles to the instructional systems model of training: Implications for needs assessment, design, and transfer. In C. L. Cooper & I. T. Robinson (Eds.), *International review of industrial and organizational psychology* (Vol. 10, pp. 1–48). London: Wiley.

Ford, J. K., Quiñones, M. A., Sego, D. J., & Sorra, J. S. (1992). Factors affecting the opportunity to perform trained tasks. *Personnel Psychology, 45,* 511–527.

Francis, D., & Young, D. (1979). *Improving work groups: A practical manual for team building.* San Diego, CA: University Associates.

Gabarro, J. (1990). The development of working relationships. In J. Galegher, R. Kraut, & C. Egido (Eds.), *Intellectual teamwork* (pp. 79–110). Hillsdale, NJ: Erlbaum.

Gersick, C.J.G. (1988). Time and transition in work teams: Toward a new model of group development. *Academy of Management Journal, 31,* 9–41.

Gersick, C.J.G., & Hackman, J. R. (1990). Habitual routines in task-performing groups. *Organizational Behavior and Human Decision Processes, 47,* 65–97.

Gibb, J. R. (1964). Climate for trust. In L. P. Bradford, J. R. Gibb, & K. D. Benne (Eds.), *T-group therapy and laboratory method: Innovation in re-education.* New York: Wiley.

Ginnett, R. C. (1987). *First encounters of the close kind: The first meetings of airline flight crews.* Unpublished doctoral dissertation, Yale University.

Gist, M. E., & Mitchell, T. R. (1992). Self-efficacy: A theoretical analysis of its determinants and malleability. *Academy of Management Review, 17,* 183–211.

Glickman, A. S., Zimmer, S., Montero, R. C., Guerette, P. J., Campbell, W. J., Morgan, B. B., & Salas, E. (1987). *The evolution of teamwork skills: An empirical assessment with implications for training* (Tech. Rep. TR-87–016). Orlando, FL: Naval Training Systems Center.

Goodman, P. S. (Ed.). (1986). *Designing effective work groups.* San Francisco: Jossey-Bass.

Graen, G. B., & Scandura, T. A. (1987). Toward a psychology of dyadic organizing. In B. M. Staw & L. L. Cummings (Eds.), *Research in organizational behavior* (Vol. 9, pp. 175–208). Greenwich, CT: JAI Press.

Gully, S. M. (1997). *The influences of self-regulatory processes on learning and performance in a team training context.* Unpublished doctoral dissertation, Michigan State University, Department of Psychology.

Gully, S. M. (in press). Work team research since 1985: Recent findings and future trends. In M. Beyerlein (Ed.), *Work teams: Past, present, and future.* Amsterdam: Kluwer Academic.

Hackman, J. R. (1987). The design of work teams. In J. W. Lorsch (Ed.), *Handbook of organizational behavior* (pp. 315–342).Upper Saddle River, NJ: Prentice Hall.

Hackman, J. R. (1990). Creating more effective work groups. In J. R. Hackman (Ed.), *Groups that work (and those that don't): Creating conditions for effective teamwork.* San Francisco: Jossey-Bass.

Hackman, J. R. (1992). Group influences on individuals in organizations. In M. D. Dunnette & L. M. Hough (Eds.), *Handbook of industrial and organizational psychology* (Vol. 3, pp. 199–267). Palo Alto, CA: Consulting Psychologists Press.

Hill, W. F., & Gruner, L. (1973). A study of development in open and closed groups. *Small Group Behavior, 4,* 355–381.

Hollenbeck, J. R., Ilgen, D. R., Sego, D. J., & Major, D. A. (1995). The multi-level theory of team decision making: Decision performance in heirarchical teams incorporating distributed expertise. *Journal of Applied Psychology, 80,* 292–316.

Jackson, S. E., May, K. E., & Whitney, K. (1995). Understanding the dynamics of diversity in decision-making teams. In R. A. Guzzo & E. Salas (Eds.), *Team effectiveness and decision making in organizations* (pp. 204–261). San Francisco: Jossey-Bass.

Karoly, P. (1993). Mechanisms of self-regulation: A systems view. *Annual Review of Psychology, 44,* 23–52.

Katz, D., & Kahn, R. L. (1978). *The social psychology of organizations* (2nd ed.). New York: Wiley.

Katz, R. (1978). Job longevity as a situational factor in job satisfaction. *Administrative Science Quarterly, 23,* 204–223.

Katz, R. (1980). Time and work: Toward an integrative perspective. *Research in Organizational Behavior, 2,* 81–127.

Katz, R. (1982). The effects of group longevity on communication and performance. *Administrative Science Quarterly, 27,* 81–104.

Klaus, D. J., & Glaser, R. (1970). Reinforcement determinants of team proficiency. *Organizational Behavior and Human Performance, 5,* 33–67.

Kleinman, D. L., & Serfaty, D. (1989). Team performance assessment in distributed decision making. In R. Gilson, J. P. Kincaid, & B. Goldiez (Eds.), *Proceedings of the Interactive Networked Simulation for Training Conference.* Orlando, FL: Naval Training Systems Center.

Kormanski, C., & Mozenter, A. (1987). A new model of team building: A technology for today and tomorrow. In J. W. Pfeiffer (Ed.), *The 1987 annual: Developing human resources* (pp. 255–268). San Diego, CA: University Associates.

Kozlowski, S.W.J. (1998). Training and developing adaptive teams: Theory, principles, and research. In J. A. Cannon-Bowers & E. Salas (Eds.), *Decision making under stress: Implications for training and simulation* (pp. 115–153). Washington, DC: APA Books.

Kozlowski, S.W.J., & Doherty, M. L. (1989). Integration of climate and leadership: Examination of a neglected issue. *Journal of Applied Psychology, 74,* 546–553.

Kozlowski, S.W.J., Gully, S. M., McHugh, P. P., Salas, E., & Cannon-Bowers, J. A. (1996a). A dynamic theory of leadership and team effectiveness: Developmental and task contingent leader roles. In G. R. Ferris (Ed.), *Research in personnel and human resource management* (Vol. 14, pp. 253–305). Greenwich, CT: JAI Press.

Kozlowski, S.W.J., Gully, S. M., Salas, E., & Cannon-Bowers, J. A. (1996b). Team leadership and development: Theory, principles, and guidelines for training leaders and teams. In M. Beyerlein, D. Johnson, & S. Beyerlein (Eds.), *Advances in interdisciplinary studies of work teams: Team leadership* (Vol. 3, pp. 251–289). Greenwich, CT: JAI Press.

Kozlowski, S.W.J., Gully, S. M., Smith, E. M., Brown, K. G., Mullins, M. E., & Williams, A. E. (1996c, April). Sequenced mastery goals and advance organizers: Enhancing the effects of practice. In K. Smith-Jentsch (Chair), *When, how, and why does practice make perfect?* Symposium conducted at the Eleventh Annual Conference of the Society for Industrial and Organizational Psychology, San Diego, CA.

Kozlowski, S.W.J., Gully, S. M., Smith, E. A., Nason, E. R., & Brown, K. G. (1995, May). Sequenced mastery training and advance organizers: Effects on learning, self-efficacy, performance, and generalization. In R. J. Klimoski (Chair), *Thinking and feeling while doing: Understanding the learner in the learning process.* Symposium conducted at the Tenth Annual Conference of the Society for Industrial and Organizational Psychology, Orlando, FL.

Kozlowski, S.W.J., & Hattrup, K. (1992). A disagreement about within-group agreement: Disentangling issues of consistency versus consensus. *Journal of Applied Psychology, 77,* 161–167.

Kozlowski, S.W.J., & Hults, B. M. (1986). Joint moderation of the relation between task complexity and job performance for engineers. *Journal of Applied Psychology, 71,* 196–202.

Kozlowski, S.W.J., & Salas, E. (1997). An organizational systems approach for the implementation and transfer of training. In J. K. Ford, S.W.J. Kozlowski, K. Kraiger, E. Salas, & M. Teachout (Eds.), *Improving training effectiveness in work organizations* (pp. 247–287). Hillsdale, NJ: Erlbaum.

Levine, J. M., & Moreland, R. L. (1990). Progress in small group research. *Annual Review of Psychology, 41,* 585–634.

Locke, E. A., Frederick, E., Lee, C., & Bobko, P. (1984). Effect of self-efficacy, goals, and task strategies on task performance. *Journal of Applied Psychology, 69,* 241–251.

Louis, M. R. (1980). Surprise and sense-making: What newcomers experience in entering unfamiliar organizational settings. *Administrative Science Quarterly, 25,* 226–251.

Major, D. A., & Kozlowski, S.W.J. (1997). Newcomer information seeking: Individual and contextual influences. *International Journal of Selection and Assessment, 5,* 16–28.

Major, D. A., Kozlowski, S.W.J., Chao, G. T., & Gardner, P. D. (1995). Newcomer expectations and early socialization outcomes: The moderating effect of role development factors. *Journal of Applied Psychology, 80,* 418–431.

McGrath, J. E. (1990). Time matters in groups. In J. Galegher, R. Krout, & C. C. Egido (Eds.), *Intellectual teamwork* (pp. 23–61). Hillsdale, NJ: Earlbaum.

McIntyre, R. M., & Salas, E. (1995). Measuring and managing for team performance: Lessons from complex environments. In R. A. Guzzo & E. Salas (Eds.), *Team effectiveness and decision making in organizations* (pp. 9–45). San Francisco: Jossey-Bass.

Mitchell, R. (1986). Team building by disclosure of internal frames of reference. *Journal of Applied Behavioral Science, 22,* 15–28.

Mitchell, T. R., & Silver, W. S. (1990). Individual and group goals when workers are interdependent: Effects on task strategies and performance. *Journal of Applied Psychology, 75,* 185–193.

Modlin, H. C., & Faris, M. (1956). Group adaptation and integration in psychiatric team practice. *Psychiatry, 19,* 97–103.

Moreland, R. L., & Levine, J. M. (1988). Group dynamics over time: Development and socialization in small groups. In J. E. McGrath (Ed.), *The social psychology of time: New perspectives* (pp. 151–181). Thousand Oaks, CA: Sage.

Moreland, R. L., & Levine, J. M. (1989). Newcomers and oldtimers in groups. In P. Paulus (Ed.), *Psychology of group influence* (pp. 143–186). Hillsdale, NJ: Earlbaum.

Moreland, R. L., & Levine, J. M. (1992). The composition of small groups. In E. E. Lawler III, B. Markovsky, C. Ridgeway, & H. Walker (Eds.), *Advances in group processes* (Vol. 9, pp. 237–280). Greenwich, CT: JAI Press.

Morgan, B. B., Glickman, A. S., Woodard, E. A., Blaiwes, A. S., & Salas, E. (1986). *Measurement of team behaviors in a Navy environment* (Tech. Rep. NTSC TR-86–014). Orlando, FL: Naval Training Systems Center.

Morrison, E. W. (1993). Newcomer information seeking: Exploring types, modes, sources, and outcomes. *Academy of Management Journal, 36,* 557–589.

Nason, E. R. (1995). *Horizontal team member exchange (HMX): The effects of dyadic relationship quality on team processes and outcomes.* Unpublished doctoral dissertation, Michigan State University, Department of Psychology.

Nieva, V. F., Fleishman, E. A., & Rieck, A. (1978). *Team dimensions: Their identity, their measurement and their relationships* (Contract No. DAHC 19–78-C-0001). Washington, DC: Response Analysis Corporation.

Orasanu, J. (1990). *Shared mental models and crew performance.* Paper presented at the Thirty-Fourth Annual meeting of the Human Factors Society, Orlando, FL.

Ostroff, C., & Kozlowski, S.W.J. (1992). Organizational socialization as a learning process: The role of information acquisition. *Personnel Psychology, 45,* 849–874.

Ostroff, C., & Kozlowski, S.W.J. (1993). The role of mentoring in the information gathering processes of newcomers during early organizational socialization. *Journal of Vocational Behavior, 42,* 170–183.

Pritchard, R. D., Jones, S. D., Roth, P. L., Stuebing, K. K., & Edeberg, S. E. (1988). Effects of group feedback, goal setting, and incentives on organizational productivity. *Journal of Applied Psychology, 73,* 337–358.

Roth, J. T., Hritz, R. J., & Lewis, C. M. (1984). *Methods for understanding, describing, assessing, and training teamwork* (Contract No. MDA903–81–C-0198). Alexandria, VA: U.S. Army Research Institute for the Behavioral and Social Sciences.

Rousseau, D. M. (1985). Issues of level in organizational research: Multi-level and cross-level perspectives. In L. L. Cummings & B. M. Staw (Eds.), *Research in organizational behavior* (Vol. 7, pp. 1–37). Greenwich, CT: JAI Press.

Salas, E., Cannon-Bowers, J. A., & Kozlowski, S.W.J. (1996). The science and practice of training: Current trends and emerging themes. In J. K. Ford, S.W.J. Kozlowski, K. Kraiger, E. Salas, & M. Teachout (Eds.), *Improving training effectiveness in work organizations* (pp. 357–368). Hillsdale, NJ: Erlbaum.

Salas, E., Dickinson, T. L., Converse, S. A., & Tannenbaum, S. I. (1992). Toward an understanding of team performance and training. In R. W. Swezey & E. Salas (Eds.), *Teams: Their training and performance* (pp. 3–29). Norwood, NJ: Ablex.

Seers, A. (1989). Team-member exchange quality: A new construct for role-making research. *Organizational Behavior and Human Decision Processes, 43,* 118–135.

Shiflett, S. (1979). Toward a general model of small group productivity. *Psychological Bulletin, 86,* 67–79.

Shiflett, S., Eisner, E. J., Price, S. J., & Schemmer, F. M. (1982, July). *The definition and measurement of team functions* (ARRO Rep. No. 3068-FR-R81-4). Washington, DC: Advanced Research Resources Organization.

Smith, E. M., Ford, J. K., & Kozlowski, S.W.J. (1997). Building adaptive expertise: Implications for training design. In M. A. Quiñones & A. Ehrenstein (Eds.), *Training for a rapidly changing workplace: Applications of psychological research* (pp. 89–118). Washington, DC: APA Books.

Smith, E. M., & Kozlowski, S.W.J. (1994, April). Socialization and adaptation: Individual and contextual influences on social learning strategies. In S.W.J. Kozlowski (Chair), *Transitions during organizational socialization: Newcomer expectations, information-seeking, and learning outcomes.* Symposium conducted at the Ninth Annual Conference of the Society for Industrial and Organizational Psychology, Nashville, TN.

Steiner, I. D. (1972). *Group process and productivity.* New York: Academic Press.

Stevens, M. J., & Campion, M. A. (1994). The knowledge, skill and ability requirements for teamwork: Implications for human resource management. *Journal of Management, 20,* 503–530.

Sundstrom, E., De Meuse, K. P., & Futrell, D. (1990). Work teams: Applications and effectiveness. *American Psychologist, 45,* 120–133.

Terreberry, S. (1968). The evolution of organizational environments. *Administrative Science Quarterly, 12,* 590–613.

Thompson, J. (1967). *Organizations in action: Social science bases of administrative theory.* New York: McGraw-Hill.

Tuckman, B. W. (1965). Developmental sequence in small groups. *Psychological Bulletin, 63,* 384–399.

Tuckman, B. W., & Jensen, M.A.C. (1977). Stages of group small-group development revisited. *Group and Organization Studies, 2,* 419–427.

Tuckman, B. W., & Sexton, T. L. (1991). The effect of teacher encouragement on student self-efficacy and motivation for self-regulated performance. *Journal of Social Behavior and Personality, 6,* 137–146.

Tziner, A., & Eden, D. (1985). Effects of crew composition on crew performance: Does the whole equal the sum of its parts? *Journal of Applied Psychology, 70,* 85–93.

Van de Ven, A. H., Delbecq, A. L., & Koenig, R. (1976). Determinants of coordination modes within organizations. *American Sociological Review, 41,* 322–338.

Volpe, C. A., Cannon-Bowers, J. A., Salas, E., & Spector, P. (1996). The impact of cross-training on team functioning: An empirical investigation. *Human Factors, 38,* 87–100.

Whittaker, J. (1970). Models of group development: Implications for social group work practice. *Social Service Review, 44,* 308–322.

Yalom, I. E. (1970). *The theory and practice of group psychotherapy.* New York: Basic Books.

Zalesny, M. D., Salas, E., & Prince, C. (1995). Conceptual and measurement issues in coordination: Implications for team behavior and performance. In G. R. Ferris (Ed.), *Research in personnel and human resources management* (Vol. 13, pp. 81–115). Greenwich, CT: JAI Press.

Zander, A. (1982). *Making groups effective.* San Francisco: Jossey-Bass.

PART 2

The Effect of Change on Three Key Processes— Staffing, Motivation, and Employee Development

CHAPTER 9

The Challenge of Staffing a Postindustrial Workplace

Kevin R. Murphy

In Chapter One, Ilgen and Pulakos concisely define the task of staffing as "linking human knowledge, skills, abilities, and dispositions to the demands of the work setting." They also note that performance effectiveness depends on the match between the demands of the job and the characteristics of the jobholder. They go on to say that definitions of *jobs* and *job performance* are becoming increasingly complex, fuzzy, and dynamic. One implication is that familiar models for staffing may no longer apply in many organizations, or at least may no longer prove as useful as they did in the past. The familiar model I have in mind is one that uses stable characteristics of individuals (such as general cognitive ability and personality traits) to predict their future performance in stable, well-defined, thoroughly analyzed, and well-understood jobs; validates those predictions by correlating measures of the individual differences with indices of job performance; and then permits long-term forecasts of the success of various staffing strategies. The goal of these staffing models is to do the best job possible (given various practical constraints, such as the quality of the applicant pool and individual preferences) of fitting people to jobs.

The cumulative message of the chapters in this book is that changes in organizations and in methods of organizing work may render current models and methods of staffing at least partially obsolete. It is important to keep in mind that there is a great deal of uncertainty in describing changes or future directions in the workplace.

The extent to which the changes suggested in these chapters have actually occurred, or are likely to persist beyond the normal life span of other managerial fads, is far from clear (the ratio of hype to evidence in this area is alarming), and it is difficult to distinguish true and lasting changes in the organization of work from mere speculation about the future of organizations. Nevertheless, there does seem to be credible evidence of meaningful changes in the way many organizations approach work, and these changes will have important implications for staffing.

This chapter makes three general propositions. First, changes in the way organizations are structured and work is performed may be more fundamental than most commentators suggest, and may require substantial changes in the way we think about the goals, methods, and evaluation of staffing programs. Throughout the chapter I will use the term *postindustrial workplace* as a bit of short-hand to describe the sorts of organization that seems to be emerging. I will expand on the meaning and implications of this term in the sections that follow.

Second, current assumptions about the impact of staffing decisions on organizations (such as the assumption that relatively small changes in the validity of selection tests can translate into large changes in organizational productivity) may need to be re-examined in light of ongoing changes in organizations. Many of the key concepts in current staffing models rely on the assumption that the duties, tasks, and demands of jobs often remain stable for relatively long periods (making it possible to forecast success in one's current job and in other jobs in a well-defined career path). As jobs become more fluid, this assumption of relative stability may become increasingly problematic.

Third, there are reasons to question the sustainability of a number of changes in organizations described in the preceding chapters. As I note later, relatively little is known about the extent to which such changes are actually occurring in the workplace, or the extent to which jobs in organizations that implement the postindustrial model described here are really different from jobs in organizations that follow the "industrial" model. If the changes outlined in this book's earlier chapters are taken to the extreme, they would be difficult to sustain for any prolonged period. Conversely, if these changes are in fact happening only in isolated pockets of the economy, speculation about broad shifts in the organization of work, the types of staffing models needed, and so on may be premature. Although the true extent of such changes may be unknown, it is possible to build some models of the extent to which such changes in the organization of work might reasonably be sustained, helping to establish some of the boundary conditions for the emergence of a truly new model for the organization of work.

A key theme linking these three points, and linking them to the chapters in the first part of the book, is that the definition of effective job performance is changing as organizations change, and that models and methods for assessing and increasing job performance that have been successful in the past may not be as successful in the future. To understand why this might occur, it is useful to consider briefly where we seem to be heading.

The Postindustrial Workplace

The first eight chapters of this book paint a picture of a workplace in transition. Perhaps the most notable feature of this evolving workplace is the idea that job descriptions will normally be fluid rather than fixed, abstract and general rather than presenting a detailed picture of exactly what each individual should do to perform his or her job. A key assumption of the postindustrial workplace is that the turbulent external environment faced by organizations (such as the need to change products or services frequently in response to market demands or competitors' innovations) will lead to the need for frequent changes in workers' responsibilities, tasks, and work relationships. This implies that organizations that develop and hold on to rigid specifications of exactly what each employee is supposed to do will find it difficult to respond to changes in the marketplace or in the competitive environment in which they function.

In organizations that attempt to maintain the flexibility required to adapt to frequent changes of the sort just described, job responsibilities are likely to be defined only in the most general terms, and decisions regarding what behaviors specific workers should engage in at a given point in time are likely to be complex and to be affected by a number of contextual factors. The best answer to the question, What am I supposed to do in my job? is likely to be, It depends.

Fluid and flexible job descriptions will almost certainly lead to ambiguity and disagreement about the definition of good or poor job performance (Bowen, 1997; Campbell, 1990; London & Mone, Chapter Five, this volume). They are also likely to lead to fundamental shifts in the balance of power between labor and management. In the past, labor contracts have often included very specific provisions regarding the tasks performed by incumbents in particular jobs, and disagreements regarding responsibilities and performance standards could be resolved by referring to job descriptions. As the parameters of the job become less distinct, determinations of who is supposed to do what and how well a specific incumbent has done are likely to become increasingly contentious.

Another noteworthy aspect of the postindustrial workplace is the extensive use of teams (Driskell & Salas, 1992; Kozlowski, Gully, Nason, & Smith, Chapter Eight, this volume). Rather than assigning jobs, responsibilities, tasks, and so forth to individuals, many organizations are moving in the direction of assigning broad responsibilities to teams (which may be assembled for specific projects or may continue to function as units across many projects). As noted in Chapter Eight, teams must often negotiate and define roles for particular members, and the actual responsibilities of an individual's job may depend as much on the decisions of the team as on the decisions of the broader organization.

A third noteworthy feature of the postindustrial workplace is the assumption that individuals will change jobs, organizations, and even careers with some frequency. Career systems in many organizations are still based on the assumption that people will stay with the organization for long periods and move through well-defined career steps (often based on progression in the hierarchy of the organization). This model of career progression may become increasingly unrealistic as organizations change their strategies and structures. First, the stable organizational environments that provided a basis for this career model seem to be eroding. In contrast to the period 1940–1975, when industrial production underwent continuing expansion and the demand for American goods and services was virtually insatiable (and when there was virtually no foreign competition in several key industries), workers in postindustrial organizations can no longer count on having stable jobs or careers. Second, the organizational structures that supported such a model of career development (that is, well-defined hierarchical structures with many levels and large numbers of positions to be filled in each of several career tracks) appear to be losing favor in many organizations.

Finally, there is evidence that many organizations are developing a two-tiered workforce—a workforce made up of core and contingent employees (Hulin & Glomb, Chapter Four, this volume). Contingent employees have a limited relationship with the organization and may be employed only for the duration of a project or product run, whereas core employees have a more ongoing relationship with the organization, although the terms of this relationship might be undefined. One implication of the increasing use of contingent labor is that many workers may have no real connection to the organization that currently employs them. As I note in a later section of this chapter, the division of labor between core and contingent employees may represent a complex and controversial set of decisions about the roles that employees should occupy in an organization.

The emerging organizations I refer to as postindustrial represent a sharp deviation from the sort of organization that has dominated the landscape over the past century or two. The first proposition put forth in this chapter is that changes in the fundamental organization of work have not yet been accompanied by changes in the way we think about staffing organizations.

Proposition 1: The Industrial Revolution May Be Over: Implications for Staffing

The effective use of technology in the workplace has always been a concern of managers and employees, and examples of the successful application of the technology of the day survive from the Stone Age (debates continue about the technologies and methods of work organization used to construct Stonehenge and other surviving monuments of the period) to the preindustrial period of the eighteenth century. By the 1780s fundamental changes in the design of work and the application of technology to industrial production (and the monumental changes in productivity that accompanied new methods of work organization and new technologies) had become sufficiently well established to be called the industrial revolution.

Historians tend to focus on the technological bases of the industrial revolution (steam power, the cotton gin, the spinning jenny, railroads, and so on), but the human side of this revolution was equally important, and it shaped the way we still think about work and organizations.

One reason for the success of the industrial revolution was that the nature and organization of work changed to take maximum advantage of emerging technologies. A distinguishing feature of the industrial system was the development of jobs that were simple, stable, and standardized. This meant that industrial jobs could be easily learned (even by the largely illiterate workforces of the time), that performance could be defined in relatively simple terms, and that jobs could be staffed by workers who did not possess specialized skills or knowledge. This model of work organization provided a foundation for many of the defining features of the industrial system (ranging from scientific management to continuous process production methods) and set the stage for the development of staffing models that are still in use today.

The standardization and simplification of work in industrial settings made possible what is still a cornerstone of human resource management—a focus on the job rather than on the position as a unit of analysis. That is, work was designed in such a way that it could be rationally planned in the abstract, and the essential characteristics of the work could be described without consideration of the individuals holding particular positions. Familiar human resource functions ranging from job analysis, selection testing, development of job families and career ladders, development of generalizable performance appraisal systems and criteria, and so on all rest on systems of work design that separate decisions about the design and flow of work from decisions about the workers themselves.

Systems of work organization that feature standardization and stability greatly facilitate many aspects of human resource management. First, it is possible to analyze jobs systematically and to have some confidence that essential features of the job will not change as incumbents change, or as jobs or job incumbents in other parts of the organization change. Second, it is possible to define concretely the dimensions of job performance and to scale performance in such a way that the implications of various levels of job performance are understood. By understanding both the dimensions and the concrete meaning of various levels of performance, it is possible to forecast the probable outcomes of various human resource interventions.

This system of work organization allows one to use systematic personnel selection to identify the individuals who are most likely to perform well, and to tailor training to maximize the job-related knowledge and skills of those who are selected. It is possible to design sensible career paths, based on the reasonable supposition that experience in particular jobs will develop specific skills and that effective performance in those jobs can be used to forecast effective performance later in one's career.

Research on the validity and utility of personnel selection tests (Hunter & Hunter, 1984; Hunter & Schmidt, 1982) illustrates many of the strengths of this system. At a practical level, research on the utility of selection tests suggests that the use of valid predictors can result in substantial increases in the productivity of the workforce. At a scientific level, this research suggests that broad principles can be articulated about the sorts of individuals who are most likely to succeed or fail in many jobs. Most generally, performance can be substantially improved in virtually any job by hiring individuals who are relatively high on general cognitive ability and who show a few key personality traits (such as conscientiousness). Specific improvements on this general formula can sometimes be offered, through a fine-grained analysis of the tasks and the demands of a job, but the high degree of standardization inherent in the industrial model that has dominated our thinking for the last two hundred years allows the human resource manager to accomplish a great deal with a relatively simple set of tools.

One of the ironies suggested by the first eight chapters of this book is that just as we have reached a consensus on how to do things such as personnel selection simply and well (developments in meta-analysis and validity generalization in the last fifteen to twenty years have led personnel psychologists and human resource managers to become much more optimistic about our success in these endeavors), the foundation of our success may be crumbling (Murphy, 1996). Organizations that feature loosely defined jobs, teams, definitions of effective job performance that depend substantially on contextual factors (that is, doing whatever is most effective at the moment) rather than well-defined prescriptions (that is, doing what you are supposed to do), and mixes of core and contingent employees are likely to require different staffing systems than those that follow the traditional industrial model. I illustrate this by discussing two changes in personnel selection systems that might be anticipated in postindustrial organizations: the need for different types of selection devices, and the need for new decision models. Subsequent sections of this chapter consider the implications of these changes for defining and measuring performance and for understanding careers.

The Need for New Predictors and New Selection Criteria

In recent years, researchers have reached consensus that both general cognitive ability and broad personality traits are relevant to predicting success in a wide array of jobs (Barrick & Mount, 1991; Hunter & Hirsh, 1987; Hunter & Hunter, 1984; Murphy & Shiarella, 1997; Ree & Earles, 1994; Tett, Jackson, & Rothstein, 1991). Broad characteristics such as "g" and conscientiousness explain only a portion of the variance in job performance; this proportion depends on precisely how *performance* is defined and on how information about cognitive ability and personality is integrated (Murphy & Shiarella, 1997), and the proportion of variance in job performance *not* explained by these factors is almost certainly larger than the proportion explained. Nevertheless consistent findings of validity for measures of these constructs has led to considerable optimism about our ability to predict job performance on the basis of a relatively simple, and perhaps universal, set of constructs. As jobs and the nature of job performance change, however, it is likely that the antecedents of effective job performance are likely to change as well. As I note later, some of the changes may lead to an even heavier emphasis on general cognitive abilities and global personality characteristics as predictors of performance across jobs, whereas other changes may lead to an increasing emphasis on abilities, skills, and attributes that are not currently considered essential predictors of performance.

First, changes in technology are likely to change the types of cognitive operations (and abilities) used at work. Workers' access to information technology is likely to lead to less emphasis on the ability to retrieve prior knowledge from memory and to more emphasis on abstract knowledge as determinants of effective performance (Hesketh & Neal, Chapter Two, this volume). Furthermore, changes in technology may change the job in ways that make particular personality characteristics more or less relevant to success. For example, one reason that conscientiousness appears to be related to performance in a wide variety of jobs (Barrick & Mount, 1991) is that conscientious people are organized, planful, and responsible. Technology (such as project planning software, automated paging and reminder systems, and automatic monitoring systems) is increasingly used to perform functions that were once the province of organized, responsible, and planful workers.

Several chapters in Part One of this volume (notably Chapter Five by London & Mone) stress the need for continuous learning in jobs of the future. Individual differences in self-efficacy perceptions (Bandura, 1994) and learning orientation (Dweck, 1986) are likely to be important determinants of the success of continuous learning, independent of one's level of cognitive ability. Individuals who believe that they are not capable of learning and mastering new information, work methods, and so on may be at a substantial disadvantage in jobs that require continuous learning. Increasing emphasis on continuous learning also suggests that people's current levels of performance, and the resources they have at their disposal, will be an important antecedent of future performance. Continuous learning involves investing resources, which suggests that the rich will get richer. As noted in Chapter Five, continuous learning is most likely in people willing to devote the time, energy, and financial resources needed to pursue learning opportunities. This implies that good performers, and people with time and money on their hands, are most likely to engage in continuous learning, and that people who are marginal performers in relatively stable and simple jobs will increasingly be left behind in jobs that require continuous learning.

The increasing use of teams is likely to lead to greater emphasis on social skills as determinants of effective job performance. The individual difference variables relevant to success in a team environment may include interpersonal sensitivity and collectivism (Driskell & Salas, 1992; Kozlowski et al., Chapter Eight, this volume).

Transcultural skills (ability to manage interpersonal relationships across cultures) are also likely to become increasingly important, especially in multinational ventures.

Technological changes in work (see Hesketh & Neal, Chapter Two, this volume) may pose special challenges for managing interpersonal relationships. Although there is an increasing emphasis on teams in many organizations, this does not necessarily mean that there will be an increasing emphasis on face-to-face interaction. In many settings it is possible to assemble "virtual teams" made up of members working in different locations who interact via computers, teleconferencing, and so on. It is unlikely that the types of interpersonal issues that arise in virtual teams will be the same as those that arise in teams that work in the same location, or that the same skills will be needed to work effectively in both sorts of teams. At this point, very little is known about the skills, personality characteristics, and so on that are most likely to be critical for functioning effectively in jobs where telecommuting, virtual teams, electronic brainstorming, and so forth are part of the landscape.

In service-oriented organizations, the individual differences most likely to be relevant to effective job performance are personality and temperament variables (Hogan, Hogan, & Busch, 1984). Examples of personal characteristics and personality traits that have been cited as relevant to success in service occupations include motivational constructs (such as a service orientation), "upbeat" behavior, attractiveness, courtesy. The same traits that are relevant in many other jobs (such as "g" and conscientiousness) are also important in service jobs, but the unique demands of service work may lead to a broader conception of the optimal set of predictors.

Finally, changes in organizations may lead to significant changes in the sorts of criteria we try to maximize with selection tests. In the past, the emphasis in selection has been on identifying individuals who are most likely to perform their individual jobs well. That is, the goal of hiring has typically been described in terms of maximizing performance in the current job by fitting people appropriately to jobs. The increasing fluidity and instability in job descriptions and job demands suggests that organizations should emphasize person-organization fit rather than person-job fit in making selection decisions (Bowen, 1997). Current models emphasize hiring for the job, but if jobs are constantly changing and individuals are constantly moving from one job to another as the nature and demands of the jobs change, it is likely that the ultimate criterion will be an individual's overall contribution to the organization rather than his or her performance in the current job assignment (Motowidlo & Schmit, Chapter Three, this volume).

The Need for New Decision Models

Personnel selection has traditionally been thought of as the problem of finding the best k candidates (out of a pool of N applicants, where $N > k$) for a particular job. In a postindustrial workplace, it is not clear whether the concept of applying for a job will even make sense. Rather than deciding which applicants best fit a particular job, organizational decision makers are likely to consider two questions: Should the applicant become a member of this organization? and How should the abilities, skills, and experiences of this applicant be best used? The first decision involves an assessment of person-organization fit, as described earlier. The second decision represents the type of decisions that organizations have rarely been called upon to face—that is, classification decisions. (The armed services represent a notable exception.)

The technical issues involved in making classification decisions have long been understood, and numerous models exist for optimizing the quality of such decisions (Brogden, 1959; Hunter & Schmidt; 1982, Kroeker & Rafacz, 1983; Zeidner & Johnson, 1994). The biggest barriers to adopting a classification model rather than a selection model are likely to be psychological and political rather than technical. Classification decisions are a decidedly unfamiliar approach in the civilian workplace; organizations have little experience with deciding what job is best for the individual. Current models of personnel selection are almost uniformly oriented toward determining which individuals are best suited for the job, and switching to determining which position is best for each person rather than which person is best for each position may require management, labor, and personnel specialists to adopt fundamentally different mind-sets in approaching this task.

Decisions about how best to use the talents, experience, and knowledge of organization members are typically more complex than simple selection decisions (Zeidner & Johnson, 1994). The increasing use of teams in organizations adds another layer of complexity to this decision, because an individual might fit better into a particular job assignment than in the team where that job now resides. Indeed, one model for classifying employees might be to find the best team for each worker and let the team negotiate his or her job assignment. Even this model has its complexities, because teams are no more a fixed feature of organizations than jobs. That is, there may be cases in which the organization must decide who to move out of a team to make room for a new member (and where to place the member who has been moved from that team) rather than searching for the team that has a vacancy. Research on classification models (such as Zeidner & Johnson, 1994) suggests that the optimal assignment of individuals to jobs provides an opportunity for tremendous increases in performance and productivity, even compared to the gains associated with valid selection (see Hunter & Schmidt, 1982). Few human resource professionals, however, have the information or the authority to make true classification decisions in organizations, and it is not clear whether organizations will be able to take advantage of the opportunities afforded by a classification framework.

Staffing decisions do not occur in a vacuum; rather, they occur in a context—social, legal, economic, technological, and so forth—that substantially affects those decisions. The most obvious barrier to moving from a select-the-person-for-the-job model to a select-the-job-for-the-person model is the legal environment in which personnel decisions now occur. For example, the Uniform Guidelines on Employee Selection Procedures (1978) specify in great detail the strategies and evidence needed to develop and defend a personnel selection system that appears to have an adverse impact on protected groups. These guidelines codify the selection-for-the-job model, requiring detailed job analyses, substantial evidence for the validity and fairness of selection systems, and most generally, "job-relatedness." If the job is indeed an endangered species, job-relatedness may also become an outdated concept. It is unlikely, however, that the legal environment surrounding personnel decisions will change sufficiently in the foreseeable future to allow for radically different models for assessing and validating personnel selection and classification systems. Even if the "job" disappears from some organizations, it is likely that concepts such as job-relatedness will retain their influence on staffing system development and validation.

Making Selection an Easier Task and a Harder Job

The model for staffing that arose with the industrial system was based on an analysis of the demands of each job and the identification of individuals who were most likely to meet those job demands. Changes in organizations and work systems are likely to complicate many aspects of personnel selection (such as the need to identify new predictors and to develop new decision models), and may make the staffing manager's task more difficult. Conversely, these changes might make some aspects of hiring easier. If the job is no longer the focus of staffing decisions, it follows that many of the activities that currently consume the time and energy of human resource departments will change dramatically. For example, in an organization where there are no jobs, the traditional model for job analysis might not apply. Rather than analyzing the precise duties, responsibilities, and knowledge, skill, and ability requirements of specific jobs, there is likely to be a greater emphasis on identifying the best methods of using the available workforce to accomplish particular tasks or projects (that is, rather than analyzing existing jobs, the human resource manager's task may be to configure a set of roles in the organization that are needed to accomplish a project). In organizations where jobs are relatively fluid, there will be less need to identify people who fit existing jobs, and less of a need to tailor hiring practices (such as selection and validation of tests, and setting cutoff scores) to particular jobs. Organizations that follow this model of work organization are likely to seek generalists (individuals who rate high on "g," conscientiousness, self-efficacy, and social skills) rather than specialists who do specific jobs.

If we no longer need to tailor staffing to the demands of particular jobs, it should be possible to develop generic staffing criteria that apply across jobs and organizations. This solves the problem of reinventing the wheel every time we develop a new selection system, but it introduces a new problem. Because selection in organizations with highly fluid job descriptions is not tied to specific jobs, many other organizations are likely to seek the same generalists that your organization seeks. If you accept the proposition that individuals who are high on a relatively small number of cognitive, personality, and social attributes are more likely to succeed in a variety of roles in a given organization, it seems likely that they would also be expected to succeed in many different organizations. Therefore, while you might know what sorts of individuals you should seek (without having to do detailed analyses of specific jobs), it is likely that other organizations will also seek out the same individuals. Competition between organizations for individuals who are high on the variety of attributes just cited is likely to be intense, and organizations might need a personnel staffing system that emphasizes attracting the best candidates rather than winnowing a large pool of applicants.

Proposition 2: We Might Not Know Staffing Success When We See It

Traditionally, the goal of staffing has been to maximize performance and effectiveness by fitting people to jobs. Thus one index of the success of staffing would be increases in average performance levels, or perhaps decreases in the variability of performance across individuals. Expected changes in performance can be used as a basis for forecasting organizational profitability via the application of utility models (Boudreau, 1991; Boudreau, Sturman, & Judge, 1994). If, however, the definition of *job performance* is indeed changing in fundamental ways, assumptions about how we evaluate staffing success may also have to change.

What Is Successful Performance?

Current models of job performance tend to focus on two broad facets of work behavior: individual task performance, and behaviors that create and maintain the social and organizational context that allows others to carry out their individual tasks. Individual task performance involves learning the core tasks of the job, and the contexts in which they are performed, as well as being able and motivated to perform the tasks when called for. Many validity studies appear to equate individual task performance with overall job performance (Hunter, 1986; Murphy, 1989, 1996).

In addition to the specific tasks that are included in most job descriptions, the domain of job performance includes a wide range of behaviors such as teamwork, customer service, and organizational citizenship that are not always necessary to accomplish the specific tasks in an individual's job but that are absolutely necessary for the smooth functioning of teams and organizations (Brief & Motowidlo, 1986; Borman & Motowidlo, 1993; Edwards & Morrison, 1994; McIntyre & Salas, 1995; Murphy, 1989; Organ, 1988; Smith, Organ, & Near, 1983). For example, Campbell's model of performance (1990) includes behaviors such as volunteering, persisting, helping, and maintaining individual discipline (see also Campbell, McCloy, Oppler, & Sager, 1993). Labels such as "contextual performance," "organizational citizenship," and "prosocial behaviors" have been applied to this facet of the performance domain, and although these three terms are not interchangeable, they all capture aspects of effective job performance that are not always directly linked to accomplishing specific tasks.

A theme running through many discussions of the changing nature of job performance is that contextual performance is becoming increasingly important, and that effective performance of individual job tasks is becoming relatively less important in determining whether an individual is effective in his or her job. It is important to emphasize that the importance of core task performance relative to contextual performance is changing, and both of these aspects of job performance are likely to be critical, no matter how extensive the changes in the definition of the performance domain. Nevertheless, there does seem to be some consensus that as organizations and methods of work organization change, behaviors that are directed toward building and maintaining the social context in which work can be effectively performed will become increasingly important in defining an effective worker.

Earlier I noted that some organizations are likely to orient staffing models toward identifying generalists rather than specialists (that is, people likely to do well in a variety of roles rather than people who best fit a specific role). An increasing emphasis on contextual performance is likely to accelerate this trend. The dimensions of contextual performance appear to be more nearly universal than core technical performance dimensions. The behaviors that constitute core technical performance vary substantially across jobs (Lord & Smith, 1997; Motowidlo & Schmit, 1997), but the behaviors that constitute contextual performance may not change as much as jobs or assignments change. As a result, it seems likely that in developing selection systems aimed at maximizing contextual performance, organizations are more likely to emphasize the same core sets of performance behaviors across most roles or jobs than to tailor their emphasis on specific contextual performance behaviors to specific jobs.

Most discussions of the definition of *performance* have focused on the changing content of jobs—that is, what constitutes good performance (Murphy, 1989). Questions are also emerging about who should define good or poor job performance. Standards for defining performance were once determined internally by the organization, but they are becoming increasingly customer determined (Bowen, 1997). Customers might be either internal or external, and human resource systems often fail to include any mechanism for obtaining performance input from customers. Although organizations seem to pay more and more attention to customers' definitions of effective performance, it is important to note that customers sometimes do not know what they are talking about. Except in boundary roles, customers have relatively little information about individual performance, although they might have some information about the results of performance (which will generally be difficult to trace back to specific individuals).

Finally, changes in technology are likely to have important implications for determining why people perform well or poorly. Performance is probably a function of the person (P), the technology (T), and the $P \times T$ interaction, which complicates both staffing decisions and the evaluation of the success of those decisions (Hesketh & Neal, Chapter Two, this volume). You might select the right person but pair him or her with the wrong technology. This may make it difficult to evaluate performance sensibly because it may not be possible to separate successfully different sources of performance variance (P, T, or $P \times T$).

Do We Want Performance Now or Performance Later?

Three different conceptions of job performance are encountered in the literature on the changing nature of organizations. Psychologists (such as Campbell, 1990; Murphy & Cleveland, 1995) tend to focus on what someone has done—that is, on behaviors;

managers tend to focus on the results, or outcomes, of behavior. Many emerging models of performance pay attention to what a person *might* do in the future. In this volume, assessments of continuous learning (London & Mone, Chapter Five; Lord & Smith, Chapter Seven), adaptive performance (Hesketh & Neal, Chapter Two), distal performance capabilities (Kozlowski et al., Chapter Eight), and so forth are predicated on the idea that it is valuable to obtain knowledge and skills now, because they might be needed in the future (London & Mone, Chapter Five). In a continuous learning environment, the question of whether these skills and this knowledge are actually used is more a matter of organizational strategy and planning (Can an organization correctly anticipate what skills and knowledge will be needed and used at some future point?) than of individual effectiveness. This emphasis on continuous learning, however, does raise the question of the extent to which we ought to focus on performance now rather than think about performance later when evaluating staffing success.

Discussions of continuous learning in this volume and elsewhere imply that it can sometimes be more useful to devote time and energy to preparing for the future than to performing one's current job assignment. The pitfalls to this orientation, if taken to extremes, are obvious. First, because future performance requirements are often unknown, planning future needs will involve a great deal of uncertainty and error. This implies that continuous learning must be broad (and time-consuming) to have a reasonable chance of being useful. It also implies that much of what is learned now will turn out to be of limited use later. In the worst-case scenario, continuous learning might become a substitute for current performance. It can be more fun and interesting to engage in continuous learning than to execute the core technical performance tasks in many jobs. Time and energy devoted to continuous learning must come from somewhere, and some of this will be taken away from core performance. An inappropriately high emphasis on continuous learning could lead to a dilettante mentality—always learning and never doing.

Earlier in this chapter I alluded to the need for research on the extent to which the changes in the nature of work so widely discussed in the popular and scientific press are actually being implemented in the workplace. For example, continuous learning is widely cited as an important attribute of the modern workplace, but little is known about how much time, resources, energy, and so on are actually devoted to continuous learning activities by workers in different industries or in different types of organizations. In the absence of good descriptive research on the true extent of continuous learning requirements in industry today, it might be necessary to construct a model that at least identifies boundary conditions for determining whether there has in fact been a meaningful shift in the requirement that workers engage in continuous learning, and whether the emphasis on continuous learning is sufficiently strong that those learning activities do more to detract from than to support the core tasks of the organizations (by directing more resources toward learning and away from core tasks than are recouped by the productivity gains that accompany learning activities).

Modeling the Dynamics of Continuous Learning: Boundary Conditions

Suppose you wanted to test the hypothesis that there have been no real changes in the continuous learning requirements of jobs in a particular industry. It might be possible, for example, that the extensive discussions of continuous learning in the recent literature represent hype rather than real changes in the nature of work. The process of thinking about the sorts of data that would be needed to credibly test this hypothesis helps to identify some of the boundary conditions for models that posit that an increased emphasis on continuous learning represents a real, widespread, and sustainable change in the nature of work.

To determine whether there has been a real change in continuous learning requirements, one must first grapple with the precise definition of *continuous learning*. In particular, what is the distinction (if any) between training, development, updating, and continuous learning, and what are the indicators that are most appropriate for measuring each? Once an acceptable definition of the construct and an acceptable set of operational indicators has been identified, it is then important to determine the extent to which these activities are (and have in the past been) present in organizations and jobs that follow the industrial model; to assess the variability (over jobs, organizations, and time) in the presence and extent of these activities; and to evaluate the extent to which these are part of postindustrial jobs. The hypothesis that there has been a meaningful increase in continuous learning requirements suggests that there should be measurable increases in the frequency, intensity, and extent of such activities, and that the difference between industrial and postindustrial jobs should be relatively large, compared to the variability across organizations, jobs, and so on within the industrial and postindustrial categories. To my knowledge, there has never been an empirical test of this sort of the hypothesis that continuous learning is more important in jobs now than it was in the past.

Suppose you had established that there was indeed more emphasis on continuous learning activities now than in the past, and were worried that there might be too much emphasis on these activities in some organizations. To evaluate this possibility empirically, you would need to know the resources (time, money, and so on) devoted to continuous learning activities in that organization; the approximate payoff of these activities, in terms of predicted increases in productivity resulting from them; and the productivity payoff if these resources were devoted elsewhere in the organization (such as if time devoted to continuous learning activities were instead devoted to carrying our core tasks using present skills and knowledge, thus taking the risk that skills and knowledge being developed through these activities will not be needed in the future). In theory, the extent to which continuous learning is emphasized in an organization might be at any point on a continuum from no real changes, or even real decreases in continuous learning requirements, to an overemphasis on continuous learning, to the point that learning activities interfere with more than they aid the accomplishment of core tasks. As the preceding paragraphs suggest, the task of establishing the upper and lower bounds of this continuum may be a complex one; the problem of finding where on this continuum your organization lies might be even more complex.

Staffing Success: Helping, Preparing, or Doing?

The preceding sections suggest three criteria that might be used to evaluate the success of staffing. First, we might focus on contextual performance and argue that staffing is successful if we attract, hire, and retain people who create the conditions that most frequently support the core technical functions of the organization. Thus one model of staffing success focuses on *helping*—on maximizing contextual performance—based on the assumption that this will create conditions that also maximize core technical performance. This approach could be thought of in terms of the mediation model, in which the ultimate outcome is similar to the outcome emphasized in traditional staffing approaches (that is, maximizing core technical performance), but in which staffing activities are directed toward maximizing contextual performance (which will in turn enhance core technical performance) rather than focusing directly on matching the technical skills and abilities of applicants with the requirements of jobs. In this model, it will be important to consider both the links between staffing activities and contextual performance, and those between contextual performance and enhanced core technical performance.

A second model for evaluating staffing success is a *preparing* model. That is, we could envision the goal of staffing to be attracting, selecting, and retaining people who are most likely to learn new roles, adapt to changing circumstances, and so forth. This version of staffing also implies a mediation model, but in this case continuous learning is the mediator. That is, we might try to select those applicants most likely to engage in continuous learning, on the assumption that they are most likely to perform well in the long run. As with the previous model, care will have to be taken to evaluate both of the links in the model; organizations that successfully attract people who engage in continuous learning will flourish only if that learning can be linked closely with future performance.

In contrast to the helping and preparing models just described, I would characterize traditional staffing models as *doing* models. That is, the goal of these models has generally been to maximize current core technical performance. One great advantage of a doing model is its simplicity. If staffing is indeed successful, there should be clearly observable changes in productivity and performance outcomes. The helping and planning models are indirect, and it is therefore possible that staffing success will not be accompanied by performance increases. That is, organizations that successfully maximize continuous learning and contextual performance have won only half the battle. They will still need to put into place systems that maximize the links between these constructs and core technical performance. As organizations and systems for organizing work change, however, it is likely that mediated models, in which the immediate goal of selection is to maximize contextual performance of continuous learning, will present a more realistic vision of the staffing process, and of the problems that must be considered in evaluating the reasons for the success or failure of staffing.

Proposition 3: Current Trends, If Taken Too Far, May Not Be Sustainable

Throughout this chapter I have contrasted the traditional industrial model—in which jobs are relatively simple, stable, and well understood—with the postindustrial model, in which jobs and relationships between individuals and organizations are assumed to be in flux. If we think about an organization in which all of the trends discussed in the literature are implemented fully, the picture that emerges is a workplace in which individuals frequently move from one assignment to another (and from one organization to another), in which teams rather than individuals are the natural unit of analysis, in which job descriptions have little stability or meaning, and in which the assumption of long-term relationships between individuals and organizations, accompanied by predictable movement through hierarchical levels of the organization, is no longer tenable. I use the term *radical postmodern* to describe this sort of organization, and I distinguish between the radical postmodern model, in which virtually all of the trends discussed in this book are implemented to the greatest extent possible, and the more general postindustrial model, in which organizations move in the direction suggested by these trends without necessarily abandoning all facets of the traditional industrial model of work organization. To see why the trends described in previous chapters of this book are not sustainable, if taken to extremes, consider the problems that would be faced by a radical postmodern organization.

Time Isn't on the Organization's Side

There is clear evidence that attitudes toward the job, the organization, and job performance itself develop over time and may take time to stabilize (Hulin & Glomb, Chapter Four, this volume). It takes repeated practice on a task to develop true expertise, and time to develop thorough understanding of performance systems (Hesketh & Neal, Chapter Two; Lord & Smith, Chapter Seven). Similarly, it can take a good deal of time for teams to develop and stabilize, especially if the goal of forming teams is to develop smooth coordination, and for people to settle into their roles (Kozlowski et al., Chapter Eight). If jobs change in meaningful ways at frequent intervals, there may not always be sufficient time for stable attitudes or stable relationships within teams or stable differences in performance to develop.

The first roadblock to success in a radical postindustrial organization is that constant updating and change is not a sustainable pattern. Organizations that would undergo continuous change along the lines described in several of the chapters in this book would eventually crash to a halt, because workers would rarely have the time needed to move from early socialization and learning stages, in which they are acquiring skills, working out interrelationships, learning to use new performance systems, and so on, to more mature production stages, where they had acquired the expertise and had developed work systems that would actually allow them to get much done.

Who Does the Work?

Earlier I noted that an overemphasis on continuous learning (or on contextual performance for that matter) might make it difficult for organizations to actually carry out their core tasks, because their focus would so often be on preparing and helping, and not often enough on doing. Some organizations appear to solve this dilemma by developing a two-tiered workforce, in which there are a relatively small number of employees who have ongoing relationships and relatively stable futures with the organization (core employees), and a relatively large number of contingent workers. In particular, radical postindustrial organizations, in which core employees are heavily engaged in activities other than core task performance, might find this two-tiered structure almost irresistible.

Contingent workers are employed to accomplish particular tasks or projects, with no implicit or explicit promise of an ongoing relationship with the organization. Although the literature on changing organizations is not always explicit about this point, it seems obvious that many of the changes described in this volume apply more to core employees than to contingent workers. In fact, I argue that the traditional industrial model of work organization is alive and well in the contingent workforce, and that the radical postmodern model described here would at best be relevant to a relatively small portion of the workforce.

Contingent employees are likely to devote most of their time to core technical performance, and to orient their work behavior to specific requirements of the work role (Hulin & Glomb, Chapter Four, this volume). They should not be expected to engage in contextual performance behaviors, and they are unlikely to be rewarded for doing so. In this way, contingent work is pretty much like work under the traditional industrial model. That is, contingent workers generally have specific, well-understood tasks to perform; need relatively little preparation or training to do them; and are evaluated and rewarded strictly in terms of their core technical performance.

Viewed in this light, it seems misleading to label the small section of the workforce that does not consist of contingent workers the core employees, because the core technical tasks of the organization are more likely to be done by the contingent workforce than by the core workers. The core workforce members will be responsible for contextual performance—that is, for creating the conditions under which contingent workers can be successful. It seems likely, however, that most of the work of the organization will be done by the contingent employees, whereas work activities regarded as peripheral under the traditional models of work organization will be done by core employees.

Depleting the Resource Pool

Companies that rely too heavily on contingent workers run the risk of depleting the pool of available high-quality workers and are likely to fail to develop the core workforce they need (Hulin & Glomb, Chapter Four, this volume). Organizations typically do not invest in the development of contingent employees, but these are the people they must rely on over the long run to produce their goods and services. Although some short-term gains might be realized by replacing permanent employees with contingent workers, the long-run implications of an overreliance on contingent workers might be fatal to organizations.

The extensive use of contingent employees is likely to raise a number of political and societal problems. First, there is some evidence that the development of a two-tiered workforce (core versus contingent) will increase the racial and sexual segregation of the workforce (Hulin & Glomb, Chapter Four, this volume). Full-time core employees are more likely to be white and male, whereas contingent employees are more likely to be females and members of minority groups. Second, the pay and benefits associated with contingent employment are often so much lower than those associated with similar but more permanent work that many full-time workers will find it difficult to make ends meet.

Who Wants This Sort of Career?

Ongoing change in organizations is likely to have implications for both the definition and the attractiveness of a career. In the traditional model, career implied long-term attachment to the organization, stable employment, progression through the hierarchy, and so on. As organizations become flatter, more team-oriented, more willing to rely on contingent work, and so on, the viability and attractiveness of the traditional career is likely to diminish. Consider, for example, three of the problems encountered when an organization moves from individual-based to team-based production methods.

First, team-based organizations are likely to be flatter than organizations that employ more traditional methods of work (that is, they will feature fewer hierarchical levels). There will be fewer promotions than in a traditional organization. This means that many individuals will have the same job title for long periods and that substantial changes in roles in organizations (such as moving from labor to management) may be rare. Current definitions of career success are so heavily laden with the assumption of upward movement that individuals who remain members of a team for long periods may come to regard themselves as failures (even though, as compared to contingent workers, their circumstances might be very favorable).

A movement toward teams often implies a change from individual-oriented to team-oriented performance measures. One problem associated with team performance measurement is the role of such measures in the organization's career system. I noted earlier that the opportunities for promotion in relatively flat organizations may be relatively infrequent, but there is still is a need to make decisions about who moves into what roles in the organization. Team-based evaluations may mean that performance appraisals will have less of role in the career system than has been typical for individual-based appraisal systems. Organizations are unlikely to promote or transfer an entire team; if the team is the unit of analysis for job performance measurement, it is unlikely that appraisals will be useful for a wide array of career-oriented applications.

One could argue that under traditional methods of work organization career success was at least in part a function of one's individual efforts and accomplishments. In team-based organizations, the link between individual behavior and career success is likely to be much weaker, suggesting that career progression will not serve as an important motivator in postindustrial organizations.

On the whole, radical postindustrial organizations, in which all of the trends described in earlier chapters are implemented to the fullest extent possible, do not seem very appealing. Indeed, organizations that follow more traditional models might find it easier to attract and retain people whose values and preferences are more in line with the traditional model of work organization. In fact, one might argue that even if the postindustrial method of work organization is better, organizations might still be more successful with a traditional model than with a radical postindustrial model, because of their ability to attract and retain high-quality employees who value the traditional career. At this point we do not know enough about the possible trade-offs between optimal models of work organization and individual preferences about careers to know whether or when adopting suboptimal models leads to a long-term gain (because of the relative ease of staffing a traditional organization). The relative unattractiveness, however, of careers in radical postindustrial organizations does open the possibility that this form of organization would not last.

Optimizing the Balance Between the Industrial and Postindustrial Models of Work Organization

The radical postindustrial model, in which all of the trends discussed in this book are taken to their limit, is unlikely to represent a sustainable strategy for organizing work. Conversely, the traditional industrial model is probably no longer appropriate for some organizations. The question that most organizations are likely to face is not which of these two forms they should choose but rather what is the optimal mix of elements from the industrial model (such as stable, well-defined jobs) and the postindustrial model (such as teams and enhanced emphasis on continuous learning). I believe that the optimal mix of features from these two models of work organization, as well as the optimal strategy for staffing, depends substantially on the turbulence of the environment in which the organization functions (Thompson, 1967), as illustrated in Figure 9.1.

Figure 9.1. Optimal Mix of Industrial and Postindustrial Features in Relation to Environmental Turbulence.

Environment

Highly Stable	Highly Turbulent

Model for Organizing Work

Traditional Industrial	Radical Postindustrial

Staffing Strategy

Emphasis on Specialists	Emphasis on Generalists

An organization that produces a limited range of products and services in an environment where there is a relatively steady demand and minimal competition is one in which traditional structures (such as stable, well-defined jobs, and staffing strategies that fit individuals to specific jobs or career paths) are likely to work well. In light of all the recent attention given to changes in the world of work, it is worth remembering that the traditional industrial structure, and the human resource practices that developed out of this model, can be highly efficient and effective when applied in a receptive environment. Conversely, an organization that functions in a highly turbulent environment is likely to function best if the system for organizing work puts a premium on flexibility and adaptation (the postindustrial model). Most organizations probably fall nearer to the middle of the various continua shown in Figure 9.1 (that is, somewhat turbulent environments with periods of relative stability, and attention to both specialist and generalist attributes when hiring). The challenge that these organizations will face is the choice of specific features from each model that best fit their strategic needs. For example, teams, fluid job descriptions, and continuous learning are all part of the postindustrial model, but the decision to adopt one of these elements does not and should not imply that the others are also appropriate and useful. Human resource managers in such organizations face a difficult challenge in finding the mix of organizational characteristics (including staffing strategies) that is appropriate for the tasks and environment that characterize their particular organization.

Conclusion

Figure 9.1 suggests the staffing dilemma that organizations will face as they move from the traditional industrial model for organizing work toward a postindustrial model: the need to strike a balance between the staffing strategies aimed at locating and developing specialists (fine-grained job analysis, tailored selection and training) and staffing strategies aimed at locating and developing generalists (selecting for person-organization fit, continuous learning programs). Radical postmodern organizations are likely to be rare (and those that emerge are unlikely to last), but in many industries, traditional industrial forms of work organization may become increasingly rare as well. Perhaps the most pressing priority in the area of human resource management is the need to develop models for staffing postindustrial organizations. Current staffing models, which emphasize job analysis, development of specific recruitment, selection and evaluation systems for different jobs, and development of well-specified career paths, work well in stable environments, but as organizations face increasingly turbulent internal and external environments they will need to incorporate much more flexibility and adaptability into their staffing function. Many of the technical underpinnings of a generalist staffing model are already in place (for example, there is broad consensus about general cognitive abilities and global personality traits that are likely to be relevant across most jobs and roles in organizations), but we have not yet developed ways of thinking about staffing that are fully compatible with the demands of the postindustrial age. Furthermore, there is little indication that the external constraints on staffing decisions (such as the legal environment, bargaining agreements, and workers' expectations) have changed or will change in the near future in a way that will make the generalist model fully workable. It is likely that the way psychologists and human resource managers think about staffing and the way key constituencies think about staffing will have to evolve significantly before a smooth transition can be made from the industrial to the postindustrial model for organizing work.

References

Bandura, A. (1994). Regulatory function of perceived self-efficacy. In M. G. Rumsey, C. B. Walker, & J. H. Harris (Eds.), *Personnel selection and classification: New directions* (pp. 261–272). Hillsdale, NJ: Erlbaum.

Barrick, M. R., & Mount, M. K. (1991). The Big Five personality dimensions and job performance: A meta-analysis. *Personnel Psychology, 44,* 1–26.

Borman, W. C., & Motowidlo, S. J. (1993). Expanding the criterion domain to include elements of contextual performance. In N. Schmitt & W. C. Borman (Eds.), *Personnel selection in organizations* (pp. 71–98). San Francisco: Jossey-Bass.

Boudreau, J. W. (1991). Utility analysis for decisions in human resource management. In M. D. Dunnette & L. M. Hough (Eds.), *Handbook of industrial and organizational psychology* (Vol. 2, 2nd ed., pp. 621–745). Palo Alto, CA: Consulting Psychologists Press.

Boudreau, J. W., Sturman, M. C., & Judge, T. A. (1994). Utility analysis: What are the black boxes, and do they affect decisions? In N. Anderson & P. Herriot (Eds.), *Assessment and selection in organizations: Methods and practice for recruitment and appraisal* (pp. 77–96). New York: Wiley.

Brief, A. P., & Motowidlo, S. J. (1986). Prosocial organizational behaviors. *Academy of Management Review, 10,* 710–725.

Brogden, H. E. (1959). Efficiency of classification as a function of number of jobs, percent rejected, and the validity and intercorrelations of job performance estimates. *Educational and Psychological Measurement, 19,* 181–190.

Campbell, J. P. (1990). Modeling the performance prediction problem in industrial and organizational psychology. In M. D. Dunnette & L. M. Hough (Eds.), *Handbook of industrial and organizational psychology* (Vol. 1, 2nd ed., pp. 687–732). Palo Alto, CA: Consulting Psychologists Press.

Campbell, J. P., McCloy, R. A., Oppler, S. H., & Sager, C. E. (1993). A theory of performance. In N. Schmitt & W. C. Borman (Eds.), *Personnel selection in organizations* (pp. 35–70). San Francisco: Jossey-Bass.

Driskell, J. E., & Salas, E. (1992). Collective behavior and team performance. *Human Factors, 34,* 277–288.

Dweck, C. S. (1986). Motivational processes affecting learning. *American Psychologist, 41,* 1040–1048.

Edwards, J. E., & Morrison, R. F. (1994). Selecting and classifying future naval officers: The paradox of greater specialization in broader arenas. In M. G. Rumsey, C. B. Walker, & J. H. Harris (Eds.), *Personnel selection and classification: New directions* (pp. 69–84). Thousand Oaks, CA: Sage.

Hogan, J., Hogan, R. T., & Busch, C. M. (1984). How to measure service orientation. *Journal of Applied Psychology, 69,* 167–173.

Hunter, J. E. (1986). Cognitive ability, cognitive aptitudes, job knowledge, and job performance. *Journal of Vocational Behavior, 29,* 340–362.

Hunter, J. E., & Hirsh, H. R. (1987). Applications of meta-analysis. In C. L. Cooper & I. T. Robertson (Eds.), *International review of industrial and organizational psychology* (pp. 321–357). New York: Wiley.

Hunter, J. E., & Hunter, R. F. (1984). Validity and utility of alternative predictors of job performance. *Psychological Bulletin, 96,* 72–98.

Hunter, J. E., & Schmidt, F. L. (1982). Fitting people to jobs: Implications of personnel selection for national productivity. In E. A. Fleishman & M. D. Dunnette (Eds.), *Human performance and productivity: Vol. 1. Human capability assessment* (pp. 233–284). Hillsdale, NJ: Erlbaum.

Kroeker, L. P., & Rafacz, B. (1983). *Classification and assignment with PRIDE(CLASP): A recruit assignment model* (Tech. Rep. NPRDC-TR-84–9). San Diego, CA: Navy Personnel Research and Development Center.

McIntyre, R. M., & Salas, E. (1995). Measuring and managing for team performance: Emerging principles from complex environments. In R. A. Guzzo & E. Salas (Eds.), *Team effectiveness and decision making in organizations* (pp. 9–45). San Francisco: Jossey-Bass.

Murphy, K. R. (1989). Dimensions of job performance. In R. Dillon & J. Pelligrino (Eds.), *Testing: Applied and theoretical perspectives* (pp. 218–247). New York: Praeger.

Murphy, K. R. (1996). Individual differences and behavior in organizations: Much more than "g." In K. R. Murphy (Ed.), *Individual differences and behavior in organizations* (pp. 3–30). San Francisco: Jossey-Bass.

Murphy, K. R., & Cleveland, J. N. (1995). *Understanding performance appraisal: Social, organizational, and goal-oriented perspectives.* Thousand Oaks, CA: Sage.

Murphy, K. R., & Shiarella, A. H. (1997). Implications of the multidimensional nature of job performance for the validity of selection tests: Multivariate frameworks for studying test validity. *Personnel Psychology, 50,* 823–854.

Organ, D. W. (1988). *Organizational citizenship behavior: The good soldier syndrome.* San Francisco: New Lexington Press.

Ree, M. J., & Earles, J. A. (1994). The ubiquitous productiveness of "g." In M. G. Rumsey, C. B. Walker, & J. H. Harris (Eds.), *Personnel selection and classification: New directions* (pp. 127–136). Hillsdale, NJ: Erlbaum.

Smith, C. A., Organ, D. W., & Near, J. P. (1983). Organizational citizenship behavior: Its nature and antecedents. *Journal of Applied Psychology, 68,* 653–663.

Tett, R. P., Jackson, D. N., & Rothstein, M. (1991). Personality measures as predictors of job performance: A meta-analytic review. *Personnel Psychology, 44,* 703–745.

Thompson, J. D. (1967). *Organizations in action.* New York: McGraw-Hill.

Uniform Guidelines on Employee Selection Procedures. (1978, August 25). *Federal Register, 43,* 166.

Zeidner, J., & Johnson, C. D. (1994). Is personnel classification a concept whose time has passed? In M. G. Rumsey, C. B. Walker, & J. H. Harris (Eds.), *Personnel selection and classification: New directions* (pp. 377–410). Hillsdale, NJ: Erlbaum.

CHAPTER 10

Managing Work Role Performance

Challenges for Twenty-First-Century Organizations and Their Employees

Patrice R. Murphy
Susan E. Jackson

Our charge in writing this chapter was to focus on the implications of the changing context of work for all personnel actions other than those directly related to staffing (the domain of Chapter Nine) or training and development (the domain of Chapter Eleven). To make this task manageable, we chose to focus on two aspects of the motivational system: specification of performance criteria and administration of reward systems. These two activities are central to the organization's motivational system, although they are not the only elements in the system. More generally, an organization's motivational system includes all elements of the system intended to shape the direction, intensity, and persistence of performance-relevant behaviors. (Determining which actors are in the set and the competencies of those actors is assumed to fall within the domains of staffing and learning.) Ordinarily, this broad definition of an organization's motivational system would include the elements of job and organization design, among other things. However, because most of the preceding descriptions of the changing nature of work address these design elements, here we consider job and organization design elements as exogenous to the motivational system. Thus the question we address is, What are the implications of the identified changes in job and organization design for the specification of performance criteria and the administration of reward systems?

As Ilgen and Pulakos summarized in Chapter One, the critical job and organizational changes described throughout this volume include:

- Moving from stable work responsibilities to unstable responsibilities
- Shifting from having many employees with similar responsibilities to having many employees with unique responsibilities
- Moving away from person-technology interfaces that are machine driven and relatively standardized toward interfaces that are person driven and more variable
- Shifting from internally defined performance standards to customer-defined performance standards
- Changing from designs that maximize present performance to designs that enable future performance
- Leaning toward less reliance on individual-based structures to greater use of team-based structures

In our view, all of these trends reflect a shift from organizational forms that rely on bureaucratic jobs as the basic structural components of organizations to forms that rely on work roles as the fundamental structural components.

Closely associated with the shift from bureaucratic jobs to work roles, which is occurring gradually and does not encompass all organizations, are two more specific consequences: *emergent, unformalized* performance criteria are replacing *specified, formalized* performance criteria; and *social* performance criteria are replacing *asocial* performance criteria. Figure 10.1 depicts the connections we see between specific job and organizational changes and these two consequences. As we describe throughout the remainder of this chapter, the evolution toward work organizations that ask people to perform in an environment that places relatively more emphasis on emergent, social performance and relatively less emphasis on specified, task-based performance creates numerous challenges for performance management systems. To meet these

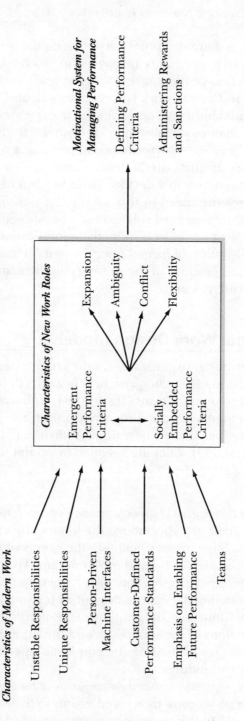

Figure 10.1. Challenges in Managing Work Role Performance.

Characteristics of Modern Work

Unstable Responsibilities

Unique Responsibilities

Person-Driven
Machine Interfaces

Customer-Defined
Performance Standards

Emphasis on Enabling
Future Performance

Teams

Characteristics of New Work Roles

Emergent
Performance
Criteria

Socially
Embedded
Performance
Criteria

Expansion

Ambiguity

Conflict

Flexibility

*Motivational System for
Managing Performance*

Defining Performance
Criteria

Administering Rewards
and Sanctions

challenges, organizations need to examine the assumptions inherent in current performance management practices, to identify those that are likely to be inconsistent with some of the changes being experienced in the way work is accomplished, and to begin experimenting with alternative performance management approaches.

In this chapter we move quickly from the traditional job-based conceptualization of performance to propose a role-based view of performance against criteria that are emergent, unformalized, and social. We then turn to a detailed consideration of the implications of the trends discussed in this volume for defining work performance in the context of role expansion, ambiguity, conflict, and flexibility. Next we address immediate implications for the design and administration of formal reward systems. Finally we raise some long-term implications of the shifting employment contract and issues for future research.

Traditional Work Design Model

In the traditional organization, jobs are the basic units around which performance management is organized. Jobs serve to link individuals to organizations (Ilgen, 1994). Jobs have been defined as "task elements grouped together under one job title and designed to be performed by a single individual" (Ilgen & Hollenbeck, 1991, p. 173). They are assumed to exhibit the following four characteristics:

1. *Jobs are the creation of the organization's prime beneficiaries or agents,* whose goals or expectations the job incumbents are intended to meet. Supervisors usually are the agents whose goals and expectations considered most relevant. That is, from a job incumbent's perspective, supervisors are responsible for distilling and funneling the expectations of all relevant agents to the employee. Ultimately, the employee is responsible for meeting the expectations of the supervisor, and the supervisor in turn is responsible for evaluating the employee's performance against those expectations.
2. *There is presumably a shared consensus about the task elements that constitute a job*—a consensus based mainly in the formal description of the job. In this sense, jobs are presumed to be objective.

3. *Jobs are bureaucratic, existing independently of job incumbents.* That is, people are assumed to move in and out of jobs with no consequences for the job's definition.
4. *Jobs are quasi-static*—that is, they are fairly constant over time, with changes to the job being evolutionary and somewhat predictable rather than revolutionary and unpredictable.

In such a bureaucratic, rationalized model of jobs it is recognized that the work environment within which jobs are performed is composed of diverse constituencies. The work environment is thus subjectively construed, personalized, political, and dynamic (see, for example, Ferris & Judge, 1991). Nevertheless, the job is considered to be an entity that can and should be understood and measured separate from the "messy" environment in which it is performed. Perhaps the environment cannot be tamed, but the job can be. For example, to bridge the gap between the job and the work environment, performance expectations specified by sources other than the immediate supervisor—including managers in other work units or at several levels above the employee, peers, and perhaps subordinates—can be acknowledged and formalized. To ensure consensus about the job definition, uniformity in the way the job is carried out, and relative stability over time, job descriptions can be promulgated and used by both supervisors and incumbents as the basis for key personnel decisions. Both supervisors and incumbents can be trained to rely on job descriptions to anchor their expectations for job performance.

In traditional bureaucratic organizations, performance is measured against the formally defined job, and "accurate" job specification is a goal worth striving toward. In the best run of these organizations, job analysts struggle continually to ensure that the expectations of all relevant social actors are formally captured, that personal interpretations of the job do not stray from the formal job description, and that job descriptions are revised on a timely schedule to reflect changes in technologies and in supervisors' expectations. Although it is recognized that jobs are not always well-specified, it is assumed that they can and should be (such as by a skilled job analyst). Well-specified jobs are the foundation on which performance management systems are built.

Ambiguity can arise from administrative failure to formalize expectations that were widely held but seldom stated or from failure to reconcile and define task senders' expectations in an accurate or timely manner. However, within the bureaucratic model, ambiguity is seldom deliberately designed into a job description (see, for example, Lawler & Jenkins, 1992). Figure 10.2 graphically compares a well-specified bureaucratic job with an underspecified bureaucratic job.

In bureaucratic organizations, underspecified jobs create a number of problems for performance assessment and the administration of rewards. These include perceived inequity, lack of a perceived link between performances and rewards, and misallocation of financial resources. In addition, failure to specify emergent expectations creates ambiguity, conflict, and possibly overload. These maladies can in turn directly undermine performance by increasing the risk of misplaced effort and mistaken work priorities. In addition, an underspecified job means that measured performance criteria are deficient. Thus the effect of subsequent performance management actions (such as giving performance feedback, setting goals for future performance, giving recognition, and adjusting compensation to reward excellent performance) is likely to be weakened, which in turn constrains both morale and productivity. In fact, the importance of fully specifying the content of a job was codified in the 1978 Uniform Guidelines

Figure 10.2. Job Specifications in Bureaucratic Organizations.

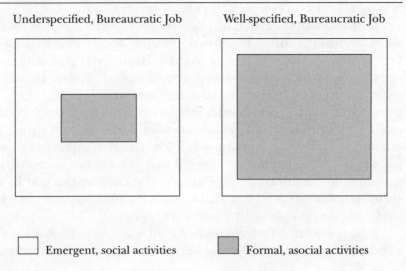

Underspecified, Bureaucratic Job   Well-specified, Bureaucratic Job

☐ Emergent, social activities   ▨ Formal, asocial activities

on Employee Selection Procedures (Equal Employment Opportunity Commission, 1978), which state: "Job analysis—content of the job . . . the work behavior(s), the associated tasks, and, if the behavior results in a work product, the work products should be completely described (essential)" (p. 4).

In the traditional bureaucratic approach to conceptualizing performance, there are two main ways to "fix" an underspecified job: formalize emergent tasks and add them to the job definition, or explicitly eliminate them from the formal job definition. A completely accurate job description would presumably reduce ambiguity, conflict, and severe overload for the incumbent; minimize subjectivity in personnel decisions; and eliminate the problem of a deficient performance criterion. The performance management process then consists of selecting qualified people to do the job, communicating the formal job requirements, training the incumbent to perform the required tasks, evaluating performance on those tasks, and taking corrective steps in terms of training and discipline if performance is inadequate. Corrective action is expected to improve directly the organization's ability to manage performance by increasing its control over employees' behaviors.

Employees and employers alike suffer from the negative consequences of underspecified jobs in bureaucratic organizations. So, in such organizations the message is clear: ambiguity, conflict, and overload create inefficiencies, waste, and deterioration of human resources. Get rid of them.

Within a bureaucracy, the situational context of jobs is presumed to be of little consequence. Indeed, obliteration of the disturbances caused by situational idiosyncrasies are a bureaucracy's raison d'être. Turbulent environments are dealt with by the creation of buffering mechanisms to protect the technical core of the organization from environmental fluctuation (Thompson, 1967). This approach works up to a point. But eventually the costs (in both time and resources) of buffering the organization become too great and the organization's failure to be responsive to changes in the environment interferes with organizational effectiveness.

To survive within their increasingly turbulent environments, modern organizations are experimenting with new organizational forms. Layers of management are being removed, vertically integrated firms are being unbundled, boundaries within and between organizations are becoming blurred, and network structures are replacing line-and-box pyramids. The rules and regulations that govern behavior within bureaucracies are giving way to empowerment and self-managed teamwork. Hierarchical control is giving way to lateral coordination. Stable organizations are being reformed into flexible structures that can readily adapt to the changing competitive landscape (see, for example, Mohrman, Mohrman, & Tenkasi, 1997).

It is within this more macrocontext that many of the specific changes described elsewhere in this volume are unfolding. In such a context, the performance management "problem" is no longer an underspecified job, and the solution is no longer simply to invest more resources in job specification. The new performance management problem is that jobs as they existed in bureaucratic organizations are disappearing. In their place are expanded, ambiguous, and evolving performance expectations that resist formalization. Consequently, our focus must shift to a different set of performance management issues. The dynamic processes associated with role invention, negotiation, and modification take center stage. To be effective, systems for managing work performance must recognize, accept as legitimate, and attempt to influence these dynamic processes.

Newly Emerging Work Designs

Years ago, the Hawthorne studies taught us that even routine, mechanistically designed jobs found in prototypic bureaucracies are performed in a powerful social context (Yorks & Whitsett, 1985). Nevertheless, during the decades that followed, the dominant paradigm in industrial (personnel) psychology largely ignored the social context as important to the definition of job performance. The job was viewed as the most important defining element of performance. In fact, long before validity generalization became a subject for debate, the Uniform Guidelines reflected the assumption that context was not particularly important. Describing tasks, behaviors, and work products was essential. Measuring importance and criticality was essential. And describing knowledge, skills, and abilities was essential. But describing the work situation was merely recommended.

To the extent that work organizations become less bureaucratic and more responsive to a dynamic external environment, performance management systems are moving away from reliance on the job as the basis for managing performance. Signs of this shift are reflected in the field of industrial and organizational psychology. For example, recognizing that performance beyond the boundaries of a defined job may sometimes be more important than performance falling within the boundaries of a job, a few mavericks have argued that the job should be abandoned as the object of selection decisions. Instead of maximizing person-job fit, we should seek to match person-organization fit (Bowen, Ledford, & Nathan, 1991). Growing interest in models for assessing and developing employees' competencies and capabilities also reflects the realization that the work to be done in organizations no longer comes bundled in neatly packaged jobs. In an era of downsizing, reengineering, quality improvement, teamwork, lateral processes, and increased customer focus, employees are responsible for a constantly changing mix of responsibilities (Lawler & Ledford, 1997). Their responsibilities are determined not by job descriptions but by the demands of various stakeholders who have the right to claim employees' time, attention, energy, and capabilities.

As organizations evolve away from the bureaucratic form, how should we conceptualize and manage work performance? During the past several years, a variety of suggestions have been offered for conceptualizing performance in a way that recognizes the importance of the situational context within which work tasks are performed. One approach argues for assessing the situational context and then treating it as an additional, independent factor that must be taken into consideration when interpreting performance scores and the relationship between measured performance and other constructs (see, for example, James, Demaree, Mulaik, & Ladd, 1992). Another approach argues for recognizing that job performance is not the only type of performance of interest. Constructs intended to describe performance falling outside the domain of well-specified jobs include organizational citizenship, prosocial behavior, extrarole behavior, and contextual performance (see Van Dyne & Le Pine, 1998; Motowidlo & Schmit, Chapter Three, this volume). Consistent with the traditional approach, this new approach shares the assumption that performance can be meaningfully separated into that which falls within the boundaries of a well-specified job and that which falls outside the job. Notably, the behaviors identified as falling outside the boundaries of jobs almost always involve the management of social relationships. The assumption that these behaviors are peripheral to, rather than inherent in, the central aspects of the work that employees are hired to do implies a view of work as comprised primarily of well-specified, formalized tasks that can be carried out by an individual.

To capture the nature of performance required within newly emerging work designs, it may be useful to use a different vocabulary to describe what people are employed to do. By using a different vocabulary—one that does not carry with it all the assumptions of a bureaucratic model—it may be easier to acknowledge the complexity of performance expectations that define work that is largely socially constructed rather than mechanical. The vocabulary of role theory is one alternative worthy of consideration.

Understanding Newly Emerging Work Designs: From Job Performance to Work Role Performance

In this section we illustrate how role theory can be used to conceptualize performance within a context in which the importance of well-specified, formalized job tasks is shrinking and the importance of so-called nonjob activities is growing. As a general theory intended to describe all social systems, role theory is not constrained by the assumptions of bureaucratically organized work (see Kahn et al., 1964; Katz & Kahn, 1978; Stryker & Statham, 1985).

Briefly, role senders are those people who influence or are concerned with the behavior of the person in a focal role: they comprise the *role set*. Role senders communicate their expectations for the role incumbent's performance using both formal and informal means. They may be members of the same organization (coworkers, supervisors, subordinates, internal or external customers) or nonmembers (external customers and suppliers, family, professional colleagues). Importantly, role sending is "a continuing cyclical process" (Katz & Kahn, 1978, p. 187) in which role incumbents influence role expectations in two ways: indirectly, through their behavior in response to received role signals; and directly, through their participation in a dynamic process of role negotiation (Graen, 1976; Graen & Scandura, 1987).

To describe job and nonjob spheres of behavior and performance, Ilgen and Hollenbeck (1991) proposed a model of job-role differentiation. In their model, jobs are differentiated from roles, as follows: jobs comprise established tasks and formalized expectations, while roles comprise emergent tasks and informal expectations. Because it is grounded in role theory, this conceptualization helps shift attention away from the question of the particular content that falls within the job-tasks boundary, and instead focuses attention on the dynamic processes related to managing the entire performance domain.

To underscore the usefulness of this shift in focus, we argue that new approaches to performance management should abandon the concept of job altogether. (An alternative solution would be to fold role performance into the concept of the job; this solution is unlikely to stimulate a reanalysis of the flawed assumptions associated with the concept of jobs, however, which is reason enough to reject it.) In place of the old vocabulary, we use the term *work role* to refer to the total set of performance responsibilities associated with one's employment. This approach (which Ilgen and Hollenbeck were not advocating, we should note) is consistent with role theory's assumption that roles (not jobs) are the building blocks of social organization. (To emphasize the importance of abandoning old assumptions and starting anew, we considered using a completely new term—*joles*—throughout the remainder of this chapter. But we are not sure the field is ready, yet.)

Dimensions of Work Roles

Work roles usually consist of many responsibilities, which vary along two continuous dimensions: social embeddedness and formalization. The dimension of social embeddedness is a continuum ranging from asocial to social. The dimension of formalization is a continuum ranging from formalized to emergent.

Social Embeddedness

Asocial tasks are activities that can be carried out by an incumbent working more or less alone. To the extent that tasks require *coordination* (not merely co-action) with one or more other people, they are more socially embedded. Many work activities involve a mix of asocial and social elements. For ease of expression, however, we refer to tasks that involve relatively little social coordination as asocial and to tasks that involve relatively large amounts of coordination as social.

Formalization

Formalized tasks, as just described, are those that are clearly specified and for which there is a high degree of consensus that they are to be performed as part of the employment relationship. When tasks cannot be clearly specified, it is often because they emerge in response to changing environmental conditions and technologies, or because they emerge through unique interactions with individual customers, suppliers, peers, subordinates, and so on.

In flexible organizations that emphasize lateral coordination, few employees carry out tasks such as handling goods, operating a machine, or processing information in social isolation. The use of teams to carry out complex planning, research, and production activities that are beyond the capacity of a single individual enmeshes the performance of individual employees with those of other employees—team members, internal customers, internal suppliers, supervisors, subordinates, and so on. Assignment to multiple teams, projects, or work areas expands the role set in unique jobs to include multiple groups of coworkers whose interests and priorities may conflict (see Motowidlo & Schmit, Chapter Three, this volume). Coproduction by employees and customers, particularly in a services environment, further expands the role set beyond the organization's boundary, enmeshing the task performance of employees with others whose activities are governed primarily by a different social system in which the focal employee does not hold membership (Rafaeli, 1997). It is not merely role sets that are expanding, however; the very nature of employees' relationships with many of the members of a role set is changing. As employers emphasize the importance of internal and external customer relationships, the expectations for employees shift away from norms that fit a one-time *encounter,* which may be formalized and carried out in a relatively asocial manner, and toward norms appropriate to a continuing *relationship* (Gutek, 1995), which is more emergent and socially embedded.

In Chapter Three, Motowidlo and Schmit point to a number of problems that arise in managing performance in unique jobs.

In such jobs, responsibilities are often emergent and may be socially embedded: we believe that it is these qualities of the work that underlie many of the problems associated with managing performance. Such problems are not unique to employees who work with the company's external customers, suppliers, and strategic partners. As Hulin and Glomb point out in Chapter Four, workers from a range of backgrounds (such as retirees, involuntary part-timers, student part-timers, and contract employees) bring a variety of role expectations to the workplace. Many of the likely differences in employees' work motivation and performance can be traced to the employees' responsiveness to the competing and complementary expectations of people from other role sets. People in an employee's numerous role sets are often beyond the control or even the knowledge of the employer. But this does not diminish their influence—positive or negative—on work performance or other outcomes, such as stress or dissatisfaction (see, for example, Krupnick, 1992; Thoits, 1991).

Characteristics of Emergent, Socially Embedded Work Roles

We turn now to a more detailed discussion of the complex role demands faced by employees in many modern organizations. Our objective is to show how the changing nature of work brings into greater focus the problems associated with specifying performance criteria in the context of role expansion, ambiguity, conflict, and flexibility. These problems arise when organizations attempt to use performance management systems designed for bureaucratic jobs in organizations where work responsibility is characterized by increasingly emergent, socially embedded roles.

Role Expansion

Role expansion occurs through the addition of emergent tasks to a formal job. Emergent tasks are those for which there are no established and accepted norms that govern interdependent behavior. They arise in unstructured, problematic situations. The process of role expansion can be understood in terms of Graen and Scandura's theory of dyadic organizing (1987), which was developed to understand the dynamic processes through which job incumbents and their supervisors establish role expectations for one another. In this model, role relationships are established in three phases: role taking, role making, and role routinization. Early in the relationship (which is assumed to be hierarchically structured), when new, unstructured situations arise, the one-way process of role sending is dominant for the supervisor and the one-way process of role taking is dominant for the job incumbent. In the next phase (role making), a dynamic interchange occurs. Because job incumbents are highly motivated to possess roles in which they can perform successfully, they attempt to move from passive acceptance of their supervisor's sent role to a more active process of influencing those expectations through negotiation and persuasion. Eventually, according to this model, the third phase of role routinization sets in. When an incumbent encounters a new situation that is similar to those for which roles have already been negotiated and routinized, the incumbent knows what to do. The incumbent and supervisor are able to coordinate their behaviors with little negotiation or uncertainty. In fact, it is possible that by this point the incumbent's previously negotiated role has become a part of his or her formal job documentation.

In the traditional model of a bureaucratic organization, role expansion would be unusual for most employees. Graen and Scandura (1987) proposed that it would occur only when supervisors have high degrees of latitude for assigning tasks, when they need to use this latitude to get work done, when they possess the personal and positional resources required to convince job incumbents to take on new tasks, and when incumbents have both the ability and the motivation to accept challenges beyond their job descriptions.

Graen and Scandura (1987) depicted role expansion, and the associated dynamic process of role making, as optional in the context of employment relationships. This view was consistent with studies conducted in the 1970s, which found that many employees reported low involvement in role-making processes (Dansereau, Graen, & Haga, 1975; Graen & Cashman, 1975). But in the emerging nonbureaucratic organizations, role expansion is no longer optional for many employees. For example, Hesketh and Neal (Chapter Two, this volume) argue that with the pervasiveness of technology in virtually every work context, an individual's responsiveness to technology is a central criterion for work role performance.

Providing Services

Growth in services has been argued by Bowen and Waldman (Chapter Six, this volume) to broaden the range of performance criteria to include employee attitude, mood, and dress. In attempting to control these aspects of their employees' behaviors, employers recognize that perceptions of how well an employee performs the asocial aspects of a job can depend on their customers' reactions to the social contexts in which tasks are performed. Furthermore, employees are held responsible for creating and managing this social context. For services that involve primarily the delivery of an encounter, where the social aspects of the task require little coordination between the service provider and the customer, expectations concerning employees' displaying appropriate attitude, mood, and dress can be readily specified and formalized. They can be easily incorporated in a job description, and the bureaucratic model for managing performance can be applied without much modification.

Increasingly, however, effective service delivery involves more than simple, routine encounters between employees and customers— it involves establishing long-term relationships. As firms move away from delivering service encounters toward competing on the basis of their ability to establish and maintain service relationships, role-making processes become integral to the conduct of the employee's work. To establish effective relationships, employees must be given latitude to negotiate their roles with clients. Different clients may have different preferences for employee displays of attitude, mood, and dress. Under these circumstances, role routinization and formalization could be detrimental to the delivery of excellent service. Thus, negotiating these and other social aspects of each service relationship becomes part of the work itself. As many employees learn, it is not sufficient to *meet* their customers' expectations; they must *exceed* them and so create feelings of customer "delight." Employees are expected to accept role expansion as a legitimate means for ensuring high levels of customer satisfaction.

The problem of variance in customer expectations and perceptions of performance were discussed by Motowidlo and Schmit in Chapter Three and Bowen and Waldman in Chapter Six. Motowidlo and Schmit argue that both task-focused and context-focused (that is, social) efforts should be assessed as performance, taking account of both main and interaction effects of situations and the total distribution of behavioral episodes in the performance domain. Their summary of the problems likely to arise in measuring performance using performance standards and evaluations from multiple sources is sobering. These include problems of holding raters accountable for their ratings, dealing with differences between raters' evaluations, combining ratings into a meaningful single rating for an individual, and making fair comparison among ratees. Clearly, new approaches to performance assessment are needed to address the problem of variance in expectations.

Teaming

A second trend—the proliferation of team-oriented and collaborative work arrangements—increases the number and variety of legitimate role senders with whom employees are interdependent, reflected in the increasing popularity of 360-degree performance assessment systems. Increasingly, employees are being asked to meet the role expectations of an expanded range of legitimate role senders. An expanded role set, in turn, may increase the pressure on role incumbents to move more rapidly from role taking to role making. As just described, customers' performance expectations have been added to supervisors' expectations. Furthermore, the meaning of *customer* has been expanding to include both internal customers and external customers. Suppliers, coworkers, multiple supervisors, and subordinates may also be involved in performance assessments. Indeed, Motowidlo and Schmit in Chapter Three call for performance appraisal to include ratings from multiple supervisors, peers, subordinates, customers, and "virtually anyone else who observed the ratee's performance." Any or all of these parties may participate in role-making processes, although perhaps not from equivalent bases of power.

Graen and Scandura's model of dyadic organizing (1987) addresses leader-member dyadic exchanges, but their description of the phases through which roles develop can also form the basis for conceptualizing role expansion in such complex, multiparty role sets. With multiple role senders participating in defining how they conduct their work, and limited resources available to comply with all of the expectations expressed by members of an expanded role set, role incumbents can be expected to move more rapidly from a role-taking stance into role-making negotiations. Furthermore, these role-making processes are likely to move from dyadic to multiparty exchanges, as the subordinate-supervisor dyad is supplemented by team, customer, and coworker relationships. Kozlowski, Gully, Nason, and Smith (Chapter Eight, this volume) argue that the task interdependencies that link differentiated roles together drive the team development process from an initial individual self-focus through a dyadic to a team focus. These dense networks of interdependencies through which modern organizations coordinate work activities mean that a role negotiated with one member of the employee's role set is very likely to have implications for another role relationship.

Fundamentally, organizations must struggle with the reality of multiparty involvement early in the performance management process. Not only do customers and other members of the role set have a say in evaluating performance, but they also have been invited to participate in the process of negotiating and specifying the behaviors expected for good performance. That is, they have been invited to expand employees' roles. In particular, customers and subordinates are likely to be in this situation. Such members of the role set may, however, have neither the formal responsibility nor the resources needed to support and facilitate employees' performance in the defined role. Although they participate in performance assessments, they have no ability or incentive to redirect organizational resources to support the levels of performance they demand. Thus, a key challenge for organizations is to ensure that criteria for assessing performance do not become unrealistic given an employee's access to needed resources.

Role Ambiguity and Role Conflict

Role ambiguity is experienced when incumbents are uncertain about the expectations they must meet in order to perform their roles satisfactorily. It can arise from three sources: the role sender's uncertainty as to what the role comprises may result in weak signals being sent to the role incumbent, the role incumbent may fail to accurately decode signals sent by role senders, or the role incumbent may be uncertain about which of the multiple role senders are most powerful, and hence whose expectations should be attended to (Ilgen & Hollenbeck, 1991; Jackson & Schuler, 1985; Salancik & Pfeffer, 1977).

Role conflict is experienced when the role incumbent believes that satisfactory performance in one role (or in one domain of a complex role) interferes with satisfactory performance in another role (or role domain). It can arise from conflicting expectations among the most powerful role senders, or from uncertainty by a role incumbent as to which role expectations should be given higher priority when the inevitable conflicts arise.

High levels of role ambiguity and role conflict can be expected to accompany the shift from well-specified bureaucratic jobs to work roles that are defined by multiple legitimate role senders. As Figure 10.3 illustrates, employers are giving more role senders legitimate power with which to negotiate and assess the performance of employees. However, the use of practices such as 360-degree feedback systems and customer satisfaction surveys may confuse employees about the relative priority to be given to each member or constituency within their full work role set. Thus workers may experience more uncertainty as to which role senders are most powerful, and hence which role relationships should receive the most attention.

Multiple role senders, in turn, may be unaware of one another's conflicting expectations (Ilgen & Hollenbeck, 1991) and hence be unable to moderate their performance expectations. Even if they are aware of the conflicting role expectations among members of the focal role set, role senders may vary in terms of their willingness or ability to moderate their own role expectations. Thus, for employees embedded in a large, diverse network of relationships (such as employees who are members of multiple project teams), proactively managing role conflict and role ambiguity becomes a prerequisite for satisfactory work performance.

As some of the chapters in this volume make clear, employees' role sets are not only growing in size, but within a single organization there is also growing variety in the role sets of different groups of workers (see, for example, Hulin & Glomb, Chapter Four, this

Figure 10.3. Opportunities for Role Conflict and Ambiguity Created by Role Expansion.

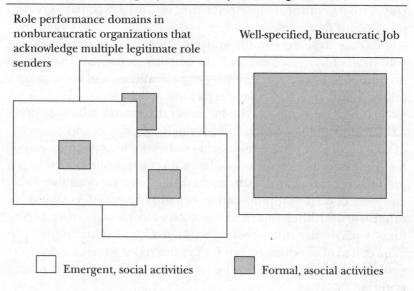

Role performance domains in nonbureaucratic organizations that acknowledge multiple legitimate role senders

Well-specified, Bureaucratic Job

☐ Emergent, social activities   ▨ Formal, asocial activities

volume). This variation among members of an organization's workforce increases the difficulty of predicting which role senders will be given highest priority by a particular worker, in light of that individual's role set, and which role senders are most likely to hold conflicting expectations. For example, contingent workers may be more sensitive than full-time, permanent employees to the role expectations of external professional colleagues, family members, and alternative employers such as employment agencies. A contingent worker who places great importance on family expectations and the expectations of the employment agency that serves as a regular source of work might be contrasted with a core employee who is assigned the same formal tasks but pays relatively more attention to supervisory expectations about overtime or to customer expectations and less attention to family expectations. In such a case, the full set of received and negotiated role expectations for the two workers may be fundamentally different, even though they are formally responsible for the same core set of established tasks.

When role expectations conflict, whose will be attended to? It will be more difficult to predict, for a worker in a particular job, which role senders constitute his or her role set and which have greatest salience for that worker.

To date, research on the consequences of role ambiguity and role conflict have focused on their negative consequences for role incumbents, for their employing organizations, and for nonwork relationships (see, for example, Jackson & Schuler, 1985). This approach is consistent with the bureaucratic model, which assumes a relatively stable environment in which role clarity and low levels of role conflict are achievable and contribute to organizational effectiveness. Little attention has been directed toward considering the possibility that ambiguity and conflict may be both inevitable and beneficial for employees and organizational effectiveness. In other words, rather than attempt to specify clearly either behaviors or particular outcomes to be used when evaluating performance, it may be advantageous for organizations to rely on only very general job descriptions and general descriptions of performance criteria.

An example of how such role ambiguity may generate potentially positive consequences is the facilitation of *role improvisation* and, hence, organizational change. Stryker and Statham (1985) argue that during periods of upheaval or discontinuity, role senders are willing to accept deviation from their normal role demands, in effect permitting temporary or even permanent role improvisation. Conditions of crisis often cause role boundaries to dissolve or "dedifferentiate"; behaviors normally seen as inappropriate may become acceptable as a temporary solution to managing problematic or threatening situations (Lipman-Blumen, 1973). Many modern organizations seek to undergo significant change—and the ideal is to effect needed changes in anticipation of future demands rather than in reaction to a crisis. Thus, allowing conditions that facilitate role improvisation (such as moderate levels of chronic ambiguity and conflict) to persist within the organization may enhance long-term adaptability and effectiveness (see, for example, Schneider, 1987). Specification of very general performance criteria may enable more flexible performance appropriate to the rapidly shifting needs of the organization. Benefits of role conflict and ambiguity for the individual employee are discussed in the next section in terms of the motivational systems of rewards and sanctions.

Role Flexibility

Role flexibility refers to the process of changing established or emergent role expectations. The extent to which individuals or groups are able to shift between different combinations of expectations constitutes the degree of role flexibility. Flexibility can be expected to occur more frequently in the context of unpredictable social or technological change. Social structures also can facilitate or hinder flexibility. Figure 10.4 depicts the complex nature of an employee's full set of roles and related role expectations, taking into account their multiple work and nonwork roles. Within the span of a typical day or week, an employee may repeatedly move between these diverse sets of work and nonwork role expectations, adapting to the demands of each with varying degrees of ease. Increasingly, within the context of work, employees are being expected to demonstrate similar flexibility as they change roles within the organization, either because they are managing multiple roles simultaneously or because their roles are shifting rapidly across time.

Stryker and Statham (1985) point out that highly structured rites of passage that mark dramatic shifts in one's roles may facilitate role transitions by creating a social system that assures the individual that the new role is valued and provides support for the change. Similarly, in organizations the stress associated with role changes and flexibility should be reduced to the degree that the organization provides a supportive social climate and positive peer experiences related to role transitions. Hesketh and Neal argue in Chapter Two that role flexibility (or what they termed adaptive performance) should be treated as a component of performance that is separate from task and contextual performance. Measures of adaptive performance would reflect the ease with which employees learn new tasks, their confidence in approaching new tasks, and their flexibility and capacity to cope with change. The need for role flexibility or adaptive performance is being influenced by a number of trends discussed in this volume, including the increasing incidence of teamwork, contingent work, and use of technology.

Figure 10.4. Multiple Roles and Unpredictable Change Require Role Flexibility.

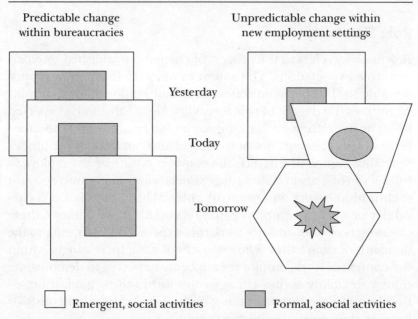

Predictable change within bureaucracies

Unpredictable change within new employment settings

Yesterday

Today

Tomorrow

☐ Emergent, social activities   ▩ Formal, asocial activities

Teams

The shift to teams is often driven by a perceived need for increased flexibility. Managers may be assuming that teams provide the best social structure within which to facilitate easy shifts in both established and emergent tasks. Teams may provide the ability to change both the tasks and the roles performed by team members. Tasks can be redistributed within a stable configuration inside the team to cover absence, to flex production, and so on. Alternatively, tasks can be redistributed in completely new configurations but within a stable social structure, allowing teams to evolve new roles to meet changing customer needs or environmental shifts, or to make rapid transformations to adjust to environmental turbulence.

Contingent Work

Contingent workers are increasingly being asked to self-manage their career development. The true meaning of this can range from simply maintaining basic technical skills in a state of job readiness, to steady career progression (London & Mone, Chapter Five, this volume). At either extreme, it is probable that career self-management will require skills to be deployed in varying combinations over time, refreshed and applied to varying task combinations. Employees are therefore more likely to be sensitive to configurations of tasks across different roles. Employers, in turn, may reserve the increasingly rare reward of employment security for employees who demonstrate a high degree of flexibility and the willingness to prepare for the organization's future, unpredictable performance expectations.

Technology

The diffusion of technology as a ubiquitous feature of working life is increasing the requirement for flexibility by workers exposed to rapid shifts in technology. Across the full gamut of service, manufacturing, professional, managerial, and technical jobs, technology can change established and emergent role expectations, and hence performance criteria, in two ways. First, as Bowen and Waldman illustrate in Chapter Six, technology can alter the social context in which tasks are performed, creating interdependencies among workers, customers, and suppliers where none previously existed, and broadening and deepening the range of social relationships to be managed by a worker. Second, as Hesketh and Neal argue in Chapter Two, the extent to which an individual is able to interact with technology to enhance performance is in itself a critical performance criterion. Role flexibility can thus broaden the criteria for performance to include the interaction between the person and technology, as well as interpersonal or contextual performance.

Using Rewards and Sanctions to Manage Work Role Performance

So far, we have argued for using role theory concepts to conceptualize work performance criteria. In comparison to traditional terminology, which presumes a bureaucratic model of work and organization design, the language of role theory brings to center stage the dynamic processes that shape work expectations over time and across social constituencies. These processes in turn have implications for how performance is defined and measured.

Conceptualizing performance is an important first step in constructing a motivational system, but it is just the beginning. Thus, we next turn to a consideration of issues in the design of systems of rewards and sanctions. To focus this discussion, we address five issues relating to the design and implementation of formal reward systems: short-term versus long-term perspectives, behavior versus outcomes, individuals versus aggregated social units, monetary versus nonmonetary rewards, and control.

Short-Term Versus Long-Term Perspectives

Both employers and employees develop preferences for either a short-term or long-term perspective on rewards. London and Mone contend in Chapter Five that the need to motivate continuous learning as a central dimension of performance requires that workers be rewarded today for learning or developmental potential they may use tomorrow. They suggest rewarding "vitality-related performance dimensions" such as anticipating learning requirements and setting developmental goals. They also acknowledge, however, the need to address basic questions such as the extent to which improved or increased skills are worth more to an organization, the extent to which workers should be rewarded for learning that may or may not be transferred effectively to the job-work role, and the problem of maintaining the freshness of skills. Future research into the effectiveness of such pay systems in different kinds of organizations would be valuable.

Taking an alternative view of the long term, some employers seek to structure compensation around a "cumulative earnings perspective" (Gerhart & Milkovich, 1992) based on a calculation of the value of earnings expected to be accumulated over future periods. In a secure job environment, such as teaching, where employees can be relatively sure of their ability to reap long-term salary benefits and the maximum potential pay point is known, new employees have been found to focus more on the top pay rate available than on the entry point (Wazeter, 1991). Employees are likely to have less regard to cumulative earnings when they perceive a less secure work environment. Contingent workers, those with more transferable skills, and those who have experienced layoffs may therefore be more inclined to seek a higher salary premium to offset employment insecurity, and to reject compensation that has a long-term structure. Where an organization seeks to integrate contingent workers into the ranks of permanent employees, problems may therefore emerge. Two groups of workers engaged in similar roles may require different compensation structures, resulting in different monetary rewards and the inherent risks of perceived inequity that may result. Indeed, the problem of perceived inequity may be intractable: the absence of a wage premium to compensate for job insecurity and the lack of access to long-term benefits may be seen as inequitable by contingent workers in much the same way that their presence is resented by permanent employees. This equity dilemma may moderate an organization's ability to integrate contingent workers seamlessly alongside core employees.

Behaviors Versus Outcomes

The second choice in the design of reward systems concerns the focus on behaviors versus outcomes. Industrial and organizational psychologists have traditionally focused on the importance of paying for behaviors that can be specified in advance by the employer. Role ambiguity and conflict, however, which make it difficult to clearly define role behaviors, may have some beneficial consequences for employees that serve to motivate performance. For example, the inevitability of conflict in modern work situations combined with increased pressures for organizations to reduce cycle times while being responsive to customers' varied concerns may be best handled by empowering employees to resolve conflicts on their own (for instance, see Evans & Sims, 1997; Sprietzer, 1996). Empowerment shifts control of work processes from external sources to employees. Increased control in turn contributes to employees' positive physical and mental health (Ganster, 1989; Jackson, 1989; Shapiro, Schwartz, & Astin, 1996). Thus, improved worker health may result when strategies such as empowerment form part of a prescription whereby organizations actively manage conflict and ambiguity, rather than treating conflict and ambiguity as something to be cured, and empowerment as an unrelated, discretionary activity.

The process of career self-management may also benefit from role conflict and ambiguity. In Chapter Five, London and Mone refer to the "protean career" managed by the person rather than the organization, emphasizing the responsibility of the individual role incumbent to seek out opportunities to develop, practice, and exploit their knowledge, skills, and abilities (see Hall, 1996). Role ambiguity may give role incumbents flexibility in selecting work activities that match their interests and developmental needs. Seizing opportunities to shape one's employment obligations to fit one's own interests can lead to the creation of idiosyncratic (that is, person specific) work roles. Idiosyncratic jobs can develop even in bureaucratic organizations (Miner, 1990). Their frequency and range can be expected to increase in less bureaucratic organizations with higher levels of role ambiguity and conflict.

In terms of formal reward systems, agency theorists take an economic perspective, predicting that behavior-based rewards are more efficient than outcomes-based rewards when employees' efforts can be easily monitored (Eisenhardt, 1988, 1989). As roles become less programmable and more difficult to monitor, outcome-oriented rewards should thus become both necessary, because of the problem of specifying desired behaviors, and economically rational. Outcome-oriented contracts may contribute to higher compensation costs, because employees' inability to diversify the outcome risk may motivate them to seek a compensating pay differential. Organizations may thus find that their efforts to trim labor costs by shifting performance risk onto employees are undone by the demand for a risk premium (Conlon & Parks, 1990).

Another problem with outcome-based pay is that it provides little opportunity for an organization to specify the kind of behaviors, roles, or skill sets that are believed to facilitate the achievement of its business strategy. In the case of customer-driven services work, organizations risk rewarding the wrong things precisely because of their inability to define desired behaviors and make them tangible (Bowen & Waldman, Chapter Six, this volume). Skill-based pay lies between rewards based on fully specified behaviors and those based solely on outcomes. For example, Lawler and Jenkins (1992) argue that skill-based individual rewards are one way to motivate the development of the skills required in team environments. Skill-based pay has been associated with increased flexibility, higher quality output, and lower absenteeism and turnover, although as Lawler and Jenkins point out, these relationships may be confounded by above-market pay rates. Nevertheless, skill-based pay may be an increasingly important means by which organizations can specify broad groups of competencies required in a role or a group of roles, without being too prescriptive about specific behaviors or outcomes.

As the issue of what to reward becomes more complex, the issue of which types of processes to engage when designing and delivering rewards may also become more important. Two foundational concerns in the design of reward systems are managing perceptions of procedural and distributive justice. Of these, Lord and Smith, in Chapter Seven, emphasize the particular importance of procedural justice when direct monitoring of behavior is difficult, such as when workers are at different sites from their superiors, work at home, or work different hours than their supervisors. In work settings such as these, authority- or legitimacy-based relationships are said to be more enduring than one-time outcomes based on distributive justice (Tyler & Lind, 1992). Employee motivation through the effective management of justice concerns will be an increasingly challenging leader responsibility given greater workforce diversity, variation among jobs, temporary work, frequent jobs changes, and compensation policies such as pay for skills.

Individual-Based, Team-Based, or Organization-Based Rewards

The third choice concerns the level of the unit to be rewarded: Should rewards be tied to the performance of individuals or to the performance of some higher level unit, such as the team, work unit, or division? Rewards may be offered at supra-individual levels because doing so provides a link with the unit responsible for achieving some work performance, or because a group reward is seen to be culturally appropriate. As Lord and Smith point out in Chapter Seven, rewards that benefit a group rather than the individual may be more appropriate in cultures that emphasize collectivism rather than individualism. Even in strongly individualistic cultures such as that of the United States, there is increasing interest in group-based rewards (O'Dell, 1987). In spite of the profound shifts toward team-based work organization documented in this volume, however, it is clear that few innovative alternatives to individual-level reward systems have emerged.

Current pay practices leap from individual level rewards to group incentives operating almost exclusively at the level of the business or operating unit, such as profit sharing, gain sharing, and employee stock ownership (see, for example, Gerhart & Milkovich, 1992; Lawler & Jenkins, 1992). The research literature has yet to provide evidence that can be used with reasonable confidence to design an effective approach to linking formal rewards to the accomplishments of unstable teams and loosely structured and shifting work groups, although practitioners appear to be seeking alternatives at this level.

Monetary and Nonmonetary Rewards

The fourth choice concerns monetary versus nonmonetary rewards. Both practice and research agree that pay is a reward of unique importance because it is instrumental in obtaining a range of other rewards (Lawler, 1971). The increasing demand for emotional labor discussed by Bowen and Waldman in Chapter Six points to the need for a range of performance incentives aimed at encouraging role-relevant behaviors (or sanctioning deviant behaviors) that may be difficult to define. Service work in particular may require performance standards that address emotional labor or emotional displays (Hochschild, 1983), but the exercise of discretion is also necessary to ensure that emotional labor is sensitive to subtle situational variances (see, for example, Rafaeli & Sutton, 1987, 1991).

Three problems interfere with the prompt use of monetary rewards in these circumstances: the difficulty of fully codifying the desired discretionary behavior, the difficulty of monitoring and reporting on such behavior, and the continued hierarchical arrangement of work, in which many of the crucial service encounters are undertaken by low-paid, low-status frontline employees. Organizations may therefore find it difficult to define discretionary behaviors accurately and even harder to measure them; they may find themselves reluctant to pay for them. In such circumstances, nonmonetary rewards such as recognition, access to training, or developmental opportunities may be more readily available, more flexibly applied, and less expensive.

When nonmonetary rewards are used as a deliberate component of the formal reward system, the question arises of whether extrinsic rewards that are contingent on performance are nonadditive, with monetary rewards actually detracting from intrinsic motivation (De Charms, 1968; Deci, 1972). The argument for such an effect is based in expectancy theory, which posits that the key aspect of intrinsic motivation is a feeling of personal causation: extrinsic rewards undermine intrinsic motivation by shifting the locus of causation to external sources (De Charms, 1968). Research has found support for this argument when the task is interesting and usually intrinsically motivated (Ryan, Mims, & Koestner, 1983). Gerhart and Milkovich (1992) cite more recent research by Phillips and Freedman (1985) which suggests that the effects of work motivation might be additive for individuals with high intrinsic work values, but nonadditive for individuals with high extrinsic work values. Hulin and Glomb's discussion of contingent workers in Chapter Four illustrates the problem of assuming that all workers have similar behavior-reward contingencies, expectancies, and instrumentalities. They argue that employees working side by side may need to be motivated differently, according to their unique circumstances. The effects of combining intrinsic and extrinsic rewards remains unclear, however. Further research into the use of both forms of reward simultaneously and into the importance of task context would help illuminate the effectiveness of different reward strategies.

Control

The fifth issue that has plagued the design of reward systems, even in traditional bureaucratic organizations, is the nature and extent of employee control over the performance of work, and the effect of this control on the acceptance of contingent and group-based rewards. Two of the three concepts that underpin expectancy theory (Vroom, 1964) may be moderated by the degree of control employees perceive they have: the belief that behavior will lead to certain outcomes and the belief that performance at the desired level is achievable with effort. Low expectancy in either respect is predicted to have a negative effect on motivation. Performance-contingent rewards are intended to increase employee motivation by eliciting greater effort, care, skill, or creativity. Performance-related pay systems thus assume that an employee can exercise control over performance, first by controlling the necessary means (including both personal and other resources) to effect some change in effort, and then by having a direct line of sight from that effort to the desired performance outcome. Individual differences in generalized self-efficacy will affect these values. Exogenous constraints on performance will also influence an employee's reward expectancy and hence motivation. Situational factors such as employees' access to resources, the embeddedness of individuals in interdependent team structures, and the impact of technology are of particular interest in the context of the trends discussed in this volume.

Access to resources will vary with the degree of role flexibility. When role flexibility is conceptualized as role diversity, a number of potentially positive outcomes for employees become apparent. Boundary spanners, for example, almost always are expected to exhibit role flexibility. While this has often been construed as a source of stress, it may also increase the resources available to the employee. Boundary spanners often can access resources available through one set of role relationships and use them to relieve the strain and overload created by a different set of role expectations. Adding roles may thus serve to increase access to resources.

Access to resources will also vary with the degree to which employees are empowered at different levels within the organizational hierarchy. The wide application of performance-related rewards to low-level employees raises questions concerning the boundary conditions of existing research on performance-related pay, and about the need for new research in the context of greater employee control of resources. For example, in their review of the extant literature on performance-based pay, Lawler and Jenkins (1992) identify merit pay, based on supervisor ratings of performance, as the most widely used approach to paying for performance. They argue that in spite of merit pay's continuing popularity (O'Dell, 1987), there is considerable evidence that most systems fail to create a clear relationship between pay and performance, and consequently do not produce the positive motivational effects expected of them. Among the possible reasons suggested for these findings are poor performance measures and poor communication, both of which may be affected by the level of control that employees perceive themselves as exercising over performance. If delayered organizations are indeed empowering employees with greater problem-solving autonomy and access to resources, future research tracking the effects of performance-related pay, which organizations appear to be experimenting with at multiple levels within organizational hierarchies, may uncover more precise effects for control and reward expectancy.

The growth of teams also suggests the need to revisit some of the established research on reward systems. Expectancy theory suggests that motivation will be greater under reward systems that tie pay to individual rather than group performance, because instrumentality perceptions are believed to be greater for individual performance. Empirical research going back to Schwab (1973) supports this hypothesis. Research conducted in less complex laboratory settings, however, or in traditional bureaucratic organizations, may not be informative about the group instrumentality perceptions of individuals in complex, highly interdependent work settings. Individuals working in high-control, self-managing work teams, performing complex work tasks that are clearly beyond the capability of any one individual, may display a higher level of group instrumentality than has been found in past research (Guzzo & Dickson, 1996).

Finally, the interaction of individual differences with technology has implications for the design of reward systems. Hesketh and Neal argue in Chapter Two that the extent to which an individual is able to use technology to enhance performance is the very essence of performance. Organizations' efforts to create reward systems that take into account such abilities have to date focused on the development of competency standards for performance that increasingly incorporate use of existing technology. Hesketh and Neal's chapter, however, suggests considerable challenges for the creation of technology-sensitive reward systems. First, the distinction between weak and strong technology situations (Weiss & Adler, 1984) points to the potential for a constant technology to be utilized in situations of varied predictability and control. In strong technology situations, individual differences may have little power to influence performance. In weak technology situations, individual differences may be more evident. Thus organizations should not assume a constant person-technology interaction: the context may moderate the ability of the individual to interact with technology to improve performance.

A second issue is the role of technology in performance monitoring, and the risk that the definition of performance may become dictated by the limits of technology. Performance definition and performance measurement always have been mutually dependent—and the tools for detecting and processing information underpin both. The potential, however, for performance self-management using electronic monitoring, suggested by Hesketh and Neal, is an alternative view of the performance management potential of technology. Research on the design of effective self-monitoring systems could be quite useful.

Long-Term Implications of the Shifting Employment Contract

Finally, we consider a more general issue that must be addressed by organizations as they attempt to realign their reward systems to better fit work organized around roles instead of jobs—the motivational implications of changing employment relationships. The ability of firms to create and manage flexible, ambiguous roles that are based in established relationships may be inhibited by the simultaneous development of increasingly contingent, transactional employment contracts.

In Chapter Four, Hulin and Glomb review a considerable although inconclusive body of research comparing the attitudes of part-time and full-time workers. A number of studies found that in the short run part-timers are no less satisfied than core workers when demographics are controlled. Hulin and Glomb suggest that different framing and anchoring of expectations by part-time and full-time workers may partly explain these findings. Contingent workers may simply expect less from their work life in terms of both intrinsic and extrinsic rewards. Differences in pay and conditions for core and contingent workers may not, therefore, result in differences in motivation. Conversely, the provision of equal rewards may, in the short term, result in higher motivation among contingent workers because their expectations are exceeded.

In the long term, however, a more complex motivational scenario may emerge. A U.S. Bureau of Labor Statistics survey of workers engaged in contingent and alternative work structures in the United States found that almost two-thirds of respondents worked in such jobs involuntarily (U.S. Department of Labor, 1995). The exception was independent contractors, four-fifths of whom preferred their current work arrangements. Among contingent, on-call, and temporary agency hires, however, almost two-thirds would prefer a traditional, permanent job if they had the chance. If the trends identified in this volume are correct and the shift toward contingent work constitutes a permanent change in the structure of the U.S. labor market, it will be important to observe whether workers' preference for permanent work adjusts itself to this new reality. A growing preponderance of low-cost work structures may lead to resigned acceptance of contingent worker status.

A paradox is evident when we consider the implications of an erosion of employee trust and expectations for the design and operation of the organization's motivational system. In Chapter Four, Hulin and Glomb point to the possible negative effect of contingent work arrangements on individual cognitive responses such as organizational commitment and perceived organizational support. In Chapter Six, Bowen and Waldman discuss the importance of perceived fairness in human resource management policies and practices, and the risk that perceived violation by the organization of a worker's psychological contract may cause employees to withhold customer service behaviors that are central to the delivery of service quality. In the long term, the creation at the societal level of a pool of contingent workers will have important effects on the psychological contract that those workers are able to fulfill. Contingent workers' repeated exposure to short-term, transactional contracts of employment and lack of experience with more relational, long-term contracts is likely to lead to a fundamental change in their social expectations of work (Rousseau & Parks, 1993; Rousseau, 1995). Increasing numbers of workers will come into contact with the transactional assumptions that underpin the contingent contract of employment, either directly through their own experience or indirectly through the experience of family, friends, or peers (Barling, Dupre, & Hepburn, 1998; Skarlicki, Ellard, & Kelln, 1998). Having become accustomed to more transactional contracts through repeated exposure, it is an interesting question whether more relational contracts could then be successfully created between workers and their employers or between employees and the clients they serve.

If individual-level effects include some erosion of the foundational trust and implicit relational expectations of the employer-employee relationship, it may be impossible for employees to participate in high-trust employment relationships even when they are offered, and it may be more difficult for them to adopt long-term, relational orientations with clients. At the societal level, such an effect could cause the psychological landscape of work to be so fundamentally altered that employment structures based on relational contracts may become increasingly difficult to retrieve. Firms that do wish to enter into a more relational contract with employees may find themselves attempting to recruit from a labor pool that no longer trusts employers to deliver on relational contract elements such as job security and personal development in return for loyalty, hard work, and long service. A useful body of research already exists on the indirect effect of layoffs on survivors. Further research is needed to understand the long-term direct effect of layoffs or repeated experience of contingent work, to trace the work attitudes and motivation of those types of employees in their subsequent jobs.

Conclusion

The depth and complexity of the organizational changes discussed in this volume are already having profound effects in many organizations and, as we have suggested, may have long-term consequences that reach well beyond those organizations that are seeking to adopt new organizational forms. These changes are testing the boundary conditions of some widely applied tenets of industrial and organizational psychology and long-established human resource management practices. Many of the unanswered issues raised in this chapter are concerned with the development of performance criteria and with the design and administration of reward systems. When addressing these issues, future researchers will need to attend carefully to organizational contexts. As we have noted, organizational context may be treated as an independent variable that directly or indirectly influences job performance, or performance may be conceptualized more broadly in terms of role performance that is integrally linked with context. In either case, it is clear that the growing diversity of organizational contexts and work arrangements means that future research should more explicitly consider the possible effects of context (see Hattrup & Jackson, 1996; Jackson & Schuler, 1995). Design choices that are effective in relatively bureaucratic organizations structured around well-specified jobs may have unexpected negative consequences in organizations structured around work roles characterized by role expansion, ambiguity, and conflict, and where creativity and flexibility are valued over adherence to routines and predictability.

For future researchers to investigate the question of whether the changing nature of work requires new approaches to performance management, they must have means for conceptualizing differences in organizational contexts. We have suggested that variations in work role performance criteria can serve as the basis for describing organizational differences. Specifically, two dimensions that differentiate among organizational contexts are the degree to which performance criteria are formalized or emergent and the extent to which performance criteria are defined and assessed socially or asocially. In contexts characterized by work performance criteria that are both formalized and unaffected by a dynamic and complex social environment, performance management systems should perhaps be designed to minimize role expansion, ambiguity, and conflict. When work performance criteria are emergent, however, and when the definitions and assessments of criteria must be responsive to a socially complex and dynamic system of legitimate role senders, a different approach to performance management may be required. In such settings, motivational systems may be effective only when they acknowledge the inevitability of role expansion, ambiguity, and conflict, and when they facilitate the role flexibility that employees need to be effective within such environments.

In addition to this broad suggestion for future research on performance management, we have suggested several more specific topics needing attention, including the following:

How can multirater participation in the definition and assessment of performance best be structured so as to maximize performance? Key issues here include understanding how employees process and respond to performance expectations that vary across constituencies with differing levels of salience, accountability, power, and access to the resources needed by employees to respond to those expectations.

How do employees attempt to manage their performance when faced with conflicting expectations and disagreements among raters? To address this question, the measurement of expectations becomes a key issue. Combining the technology of 360-degree feedback systems with Jackson's measurement approach for assessing norms (1966) might be useful here.

Can self-monitoring systems that use information technology to inform individuals and groups of their performance be designed to stimulate prompt corrective action and learning while avoiding negative employee reactions to close supervision and the frustration that often accompanies continuing negative feedback? As Frese (1997) observed, we seem to know more about the conditions that lead to helplessness than about the conditions that support self-reliance, initiative, and self-training. His model of organizational and personal factors that support the development of personal initiative is a useful starting point for new research on this topic.

How can traditional performance assessment techniques be revised for use in evaluating dynamic phenomena, such as role flexibility, role innovation, and adaptive performance? In turn, should pay systems be redesigned to reward employees for the degree to which these characteristics are present in their jobs, or for the degree to which they show proficiency in these areas?

What are the motivational consequences of various work arrangements (such as employees engaged in a short-term, contingent contract for full-time employment or independent contractors engaged through a temporary help agency but with the expectation of a continuing employment relationship)? The markedly different employment preferences among independent contractors versus part-time and temporary hires found by the U.S. Department of Labor (1995) shows the importance of identifying the employment relationship more precisely, rather than aggregating results across workers in various contingent or alternative work arrangements. Future research into motivation, performance, and workers' affective response to performance feedback should model the effect of situational differences arising from the employment relationship. This would provide a valuable extension of the extensive research on part-time work cited by Hulin and Glomb in Chapter Four.

Under what conditions are role ambiguity and conflict beneficial for performance? Research to date has focused on the negative consequences of these phenomena. Future research into the possible positive effects of role ambiguity and conflict for individuals, organizations, and nonwork relationships would extend this field.

How can reward systems be designed to support the complex combinations of individual, dyadic, and group-level performances required in work roles characterized by high degrees of social embeddedness? Few innovative alternatives to individual and business-unit-level reward systems are widely understood. Research exploring the effect of dyadic and group rewards could usefully address two particular developments. First, experimental research should attempt to replicate the task complexity and social interdependence increasingly found in organizations in order to more accurately assess individuals' perceived instrumentalities and expectancies in modern group environments. A second valuable research stream could focus on motivation and performance within unstable teams and loosely structured, shifting work groups.

References

Barling, J., Dupre, K., & Hepburn, C. G. (1998). Effects of parents' job insecurity on children's work beliefs and attitudes. *Journal of Applied Psychology, 83,* 112–118.

Bowen, D. E., Ledford, G. E., Jr., & Nathan, B. N. (1991). Hiring for the organization, not the job. *Academy of Management Executive, 5,* 35–51.

Conlon, E. J., & Parks, J. M. (1990). Effects of monitoring and tradition on compensation arrangements: An experiment with principal-agent dyads. *Academy of Management Journal, 33,* 603–622.

Dansereau, F., Graen, G. B., & Haga, W. J. (1975). A vertical dyad linkage approach to leadership within formal organizations. *Organizational Behavior and Human Performance, 13,* 46–78.

De Charms, R. (1968). *Personal causation: The internal affective determinants of behavior.* New York: Academic Press.

Deci, E. L. (1972). The effects of contingent and non-contingent rewards and controls on intrinsic motivation. *Organizational Behavior and Human Performance, 8,* 217–229.

Eisenhardt, K. M. (1988). Agency and institutional theory explanations: The case of retail sales compensation. *Academy of Management Journal, 31,* 488–511.

Eisenhardt, K. M. (1989). Agency theory: An assessment and review. *Academy of Management Review, 14,* 57–74.

Equal Employment Opportunity Commission. (1978). Uniform guidelines on employee selection procedures. *Federal Register, 43,* 38290–38315.

Evans, K. B., & Sims, H. P., Jr. (1997). Mining for innovation: The conceptual underpinnings, history, and diffusion of self-directed work teams. In C. L. Cooper & S. E. Jackson (Eds.), *Creating tomorrow's organizations: A handbook of future research in organization behavior* (pp. 269–292). New York: Wiley.

Ferris, G. R., & Judge, T. A. (1991). Personnel/human resources management: A political influence perspective. *Journal of Management, 17,* 447–488.

Frese, M. (1997). Dynamic self-reliance: An important concept for work in the twenty-first century. In C. L. Cooper & S. E. Jackson (Eds.), *Creating tomorrow's organizations: A handbook of future research in organization behavior* (pp. 399–416). New York: Wiley.

Ganster, D. C. (1989). Worker control and well-being: A review of research in the workplace. Effect of job control on worker health: A look at the evidence. In S. L. Sauter, J. J. Hurrell Jr., & C. L. Cooper (Eds.), *Job control and worker health* (pp. 3–24). New York: Wiley.

Gerhart, B., & Milkovich, G. T. (1992). Employee compensation: Research and practice. In M. D. Dunnette & L. M. Hough (Eds.), *Handbook of industrial and organizational psychology* (Vol. 3, 2nd ed., pp. 481–569). Palo Alto, CA: Consulting Psychologists Press.

Graen, G. B. (1976). Role making processes within complex organizations. In M. D. Dunnette (Ed.), *Handbook of industrial and organizational psychology.* Chicago: Rand McNally.

Graen, G. B., & Cashman, J. (1975). A role-making model of leadership in formal organizations: A developmental approach. In J. G. Hunt & L. L. Larson (Eds.), *Leadership frontiers* (pp. 143–166). Kent, OH: Kent State University.

Graen, G. B., & Scandura, T. A. (1987). Toward a psychology of dyadic organizing. In L. L. Cummings & B. M. Staw (Eds.), *Research in organizational behavior* (Vol. 9, pp. 175–208). Greenwich, CT: JAI Press.

Gutek, B. A. (1995). *The dynamics of service: Reflections on the changing nature of customer-provider interaction.* San Francisco: Jossey-Bass.

Guzzo, R. A., & Dickson, M. W. (1996). Teams in organizations: Recent research on performance and effectiveness. *Annual Review of Psychology, 47,* 307–338.

Hall, D. T. (1996). *The career is dead—Long live the career.* San Francisco: Jossey-Bass.

Hattrup, K., & Jackson, S. E. (1996). Learning about individual differences by taking situations seriously. In K. R. Murphy (Ed.), *Individual differences and behavior in organizations* (pp. 507–547). San Francisco: Jossey-Bass.

Hochschild, A. R. (1983). *The managed heart: The commercialization of human feeling.* Berkeley: University of California Press.

Ilgen, D. R. (1994). Jobs and roles: Accepting and coping with the changing structure of organizations. In M. G. Rumsey, C. B. Walker, & J. H. Harris (Eds.), *Personnel selection and classification* (pp. 13–22). Hillsdale, NJ: Erlbaum.

Ilgen, D. R., & Hollenbeck, J. R. (1991). The structure of work: Job design and roles. In M. D. Dunnette & L. M. Hough (Eds.), *Handbook of industrial and organizational psychology* (Vol. 2, 2nd ed., pp. 165–207). Palo Alto, CA: Consulting Psychologists Press.

Jackson, J. (1966). A conceptual and measurement model for norms and roles. *Pacific Sociological Review, 9,* 35–47.

Jackson, S. E. (1989). Does job control control job stress? In S. L. Sauter, J. J. Hurrell Jr., & C. L. Cooper (Eds.), *Job control and worker health* (pp. 25–54). New York: Wiley.

Jackson, S. E., & Schuler, R. S. (1985). A meta-analysis and conceptual critique of research on role ambiguity and role conflict in work settings. *Organizational Behavior and Human Decision Processes, 36,* 8–104.

Jackson, S. E., & Schuler, R. S. (1995). Understanding human resources management in the context of organizations and their environments. *Annual Review of Psychology, 46,* 237–264.

James, L. R., Demaree, R. G., Mulaik, S. A., & Ladd, R. T. (1992). Validity generalization in the context of situational models. *Journal of Applied Psychology, 77,* 3–14.

Kahn, R. L., Wolfe, D. M., Quinn, R. P., Snoek, J. D., & Rosenthal, R. A. (1964). *Organizational stress: Studies in role conflict and ambiguity.* New York: Wiley.

Katz, D., & Kahn, R. L. (1978). *The social psychology of organizations* (2nd ed.). New York: Wiley.

Krupnick, R. N. (1992). *Profiles in commitment: Work and nonwork commitments and their relation to work and nonwork outcomes.* Unpublished doctoral dissertation, New York University.

Lawler, E. E., III. (1971). *Pay and organizational effectiveness: A psychological review.* New York: McGraw-Hill.

Lawler, E. E., III, & Jenkins, G. (1992). Strategic reward systems. In M. D. Dunnette & L. M. Hough (Eds.), *Handbook of industrial and organizational psychology* (Vol. 3, 2nd ed., pp. 1009–1055). Palo Alto, CA: Consulting Psychologists Press.

Lawler, E. E., III, & Ledford, G. E., Jr. (1997). New approaches to organizing: Competencies, capabilities, and the decline of the organizational model. In C. L. Cooper & S. E. Jackson (Eds.), *Creating tomorrow's organizations: A handbook for future research in organizational behavior* (pp. 231–250). New York: Wiley.

Lipman-Blumen, J. (1973). Role de-differentiation as a system response to crises: Occupational and political roles of women. *Sociological Inquiry, 43,* 105–129.

Miner, A. (1990). Structural evolution through idiosyncratic jobs: The potential for unplanned learning. *Organization Science, 1,* 195–211.

Mohrman, S. A., Mohrman, A. M., Jr., & Tenkasi, R. (1997). The discipline of organizational design. In C. L. Cooper & S. E. Jackson (Eds.), *Creating tomorrow's organizations: A handbook of future research in organizational behavior* (pp. 191–206). New York: Wiley.

O'Dell, C. (1987). *People, performance, and pay.* Houston, TX: American Productivity Center.

Phillips, J. S., & Freedman, S. M. (1985). Contingent pay and intrinsic task interest: Moderating effects of work values. *Journal of Applied Psychology, 70,* 306–313.

Rafaeli, A. (1997). What is an organization? Who are the members? In C. L. Cooper & S. E. Jackson (Eds.), *Creating tomorrow's organizations: A handbook for future research in organizational behavior* (pp. 121–138). New York: Wiley.

Rafaeli, A., & Sutton, R. I. (1987). Expression of emotion as part of the work role. *Academy of Management Review, 12,* 23–37.

Rafaeli, A., & Sutton, R. I. (1991). Emotional contrast strategies as social influence tools: Lessons from bill collectors and criminal interrogators. *Academy of Management Journal, 34,* 749–775.

Rousseau, D. M. (1995). *Psychological contracts in organizations: Understanding written and unwritten agreements.* Thousand Oaks, CA: Sage.

Rousseau, D. M., & Parks, J. M. (1993). The contracts of individuals and organizations. *Research in Organizational Behavior, 15,* 1–43.

Ryan, R. M., Mims, V., & Koestner, R. (1983). Relation of reward contingency and interpersonal context to intrinsic motivation: A review and test using cognitive evaluation theory. *Journal of Personality and Social Psychology, 45,* 736–750.

Salancik, G. R., & Pfeffer, J. (1977). An examination of need-satisfaction models of job attitudes. *Administrative Science Quarterly, 2,* 427–456.

Schneider, B. (1987). The people make the place. *Personnel Psychology, 40,* 437–454.

Schwab, D. P. (1973). Impact of alternative compensation systems on pay valence and instrumentality perceptions. *Journal of Applied Psychology, 58,* 308–312.

Shapiro, D. H., Schwartz, C. E., & Astin, J. A. (1996). Controlling ourselves, controlling our world: Psychology's role in understanding positive and negative consequences of seeking and gaining control. *American Psychologist, 51,* 1213–1230.

Skarlicki, D. P., Ellard, J. H., & Kelln, B. R. (1998). Third-party perceptions of a layoff: Procedural, derogation, and retributive aspects of justice. *Journal of Applied Psychology, 83,* 119–127.

Sprietzer, G. M. (1996). Social structure characteristics of psychological empowerment. *Academy of Management Journal, 39,* 483–504.

Stryker, S., & Statham, A. (1985). Symbolic interaction and role theory. In G. Lindzey & E. Aronson (Eds.), *Handbook of social psychology* (Vol. 1, pp. 311–378). New York: Random House.

Thoits, P. A. (1991). On merging identity theory and stress research. *Social Psychology Quarterly, 54,* 101–112.

Thompson, J. D. (1967). *Organizations in action.* New York: McGraw-Hill.

Tyler, T. R., & Lind, E. A. (1992). A relational model of authority in groups. In M. P. Zanna (Ed.), *Advances in experimental social psychology* (Vol. 25, pp. 115–191). New York: Academic Press.

U.S. Department of Labor. (1995). Contingent and alternative employment arrangements. Bureau of Labor Statistics, Rep. No. 900. Washington, DC: U.S. Department of Labor.

Van Dyne, L., & Le Pine, J. (1998). Helping and voice extra-role behaviors: Evidence of construct and predictive validity. *Academy of Management Journal, 41,* 108–119.

Vroom, V. H. (1964). *Work and motivation.* New York: Wiley.

Wazeter, D. L. (1991). *The determinants and consequences of teacher salary schedules.* Unpublished doctoral dissertation, Cornell University.

Weiss, H. M., & Adler, S. (1984). Personality and organizational behavior. In B. M. Staw & L. L. Cummings (Eds.), *Research in organizational behavior* (Vol. 6, pp. 1–50). Greenwich, CT: JAI Press.

Yorks, L., & Whitsett, D. A. (1985). Hawthorne, Topeka, and the issue of science versus advocacy in organizational behavior. *Academy of Management Review, 10,* 21–30.

CHAPTER 11

Performance and Employee Development

Kurt Kraiger

As noted throughout this book, employee performance remains a critical component of organizational effectiveness. As new models of technology, organizational systems, and requisite skill sets are advanced and popularized, the need to understand, ensure, and assess human performance in organizations remains unchanged. Although the authors of this book each offer their perspectives on how various aspects of performance and performance measurement may change given current changes in technological, social, political, and economic systems, the centrality of employee performance to today's organization remains constant.

As noted by Ilgen and Pulakos in Chapter One, three key human resource processes are necessary to link employees to the services and work output of an organization: staffing, motivation, and employee learning. Other chapters in the book examine the impact of the changing nature of performance on staffing (Murphy, Chapter Nine) and motivation issues (Murphy & Jackson, Chapter Ten). The purpose of this chapter is to reflect on the implications for employee learning given the various perspectives on employee performance in today's organizations offered by the authors of this book.

Traditionally, employee learning has been conceptualized by industrial/organizational (I/O) psychologists in terms of three core activities: training, development, and career progression.

Training is the systematic acquisition of knowledge, skills, and attitudes that result in improved performance in another environment (Goldstein, 1993). Systematic training may be formal (such as a lecture or computer-based training) or informal (such as on-the-job training). *Development* activities are generally less systematic or planned than training. These are defined as any organizationally relevant event that results in the acquisition of knowledge, skills, and attitudes that are not immediately applicable to one's job but that benefit the employee as an individual or in a potential future job (Noe, Wilk, Mullen, & Wanek, 1997). Examples of development activities include formal courses, performance assessment and feedback, job experiences, and mentoring. *Career progression* is the sequencing of assignments or jobs to advance the knowledge or skill sets of workers. Examples of career progression activities include job rotation (Vobejda, 1987) and challenging initial work assignments (Kauffman, 1978).

In general, I will refer to these three systems in discussing the linkage between employee learning and how we are reconceptualizing employee performance. It should be recognized, however, that employee learning itself is being reconsidered, with the emerging definition being much broader than prior conceptualizations (Ford & Kraiger, 1995; Kraiger, Ford, & Salas, 1993). For example, research on continuous learning (see London & Mone, Chapter Five, this volume) recognizes that learning and development may occur both within and outside of the job (at the discretion of the employee), and may occur through learning media unrelated to the job. Similarly, research on transfer of training and learning climates (such as Ford & Weissbein, 1997) and employee socialization (Major & Kozlowski, 1997) is placing increasing emphasis on the role of everyday work experience in employee development. From the perspective of organization design, the concepts of a learning organization (Senge, 1990) and learning cultures (Tracey, Tannenbaum, & Kavanagh, 1995) have been proposed to describe how organizations may create environments conducive to employee learning, irrespective of the impact of traditional training and development. Although the focus of the chapter is on more traditional forms of training and development, references to these emerging forms of employee learning are offered as necessary.

Performance and Training

Before examining how the changing nature of performance may affect employee learning, it is advantageous to consider what role employee performance plays in the design, delivery, and evaluation of training. A general instructional systems approach to training consists of five primary phases: (1) assessing needs and establishing learning objectives; (2) designing training through activities such as choosing media, selecting trainers, and creating training content; (3) delivering the training; (4) specifying evaluation criteria and evaluating training; and (5) ensuring transfer of training through measurement and follow-up (Goldstein, 1993; Kraiger, 1995/1996). Note that, considered more broadly, these five phases may apply to other forms of employee learning such as developmental and career progression activities. How does an understanding of the construct of performance support the execution of any or all of these phases?

As other authors in this volume have done, I consider the recent performance model of Campbell (1990; Campbell, McCloy, Oppler, & Sager, 1993) to address the link between performance and training subsystems. Campbell distinguished performance from effectiveness, reserving the latter term for the evaluation of the results of performance. Performance is the goal-relevant actions of an individual that *may* produce such results. In the same way, I have argued that in a training evaluation context it is important to distinguish between posttraining behaviors, which are readily apparent and related to the goals of training, and posttraining results, which represent the impact of training on the environment (Kraiger, 1995/1996; Kraiger & Jung, 1997). If the trainee is behaving in ways that are consistent with the learning objectives, then training is successful, whether or not positive results ensue. Evidence of behavioral change with no positive results may also suggest a nonsupportive environment or a misdirected training program.

In his model, Campbell proposed that performance in *any* job may comprise eight factors or eight things that people do: job-specific task proficiency, non-job-specific task proficiency, written and oral communication task proficiency, demonstrating effort, maintaining personal discipline, facilitating peer and team performance, supervision and leadership, and management and administration. Not all jobs require performance within all eight factors; for example, many jobs have no team, supervision, or management components. However, Campbell and colleagues (1993) suggested that *all* jobs consist of at least three performance components: core task proficiency, demonstrated effort, and maintenance of personal discipline. Borman and Motowidlo (1993) proposed that a simpler model of job performance results from distinguishing between behavior that contributes or does not contribute to organizational goal accomplishment. Thus all goal-relevant behavior can be categorized as episodes of either task performance or contextual performance. Both models of job performance have proven to be valuable heuristics for discussing changes in jobs and performance implications, and both are very much at odds with implicit models of job performance that underlie the classic instructional systems design model of training.

The classic design model emphasizes the critical role of a needs assessment in determining training content and evaluation criteria (Dick & Carey, 1990; Goldstein, 1993). A needs assessment is initiated whenever there is a perceived performance gap, an apparent discrepancy between actual performance and desired performance. As Campbell and colleagues (1993) and Borman and Motowidlo (1993) noted, an important implication of a multifactor performance model is that various organizational participants may differentially value each performance component. Thus, perceptions of a performance gap by one type of audience (such as customers who are concerned about the speed and accuracy of service delivery) may be equally as valid as but completely inconsistent with perceptions of no performance gap by another type of audience (such as supervisors who are concerned with employee attendance and store cleanliness). Depending on who raises the question of a performance gap, a needs assessment may or may not be conducted, and very different types of training content may result.

In general, the classic instructional systems design approach has concerned itself with the training of what Borman and Motowidlo refer to as task performance, and with Campbell's performance components of job-specific task proficiency, written and oral communication, supervision and leadership, and management and administration. For example, in a survey of management and training practices of companies, Saari, Johnson, McLaughlin, and Zimmerle

(1988) reported that communicating the company's approach to management and training in job-specific knowledge and skills were the two primary purposes for enrolling managers in internal training courses. Campbell's performance component of facilitating peer and team performance may be emphasized within the classic instructional systems approach if, and only if, the task analysis reveals the centrality of team roles. Campbell's components of non-job-specific task proficiency, demonstrating effort, and maintaining personal discipline, however, as well as Borman and Motowidlo's contextual performance, will typically be ignored in the classic instructional systems design approach, although they may be defined as core competencies in developmental activities within some organizations.

It is important to recognize that current, well-accepted training models do not account for several core components (demonstrated effort and maintenance of personal discipline) of job performance (those common to all jobs) in Campbell's model. There are several reasons for this. The most obvious is that the construct definitions of these components are relatively new. Further, because training departments compete for scarce organizational resources, training efforts are typically focused on more apparent job-specific task components. It is fair to suggest, however, that classic needs assessment approaches, which emphasize traditional task analysis tools, have resulted in too great an emphasis on job-specific components. As I have suggested elsewhere (Kraiger, 1995), this focus on the job-specific has come from our comfort with the observable, and the inability of the field of I/O psychology to leave behind outdated behavioral paradigms of the 1950s and 1960s. Finally, it has only been recently that nonbehavioral performance dimensions such as effort, initiative, and self-maintenance have been recognized as legitimate learning outcomes for training (Jonassen & Tessmer, 1996/1997; Kraiger et al., 1993; Royer, Cisero, & Carlo, 1993).

Before more thoroughly examining the changing impact of performance on employee learning, it is helpful to consider briefly current trends in training, particularly from an applied perspective. In terms of training research, the field has come a long way since the 1970s and 1980s, when authors of chapters in the *Annual Review of Psychology* typically reviewed new training methods and could only hope for more research, better research, or research that was theory-based (Campbell, 1971; Goldstein, 1980; Wexley, 1984; Latham, 1988). As late as 1988, the training field had seemingly become so theoretical that Latham (1988) opened his review by noting: "It may become a tradition in this journal for the authors of the chapter on training and development to lament . . . the lack of attention to theory and the lack of research influencing practice evident in the practitioner literature on this topic" (pp. 545–546).

Since Latham's review, the training field has seen considerably more theory-based research, research that provides great promise for the ability to integrate emerging models of performance into the science and practice of training. Central to this new wave of theory and research has been a series of articles linking cognitive and instructional psychology (broadly viewed as the study of how we think and learn) to the science of training (broadly viewed as the study of how we get others to think and learn about their jobs). These articles include early general works by Howell and Cooke (1989) and Lord and Maher (1991), and more focused works applying cognitive constructs to the topics of training evaluation (Kraiger et al., 1993) and needs assessment, training design, and transfer of training (Ford & Kraiger, 1995).

During the same period, the applied side of training has undergone many important changes that underscore the importance of identifying and strengthening its link to employee performance. In large part these changes are being driven by organizational issues related to increasing diversity in the workplace and by the generally declining skill base in the modern workforce. For some time now, both scientists and practitioners have been discussing the implications of the changing face of the American workforce for organizational staffing and management practices (see Goldstein & Gilliam, 1990; Offermann & Gowing, 1990). With respect to workforce diversity, organizations are either deciding that "embracing diversity" is a competitive advantage (Cox & Blake, 1991), or that avoiding litigation is an economic necessity. Accepting these goals has direct implications for learning outcomes in training which are completely consistent with Campbell's model (1990). As issues of managing workforce diversity become viewed as both necessary (given changes in applicant pools) and desirable (given changes in internal and external preferences for doing business), organizations are turning to training as an intervention for shaping and managing intercultural differences (Cox & Blake, 1991; Thomas, 1992). As issues of sexual harassment and hostile work environments become more and more prevalent across corporate America, organizations are again turning to training as a means for communicating organizational policy and providing alternative interaction patterns (Fitzgerald, Hulin, & Drasgow, 1995; Livingston, 1982). Finally, as organizations grapple with the problem of declining worker skills in jobs that are increasingly technologically complex, they are relying on basic and technical skill training to revitalize human capital. To meet all of these challenges, the training world is responding with innovations in three areas: changes in training focus, the introduction of new technology, and the emergence of new theory-based training strategies. By changes in training focus I am referring to both the need for additional training and the need for specific types of training that have been called for by proponents of modern management strategies such as total quality (Dean & Bowen, 1994; Hackman & Wageman, 1995), customer service (Bowen & Lawler, 1992; Bowen & Waldman, Chapter Six, this volume), and the use of work teams (Cannon-Bowers, Oser, & Flanagan, 1992; Kozlowski, Gully, Nason, & Smith, Chapter Eight, this volume). By the impact of technology I am referring to the use of multimedia training that provides both quality, case-sensitive hypertext systems to work applications, and contextualized training and learning environments such as intelligent tutoring systems and hypermedia instructional systems (Acker, Lester, Souther, & Porter, 1991; Choi & Hannafin, 1995). By new theory-based training I am referring to modern approaches to instruction that favor problem-based training, situated learning, and just-in-time delivery of knowledge and skills (Brown, Collins, & Duguid, 1989; Caudron, 1996; Choi, 1995; Glaser & Bassok, 1989). As I review and discuss the changes in the definition and measurement of performance suggested by the authors in this volume, I continually return to these three trends as important perspectives for understanding the implications of employee performance for employee learning.

Implications of Changes in Employee Performance for Training and Development

The various authors of the chapters in this volume agree on at least four broad changes in organizational functioning that have implications for how we will (and should) define and measure employee performance:

1. Most authors suggested that job descriptions are becoming increasingly more fluid, with responsibilities defined more generally and with employees being required to make more complex decisions about job activities based on contextual factors.

2. Most authors also agree that as jobs become more fluid, performance itself is becoming more ambiguously defined, with less agreement among job stakeholders in how performance requirements and effectiveness should be defined or measured; this ambiguity is accentuated by the simultaneous movements to use internal and external customers to set service expectations, and to increasing reliance on work teams to make decisions regarding job assignment and performance management.

3. As workers become more flexible in their choices of jobs, organizations, and careers, and as organizations become more reliant on part-time and contingent workers, the willingness of organizations to invest in employee development is changing.

4. As suggested earlier, technological enhancements will continue to change how workers perform their jobs, and will also make it more difficult to separate technological and human contributions to performance effectiveness (Hesketh & Neal, Chapter Two, this volume). In this section I review each of these changes, noting the implications of the change for employee learning and how we define and evaluate performance in training systems.

Fluid Jobs

Several authors in this volume proposed that job descriptions will become more fluid, perhaps describing general expectations rather than detailed descriptions of job responsibilities. Such descriptions may be necessary given less stability in the jobs themselves, a condition that may reflect an adaptation of organizations to volatile environments, or preferences for workers who can select appropriate behaviors based on their understanding of contextual factors.

As a result of these predicted changes in the stability of jobs and job descriptions, it can be anticipated that job responsibilities will become more general, and that workers will be responsible for making more complex decisions about job duties given their interpretations of contextual factors (Motowidlo & Schmit, Chapter Three, this volume). These changes should have several implications for understanding and evaluating performance relevant to training and development systems.

Competency Approaches

Most notably, many organizations today are choosing to base employee selection, classification, and training systems on performance potential (such as competencies) rather than on job-specific work samples or worker attributes (see Kesler, 1995; Lawler, 1994). Competencies are an individual's demonstrated knowledge, skills, or abilities (KSAs) (Ulrich, Brockbank, Yueng, & Lake, 1995). Note, however, that competencies go beyond the more traditional KSAs; they are KSAs that are *demonstrated* in a job context influenced by the organizational culture and business environment (Boyatzis, 1982). Additionally, competencies may be thought of as clusters of KSAs that make a real difference in an organizational environment (Wisher, 1994). In these ways, competencies are very much like Campbell's performance components (1990), except that competencies are generally thought of as organizationally specific and job generic (relevant to all jobs within one organization), and the performance components may be either job generic or job specific depending on the competency.

The introduction of competency frameworks has resulted in some controversy, both in the research and scientific community and within and among organizations implementing such systems. At a construct level, there is disagreement over how competencies are to be defined, over what exactly is a competency. Are they synonymous with knowledge, skills, and abilities, or do they reflect exemplary aptitudes of value to the organization? At the organizational level, companies are grappling with how to link competency measurement to other human resource systems. Should only organizationwide competencies be assessed, and if so, what is the role of job-specific task knowledge? In multinational companies, do specific competencies (such as interpersonal skills) mean the same in different cultures? At a professional level, researchers and scientists are questioning the value added by competency models over traditional models linking job-specific knowledge and skills to job tasks.

Although the debate over the competency movement undoubtedly will be carried out at all levels, it is clear now that when competencies are carefully defined, as earlier, they bear a strong enough resemblance to Campbell's model (1990) that they serve as a useful framework for discussing training and development implications.

At one level, a shift in the definition of performance requirements from job-specific tasks and attributes to generic competencies may have little surface impact on the training function. For example, I recently completed a project for an organization that provides call center functions for Fortune 100 companies. A year ago, the training department established a training program based on the specific responsibilities for handling calls for each client and on the organization's objectives for the provision of customer service. We were asked to design a customer service certification exam, which we based on twelve broad competencies drawn from an analysis of the job requirements and from benchmarking of other service organizations. This year the training department is redesigning the training around the twelve competencies. A significant proportion of the training, however—how to provide excellent customer service over the phone—remains relatively unchanged.

Impact on Needs Assessment

At another level, a shift from job-specific performance requirements to organizationwide (or industrywide) competencies may hold significant consequences for the training function. Consider the needs assessment process. Needs assessment usually consists of three primary steps: organizational analysis, job and task analysis, and person analysis. Traditionally, the value of the organizational analysis has been to provide guidance to the researcher for subsequent (more content-relevant) stages; key stakeholders define performance goals, anticipate changes in the organizational mission or goals, and identify available resources for training. With a competency-based approach, the value of organizational analysis may supersede the other two steps with respect to delineating training content. This is because stakeholders will have the opportunity to define those performance requirements that they value within the organization (such as customer-focus, flexibility, and problem solving). These performance variables expressed as values will guide training design with or without a subsequent job analysis.

As for the job analysis, the traditional approach requires researchers to study the critical tasks and worker requirements (the KSAs) of the job for which training is designed. Using a competency approach, the performance requirements are selected before this step is initiated, and the role of the job analysis is to map job-specific worker requirements onto the broad organizationwide competencies to determine training emphasis (see Ford & Wroten, 1984). Finally, during the person analysis, the traditional approach requires the determination of who needs training, typically through the use of traditional forms of performance appraisal. Using a competency approach, the objective of the person analysis remains the same, but job-based appraisals would be inadequate for this purpose, and researchers would require the use of more general measurement systems, such as 360-degree feedback systems (see London & Smither, 1995; Tornow, 1993).

Modularized Training

With respect to employee development systems, the shift toward more fluid jobs and competency-based human resource systems may result in more modularized training and development systems within organizations. Since job duties and worker requirements are becoming general across jobs, it will make increasingly less sense to design self-contained, job-specific training programs. Instead, organizations can design a series of more general training modules that reflect the broad competencies or the performance components expected by the organization. Through job-analysis matching information, the organization can recommend either specific training modules for specific jobs, or recommend sequences of training and development experiences for organizational members aspiring to long-term organizational membership and ascension.

Training Decision Making

Although such a system is appropriate given the existence of fluid jobs and organizationally defined performance requirements, it places greater responsibilities for training decision making on two segments of the organization. First, employees and their supervisors will have to assume a greater role in deciding what training individual employees should receive (London & Mone, Chapter Five, this volume; Noe et al., 1997). By selecting competency-based training or developmental experiences, employees may have the opportunity to participate in what is tantamount to cross-training, training outside the requirements for their particular jobs. The question will become whether or not it is advantageous to them or the organization that they receive this training. Moreover, if the employee perceives training and development as a useful strategy to prepare for a promotional opportunity, the appropriate learning experiences should be available, but it will be incumbent upon the employee or his or her supervisor to decide the content and timing of training.

Second, while organization-specific, job-generic competency-based training and development systems may be a reasonable reaction to fluid job descriptions and responsibilities, it is still true that employees must perform certain job-specific activities. This is emphasized in Campbell's performance model in reference to the core performance component of job-specific task proficiency. If the training function of an organization is shifted to support employee learning of the general competencies, then responsibility for teaching job-specific declarative and procedural knowledge will fall to on-the-job trainers. In general, I/O psychologists have overlooked the importance of on-the-job training and have failed to provide prescriptions for optimizing this training, even though it is estimated that on-the-job training accounts for the majority of training time in American organizations (Dertouzos, Lester, & Sokow, 1989; Semb et al., 1995). The possibility of formal training moving toward performance components or competencies implies the threat of on-the-job trainers becoming even less supported in their efforts to provide critical knowledge and skill training to workers.

Ambiguity in Defining Performance

A second major theme raised by the authors in this volume is that what constitutes performance, and performance effectiveness, will become less clearly defined. There are several possible reasons for this. Motowidlo and Schmit suggest in Chapter Three that the distinction between task and contextual performance provides two different perspectives for observing and evaluating employee performance. A middle manager may be technically proficient but display poor contextual performance by failing to support his or her peers, or by cheating on expense reports. Bowen and Waldman suggest in Chapter Six that the shift by the United States toward a service economy places a premium on service-oriented performance. In any discussion of performance, a critical question is, In whose eyes? Bowen (Bowen & Lawler, 1992; Bowen & Waldman, Chapter Six, this volume) has argued that the customer must be one (or the ultimate) determinant of whether a given set of behaviors are effective. A restaurant waiter may be technically proficient (providing wine recommendations, remembering which diners receive which meals), but his customers may not return to the restaurant if they find him distant, unfriendly, or impersonal. A number of authors, but particularly Kozlowski and colleagues in Chapter Seven note the increasing reliance on work teams to perform jobs. This adds another form of ambiguity to the definition of performance. Individuals may be good at the technical aspects of their jobs but unable to work with or support their team members. Research by the Navy on work teams has led to the distinction between teamwork and taskwork skills (see Cannon-Bowers, Tannenbaum, Salas, & Volpe, 1995; Morgan et al., 1986). Taskwork skills are synonymous with Campbell's task-proficiency component and constitute technical abilities specific to a set of tasks. Teamwork skills overlap with several of Campbell's performance components (non-job-specific task proficiency, oral communication, and facilitating peer and team performance) and are those skills that allow individuals to coordinate their behaviors with others more effectively. Finally, Hesketh and Neal note in Chapter Two that advancements in technological use may blur the distinction between individual and technological contributions to performance; that is, it may become increasingly difficult to identify who is effective at their job and who is effective applying technology to accomplish their job.

To the extent that organizations adopt a competency-based approach to human resource management, differences among constituent groups in the definition of employee performance are less important than under previous job-specific approaches. For example, if capacity to use or react to new technology is defined as an organizationally relevant competency, then the organization will seek to bring in technologically competent individuals, and the issue of whether it is the worker or the technology that is responsible for performance effectiveness becomes trivial.

Identifying Subject Matter Experts

Whether the organization builds it human resource systems on competencies or traditional job-specific requirements, ambiguities and disagreements about the definition of effective performance have several important implications for understanding and evaluating performance in training systems. One set of implications centers on the identification and use of subject matter experts (SMEs) throughout the instructional systems design model. SMEs are used at several points during the design process to determine or verify performance standards, to define critical tasks for training, or to review training content. The concept of multiple, valid observers of job performance suggests that in contrast to traditional instructional systems design models, the selection of SMEs is not straightforward; and it may not be reasonable to expect consensus among job experts regardless of which performance component is studied. Numerous persons related to a job may be considered expert, depending on the perspective by which one views performance. It may be possible to define different pools of SMEs depending on the performance component that is determined to be the focus of training. For example, high-performing incumbents may be asked to provide input toward defining performance standards for content related to the various task-specific proficiencies, but other incumbents may be better sources of information on communication or team-related performance components. Similarly, multiple experts may not agree on the criticality or importance of various tasks and KSAs during the needs assessment process. Since interrater agreement is usually required for ratings to be considered viable, in some circumstances it may be necessary for organizations to use (and accept as valid) needs assessment ratings with low consensus.

Training Evaluation

Another set of implications of ambiguity in the definition of performance are concerned with the evaluation of training. Generally, training evaluation is conducted for one of three purposes (Kraiger, 1995/1996): to provide input into decision making about the status of training courses; to provide feedback to trainers, trainees, or training designers regarding course success; and to provide data to market the training to other organizations or future trainees. Recognition of the existence of multiple, valid observers of job performance may increase the value of training evaluation data for any of these three purposes.

Organizations may collect training evaluation data to make decisions about the future of existing training programs. Training programs may be eliminated or abbreviated given evidence that training is not successful, or additional resources may be expended on training if there is perceived to be a need for the training but there is an absence of data confirming training success (McLinden, 1995). In general, performance-oriented data will be the most useful for these decisions. By recognizing that multiple constituents will differentially view and evaluate posttraining performance, training designers can structure training development to meet each set of expectations. For example, in a retail store in which associates are expected to be responsive to customer needs, to maintain on-the-floor stock, and to support coworkers with questions or problems, training objectives—and related training criteria—can be established for each job demand. By using multiple sources of information (customers, managers, and coworkers) who evaluate discrete performance dimensions (see also Borman, 1974), organizational decision makers can make better informed decisions about the utility of each component of training. Thus, rather than addressing the simplistic question of whether or not training works, the multiple constituent–multiple dimension approach permits a more informed analysis of each training component.

It may also be important for trainees to learn during training to appreciate that various constituents will view their performance differently. For example, a management trainee focuses on pleasing his or her supervisors but fails to win the support of coworkers. Impressing upon this trainee that promotions are based on both supervisory evaluations and peer nominations, and clarifying the performance expectations of coworkers or subordinates, may provide valuable personal feedback to the trainee.

The value of training evaluation data for marketing training programs has been generally underappreciated in the literature. It is often necessary, however, to sell organizations or managers within organizations on the need for training. Likewise, knowledge of previous training success may be useful in improving new trainees' motivation for training and their self-efficacy regarding training success (Mathieu & Martineau, 1997; Noe, 1986). Depending on the audience, evidence of training impact on different performance components may be of interest. For example, indicators of greater job-specific task proficiency, personal discipline, and written and oral communication may be of interest to managers of future trainees, while the trainees themselves may be interested in evidence that training improves effort, peer performance, and supervision and leadership.

It should also be recognized that different segments of the potential audience for training evaluation results may desire performance data in different forms (Tannenbaum & Woods, 1992). McLinden (1995) argued that, more generally, training evaluation is not about *proving* that training works but about providing a preponderance of evidence that is consistent with the proposition that training works. McLinden provided the analogy of a trial attorney who does not attempt to prove that her client is not guilty, but tries instead to provide enough evidence so that a reasonable jury will accept her version of the truth. The point here is that different members of the jury judging the impact of training will look for different indicators of success. To provide meaningful training evaluation results, it is important for the analyst to be able to match the purpose of evaluation, the intended audience, and the aspect of performance being evaluated. While maintaining personal discipline may be a desired training outcome, it may be difficult to measure this performance component using normal metrics if the baseline for performance on this dimension is low (such as reports of employee theft). Anecdotal self-reports of critical incidents, however, may be very persuasive to audiences who believe that single incidences incur great costs to the organization (such as an employee who reports talking another employee out of stealing something).

Unstable Workforces

A third trend noted by several authors in this volume is that workers may become less stable in organizational membership. In the near future, workers may change jobs, organizations, or careers with greater frequency (London & Mone, Chapter Five), while organizations may draw increasingly on contingent employee pools (casual, temporary, or part-time workers) to deal with the cyclical, seasonal, or market-driven demands for their products and services (Hulin & Glomb, Chapter Four). Whether instability in organizational membership is precipitated by worker or organizational decision making, this state clearly has implications for how performance is defined and measured relevant to the training function.

Organizations are increasingly viewing corporate training as a cost center, an organizational unit that consumes more resources than it produces and one that is subject to concerns for cost containment and documentation of value added (Geber, 1995). Organizations such as these will be increasingly likely to question the value of broad-based employee training if it is probable that their employees are going to pursue careers elsewhere. Similarly, such organizations are likely to reject the notion of general training of contingent employees who have no long-term connection with the organization. Because the content, length, and timing of training programs are often established within the framework of full-time, long-term employees, there is also the possibility that traditional training programs will be mistimed or too long for part-time and temporary workers.

What to Train

A reasonable organizational response to these issues is to limit employee training to those knowledge and skills that are fundamental to effective employee performance. This strategy has the added benefit of controlling training costs, because unnecessary training is eliminated, shortened, or offered on a less frequent basis.

There are several potential costs to this approach. One is that employee skill sets may become more narrowly defined, or employees will lack cross-functional job knowledge that comes from more extensive training. A less obvious cost is that the reduction of broad skill training may be perceived by employees as a violation of a psychological contract with the organization, a contract that includes expectations regarding training and development opportunities to be provided (Wilk & Noe, 1997/1998).

A reasonable compromise would be for the organization to establish a core curriculum centered on fundamental knowledge and skills (or competencies), and to offer other training opportunities to either full-time or contingent employees either as a reward for effective performance or after an agreed-upon period of time that can be construed as a commitment to the organization by the employee.

Ideally, the recognition of instability in employee labor pools should lead organizations to conduct more extensive needs assessments at the level of organizational, job, and person analysis. At the organizational level, organizations should reconsider what training outcomes can be offered more generally to employees in order to increase commitment or tenure within the organization. At the job level, Campbell's eight performance dimensions can be used as a heuristic for organizing data collection and analysis into job aspects that are essential, helpful, or nonessential. At the person level, organizations should consider more extensive screening procedures in order to be able to build profiles of employee capability, which when combined with job analysis data can target specific employees for specific, essential job training.

How to Train

A second reasonable organizational response to unstable internal workforces is to reconsider when training should be delivered. The traditional training model positions job training early during the employment tenure, with the assumption that employees can be trained in those critical knowledge and skills that were not selected for, so that incumbents will be fully proficient on the job. Such a model also assumes that most of the training content is retained and generalized to the job, although some researchers and practitioners suggest that less than 10 percent of trained skills are transferred to the job context (Georgenson, 1982; Huczynski & Lewis, 1980). In the case of workers who are likely to leave the organization within a few years after hire, full up-front training may be inefficient in that some trained skills may never be needed before the worker leaves. In the case of contingent workers, the training may be inefficient in that temporary or seasonal workers may not be brought in at the same time as other workers, so they may need special training courses. Alternatively, the full training offered to regular workers may not be sufficient for contingent workers if the entry-level skills sets of the two vary considerably.

An alternative training model is gaining popularity in the training field: just-in-time (JIT) training (Caudron, 1996; Flynn, Sakakibara, & Schroeder, 1995). JIT training combines contextualized, hands-on training with electronic performance measurement and support systems to offer job performance training to job incumbents when it is needed, rather than all at once when starting a job. One common example is the help functions in most modern software programs. When accessed by the user, the help function provides situationally specific definitions, examples, and demonstrations. Some programs monitor user actions, and a "coach" will appear on screen to point out what a user is doing wrong or inefficiently and to demonstrate a more effective procedure. In an organizational context, JIT training is likely to include extensive on-line training manuals and job aids that are referenced by employees whenever they uncover all but the most common problems. For example, a Midwest paper company began several years ago to implement increasingly complex technologies in their production processes, using their most experienced operators to maintain and troubleshoot an automated paper-making line. As these operators began to leave through retirement, the company implemented an electronic performance support system (EPSS) that encoded the knowledge of the experienced operators. The EPSS provided replacement workers with twenty-four-hour problem-solving information in the form of JIT procedures, equipment information, and problem-solving guidance using text, photos, graphics, animation, and video.

From the perspective of dealing with an unstable workforce, JIT training has two advantages: it does not squander training resources by teaching knowledge or skills that will not be used by workers who are going to leave the organization; and it provides the minimum necessary skill training to enable part-time workers to perform effectively on the job. From a theoretical perspective, JIT training may promote better long-term retention of material because the training is embedded in a realistic context (Glaser & Bassok, 1989). For some time now, instructional psychologists have argued for the benefits of situated learning—situations that place the instruction of knowledge and skills in contexts that reflect the way they will be used in real life (see Collins, 1991; Hannafin, 1992). According to Collins (1991), there are at least three advantages of situated learning: trainees organize and apply knowledge under appropriate conditions, they learn and encode novel solutions to problems, and knowledge is stored in ways that make it accessible when solving later, real-world problems. By receiving focused training related to specific on-the-job problems, incumbents can learn to associate problem solving with situational cues, thus better organizing domain-specific knowledge and building superior problem-based goal structures (Ford & Kraiger, 1995).

Of course, the Achilles' heel of JIT training is exposed when incumbents do not access performance aids at the appropriate times, through either lack of awareness or lack of motivation. The awareness problem can be mitigated through a priori training that improves incumbents' self-monitoring skills. Considerable knowledge in cognitive psychology supports the proposition that through the acquisition of domain-specific knowledge (or increasing expertise) individuals are more likely to monitor or assess their own cognitive states accurately—for example, knowing when they have understood task-relevant information (Chi et al., 1989), knowing when to discontinue an inappropriate problem-solving strategy (Larkin, 1983), or judging the difficulty of new problems (Chi, Glaser, & Rees, 1982). Glaser and Bassok (1989) recommended four strategies for encouraging self-monitoring: questioning (posing questions about the training content), clarifying (attempting to resolve misunderstandings as they occur), summarizing (rehearsing the key elements in the training content), and predicting (anticipating future training components).

Using a performance measurement and monitoring system based on Campbell's performance model, the organization can meet the challenge of an unstable workforce by providing fundamental job training centered on the eight relevant performance components and self-monitoring skills. Training related to the performance components clarifies organizational expectations for performance, and self-monitoring training prepares employees to monitor accurately their performance and access JIT training as needed.

Technology and Performance

A final trend noted by multiple authors, and particularly Hesketh and Neal in Chapter Two, is the impact of technology on job performance. In some instances, technological advances may facilitate performance, as in the case of medical staff who are continually presented with new methods of diagnosing illnesses. In other instances, technology may change the fundamental nature of the job, as in the case of telephone repair personnel, who in one decade went from hoisting heavy cables up a pole to programming new fiber-optic pathways via a computer.

As Hesketh and Neal have noted, one implication of the technology influx has been the blurring of the boundaries between individual and technological contributions to performance. From the perspective of individual or organizational effectiveness, the distinction between the two may be trivial—if a secretary can quickly type a document with no errors, does it matter if this is due primarily to job-specific technical proficiency or to a facile word processor with auto-correct? From the perspective of designing and implementing human resource systems, however, the distinction is crucial. Is the function of training to ensure adequate typing skills, knowledge of the word processor, or reduction of computer anxiety?

Given that technological advances will continue to transform how and how well we do our jobs, it is important to understand the impact of technology on performance for purposes of designing, delivering, and evaluating training programs. There are several important implications of technology for training systems.

Needs Assessment

As noted earlier, traditional needs assessment involves determining organizational goals and training objectives, understanding critical tasks and KSAs (or job competencies), and determining who should be trained. As suggested, to make good decisions about what and who should be trained, it is critical that individual and technological contributions to performance be separated. Hesketh and Neal (Chapter Two) not only discuss some of the general problems in doing so, but also suggest some ways of partitioning performance variance into individual and technological sources. In addition to these methods, another strategy may be cognitive task analysis (Ryder & Redding, 1991). Cognitive task analysis is a technique used primarily by cognitive psychologists and knowledge engineers building expert systems. Using cognitive task analysis, the analyst would use methods such as think-aloud protocols and talk backs (where the analyst explains to the SME how to perform the task and the SME corrects inaccuracies) to uncover the mental processes required to perform the job (Ford & Wood, 1992). By selecting various SMEs who are each perceived as effective on the job but different in technological proficiency, the analyst should be able to determine performance requirements that are technologically based. For example, it should be clearer after a cognitive task analysis how SMEs perform their jobs when they are operating according to an existing mental model for task performance rather than according to one that is imposed or suggested by the desktop metaphor of the software; or how SMEs perform when they are accessing existing knowledge bases rather than databases available through the software during task execution.

Training Delivery

The influx of technology has even greater implications for the delivery of training. While not yet widely used in industry, automated training systems (ATSs) are increasingly popular in education and military settings. Broadly defined, ATSs refer to any computerized training system that attempts to adjust the stimuli, problems, or tasks presented to the trainee in response to trainee performance; or to any training system that allows sufficient learner control so that the trainee may adjust stimuli, problems, or tasks to their own learning needs. ATSs have unique advantages, most notably the reduced need for full-time trainers, the ability to be distributed to remote sites, the ability to learn by doing, and the ability for self-paced learning. Currently, the most popular ATSs used in higher education, government, and business are intelligent tutoring systems (Polson & Richardson, 1988) and hypermedia or multimedia systems

(Jonassen & Wang, 1992; Tessmer, 1995/1996). Intelligent tutoring systems provide individualized, expert-based guidance to learners as they learn by working on problems. They diagnose students' level of learning by comparing their performance with some representation of expert performance. Hypermedia systems place greater responsibility for navigation within the software on learners, but they also provide learners with a number of different tools for accomplishing learning, such as text-based discussions, video and audio segments, computer animation, and traditional computer-based instruction and testing. These systems function analogously to simulations and provide learners with information to solve problems and record the process they engage in as they work. For example, McDonald's developed a hypermedia system to train employees on customer service. Video clips of customers placing orders or registering complaints were viewed on-screen, and trainees either chose responses from pull-down menus or read about customer service options given the context. The system provided constant feedback on trainee performance, and allowed trainees to see a model transaction (on video) after each service vignette was completed. A number of other organizations are implementing intranet versions of management training, with the rationale that computer-delivered training provides flexibility to managers in when to provide training. Collectively, these automated training techniques offer the opportunity to tailor complex instructional content to meet learner needs, track learner progress, simulate equipment functions for learning and practice, and maintain a standardized training curriculum.

What is important to appreciate about these forms of training is that they appear to change the nature of the learning process. This is particularly true with respect to hypermedia systems. Unlike traditional forms of training (such as classroom style) in which passive activity by the trainee may still result in some learning, no learning occurs with a hypermedia system until the trainee actively engages the system. Because the system exists simply as a set of instructional tools to be accessed by the learner, control and responsibility for learning shifts from the trainer and system to the trainee. Because they are designed to be both user-friendly and engaging, hypermedia systems hold great potential for increasing and reinforcing trainee self-efficacy and motivation to learn (Dweck,

1986), not to mention acquisition of job-relevant knowledge and skills. From the perspective of Campbell's performance model, hypermedia systems hold the potential for training job-relevant skills (such as task proficiency and written communication) while at the same time developing other performance components such as effort and personal discipline, because these latter components are necessary to drive the learning process.

Conclusion

One of the arguments that Kevin Ford, Eduardo Salas, and I have advanced regarding learning outcomes (Kraiger et al., 1993) is that since the 1960s, I/O psychologists who studied training clung unnecessarily to behaviorism as the sole explanatory paradigm for learning, thus ignoring important developments in all other fields in psychology. This behavioral focus was evident in training and development books (such as Goldstein, 1993; Wexley & Latham, 1991) that continue to propose that all instructional objectives should be behavioral (Mager, 1984). We recognized that very often trainers and organizational leaders do not think in behavioral terms (such as, "I want my workers to be always thinking of new ways of improving job performance," or "We need workers to appreciate the safety risks that result from ignoring standard procedures"). Because for a long time we believed that learning meant (or was restricted to) behavioral change, and because we knew that observed behaviors were easier to measure than affect or cognition, we would subvert the language of our clients, rewriting their objectives in our own behavioral terms (such as, "Given a list of tasks and job responsibilities, the trainee will be able to list three methods of improving job performance," or "The worker will don the proper protective clothing prior to performing task X"). Thus, one of the key recommendations of the learning outcomes paper was that I/O psychologists who design or evaluate training programs should be able to express learning outcomes in the language of those in organizations who are invested in employee learning, and we can use a range of cognitive, affective, and behavioral descriptors to describe that learning.

Across the chapters in this volume, the authors have begun with Campbell's performance model and proposed a number of attitudinal, behavioral, and cognitive factors that either distinguish effective or ineffective performance, or are likely to lead to employees successfully adapting to performance requirements in today's organizations. Many of these factors are nonbehavioral, including team commitment and synchronous coordination (Kozlowski et al., Chapter Eight), organizational commitment (Hulin & Glomb, Chapter Four), acceptance of technology (Hesketh & Neal, Chapter Two), willingness to work independently (Motowidlo & Schmit, Chapter Three), belief in the importance of customer satisfaction (Bowen & Waldman, Chapter Six), and emotional labor (the willingness to appear customer-focused even if unhappy; Bowen & Waldman, Chapter Six). Cognitive examples include performance flexibility (being able to generate and accomplish task goals with or without the aid of technology; Hesketh & Neal, Chapter Two), demographically indexed cognitive structure (Lord & Smith, Chapter Seven), contextual knowledge (the recognition of contextual influences on performance; Motowidlo & Schmit, Chapter Three), technical vitality (anticipating learning to meet changing job demands; London & Mone, Chapter Five), and learning from experience through the acceptance of failure and expression of curiosity (London & Mone, Chapter Five).

It is impossible to say at this point how many or which particular constructs will have an impact on shaping how we define and measure employee performance. It is also beyond the scope of this chapter to discuss whether any one of these constructs should be selected for, trained for, or controlled through motivational and leadership systems. It is appropriate, however, to suggest that any or all of these *may* be constructs that could be trained, and as we suggested (Kraiger et al., 1993), if they can be trained, they can be measured.

What is important is to continue to invest in the construct validation processes initiated by Campbell (1990; Campbell et al., 1993). The most valuable aspect of Campbell's work is not the delineation of the performance components but the embedding of them in a predictor-criterion performance model. By doing so, we are able to focus on a smaller subset of variables and examine their relationship to exogenous variables (such as self-efficacy or intelligence), organizational interventions (such as selection or training), and to each other. In this regard, the similarity between the training environment and experimental settings makes training a prime domain for subsequent research. Examples of straightforward yet important questions that can be addressed in a laboratory-training setting are, Is team commitment greater when individuals are trained in intact rather than ad hoc teams? Are individuals more willing to work independently when trained in isolation rather than in groups? Is contextual knowledge enhanced through variable mapping rather than constant mapping conditions (see Schmidt & Bjork, 1992)? Does foreknowledge of organizational goals or training objectives affect trainees' belief in the importance of customer input or willingness to learn from experience? By conducting experimental research on these questions, researchers can not only uncover interventions that may improve performance effectiveness, but they can also validate aspects of Campbell's model. By conducting this research in true organizational settings, researchers can not only examine the relationship between training interventions and performance outcomes, but they can also examine the relationships among the outcomes themselves.

References

Acker, L., Lester, J., Souther, A., & Porter, B. (1991). Generating coherent explanations to answer students' questions. In H. Burns, J. W. Parlett, & C. L. Redfield (Eds.), *Intelligent tutoring systems: Evolutions in designs* (pp. 151–176). Hillsdale, NJ: Erlbaum.

Borman, W. C. (1974). The rating of individuals in organizations: An alternate approach. *Organizational Behavior and Human Performance, 12,* 105–124.

Borman, W. C., & Motowidlo, S. J. (1993). Expanding the criterion domain to include elements of contextual performance. In N. Schmitt & W. C. Borman (Eds.), *Personnel selection in organizations* (pp. 71–98). San Francisco: Jossey-Bass.

Bowen, D. E., & Lawler, E. E., III. (1992). Total quality-oriented human resources management. *Organizational Dynamics, 20,* 29–41.

Boyatzis, R. E. (1982). *The competent manager: A model for effective performance.* New York: Wiley.

Brown, J. S., Collins, A., & Duguid, S. (1989). Situated cognition and the culture of learning. *Educational Researcher, 18,* 32–42.

Campbell, J. P. (1971). Personnel training and development. *Annual Review of Psychology.*

Campbell, J. P. (1990). Modeling the performance prediction problem in industrial and organizational psychology. In M. D. Dunnette & L. M. Hough (Eds.), *Handbook of industrial and organizational psychology* (Vol. 1, 2nd ed., pp. 687–732). Palo Alto, CA: Consulting Psychologists Press.

Campbell, J. P., McCloy, R. A., Oppler, S. H., & Sager, C. E. (1993). A theory of performance. In N. Schmitt & W. C. Borman (Eds.), *Personnel selection in organizations* (pp. 35–70). San Francisco: Jossey-Bass.

Cannon-Bowers, J. A., Oser, R., & Flanagan, D. L. (1992). Work teams in industry: A selected review and proposed framework. In R. W. Swezey & E. Salas (Eds.), *Teams: Their training and performance.* Norwood, NJ: Ablex.

Cannon-Bowers, J. A., Tannenbaum, S. I., Salas, E., & Volpe, C. E. (1995). Defining competencies and establishing team training requirements. In R. A. Guzzo & E. Salas (Eds.), *Team effectiveness and decision making in organizations* (pp. 333–380). San Francisco: Jossey-Bass.

Caudron, S. (1996). Wake up to new learning technologies. *Training and Development, 50*(5), 30–35.

Chi, M.T.H., Bassok, M., Lewis, M., Reimann, M., & Glaser, R. (1989). Self-explanations: How students study and use examples in learning to solve problems. *Cognitive Science, 13,* 145–182.

Chi, M.T.H., Glaser, R., & Rees, E. (1982). Expertise in problem solving. In R. J. Sternberg (Ed.), *Advances in the psychology of human intelligence* (Vol. 1, pp. 7–75). Hillsdale, NJ: Erlbaum.

Choi, J. (1995). Situated cognition and learning environments: Roles, structures, and implications for design. *Educational Technology Research and Development, 43,* 53–69.

Choi, J., & Hannafin, M. J. (1995). Situated cognition and learning environments: Roles, structures, and implications for design. *Educational Technology Research and Design, 43,* 53–69.

Collins, A. (1991). Cognitive apprenticeship and instructional technology. In L. Idol & B. F. Jones (Eds.), *Educational values and cognitive instruction: Implications for reform.* Hillsdale, NJ: Erlbaum.

Cox, T. H., & Blake, S. (1991). Managing cultural diversity: Implications for organizational competitiveness. *Academy of Management Executive, 5,* 45–56.

Dean, J. W., Jr., & Bowen, D. E (1994). Management theory and total quality: Improving research and practice through theory development. *Academy of Management Review, 19,* 392–418.

Dertouzos, M., Lester, R., & Sokow, R. (1989). *Made in America: Regaining the productive edge.* Cambridge, MA: MIT Press.

Dick, W., & Carey, J. (1990). *The systematic design of instruction* (3rd ed.). Glenview, IL: Scott, Foresman.

Dweck, C. S. (1986). Motivational processes affecting learning. *American Psychologist, 41,* 1040–1048.

Fitzgerald, L. F., Hulin, C. L., & Drasgow, F. (1995). The antecedents and consequences of sexual harassment in organizations: An integrated model. In G. Keita & J. Hurrell Jr. (Eds.), *Job stress in a changing workforce: Investigating gender, diversity, and family issues* (pp. 55–73). Washington, DC: American Psychological Association.

Flynn, B. B., Sakakibara, S., & Schroeder, R. G. (1995). Relationship between JIT and TQM: Practices and performance. *Academy of Management Journal, 38,* 1325–1360.

Ford, J. K., & Kraiger, K. (1995). The application of cognitive constructs and principles to the instructional systems model of training: Implications for needs assessment, design, and transfer. In C. L. Cooper & I. T. Robertson (Eds.), *International review of industrial and organizational psychology* (Vol. 10, pp. 1–48). New York: Wiley.

Ford, J. K., & Weissbein, D. (1997). Transfer of training: An updated review and analysis. *Performance Improvement Quarterly, 10,* 22–41.

Ford, J. K., & Wroten, S. P. (1984). Introducing new methods for conducting training evaluation and for linking training evaluation to program redesign. *Personnel Psychology, 11,* 651–665.

Ford, J. M., & Wood, L. E. (1992). Structuring and documenting interactions with subject matter experts. *Performance Instruction Quarterly, 5*(1), 2–24.

Geber, B. (1995). Does your training make a difference? Prove it! *Training, 32*(3), 27–34.

Georgenson, D. L. (1982). The problem of transfer calls for partnership. *Training and Development Journal, 36*(10), 75–78.

Glaser, R., & Bassok, M. (1989). Learning theory and the study of instruction. *Annual Review of Psychology, 40,* 631–666.

Goldstein, I. L. (1980). Training in work organizations. *Annual Review of Psychology, 31,* 229–272.

Goldstein, I. L. (1993). *Training in organizations: Needs assessment, development, and evaluation* (3rd ed.). Pacific Grove, CA: Brooks/Cole.

Goldstein, I. L., & Gilliam, P. (1990). Training system issues in the year 2000. *American Psychologist, 45,* 134–145.

Hackman, J. R., & Wageman, R. (1995). Total quality management: Empirical, conceptual, and practical issues. *Administrative Science Quarterly, 40,* 309–342.

Hannafin, M. J. (1992). Emerging technologies, ISD, and learning environments: Critical perspectives. *Educational Technology and Development, 40,* 49–63.

Howell, W. C., & Cooke, N. J. (1989). Training the human information processor: A review of cognitive models. In I. L. Goldstein (Ed.), *Training and development in organizations.* San Francisco: Jossey-Bass.

Huczynski, A. A., & Lewis, J. W. (1980). An empirical study into the learning transfer process in management training. *Journal of Management Studies, 17,* 227–240.

Jonassen, D. H., & Tessmer, M. (1996/1997). An outcomes-based taxonomy for instructional systems design, evaluation, and research. *Training Research Journal, 2,* 11–46.

Jonassen, D. H., & Wang, S. (1992). Acquiring structural knowledge from semantically structured hypertext. *Journal of Computer-Based Instruction, 20,* 1–8.

Kauffman, H. G. (1978). Continuing education and job performance: A longitudinal study. *Journal of Applied Psychology, 63,* 248–251.

Kesler, G. C. (1995). A model and process for redesigning the HRM role, competencies, and work in a major multinational corporation. *Human Resource Management, 34,* 229–252.

Kraiger, K. (1995, August). *Paradigms lost: Applications and misapplications of cognitive science to the study of training.* Invited address for Science Weekend at the annual meeting of the American Psychology Association.

Kraiger, K. (1995/1996). Integrating training research. *Training Research Journal, 1,* 5–17.

Kraiger, K., Ford, J. K., & Salas, E. (1993). Integration of cognitive, behavioral, and affective theories of learning into new methods of training evaluation [Monograph]. *Journal of Applied Psychology, 78,* 311–328.

Kraiger, K., & Jung, K. M. (1997). Linking training objectives to evaluation criteria. In M. A. Quiñones & A. Ehrenstein (Eds.), *Training in a rapidly changing workplace: Applications of psychological research* (pp. 151–179). Washington, DC: American Psychological Association.

Larkin, J. H. (1983). The role of problem representation in physics. In D. Gentner & A. L. Stevens (Eds.), *Mental models* (pp. 75–98). Hillsdale, NJ: Erlbaum.

Latham, G. P. (1988). Human resource training and development. *Annual Review of Psychology, 39,* 545–582.

Lawler, E. E., III. (1994). From job-based to competency-based organizations. *Journal of Organizational Behavior, 15,* 3–15.

Livingston, J. A. (1982). Responses to sexual harassment on the job: Legal, organizational and individual actions. *Journal of Social Issues, 38,* 5–22.

London, M., & Smither, J. W. (1995). Can multisource feedback change perceptions of goal accomplishment, self-evaluations, and performance-related outcomes? Theory-based applications and directions for future research. *Personnel Psychology, 48,* 803–839.

Lord, R. G., & Maher, K. J. (1991). Cognitive theory in industrial/organizational psychology. In M. D. Dunnette & L. M. Hough (Eds.), *Handbook of industrial and organizational psychology* (Vol. 2, 2nd ed., pp. 1–62). Palo Alto, CA: Consulting Psychology Press.

Mager, R. F. (1984). *Preparing instructional objectives.* Belmont, CA: Pitman.

Major, D. A., & Kozlowski, S.W.J. (1997). Newcomer information seeking: Individual and contextual influences. *International Journal of Selection and Assessment, 5,* 16–27.

Mathieu, J. E., & Martineau, J. W. (1997). Individual and situational influences on training motivation. In J. K. Ford, S.W.J. Kozlowski, K. Kraiger, E. Salas, & M. Teachout (Eds.), *Improving training effectiveness in work organizations* (pp. 193–221). Hillsdale, NJ: Erlbaum.

McLinden, D. J. (1995). Proof, evidence, and complexity: Understanding the impact of training and development in business. *Performance Improvement Quarterly, 8*(3), 3–18.

Morgan, B. B., Glickman, A. S., Woodward, E. A., Blaiwes, A. S., & Salas, E. (1986). *Measurement of team behaviors in a Navy environment* (Tech. Rep. No. NTSC TR-86–014). Orlando, FL: Naval Training Systems Center.

Noe, R. A. (1986). Trainees' attributes and attitudes: Neglected influences on training effectiveness. *Academy of Management Review, 11,* 736–749.

Noe, R. A., Wilk, S. L., Mullen, E. J., & Wanek, J. E. (1997). Employee development: Issues in construct definition and investigation of antecedents. In J. K. Ford, S.W.J. Kozlowski, K. Kraiger, E. Salas, & M. Teachout (Eds.), *Improving training effectiveness in work organizations.* Hillsdale, NJ: Erlbaum.

Offermann, L. R., & Gowing, M. K. (1990). Organizations of the future: Changes and challenges. *American Psychologist, 45,* 95–108.

Polson, M. C., & Richardson, J. J. (1988). *Foundations of intelligent tutoring systems.* Hillsdale, NJ: Erlbaum.

Royer, J., Cisero, C., & Carlo, M. S. (1993). Techniques and procedures for assessing cognitive skills. *Review of Educational Research, 63,* 201–243.

Ryder, J. M., & Redding, R. E. (1991). Integrating cognitive task analysis into instructional systems development. *Educational Technology Research and Development, 41,* 75–96.

Saari, L. M., Johnson, T. R., McLaughlin, S. D., & Zimmerle, D. M. (1988). A survey of management training and education practices in U.S. companies. *Personnel Psychology, 41,* 731–743.

Schmidt, R. A., & Bjork, R. A. (1992). New conceptualizations of practice: Common principles in three paradigms suggest new concepts for training. *Psychological Science, 3,* 207–217.

Semb, G. B., Ellis, J. A., Fitch, M. A., Parchman, S., & Irick, C. (1995). On-the-job training: Prescriptions and practice. *Performance Instruction Quarterly, 8*(3), 19–37.

Senge, P. M. (1990). *The fifth discipline: The art and practice of the learning organization.* New York: Doubleday.

Tannenbaum, S. I., & Woods, S. B. (1992). Determining a strategy for evaluating training: Operating within organizational constraints. *Human Resource Planning, 15*(2), 63–81.

Tessmer, M. (1995/1996). Formative multimedia evaluation. *Training Research Journal, 1,* 127–149.

Thomas, L. S. (1992). Managing diversity: A conceptual framework. In S. E. Jackson (Ed.), *Diversity in the workplace: Human resource initiatives.* New York: Guilford Press.

Tornow, W. W. (1993). Perceptions or reality: Is multiperspective measurement a means or an end? *Human Resource Management, 32,* 221–230.

Tracey, J. B., Tannenbaum, S. I., & Kavanagh, M. J. (1995). Applying trained skills on the job: The importance of work environment. *Journal of Applied Psychology, 80,* 239–252.

Ulrich, D., Brockbank, W., Yueng, A. K., & Lake, D. G. (1995). Human resource competencies: An empirical assessment. *Human Resource Management, 34,* 473–495.

Vobejda, B. (1987, April 14). The new cutting edge in factories. *Washington Post,* p. A14.

Wexley, K. N. (1984). Personnel training. *Annual Review of Psychology, 35,* 519–552.

Wexley, K. N., & Latham, G. P. (1991). *Developing and training human resources in organizations* (2nd ed.). New York: HarperCollins.

Wilk, S. L., & Noe, R. A. (1997/1998). The role of psychological contracts in determining employees' participation in development activities. *Training Research Journal, 3,* 13–38.

Wisher, V. (1994). Competencies: The precious seeds of growth. *Personnel Management, 26,* 36–39.

Concluding Remarks

The Definition and Measurement of Performance in the New Age

John P. Campbell

For just a moment consider the "mission" of industrial and organizational (I/O) psychology to be as follows: I/O psychology is concerned with the application of psychological research and theory to understanding and enhancing individual and group behavior in work settings. This is a broad mandate and can range from issues in the cognitive processing and evaluation of performance information by a human judge to the structure of human abilities and personality as determinants of complex job performance; to the causal modeling of the entire structure of human performance determinants; to basic processes in knowledge and skill acquisition; to the identification of the most critical training needs for various segments of the current and future labor force; to basic motivational issues as they pertain to unemployment, job choice, career self-management, organizational commitment, and individual performance; to the design of effective groups and organizations; to the impact of occupational and organizational changes on satisfaction, mobility, and commitment. The bottom line is that while I/O psychology is a relatively small field, it deals with many of our most critical national problems relative to the functioning of the labor force and the enhancement of human capital. Within the field, these issues are addressed from both the individual and the institutional perspective and can range from the most basic of research issues to very applied concerns.

Research and development in I/O psychology can be characterized by the dependent variables that are of critical interest and by the major strategies (independent variables) that can explain and potentially influence them. There is a fairly clear and broad consensus about the critical dependent variables that should be explained and enhanced, at least at a general level of discussion:

- Individual job/role/occupational performance (including counterproductive behavior at work)
- Work group/team performance
- Withdrawal behavior (such as absenteeism)
- Self-evaluation of job/occupational satisfaction and organizational commitment
- Self-evaluation of "fair treatment" (such as procedural and distributive justice)

It is also true that these dependent variables can be viewed as determinants of more distal outcomes (such as organizational effectiveness) and that there may be causal relationships among them (such as individual performance as a determinant of team performance, or job satisfaction or fairness as determinants of withdrawal). To a very considerable degree, however, each of these is a valued outcome in its own right.

In general, as noted by Ilgen and Pulakos in Chapter One, the independent variables that can potentially influence the outcomes just listed can be assigned to the selection/classification system, the training and development system, the work motivation system, the work design system, and to their interactive effects. That is, what characteristics of individuals at the time of entry into the organization have significant effects on one or more of the four dependent variables? What socialization and learning strategies have significant effects? What motivational strategies have significant effects? and What parameters of work design (both process and structure) are critical? Learning strategies, motivational strategies, and changes in work design are "treatments," and Cronbach's Aptitude (that is, individual differences) × Treatment Interaction

(ATI) framework is in fact a useful way of looking at virtually every research and practice issue in I/O psychology. There are always individual differences (abilities, personality disposition, skills, expectancies) that can potentially influence the dependent variable; there are always alternative treatment effects (that is, different job assignments, different training or socialization experiences, different team structures, different reward systems) among which a choice is made, if only by default; and there is always the problem of specifying the dependent variables appropriately. There may or may not be specific interaction effects.

The ATI has four facets:

1. The dependent variable that must be specified carefully, both in terms of its intended substantive content or meaning, and in terms of its reliability, validity, relative deficiency, and relative contamination (such as all those noxious properties of the "rating" process)
2. The potentially relevant individual differences variables, and there may be a few or many
3. The alternative treatments that could be considered
4. Potential interactions, two way or N-way

Any I/O psychologist worthy of the name thinks carefully about each of these facets relative to whatever problem in basic research, applied research, system development, or practice is of concern. That is, each facet should be specified as fully as possible, in terms of both the variable and treatment conditions that are under consideration, and the relevant variables and treatments that are not under consideration, for whatever reason.

A common language for discussion of these specifications would help, but we are still a long way from having one, which does create problems. For example, to anticipate a subsequent discussion in this chapter, *technology* is a treatment effect. Regardless of whether technological changes (treatment differences) occur daily, monthly, yearly, or once a century, they are still treatment effects. Although analyzing the effects of technological changes within the ATI framework may be difficult (changes occur quickly, the N's for each treatment are small, there are many variants of the technology), they must still be discussed and examined within such a framework.

The Purpose of This Chapter

As articulated by the editors, the goals of this volume in the Frontiers of Industrial and Organizational Psychology series are based on the premise that the world of work is undergoing major changes. To go to work today is to experience a qualitatively different "treatment" effect than was going to work in the 1950s, 1960s, or 1970s. The world of work has changed because of several dynamic causal forces that are reshaping the economy, the goals and structures of organization, and the nature of the labor force.

Given this premise, the objectives of the book were to examine whether the changes being wrought by these events require changes in the way we define and measure individual work performance, for both operational and research purposes; and whether the required changes in the way performance is modeled or measured have critical implications for the selection, training, and motivational systems that constitute human resource management. The chapter authors were charged with asking and answering these two questions within their own areas of expertise.

This was a very interesting and difficult assignment for the contributors. The resulting chapters are not light reading and they are not business as usual. The goals of this final chapter are to summarize and comment on the changes identified, the issues raised, and the new directions advocated by the contributors as they addressed the two objectives put forth by the editors.

The Campbell Model

The editors wisely names this author's model of performance (Campbell, McCloy, Oppler, & Sager, 1993) as a possible framework within which to consider the book's objectives. At the risk of wasting space for those who have read it before, it is briefly summarized here. There are simply some critical points that must be made at the outset.

Again, performance is defined as behavior or action that is relevant for the organization's goals and that can be scaled (measured) in terms of the level of proficiency (or contribution to goals) that is represented by a particular action or set of actions. Performance is what employers (self or others) pay you to *do,* or what they should pay you to do. The identification of goals and the judgments concerning what is relevant for the goals are critical elements in designating what is performance and what is not. In virtually all organizations, however, large or small, the important stakeholders are not all of like mind. Consequently, there could be some disagreement over what goals are critical and what behaviors are most relevant. These facts of life have a lot to do with the issues discussed in this book.

The measurement operations, be they supervisor ratings, a simulated work sample with an "objective" scoring system, tallying the amount sold, recording customer complaints, or some variant of computerized performance assessment, besides being reliable, valid, and not deficient, should not allow contamination by sources of variation that are not under the control of the individual. To the extent that performance differences between people (the dependent variable of real intent) are the result of measurement contamination, we lose the opportunity to find out how to improve aggregate performance via improvements in selection, training, motivational, or design strategies. Measurement contamination puts the psychologist out of business, or at least at considerable risk.

Performance differences produced by technology are a case in point. If technology A is much, much better than technology B, and half of a particular research sample uses technology A because their management is ahead of its time and half the sample still uses technology B because management refuses to spend the money, the variance in performance in the total sample could be dominated by the technology differences over which the individual had no control, and which would make it difficult to determine the predictive validity of abilities, personality traits, and so on, or to evaluate the effects of training or motivational interventions using such a sample. Based on data from such a research sample, a reasonable prescription would be to give everybody technology A and forget about selection and training. We are, however, in this business because we believe that the variables that I/O psychology studies are important determinants of performance, and previous research supports this belief.

If within each technology group the correlation between ability and performance is high and it is also true that additional training would boost mean performance in each group, this is not an argument against using better technology. Everyone is in favor of using the best available technologies to improve mean performance. If at all possible, however, technology differences *within a research sample* should not contaminate the examination of other issues. It is surely also true that most people doing operational performance appraisals would discount technology differences across ratees if the raters were aware of them. If the choice of technologies (such as hardware and software for doing data analysis) is in fact under the control of the individual, then technology differences are no longer a contaminant and the individual is accountable for them. Similar reasoning applies for other potential sources of contamination.

It is also true that certain technologies, or "situations" or "contexts," could place a constraint on the mean, variance, or both of individual performance. Within the ATI framework a specific constraint situation also constitutes a treatment. Such a treatment condition may or may not change the regression of performance on specific measures of individual differences and may or may not require changes in the way performance is specified.

The Components of Performance

When defined this way, the model incorporates the notion that total performance in all jobs, occupations, or positions at the moment is multidimensional, and that each dimension is represented by a category of similar behaviors or actions (such as performance in the role of team member). Our model proposed eight primary factors. These were not idly chosen. They were meant to represent our best effort to use the available literature, from Project A to the voluminous literatures on group performance and dynamics, leadership, supervision, and management, to specify the substantive content of each dimension at a particular level of generality. For most of its history, I/O psychology has complained about the criterion problem and avoided making substantive hypotheses about how best to represent the content of performance. That situation started to change only after about 1985.

Again, at the risk of going over old ground, the briefest of definitions for each factor follows. In terms of a hierarchical factor structure, they are meant to be very high in the hierarchy. Subsequent research may show that different levels are more useful for different purposes and that the substantive definitions of the factors can be improved, which are precisely the things we need to know. It seems obvious that to accumulate research findings in the most advantageous way possible, both for future research and for practice, every study that purports to investigate the predictors or determinants of "performance" must specify the performance variable, however crudely, in terms of a model of performance—this one or a better one. The very thing we are trying to explain or improve cannot be tossed off with a general label or two, or dismissed as too difficult to specify or measure.

A Taxonomy of Higher-Order Performance Components

1. *Job-specific task proficiency.* The first factor reflects the level of proficiency with which the individual performs the core substantive or technical tasks that distinguish the substantive content of one job or position from another. A primary issue is whether this factor has a unique specification for every job, position, or role in the labor force, or whether there are major areas of expertise that have a similar specification across a number of jobs or occupations.

2. *Non-job-specific task proficiency.* In virtually every organization, individuals are required to execute performance behaviors that are not specific to their particular job.

3. *Written and oral communication proficiency.* Many jobs in the workforce require the individual to make formal oral or written presentations to audiences that may vary from one to tens of thousands. For people in those jobs, the proficiency with which they can write or speak, independent of the correctness of the subject matter, is a critical component of performance. When discussing performance issues, "poor communication" is often a catch-all description for a number of difficulties. This factor, however, does not refer to knowing what to say and when. It refers to prescribed speaking or writing tasks or assignments.

4. *Demonstration of effort.* This factor is a direct reflection of the frequency with which people expend extra effort when asked, and keep working under adverse conditions. It is a reflection of the degree to which individuals commit themselves to all job tasks, work at a high level of intensity, and keep working when it is cold, wet, or late.

5. *Maintenance of personal discipline.* This component is characterized by the degree to which negative or counterproductive behaviors, such as alcohol and substance abuse at work, law or rule infractions, and excessive absenteeism, are avoided. The high end reflects proficient self-management of time and skill resources.

6. *Facilitation of peer and team performance.* This factor represents the degree to which the individual supports his or her peers, helps them with job problems, and acts as a de facto trainer. It also encompasses how well an individual facilitates group functioning by being a good model, keeping the group goal directed, and reinforcing participation by the other group members. Two levels of lower-order subfactors are to be found in the leadership and group dynamics literature. For example, at the next level down, support for goal accomplishment and maintenance of group member relationships from the group dynamics literature (see Shaw, 1981; Zander, 1982) are the parallels to initiating structure and consideration from the leadership literature (Fleishman & Quaintance, 1984). These two factors appear in study after study, and their reality really cannot be denied.

7. *Supervision/leadership.* Proficiency in the supervisory component includes all the behaviors directed at influencing the performance of subordinates through face-to-face interpersonal interaction and influence. Supervisors set goals for subordinates, teach subordinates effective methods, model appropriate behaviors, and reward or punish in appropriate ways. The distinction between this factor and the preceding one is a distinction between peer leadership and supervisory leadership. Both that factor and this one can take advantage of previous theory and research directed at the factor structure, or a taxonomy, of leadership behavior (see Yukl & Van Fleet, 1992).

8. *Management/administration.* The eighth factor is intended to include the major elements in management that are distinct from direct supervision, such as articulating goals for the unit or enterprise, organizing people and resources to work on them, monitoring progress, helping to solve problems or overcome crises that stand in the way of goal accomplishment, controlling expenditures, obtaining additional resources, and representing the unit in dealings with other units. Subfactors that fit these specifications are summarized by Borman and Brush (1993). A distinguishing fea-

ture of the surging emphasis on team designs is that the team members take on more of the supervision (factor 7) and management (factor 8) functions.

Additional substantive specifications for performance have been offered by Borman and Motowidlo (1993), Ilgen and Hollenbeck (1991), Murphy (1989), and Organ (1997). We view all of these factors as complimentary (Campbell, Gasser, & Oswald, 1996), as do Motowidlo and Schmit (Chapter Three, this volume). When laid on top of one another, they form the beginnings of a hierarchical description of the latent structure of performance. For example, the task versus contextual distinction of Borman and Motowidlo is at a higher level, while their specific factors, and those of Organ (1997), can be thought of as specific subfactors of the eight factors just presented.

The Campbell factors, as specified in their longer versions, were intended to be as distinct as possible in terms of the work behaviors that are included in each one. That does not mean that observed measures of each factor for an appropriate sample of job incumbents will not be intercorrelated, or that a factor analysis of such intercorrelations will not yield a general factor. Given the ubiquitous effects of cognitive ability and certain personality dimensions as common determinants of virtually all components of performance, the intercorrelations simply must be there. The presence of a general factor, however, does not preclude differential prediction across factors, and certainly does not lead to the same training and development prescription for the determinants of each factor.

Another issue is the value of attempting to specify latent structure models of performance if the goals and judgments that define the relevant actions are stakeholder based and potentially idiosyncratic to a specific context. The principal answer is that the cumulative research record supports considerable generality in these kinds of latent structures across occupations and across organizations.

What cannot be emphasized too much is the importance of working toward an agreed-upon set of substantive definitions that provides a common blueprint for any investigator who wants to measure performance and any practitioner who wants to improve it. Saying that such specifications cannot be developed because organizational environments are now too dynamic is the same thing as saying that we will never understand what we are trying to do.

Performance Versus Its Determinants

The Campbell model makes a big deal about the distinction between performance itself and its determinants, and about the distinction between direct determinants and indirect determinants, as represented in Exhibit 12.1. The figure is meant to argue that the interventions that HRM has at its disposal can exert effects on performance only if they change one or more of the direct determinants. This goes for selection on the basis of general cognitive ability and personality differences, as well as for training or motivational interventions. Also, it is critical that the direct influence of motivation be represented as the three types of choices. Campbell, Gasser, and Oswald (1996) reviewed the available literature on the causal modeling of performance determinants and found it to be consistent with Exhibit 12.1, in spite of the general underspecification of the direct determinants. Knowledge, skill, and choice behavior are not themselves components of performance. Individual differences on any component of performance are a *joint function* of individual differences in knowledge, skill, and choice behavior. If the performance measurement method does not allow one or more of the three determinants to have any effects (such as when standardized simulations control for differences in the volitional choices), the measure is *determinant deficient,* which may be appropriate for some measurement goals (such as training evaluation) but not for others (such as selection research criterion measurement).

Implicit in this representation is that situations are treatments and changes in a situation are treatment effects. There are two general kinds of situational changes: those that change the work itself and thus change the performance requirements, and those that leave the job requirements the same but change the individuals knowledge, skill, or choice behavior. An intervention such as job redesign may do both. That is, in job redesign the task content is changed, which may change skill requirements, and the intervention might also change choice behavior because the new task content provides more intrinsic rewards for greater effort. Too often the term *situation* is invoked as an influence on performance, with little

Exhibit 12.1. Effects of Determinants of
Individual Differences on Components of Job Performance.

Direct Determinants

	Procedural Knowledge and Skill (PKS)	
$PC_i^a = f$ [*Declarative Knowledge (DK)*	*and Skill (PKS)*	*Motivation (M)*]
• Facts	• Cognitive skill	• Choice to perform
• Principles	• Psychomotor skill	• Choice of effort level
• Goals	• Physical skill	• Choice of duration
• Self-knowledge	• Self-management skill	of effort
	• Interpersonal skill	

Indirect Determinants

$DK = f$ [(ability, personality, interests), (education, training, experience), (aptitude-treatment interactions)]

$PKS = f$ [(ability, personality, interests), (education, training, practice, experience), (aptitude-treatment interactions)]

$M = f$ (the independent variables stipulated by research and theory in motivation)

[a]Scores on a particular performance component.

Source: Campbell, McCloy, Oppler, and Sager, 1993. Used by permission of Jossey-Bass Publishers.

or no specification for what it is supposed to mean. The word has caused much confusion and no small amount of misinformation.

Recently, considerable attention has been focused on the relationship of HRM practices to organizational effectiveness (see Becker & Gerhardt, 1996). Although still relatively small, the cumulative research record consistently shows a positive relationship between the quality of HRM practices and the overall effectiveness of the organization, when using the organization as the unit of analysis. Not measured in these studies is the linkage between changes in HRM practices and changes in individual performance (including withdrawal behavior), and the linkage between changes in individual performance and changes in organizational performance. For the causal relationship to exist at the organizational level, these two linkages simply must be there.

Within the general framework of current performance models, the types of individual changes that could improve organizational effectiveness are the following:

- Individuals could become more proficient on the technical components of what they must do.
- They could devote more time and/or a higher level of effort to the critical things they must do (such as reducing absenteeism).
- Individuals could reduce costs by assuming more responsibility for their own self-development by avoiding counterproductive behaviors.
- Individuals could improve their proficiency in leadership roles (such as peer leadership/support or team member performance).
- Individuals could effectively assume greater responsibility for particular management functions (such as controlling costs, monitoring unit performance, or representing the organization externally) or many team design requirements.

Potentially all of these changes could be influenced to some extent by the selection, training, and motivational systems or by their interactions. A major question addressed by the current contributors is whether the dynamic trends that are taking place will require changes in the HRM strategies that are used to promote the individual outcomes just listed.

The Challenges of the Future

As noted by the editors and by all of the chapter authors, the world of work is perceived to have entered a period of very dynamic change that will have major effects on research and practice in I/O psychology. Although not all contributors reflect on all the trends described in Chapter One, considerable attention was devoted to the dynamics of technological change, the changing nature of employment contracts, the increased use of new work team designs, and the use of new organizational forms (such as flatter structure, flexible staffing practices, and project focus) to meet the demands of the global economy. Three developments that did not receive much comment and which probably should not slip off our screens are the following:

1. The *Workforce 2000* report (Johnston & Packer, 1987) predicted a looming gap between the skills demanded of the labor force by the U.S. economy and the skills offered by high school

and technical school graduates (more than 50 percent of the workforce). The skills gap was projected to become most acute during the period 2000–2020. Subsequent to *Workforce 2000,* there has been some disagreement over the magnitude, pattern, and causes of the skill gap (Holzer, 1997; Penn, Rose, & Rubery, 1994). No one disputes, however, that there will be an aggregate shortfall between supply and demand during the next two to three decades. This issue incorporates a number of research questions pertaining to the basic taxonomic and substantive structure of trainable skills, the optimal identification of national training needs, the development of new methods of skills assessment and new methods for skills training, and the effective self-management of career planning and occupational training and development by each individual.

2. The composition of the labor force is changing and the pace of change will accelerate because of U.S. demographic trends. The workforce will become much more diverse *by necessity.* This will magnify racial, gender, and cultural issues as they pertain to career planning, personnel selection, training and development, performance assessment, and promotion.

3. Computerization and information technology developments since the mid-1980s have created an enormous potential for providing critical occupational information to management, policymakers, training/development specialists, jobholders, and job seekers, *if only* the processes and structures for doing so could be modeled effectively. As an example, the simple existence of the technology has literally forced the U.S. Department of Labor to begin converting its traditional data bank of occupational information, which is tied to the printed volume known as the *Dictionary of Occupational Titles,* to a computerized database that is to be fully integrated with many related databases (such as predicted employment trends, education and certification requirements, unemployment rates, compensation levels, current job openings, and so on) such that the entire information system can be accessed by virtually anyone for literally hundreds of different reasons (such as career and education planning, job search, unemployment counseling, public policy development, vocational training design, and so on). The system can be no better, however, than the substantive properties of its occupational classification structure. (What are the occupational units to which occupational information should be tied?

What model of occupational skills should be used to describe the entry-level, and expert-level, skill requirements of occupations? What individual ability, personality, and interest characteristics are required by different occupations?)

Although most of us believe with some confidence that these changes are taking place, the empirical documentation is uneven, and Murphy (Chapter Nine, this volume) worries about what is fact and what is hype. This unevenness in the empirical database has led to the creation of a National Academy of Sciences panel (Barley & Kochan, 1998) which is charged with marshaling the available evidence and specifying the nature of the data that should be collected in the future. As of this writing, the panel is in the midst of drafting its report. Its progress will be documented on a Web site maintained by the National Academy of Sciences. All that aside, it is reasonable to conclude that the aggregate effects of the above trends are making significant changes in the world of work. Will these effects necessitate changes in the way we model, assess, and attempt to enhance performance?

The Parameters of Change

The models proposed by Campbell and colleagues (1993), Borman and Motowidlo (1993), Organ (1997), and Murphy (1989) all have essentially the same form. That is, they explicitly or implicitly identify a similar set of parameters (such as the organization's goals; the behaviors, actions, and accomplishments that are goal relevant; the stakeholders who determine goals and judge what is relevant; the specifications for the components of performance; the specifications for the determinants of performance; and the specifications for the measurement methods) that must be specified before we can measure performance for some purpose. If the issue is whether the forces that are changing the world of work will, or should, require a different view of performance, then the question translates to how the specifications for these parameters will, or should, be changed. That is, a different view of performance could involve changes in one or more of the following:

- The purposes for which performance measurement is carried out

- The performance measurement methods
- The relative criticality of different performance components (given current taxonomies)
- The specifications of additional components of performance that will become critical
- The basic distinction between direct and indirect determinants
- The basic distinctions among individual, group, and organizational performance
- The basic definition of the performance content itself

With this list of possibilities in mind, the following sections summarize what the chapter contributors have to say about how our view of individual performance could, should, or might change in the future.

The Fundamental Definition of Performance

At least two of the chapters view the current nature of technological change as something that requires a change in the basic definition of performance. One that devotes considerable attention to technology in this regard, and which is cited by many of the other contributors, is Chapter Two, by Hesketh and Neal.

At first glance, the Hesketh and Neal chapter appears to take an unusual view of technology differences as determinants of differences in individual performance. On closer inspection, their discussion is quite consistent with current models. It addresses, however, the complexities of the person-technology interface in much greater, and very useful, detail. That is, choosing among alternative technologies could indeed be a choice that is under the control of the individual and that therefore would count as a legitimate determinant of individual differences in performance. Conversely, Hesketh and Neal would agree that if the choice of technologies is not under the individual's control, technology differences would function as a source of criterion contamination. For either condition, both the technology main effect and the interactive effects with individual differences could be sources of variance in individual performance and it would be useful to estimate the variance accounted for under varying degrees of individual control over technology.

The worry of Hesketh and Neal is that the pace and nature of technological change will make it very difficult to separate the two conditions and account for their effects. This is a very real worry, and it will become a larger and larger problem for criterion measurement and performance appraisal in the future. There is no easy solution. Ideally, a job or occupational analysis should identify the components of technology that are chosen by the individual and those that are not. Hesketh and Neal believe that most job analyses neglect this issue. Among others, the U.S. Army (Campbell et al., 1990) and the Federal Aviation Administration (Manning & Broach, 1992) might disagree on the basis of their past analysis work, but that does not solve the problem for the future when the pace quickens and things become more complicated. Hesketh and Neal present a convincing argument for why we might want to investigate the positive and negative effects of technology as both main effects and interactive effects on performance, and to estimate main effects and interactive effects both when the choice of technology is under individual control and when it is not. They present a number of useful methodologies that could be used to scale performance and estimate variance accounted for under various conditions. Building on their very thorough discussion, two additional suggestions would be to make the appropriate discounting of technology differences across people a part of rater training or training in performance appraisal. A second approach might be a modified simulation, similar to the walkthrough job sample developed by the Air Force (Vance, MacCallum, Coovert, & Hedge, 1988) in which individuals indicate, and perhaps demonstrate, the technology they would use to perform specific tasks or solve certain problems. The protocol could then be scored in terms of whether the individual exercised knowledgeable, discretionary choices among technologies at the appropriate places.

Chapter Five, by London and Mone, also raises fundamental questions about how the basic definition of performance might need to be reconceptualized. They seem to have two concerns about current models, both of which result from the rapid pace of technological and organizational change. First, it may not be possible to specify performance dimensions and develop measures for them that would be relevant, and therefore useful, for any significant length of time. The nature of work simply changes too quickly.

Second, in such a technologically fast-paced environment people must either be selected on the basis of having high predicted performance for a variety of subsequent assignments, the precise nature of which cannot be predicted, or the organization must almost continually lay people off and hire others as the nature of the work to be done changes and different knowledges and skills are needed. The latter strategy can be quite costly.

London and Mone wish to define performance as proficiency with regard to continuous self-directed training, which puts the measurement emphasis on two of the three direct determinants of performance in Exhibit 12.1 (knowledge and skill) rather than on performance itself. There are precedents for such a focus, as in skills-based pay (Lawler & Jenkins, 1992) and in traditional procedures for basing hiring or promotion on the level of education attained. Also, for a number of roles in the military services, the critical performance actions take place in situations that everyone hopes will never occur. In such a context, being ready (that is, having the necessary knowledge and skills) may be a very meaningful specification of performance. That is, one is in fact paid for being highly trained on certain skills.

If the London and Mone picture of change is a reasonable one, and if individuals must more or less constantly prepare for task demands that are still in the future, then the proficiency with which individuals identify and master the critical skills that will be required is a reasonable focus for performance assessments. The chapters by Bowen and Waldman (Chapter Six), Lord and Smith (Chapter Seven), and Murphy and Jackson (Chapter Ten) are consistent with this view. When viewed from current models, however, some very difficult questions still remain, such as how (that is, by what methods) a self-managed needs analysis will be able to identify which knowledge and skills will be critical in the future, and how accurately such needs can be identified if we cannot provide a substantive specification for what people must be able to do in the future. Finally, if individual proficiency in continuous self-managed learning, in the form of learning needs assessments, design of training and learning experiences, and mastery of new knowledge and skills, is made the sole focus of performance assessment, then the potential costs, as outlined by Murphy (Chapter Nine), must be recognized. Individuals could spend so much time preparing for, and trying to obtain, future assignments that their current work is neglected.

To deal with these issues, the self-directed learner will need help in the form of something akin to a synthetic validation approach and a *research-based* specification of the most critical generic skills that will be broadly applicable in the future. That is, given an interest in an occupational area, to what substantive domains of skill development should individuals assign their available training time, and what are the available training resources?

Whose Values?

If performance is viewed as those things that the organization rewards you for doing, and for doing well, then the question of whose values determine the performance specifications is a very important one. Supposedly, in a traditional, hierarchical organization with clear lines of authority and accountability, the management would be responsible for synthesizing the values of all the stakeholders and presenting clear and unambiguous performance goals to individuals. Consequently, there would be no conflicting demands on people, regardless of whether the specifications from the one voice were very general or very detailed. Although such a perfect traditional system has probably never existed, the multiplicity of important stakeholders seems to be growing. Even within the management hierarchy itself, Lord and Smith (Chapter Seven) argue that individual managers can influence the priorities assigned to specific performance components, and also the specifications for what constitutes high and low performance, if the sense-making process between leader and follower results in high levels of influence being granted to the leader.

Many chapter contributors see the trends toward a service economy; flatter, more decentralized organizations; and an accelerating pace of change as creating situations in which individuals must answer to several constituencies, be they customers (internal or external), different levels of management, peers, or subordinates. Bowen and Waldman, in Chapter Six of this volume, present this view forcefully and well in the context of customer service. The customer's value judgments about what components of performance are the most critical will become more and more important.

The customer will also play an increasing role in the actual assessment of performance proficiency. Potentially, at least, customers could be concerned with both the technical components of performance and the nontechnical components. Bowen and Waldman then argue that the variation in values or preferences among customers and the degree to which the customers' performance evaluations can indeed be influenced by the individual performer are very relevant concerns. Current performance models would not disagree.

Murphy and Jackson also note in Chapter Ten that the different stakeholders may not have equal accountability for the performance evaluations they make. That is, if you get a low performance review from customers (such as survey cards for airline flight attendants or student evaluations of instructors), the customers are not held accountable for their evaluations. As pointed out by Motowidlo and Schmit in Chapter Three, accountability has been shown to promote greater accuracy and fairness in performance ratings. Consequently, the presence of multiple, and perhaps conflicting, constituencies presents a number of important issues that both research and practice must confront, but they do not fall outside the boundaries of current performance models. In fact, current models point out the importance of such issues. Unfortunately, they do not point to easy solutions.

Resolving conflicts, real or potential, among the value systems of multiple assessors of individual performance must become an organizational development issue. That is, such conflicts will occur, and organizations must acknowledge that they occur, formulate ways of monitoring them, and develop resolution strategies that are judged to be procedurally fair. The customer is an important stakeholder with valuable information to contribute. Studying the performance goals held by customers (such as via critical incidents) is as legitimate as obtaining the same information from managers. Also, it would be useful to develop strategies for communicating to customers the degree to which the specific outcomes of interest to them can in fact be controlled by a focal individual or by the organization. Customers could also be trained with regard to the range of consequences that their assessments can have. The student as customer would be a reasonable test bed with which to begin.

Changes in Component Criticalities?

Related to the issues created by the increased presence of multiple stakeholders are the predictions of several chapter contributors that the trends currently gathering steam will change the relative importance ascribed to different components of performance. Murphy and Jackson (Chapter Ten) see the current trends as producing increased role ambiguity and increased role conflict, which will in turn place greater emphasis on the nontechnical components of performance, such as good citizenship, peer support, and so on, which are not specific to particular roles or occupations.

Hulin and Glomb (Chapter Four) raise much the same issue from a different perspective when they predict that the contingent workforce will be less concerned with the nontechnical components of performance than with the technical core. People with contingent contracts will not be expected to put forth extra effort, to be supportive of their peers, or to assume the supervisory and management responsibilities that the high performance work team requires. Hulin and Glomb also point out that the generally less favorable employment contracts to be enjoyed by contingent or consultant arrangements may produce lower job satisfaction and a greater variety of withdrawal or counterproductive job behaviors, and they argue that these dependent variables should be given much more research attention. Their points are well taken. The increasing use of such employment contracts is for real (Clinton, 1997; Cohany, 1996; Polivka, 1996) and we need to know much more about the formal, informal, and psychological clauses in such contracts and how they affect the relevant dependent variables (Rousseau, 1995). These effects could become a large national problem with serious repercussions for organizational functioning and individual welfare. It is unfortunate that we currently have no normative way of tracking changes in the relevant dependent variables for different segments of the labor force. Even national surveys of job satisfaction that are comparable across time seem not to be done anymore.

New Components of Performance?

The new dimension of performance that is most often identified as being of critical importance has to do with how well an individual adapts to new conditions or requirements. Hesketh and Neal

(Chapter Two) refer to it as adaptive performance, Murphy and Jackson (Chapter Ten) call it role flexibility, and London and Mone (Chapter Five) write about the proficiency with which individuals self-manage their new learning experiences. A clear implication is that this factor should be defined in the same way and mean much the same thing in almost all job, occupational, or role performance assessment situations. Implicitly, at least, the fullest explication is provided by London and Mone. If the variable in question is the proficiency with which individuals self-manage their continuous learning, then assessment can focus on how well individuals assess their own training needs, how well they design or select training experiences to meet their needs, how well they execute their own training experiences, and how well they evaluate whether they meet their own training objectives. Framed in this way, it would be a genuine addition to the Campbell taxonomy (Campbell et al., 1993), and it invites the development of new measures to predict it.

New Assessment Methods?

Discussions of how the new dynamics will affect methods of performance assessment are a bit sparse. The chapters by Hesketh and Neal (Chapter Two) and Motowidlo and Schmit (Chapter Three) are the only two that devote systematic attention to measurement issues. As noted by Motowidlo and Schmit, in a more complex and dynamic work environment with multiple stakeholders, potential raters can vary in terms of both the values they place on different components of performance, and the actual sample of performance components they can observe. This puts a premium on being able to match raters with the appropriate components to be rated, and procedures should be developed to improve the match. In addition, the measurement system must do its best to make the raters accountable for their ratings. That is, there must be at least the potential for raters to be asked to document, substantiate, or justify their assessments of specific individuals, even if the data are being collected for research purposes. These suggestions are well taken. This same point was raised in the previous discussion of how to deal with the differing value systems of multiple stakeholders.

Hesketh and Neal also suggest a number of methods for identifying consensus goals for different components of performance and for scaling the marginal utility (to the organization?) of different levels of goal obtainment (that is, performance). The suggestions are variations on procedures developed by Pritchard (1992) for the development of work group performance goals. This is a very useful discussion and it provides the basis for the linkage between individual performance, team performance, and organizational performance (Campbell, 1997).

Another measurement issue raised in some of the chapters pertains to the benefits and liabilities of computerized performance monitoring, or CPM. CPM has the potential to become HRM's worst nightmare. The existing literature is not positive (Aiello, 1993; Aiello & Kolb, 1995). Unless the method captures data that is a valid and not a deficient representation of the individual's technical performance goals, unless it is not contaminated by extraneous sources of variance, and unless it is perceived as procedurally fair, then it will create very negative consequences. Even if it is valid, not deficient, not contaminated, and viewed as fair, it is still potentially vulnerable to compromise or manipulation by interested parties. Hopes for CPM in anything but a very favorable "for research purposes only" environment seem naive. It has much potential, however, for training and development purposes when individuals can use the information to give themselves feedback, test the effects of different work strategies, and monitor progress toward goals.

Performance Determinants: The Generalist Versus the Specialist

A central issue addressed in many of the chapters concerns the most appropriate model for the determinants, or predictors, of performance. Recall that the Campbell model distinguishes between direct and indirect determinants, and asserts that the latter can exert an influence on performance only by influencing some combination of the former.

This highlights two issues raised by a number of the contributors. First, if the nontechnical performance components are to become generally more critical, what are the implications for the determinants of performance controlled by the selection, training, and motivational systems? If just the opposite is true, what are the implications? For either development, will the most be gained by trying to select or train for specific knowledge and skills, or should the emphasis be on selection using general traits and dispositions (such as general cognitive ability and conscientiousness)? If the nontechnical factors increase in criticality, should selection be based on general motivational and personality dispositions, or should it be based on mastery of specific interpersonal, leadership, and self-management skills? If the technical factors increase in criticality, should selection be based on cognitive ability, or should it be based on mastery of specific technical skills?

The choice among alternative strategies will not be facilitated by some radically different approach to I/O psychology or HRM. Current models do in fact point to the issues that must be addressed. We do need, however, much better information on the nature and extent of the changes that are taking place, and better forecasts of how they might continue into the future. It seems safe to assume that, in addition to basing selection on general trait characteristics, the assessment of current levels of job-relevant knowledge and skill will increase in importance—but by how much?

For example, to what extent will organizations constantly need to identify people who are project-ready, either their own people or new applicants? To what extent does being project-ready mean one is fully functional in regard to the determinants of both technical performance components and nontechnical performance components of your next assignment? In one sense, an ideal solution would be to hire people for each new project or situation who already have the necessary skills and choice behavior patterns, and then to let them go as soon as the project is finished or the situation changes. The other extreme would be to hire people only on the basis of cognitive ability and personality and make continuous learning their responsibility. We probably do not need more data or new models to know that neither extreme is feasible.

Current models say, virtually in unison, that both technical and nontechnical components of individual performance are critical for the effectiveness of the team, group, or organization, even if the optimal weights are not known. Current models also state or strongly imply that the nontechnical components, and their critical determinants, are much less occupation, role, or domain specific than the technical components. Virtually by definition, being a technically proficient psychologist, violinist, airline pilot, or police officer requires domain-specific knowledge and skill. It is also true that current data, interpreted via current models, argue convincingly that *to a certain extent* both general cognitive ability and conscientiousness/achievement orientation are related to performance on virtually all performance components in almost all work settings or roles, although the relative strengths of the relationship may be somewhat different across components of performance.

If more rapid and complex technological change is to become a permanent fixture and if the more effective organizations are to move quickly to adapt to and take advantage of such changes, then the technical components of performance will continue to be important, and low performance on these factors may become even more dysfunctional than in the past. To say it another way, the slopes of the marginal utility curves for the technical components of performance could increase, perhaps dramatically. Similarly, if team designs continue to play a bigger role in how organizations are structured, then the nontechnical performance components having to do with peer leadership and performance as a group member will also become increasingly important. If future performance demands, both technical and nontechnical, increase significantly, it puts even more pressure on education and training systems to raise the mastery level of the prerequisite skills for both areas, and we should expect even louder demands at the high school, vocational-technical, and college levels for more and better work-relevant training. For the contingent labor force, the marginal utility of performance on the nontechnical performance components may or may not decrease. Hulin and Glomb suggest that it will decrease. Murphy and Jackson suggest that it might in fact increase. We need much more research to answer these questions. However, if the same skill demands, and consequently the same reward levels, are not imposed on the contingent labor force, a two-class occupational hierarchy could become even more pronounced.

One related issue that really was not addressed by any of the contributors is how best to deal with rapidly changing knowledge and skill requirements, even after acknowledging the general validity of cognitive ability and personality, such that the adaptive capabilities of both organizations and individuals are increased. It is somewhat surprising that none of the contributors mentioned that the U.S. Department of Labor funded O*NET project (Peterson et al., 1996), which tried to do just that and which has had a reasonable amount of exposure. O*NET is an attempt to develop and evaluate taxonomies of work behavior (that is, specific performance components) and taxonomies of performance determinants (traits, knowledge domains, and skills) that could be used to describe the content and determinants of performance for broad occupational categories, not specific jobs. Among other things, the O*NET identifies a taxonomy of cross-functional skills. A subset of these are intended to be general technical skills that would be critical determinants of performance across a broad range of work requirements. That is, they are intended to address the very problem of adapting to technological change that this volume worries so much about. Another subset defines a taxonomy of interpersonal skills that would be important determinants of performance on the nontechnical components of performance in a wide variety of work settings. Although at this point it makes no claim for being optimal, the O*NET taxonomy is really the most systematically developed starting point that we have. It subsumes and in fact explicitly synthesizes the various competency models cited by Motowidlo and Schmit (Chapter Three), as well as other competency models, such as MOSAIC, developed by the U.S. Office of Personnel Management (1994). Also not mentioned is the SCANS project (Secretary's Commission on Achieving Necessary Skills, 1991), a precursor of O*NET, which was the first truly national effort to identify the general work-related skills that the noncollege population needs to acquire to best handle the dynamic trends described in this volume and to maximize their contribution to high-performance organizations.

There is one very direct implication of the above taxonomic efforts. If individuals want to maximize their chances of successfully adapting to rapid change in technology, job settings, and organizational environments, then they should develop expertise in the cross-functional skills. It is incumbent for I/O psychology, training organizations, and employers to provide the best possible substantive specifications for the most critical cross-functional skills, and to develop appropriate strategies to train people in them.

Conclusion

In the aggregate, the chapters in this volume should stimulate a careful and intense consideration of what the future world of work will be like and what our future research and practice should be like. They also, in the aggregate, exhibit a few characteristics that can distract the reader.

There is of course the tendency, commented on by Murphy (Chapter Nine), to get a bit too worked up about the perceived dynamics. Although, however, the trends may be weak or strong, examples of most of the new organizational forms probably already exist and could be studied. For one such example, we need look no further than the behavioral science contract research or the consulting firm that hires I/O psychology Ph.D.'s. In such settings, people do not have well-prescribed jobs, they move frequently from project to project, and they must continually develop new knowledge and skills, as well as write proposals for the next project before the final report of the last one is finished. Also, it is an open question as to whether current research and practice takes place mostly in organizations with the stereotypical traditional bureaucratic form, or in venues that are more like the new forms. For example, the retail industry is huge. Is it a traditional form or not?

In addition, there was sometimes a tendency in these chapters to invoke new concepts with few specifications for their meaning. Using new labels is relatively easy. Developing specifications for their meaning and substantive importance is more difficult. Finally, the word *technology* sometimes takes on mystical properties that apparently defy analysis. We have been analyzing and studying technology differences for a long time. Why mystify it?

These complaints aside, the chapters also identify a number of critical issues that need careful attention. First, if there are both technical and nontechnical skills that constitute optimal preparation for a broad variety of work assignments over an appreciable span of time, what are they? To what extent are they domain specific? Where and when should they be learned? How should they be learned? Kraiger (Chapter Eleven) reviews the new developments in training strategies that can facilitate such training objectives. In comparison, however, to abilities, personality, interests, or even performance itself, the construct of "skill" has received very little attention in the latent structure or taxonomic sense. The word itself is used freely, but seldom with any specifications for what it means. The O*NET model does constitute one such specification, and Lubinski and Dawis (1992) present a somewhat different perspective. Aside from the basic skills (such as reading, speaking, and math) and the interpersonal skills (such as giving constructive feedback), however, there is very little taxonomic research in the literature.

Second, what are the implications of a more diverse workforce for issues of bias and fairness relative to performance measurement? So far, the predictor has received most of the attention. This may change, and Equal Employment Opportunity concerns over adverse impact in selection may pale in comparison to training, pay, and promotion issues.

Third, if education, training and development, and job seeking are to become more self-managed, how, when, and by what means are such self-management skills to be developed and maintained? Can I/O psychology develop useful prototypic training models for teaching the self-management of performance improvement, as it did for teaching certain interpersonal skills via interaction modeling? How should the electronic databases that describe education and training programs, employment trends, occupational requirements, and labor market information be designed, updated, and made user friendly so as to facilitate individual self-development?

Fourth, how does moving from a traditional work group to a team design change the criticality of various performance components, and what are the most relevant knowledge, skill, and dispositional requirements? What are the best strategies for facilitating team development so as to shorten the time between team birth and maturity, maximize effectiveness at maturity, and prevent premature aging? Kozlowski, Gully, Nason, and Smith (Chapter Eight) presented a systematic set of suggestions for answering these questions.

Fifth, what will be the substantive role of leadership in the future? Where will it reside? Lord and Smith (Chapter Seven) opened the door to a wide range of possibilities. How will leadership be selected for and trained for? The functions served by the leadership components of supervision and management will not become any less important. For optimal individual and organizational performance, however, who should be responsible for these functions?

Sixth, what will be the effects of the new types of employment contracts on satisfaction, commitment, and withdrawal? What will be the effects, in turn, on organizational effectiveness and individual well-being? The specter of a two-class labor force looms larger and larger and suggests strong negative consequences. We really need longitudinal data on these issues, and it should be collected at specified intervals on national probability samples.

Seventh, what will be the effects of increased role conflict and role ambiguity on the scale that is forecasted by some of the chapter authors? Under what conditions are they adaptive, and to what extent? What is the role of individual differences in explaining the effects of increased role conflict and ambiguity?

These are just a sampling of the critical issues for research and practice that are raised by these chapters. The editors and authors are to be thanked for raising them. We should not get too distracted, however, by the mystique of technology or by the concern that our current models will not work in the new age. Current models of performance supplanted the classic model of the "criterion problem" less than fifteen years ago (Campbell et al., 1993) and they can be used to advantage to explicate the issues addressed in this volume. Those issues focus on using our applied research capabilities to determine more precisely the effects of current trends on substantive performance requirements and performance determinants, and on developing new selection, training, and motivational strategies to deal with these effects. It may be that, in the course of dejobbing the employment structure, being able to appropriately model the person-project or person-role match will become even more important. These are very exciting times for I/O psychology; and the more precisely we can identify problems and issues, formulate research questions, and develop new practices, the more rewarding it will be.

References

Aiello, J. R. (1993). Computer-based work monitoring: Electronic surveillance and its effects. *Journal of Applied Social Psychology, 23,* 499–507.

Aiello, J. R., & Kolb, K. J. (1995). Electronic performance monitoring and social context: Impact on productivity and stress. *Journal of Applied Psychology, 80,* 339–353.

Barley, S. R., & Kochan, T. A. (1998). *A study of techniques for improved occupational analysis.* Washington, DC: Division on Education, Labor, and Human Performance, Commission on Behavioral and Social Sciences and Education, National Academy of Sciences.

Becker, B., & Gerhardt, B. (1996). The impact of human resource management on organizational performance: Progress and prospects. *Academy of Management Journal, 39,* 779–801.

Borman, W. C., & Brush, D. H. (1993). More progress toward a taxonomy of managerial performance requirements. *Human Performance, 6,* 1–22.

Borman, W. C., & Motowidlo, S. J. (1993). Expanding the criterion domain to include elements of contextual performance. In N. Schmitt & W. C. Borman (Eds.), *Personnel selection in organizations* (pp. 71–98). San Francisco: Jossey-Bass.

Campbell, C. H., Ford, P., Rumsey, M. G., Pulakos, E. D., Borman, W. C., Felker, D. B., de Vera, M. V., & Riegelhaupt, B. J. (1990). Development of multiple job performance measures in a representative sample of jobs. *Personnel Psychology, 43,* 277–300.

Campbell, J. P. (1997). *The science and politics of the linkage between individual performance and organizational performance.* St. Louis, MO: Society of Industrial and Organizational Psychology.

Campbell, J. P., Gasser, M. B., & Oswald, F. L. (1996). The substantive nature of job performance variability. In K. R. Murphy (Ed.), *Individual differences and behavior in organizations* (pp. 258–299). San Francisco: Jossey-Bass.

Campbell, J. P., McCloy, R. A., Oppler, S. H., & Sager, C. E. (1993). A theory of performance. In N. Schmitt & W. C. Borman (Eds.), *Personnel selection in organizations* (pp. 35–70). San Francisco: Jossey-Bass.

Clinton, A. (1997). Flexible labor: Restructuring the American work force. *Monthly Labor Review, 120*(8), 3–17.

Cohany, S. R. (1996). Workers in alternative employment arrangements. *Monthly Labor Review, 119*(10), 31–45.

Fleishman, E. A., & Quaintance, M. K. (1984). *Taxonomies of human performance: The description of human tasks.* San Diego, CA: Academic Press.

Holzer, H. J. (1997). Is there a gap between employer skill needs and the skills of the workplace. In A. Legold, M. Feuer, & A. M. Black (Eds.), *Transitions in work and learning: Implications for assessment.* Washington, DC: National Academy Press.

Ilgen, D. R., & Hollenbeck, J. R. (1991). The structure of work: Jobs and roles. In M. D. Dunnette & L. M. Hough (Eds.), *Handbook of industrial and organizational psychology* (Vol. 2, 2nd ed., pp. 165–208). Palo Alto: Consulting Psychologists Press.

Johnston, W. B., & Packer, A. E. (1987). *Workforce 2000.* Indianapolis, IN: Hudson Institute.

Lawler, E. E., III, & Jenkins, G. (1992). Strategic reward systems. In M. D. Dunnette & L. M. Hough (Eds.), *Handbook of industrial and organizational psychology* (Vol. 3, 2nd ed., pp. 1009–1055). Palo Alto, CA: Consulting Psychologists Press.

Lubinski, D., & Dawis, R. V. (1992). Abilities, skills, and proficiencies. In M. D. Dunnette & L. M. Hough (Eds.), *Handbook of industrial and organizational psychology* (Vol. 3, 2nd ed., pp. 1–59). Palo Alto, CA: Consulting Psychologists Press.

Manning, C. A., & Broach, D. (1992). *Identifying ability requirements for operators of future automated air traffic control systems* (DOT/FAA/AM–92/26). Washington, DC: U.S. Government Printing Office.

Murphy, K. R. (1989). Dimensions of job performance. In R. Dillon & J. Pelligrino (Eds.), *Testing: Applied and theoretical perspectives* (pp. 218–247). New York: Praeger.

Organ, D. W. (1997). Organizational citizenship behavior: It's construct clean-up time. *Human Performance, 10,* 85–97.

Penn, R., Rose, M., & Rubery, J. (Eds.). (1994). *Skill and occupational change.* London: Oxford University Press.

Peterson, N. G., Mumford, M. D., Borman, W. C., Jeanneret, P. R., Fleishman, E. A., & Levin, K. Y. (1996). *O*NET final technical report* (Vols. 1 & 2). Salt Lake City: Utah Department of Employment Security.

Polivka, A. E. (1996). Into contingent and alternative employment: By choice? *Monthly Labor Review, 119*(10), 55–74.

Pritchard, R. D. (1992). Organizational productivity. In M. D. Dunnette & L. M. Hough (Eds.), *Handbook of industrial and organizational psychology* (Vol. 3, 2nd ed., pp. 443–472). Palo Alto: Consulting Psychologists Press.

Rousseau, D. M. (1995). *Psychological contracts in organizations: Understanding written and unwritten agreements.* Thousand Oaks, CA: Sage.

Secretary's Commission on Achieving Necessary Skills (SCANS). (1991). *What work requires of schools.* Washington, DC: U.S. Department of Labor.

Shaw, M. E. (1981). *Group dynamics* (3rd ed.). New York: McGraw-Hill.

U.S. Office of Personnel Management. (1994). *Professional and administrative careers: Occupational survey.* Washington, DC: U.S. Office of Personnel Management.

Vance, R. J., MacCallum, R. C., Coovert, M. D., & Hedge, J. W. (1988). Construct validity of multiple job performance measures using confirmatory factor analysis. *Journal of Applied Psychology, 73,* 74–80.

Yukl, G., & Van Fleet, D. D. (1992). Theory and research on leadership in organizations. In M. D. Dunnette & L. M. Hough (Eds.), *Handbook of industrial and organizational psychology* (Vol. 3, 2nd ed.). Palo Alto: Consulting Psychologists Press.

Zander, A. (1982). *Making groups effective.* San Francisco: Jossey-Bass.

Name Index

Subject Index